The Quiet Man

The Quiet Man

The Complete Guide To

The Complete Guide To

The Complete Guide To

The Quiet Man

The Quiet Man

The Complete Guide To

The Complete Guide To

The Complete Guide To

The Quiet Man

The Quiet Man

The Quiet Man

The Complete Guide To

The Complete Guide To

The Complete Guide To

The Quiet Man

The Quiet Man

The Complete Guide To

The Complete Guide To

The Complete Guide To

The Quiet

The Quiet

The Quiet

The Quiet Man   The Quiet Man   The Quiet Man

The Complete Guide To   The Complete Guide To   The Complete Guide To

The Quiet Man   The Quiet Man   The Quiet

The Complete Guide To   The Complete Guide To   The Complete Guide

The Quiet Man   The Quiet Man   The Quiet Man

The Complete Guide To   The Complete Guide To   The Complete Guide To

The Quiet Man   The Quiet Man   The Quiet

The Complete Guide To   The Complete Guide To   The Complete Guide

The Quiet   The Quiet   The Quiet

The Quiet Man

The Complete Guide To
The Quiet Man

The Complete Guide To
The Quiet Man

The Complete Guide To
The Quiet Man

The Complete Guide To
The Quiet Man

The Complete Guide To
The Quiet Man

The Complete Guide To
The Quiet Man

The Complete Guide
to The Quiet Man

Des MacHale

Appletree Press

Dedication

This book is dedicated to Charles Harold, Liam O'Raghallaigh,
Paddy McCormick and my wife Anne, for all their help and encouragement.

First published in hardback in 2000
and paperback in 2002 by
Appletree Press Ltd
The Old Potato Station
14 Howard Street South
Belfast
BT7 1AP

Tel: + 44 (0) 28 9024 3074
Fax: + 44 (0) 28 9024 6756
E-mail: reception@appletree.ie
Web: www.appletree.ie

Revised in 2004.

The Complete Guide to The Quiet Man

Hardback ISBN: 978-0-86281-784-8

9 8 7 6 5

Paperback ISBN: 978-0-86281-827-2

9 8 7 6 5 4 3

A catalogue record for this book is available from the British Library

AP3648

Contents

INTRODUCTION

My love affair with *The Quiet Man* began in summer 1953 when I was only seven years old. I was on holiday with my family at the seaside resort of Inniscrone, County Sligo in the West of Ireland, not a million miles away from the Isle of Innisfree made famous by W.B. Yeats. In those glorious pre-television days, the highlight of our holiday was a visit to the makeshift cinema *every evening*, sometimes seeing the movies over and over again. It was there that I saw *The Quiet Man* on the big screen for the first time and it was love at first sight. I don't remember a lot about my first viewing except of course for the dragging of Mary Kate across the countryside, of which my parents disapproved strongly, and the mother of all movie fights which was re-enacted with my three brothers for years afterwards. Curiously enough, my most abiding memory was the toadying Feeney writing the names of all those cursed by Red Will Danaher in his little book – that performance is still one of my favourites in the movie, showing the vast talents of Jack MacGowran.

The more I saw of *The Quiet Man*, the more I loved it - the macho toughness of John Wayne, the beauty of Maureen O'Hara (red is my favourite hair colour!) whom I was fortunate to meet and kiss in the flesh, the impishness of that loveable rogue Barry Fitzgerald, and the bullying of Victor McLaglen with his soft centre. At that time I had no idea who John Ford was or the huge influence that a director had on every aspect of a movie. Gradually, and maybe because of *The Quiet Man*, I became aware that I was living in a very beautiful and special part of the world, surrounded by many natural comedians and characters. I was born and brought up in Castlebar, County Mayo less than thirty miles away from Cong and other locations where most of *The Quiet Man* was shot.

Living in Cork since 1972, I became more and more interested in the *Quiet Man* phenomenon – what was the fascination of this movie for millions of people worldwide – young and old, women and men, Irish and non-Irish alike? I became curious about the locations for the shooting, the identities of the minor players, in fact every aspect of the movie. I was drawn into the profound and magical world of John Ford, surely one of the cinema's greatest directors; I became a keen fan of his work and I have viewed and collected dozens of his movies on video, not least in order to spot bit players who also featured in *The Quiet Man*!

Naturally, too, I became interested in the novels and other writings of Maurice Walsh, the incomparable Kerry writer whose original short story started the whole *Quiet Man* phenomenon. Walsh was a wonderful storyteller, a writer steeped in the oral and literary tradition of North Kerry, and he deserves a much higher place in the annals of Irish literature than he occupies at present.

As this book took shape, fate had me meet two "Quiet Maniacs", as we call ourselves, in Cork. They were to become my principal researchers and without their help I doubt if I could ever have written this book. The first was fellow-Mayoman Liam O'Raghallaigh, who worked tirelessly on my behalf, interviewing, probing the movie's background and lifting my spirits during the dark days! The second was Corkman (but honorary Mayoman) Charlie Harold, who had been assistant manager at Ashford Castle during the filming of *The Quiet Man*. He introduced me to so many people including many of the surviving extras in the movie, and opened so many doors for me as we scoured the West of Ireland for many years in search of exact locations and camera positions. He also gave me access to the unique collection of photographs he himself took during the shooting. To these two wonderful friends I owe a debt of gratitude that I can never even begin to repay. My special thanks must go to my good friend and Ulster's greatest Quiet Maniac, Paddy McCormick of Belfast, who has undertaken the graphic design of this book for love and not for money;

no fortune, but some marriage of talents! To my late parents, to my wife Anne and my children Peter, Catherine, Simon, John and Dominic, all of whom who helped in so many ways over the years I owe a special debt of gratitude also. Finally, I wish to say a big thank you to my mother-in-law, Emily Jane Gryce, for her magnificent set of a dozen oil paintings based on *Quiet Man* scenes now on display in the Collins' *Quiet Man* heritage centre in Cong and some of which are reproduced in this book.

As work progressed I became more and more convinced that *The Quiet Man* is a very deep movie and not just the 'Oirish' romp it is felt by many to be. Far from being anti-woman, it shows how a woman's determination can change the lives of all around her as she strives to attain her desired status in society. Above all, it is a movie about the dual-nationality of an Irish-American and by extension the crisis of identity faced by all emigrants since the beginning of time who are forced to straddle two cultures. The principal themes of *The Quiet Man* - love, conflict, money, fighting, comedy, music and unfortunately drinking, are eternal themes which will never go out of date, and this is just one of the many reasons for its enduring popularity.

This book could have had several other titles; for example, *All You Ever Wanted To Know About The Quiet Man But Were Afraid To Ask*, *The Quiet Maniac's Companion*, *The Quiet Man A-Z* and *All About The Quiet Man* were all contenders at various stages but eventually I settled for *The Complete Guide to The Quiet Man* as the best description of its contents. Although it contains a wealth of detail about every aspect of the movie, its making, and the origins of the story on which it was based, it is essentially a book of analysis and interpretation, written primarily for those who know and love the movie and want to deepen that love. It is not uncritical; for example some of the casting was unfortunate, with rampant nepotism, and there were not a few technical flaws mostly in the studio scenes, but like little blemishes on the faces of those we love, they serve only to increase our affection.

ACKNOWLEDGEMENTS

In the course of my own extensive researches on *The Quiet Man* I have been helped by very many people, institutions and organisations and have made many good friends in the process. In particular, I would like to express my sincere thanks to the following people for their help, hospitality and generosity:

Maureen O'Hara and her daughter Bronwyn; Lady Killanin and the late Lord Killanin; the late Maurice Walsh Jr; Mrs Mairín Walsh and Daire Walsh; Maurice Semple; Eddie and Mary Gibbons; Sean McClory; Andrew V. McLaglen; Bill Maguire; Sean Maguire; Etta Vaughan; Gerry, Margaret and Lisa Collins; Sal Mellotte and the late Joe Mellotte; John and Pat Daly; Dr Eamon Lydon; Dr John McDarby; Willie Quinn; Cormac O'Malley; John Horan; Dr Pádraigín Riggs; Dr Gwenda Young; Robert and Nellie Foy; Jack Murphy; John Murphy; Mrs May Farragher and family; Mrs Margaret Niland and family; Grace Duncan; John Cocchi; Ken Jones; Jordan Young; Michael John and Alice O'Sullivan; Sean Ryan; Tom Ryan; Sunniva O'Flynn; Sarah Hayes; Mairéad Delaney; June Beck; Chriss Nolan; Betty Hartnett; Kit Ahern; Mrs Angela Huggard; Veronica Brennan; Vera O'Leary; Aoife Bhreatnach; Tom Courell; Fr Leon O'Morcháin; Sean O'Reilly; Fergal Gaynor; Tim Robinson; Fr Benny McHale; Dominic and Oonagh Casey; Thérèse Loesberg; Peggy Clarke; Jim Cooney; Paddy Keane; Clare and Yann Kelly; Gary McEwan; Michael Byrne; Michael Walsh; Michael Donohue and David Greene.

To the staffs of the following libraries and institutions I tender my sincere thanks: Boole Library University College Cork, Cork City Library, Mayo County Library, Brigham Young University Library, Irish Film Institute, Lilly Library University of Indiana, UCLA Film and Television Archive, *The Connacht Tribune*, *Sunday World*, The Internet Movie Database, *Connaught Telegraph*.

Overall Location Map

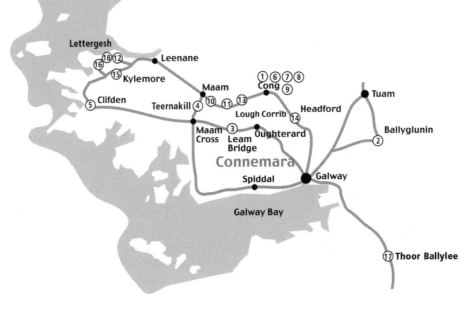

Lettergesh

Leenane

18 12
16
15 Kylemore

Clifden
5

Teernakill
4

Maam
10 11 13

1 6 7 8
Cong
9

Headford

Lough Corrib
14

Maam Cross
3

Leam Bridge

Oughterard

Connemara

Spiddal

Galway

Galway Bay

Tuam

Ballyglunin
2

17 Thoor Ballylee

North Kerry

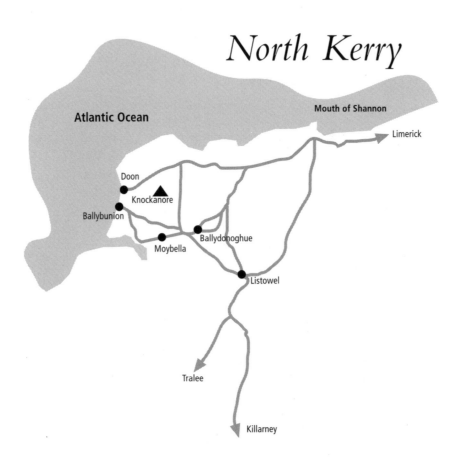

Atlantic Ocean

Mouth of Shannon

Limerick

Doon

Knockanore

Ballybunion

Moybella

Ballydonoghue

Listowel

Tralee

Killarney

Chapter One

Maurice Walsh

Our story begins in Ballydonoghue, a small village between the bigger towns of Ballybunion and Listowel in the north of the County of Kerry, in the province of Munster in the south of Ireland. It is a region renowned for its storytellers, writers and poets, and it is quite remarkable how much literary talent the region has produced and still continues to produce, out of all proportion to its size, population and resources. Names like John B. Keane, Bryan MacMahon, Eamon Kelly, Brendan Kennelly, Maurice Walsh and George Fitzmaurice are known throughout Ireland and nowadays internationally as well.

Ballydonoghue lies in the shadow of Cnucanor, anglicised as Knockanore, a hill whose name some believe is derived from the Irish "Cnoc an Áir", which means literally "The Hill of Slaughter". This, like many Irish place names, commemorates some long-forgotten battle in the time of the ancient Fenians. Others, however, believe that the hill's name comes from "Cnoc an Óir", which means "The Hill of Gold". Indeed, a Kerry beach not far away is still called Cuan an Óir after a ship from the American Colonies was washed up there in a storm, shedding its huge cargo of fool's gold which could be seen glittering in the sand for many years afterwards. In Irish legend fairy gold is a sublime substance that turns to dust in the owner's purse before he has time to spend it. Yet another derivation of the place name renders it as Cnoc an Fhomhair, which means "Hill of the Harvest". But whatever the true derivation of the name, the region is undoubtedly steeped in mythology, tradition and mystery and is an ideal breeding ground for artists, poets, dramatists, novelists and storytellers.

The area is known too for its many sporting and fighting activities. The famous Lord Kitchener was born there, as were the parents of John L. Sullivan who was to become the first heavyweight boxing champion of the world. In the first half of the nineteenth century, North Kerry was infamous for its faction fights in which hundreds of participants took part, including whole families using sticks, fists and stones or whatever else came to hand. These faction fights often took place on the flimsiest of pretexts and can be compared to mass duels. Interestingly, they were rarely suppressed by the police, who probably regarded them as safety valves for a potentially rebellious society. However, they were decidedly bloody affairs with dozens of people being killed and hundreds injured. A present-day plaque on the site of one of the most famous of these encounters reads as follows:

FACTION FIGHT AT
BALLYEIGH , BALLYBUNION

Faction fights were fights at fairs, markets, funerals, race meetings and festivals. At first the only weapons used were sticks. Faction fighting originated in Clonmel, Co. Tipperary, 1805 & spread quickly throughout the country. On the Kerry border the biggest factions were the Cooleens & the Black Mulvihills. On the 24th of June 1834 a long-standing feud between the Cooleens, Black Mulvihills & Lawlors culminated in one of the fiercest faction fights ever seen. It took place at the annual Ballyeigh festival of games & racing which dates back to pagan times. On that fateful day about 1200 men of the Cooleens crossed the Cashen River to

Ballyeigh strand & came up against a force of about 2000 of the Lawlors & Mulvihills. Despite their early attack they were forced to divide and retreat. The smaller section were driven towards the Cashen River. Their boats could not take the numbers trying to get aboard. Some were drowned & many more were beaten to death with sticks & stones. The death toll was estimated to be 20 but it was widely believed to be greater owing to the numbers who died from their injuries. No one was apprehended as a result of the inquiry. The last official race meeting was held at Ballyeigh on the 9th & 10th of September 1856. The race meeting was relocated to Listowel and it is now a very successful annual event.

Another great passion in North Kerry was horses and horse-racing and the attendant betting and wagering. The town of Listowel still boasts one of the finest racecourses in Ireland, and the Listowel Races are not just a race meet − they are a festival of enjoyment, drinking and a mini-orgy of good spirits. In fact, the whole area is rich in humour, "craic" and merriment and its people are genuinely friendly and hospitable.

Maurice Walsh's father, John, was a relatively well-to-do farmer who came from a long line of Walshs who lived in Ballydonoghue. He had a passion for horses, horse-racing and the drinking of pints of porter that often accompanies these interests, but he was also a man of learning whose house was full of books. His many other activities inclined him towards being a gentleman farmer, so it was inevitable that he would need some hired help about the farm to do the donkey work. He advertised for a strong young lad to help him, so a local woman sent her son, Paddy Bawn Enright, a stocky seventeen-year-old lad, to claim the job. His hair was as black as the crows that flew around Cnucanor so the locals, with cruel wit, nicknamed him "Paddy Bawn" which translates as "Fair Patrick". He was the original Quiet Man on whom the stories and later the movie were based.

Paddy Bawn Enright

Paddy Bawn Enright lived all his life afterwards with the Walsh family and when the movie loosely based on his character appeared in 1952 he revelled in his reputation as a local legend. He had become almost one of the Walsh family and was particularly close to the eldest son Maurice, who was born on 21 April 1879. In later life when Maurice Walsh came to write short stories and novels it was natural that his thoughts would turn to the old family retainer for inspiration. Inevitably, Paddy Bawn's character and activities were highly romanticised − he had never been to America, but like every young fellow in North Kerry, he had done a bit of boxing in his youth. He was by all accounts a quiet man noted for his hard work on the farm and his steadfast dedication to the Walsh family.

Young Maurice Walsh grew up in an intensely literary atmosphere, wallowing in his father's extensive library of classical English literature. However, like many other Irish writers, he was strongly influenced too by Celtic legends, mythology and folk tales learned at his father's knee. Luckily too, Michael Dillon, his teacher at Lisselton, fostered and encouraged his literary talent in every way. Maurice's mother Elizabeth, originally a Buckley from Cork, seems to have been a determined character, anxious for her eldest son to succeed in the priesthood or the civil service. She provided a useful and practical counterbalance to her husband John's sentimentality and lack of practicality.

Maurice Walsh – Young and Old

As a young lad, Maurice Walsh, or Mossie as he was locally known, was not tall in stature and consequently was often picked upon and bullied by bigger boys. With one bully in particular, Jack Brick, the captain of a rival football team, he had a long-running dispute. Twice they fought hand to hand and with fists, and twice the smaller Maurice had the worst of it. On the third occasion, however, he tore into his bigger opponent with a ferocity that amazed even himself, landing devastating blows to the body from which Jack Brick never recovered, although he bravely came back for more and more punishment. Local legend has it that a passing train stopped so that the passengers could watch the fight and they cheered the victorious Mossie to the echo.

Thus we see that in Maurice Walsh's own background were many of the ingredients that were to make up the story of *The Quiet Man* - faction fighting, horse-racing and betting, Paddy Bawn Enright, boxing and teaching a bully a lesson, and even a train stopping to let the passengers watch a fight.

Perhaps it was inevitable that Maurice Walsh, now with a secure if tedious job as a Customs and Excise Officer, which in his mother's eyes was the next best thing to the priesthood, should turn his hand to serious writing. From about 1905 onwards he turned out a stream of short adventure stories based mostly on the more exciting events of Irish history. These were published in periodicals such as *The Irish Emerald*, *The Dublin Magazine* and *Chamber's Journal*. Some of these stories were so successful that he later expanded them into full-length novels such as *The Key Above the Door*, *While Rivers Run*, *The Small Dark Man* and *Blackcock's Feather*.

On 11 February 1933, Maurice Walsh gained an international readership when his short story, *The Quiet Man*, appeared in the widely read popular American magazine, *The Saturday Evening Post*. In this first version of the story, Paddy Bawn Enright had become "Shawn Kelvin", perhaps because Walsh was nervous that the real individual might be recognised and object. Later, in August of 1933, the story of *The Quiet Man* appeared on the other side of the Atlantic in *Chamber's Magazine*.

From *The Saturday Evening Post* Walsh received $2000, a considerable sum of money at the time, but more importantly it brought his name to the attention of many thousands of new readers. Among these was John Ford, the Irish-American film director. Ford, reckoned by many to be the greatest director of all time and certainly high in everybody's list of the top ten directors, was born John Martin Feeney in Portland, Maine in 1894. All his life, he was intensely proud of his Irish ancestry – his father, Sean Ó Fiénne (anglicised to John A. Feeney) had been born in 1854 in Spiddal about ten miles west of Galway City and his mother Barbara, née Curran, was a native of Kilronan in the Aran Islands off the Galway coast. She was born in 1856 and, although the couple were distant cousins, they never met until their parents emigrated to the United States to escape from the ravages of post-famine Ireland. John Feeney, also known as Jack or Johnny, was the youngest of the couple's eleven children, but one of only six to survive infancy. Throughout his youth he lived in something of a dreamworld, spellbound, as Maurice Walsh was, by his father's romantic stories about fairies, leprechauns and banshees. In this spirit he claimed a fair variety of Irish names – Sean Aloysius O'Feeney (Aloysius was his confirmation name) and Sean Aloysius O'Fearna, for example. On holiday trips to Galway he picked up a smattering of the Irish language and absorbed as much as he could of Irish politics and history. He became intensely interested in the Irish struggle for freedom and a strong supporter of the Irish Republican Army. A typical Fordean romantic flight of fancy has him sharing the same ship to England with Michael Collins during the Treaty negotiations – it probably never happened, but it might just have. That was the twilight world between fact and fiction in which Ford existed.

Frank Ford and Mary Maguire on the set of The Quiet Man

John Ford's older brother, Frank T. Feeney, took up a career in the movie business working in hundreds of films as actor, director, writer and even cameraman. One night Frank was asked to stand in for a drunken actor called Francis Ford and, since the playbills had already been printed, he had to adopt the name. It stuck and it was as Francis Ford, many years later, that he became a major star of *The Quiet Man* movie. Another possible reason for the change of name was that he wanted to spare family blushes because the movie business then was not considered as respectable as it is today. John so admired his elder brother that he left college to pursue a career in the movies also. When the time came for him to take a stage name, he too took the name Ford and was afterwards known as John Ford or Jack Ford to his friends. His close friends, however, called him by the endearing name of "Pappy".

Initially John Ford acted in many of his brother's productions before branching out as a film-maker and director himself and going on to a phenomenal career that included four Academy Awards or Oscars for best director. By 1933, when he first read Maurice Walsh's story *The Quiet Man*, he already had a string of successes to his name. Many of these had Irish themes, such as *The Shamrock Handicap* (1926), *Mother Machree* (1928) and *Hangman's House* (1928). Ford had cannily realised that among

Irish-Americans and even among moviegoers worldwide, there was a huge interest in things Irish and he exploited this to the full. Besides, it gave him an unrivalled vehicle for expressing his pro-Nationalist and anti-British feelings. In 1935 he made *The Informer* which won him his first Oscar as director plus an Oscar for Victor McLaglen as best actor, and in 1937 there followed *The Plough and the Stars*, based on Sean O'Casey's famous stage play, which starred Barry Fitzgerald, Denis O'Dea, Eileen Crowe, F.J. McCormick and Arthur Shields. Ford was listed as director and Arthur Shields of the Abbey Theatre was listed as assistant director.

Ford, always on the lookout for stories with an Irish theme, saw in the story of *The Quiet Man* everything to set his imagination on fire – it was Irish, action-filled, romantic and, even before it ever appeared on the screen, involved the Irish landscape in a unique and essential way. He soon set about buying the film rights of the story from Maurice Walsh. This he accomplished in an agreement dated 25 February 1936. For the derisory but probably nominal sum of $10, Ford obtained from Walsh the exclusive motion picture rights to the story. However, in a second agreement on the same date, Walsh was to get $2500 plus half the excess over that figure if Ford managed to sell the idea to a production company. In a third and final agreement in 1951 when the film eventually got to be made, Walsh received a further $3750 through Ford from Republic Pictures. Thus, in all, Maurice Walsh received just a little over six thousand dollars from a movie which grossed millions and this was a sore point with him and his family and indeed with the many fans of Maurice Walsh to this very day.

Since the original story of *The Quiet Man* as it appeared in *The Saturday Evening Post* is no longer in print, perhaps this would be a good opportunity to revive and preserve it and allow the reader to judge the merits of this minor masterpiece at first hand. Here, by kind permission of Maurice Walsh's descendants, we reproduce it word for word as it originally appeared.

Chapter Two

The Quiet Man - The Original Story
by Maurice Walsh

I

Shawn Kelvin, a blithe young lad of twenty, went to the States to seek his fortune. And fifteen years thereafter he returned to his native Kerry, his blitheness sobered and his youth dried to the core, and whether he had made his fortune or whether he had not, no one could be knowing for certain. For he was a quiet man, not given to talking about himself and the things he had done. A quiet man, under middle size, with strong shoulders and deep-set blue eyes below brows slightly darker than his dark hair – that was Shawn Kelvin. One shoulder had a trick of hunching slightly higher than the other, and some folks said that came from a habit he had of shielding his eyes in the glare of an open-hearth furnace in a place called Pittsburgh, while others said it used to be a way he had of guarding his chin that time he was a sort of sparring-partner punching bag at a boxing camp.

Shawn Kelvin came home and found that he was the last of the Kelvins, and that the farm of his forefathers had added its few acres to the ranch of Big Liam O'Grady of Moyvalla. Shawn took no action to recover his land, though O'Grady had got it meanly. He had had enough of fighting, and all he wanted now was peace. He quietly went amongst the old and kindly friends and quietly looked about him for the place and peace he wanted; and when the time came, quietly produced the money for a neat, handy, small farm on the first warm shoulder of Knockanore Hill below the rolling curves of heather. It was not a big place but it was in good heart, and it got all the sun that was going; and, best of all, it suited Shawn to the tiptop notch of contentment; for it held the peace that tuned to his quietness, and it commanded the widest view in all Ireland –

The first warm shoulder of Knockanore Hill

vale and mountain and the lifting green plain of the Atlantic Sea.

There, in a four-roomed, lime-washed thatched cottage, Shawn made his life, and, though his friends hinted his needs and obligations, no thought came to him of bringing a wife into the place. Yet Fate had the thought and the dream in her loom for him. One middling imitation of a man he had to do chores for him, an ex-navy pensioner handy enough about the house and byre, but with no relish for the sustained work of the field – and, indeed, as long as he kept house and byre shipshape, he found Shawn an easy master.

Shawn himself was no drudge toiler. He knew all about drudgery and the way it wears out a man's soul. He ploughed a little and sowed a little, and at the end of a furrow he would lean on the handles of the cultivator, wipe his brow, if it needed wiping, and lose himself for whole minutes in the great green curve of the sea out there beyond the high black portals of Shannon mouth. And sometimes of an evening he would see, under the glory of the sky, the faint smoke smudge of an American liner. Then he would smile to himself – a pitying smile – thinking of the poor devils, with dreams of fortune luring them, going out to sweat in Ironville, or to bootleg bad whiskey down the hidden way or to stand in a breadline. All these things were beyond Shawn forever.

Market days he would go down and across to Listowel town, seven miles, to do his bartering; and in the long evenings, slowly slipping into the endless summer gloaming, his friends used to climb the winding lane to see him. Only the real friends came that long road, and they were welcome – fighting men who had been out in the "Sixteen": Matt Tobin the thresher, the schoolmaster, the young curate – men like that. A stone jar of malt whiskey would appear on the table, and there would be a haze of smoke and a maze of warm, friendly disagreements.

"Shawn, old son," one of them might hint, "aren't you sometimes terrible lonely?"

"Like hell I am!" might retort Shawn derisively. "Why?"

"Nothing but the daylight and the wind and the sun setting like the wrath o' God."

"Just that! Well,?"

"But after the stirring times beyond in the States"

"Ay! Tell me, fine man, have you ever seen a furnace in full blast?"

"A great sight."

"Great surely! But if I could jump you into a steel foundry this minute, you would be sure that God had judged you faithfully into the very hob of hell."

And then they would laugh and have another small one from the stone jar.

And on Sundays Shawn used to go to church, three miles down to the grey chapel above the black cliffs of Doon Bay. There, Fate laid her lure for him.

Sitting quietly on his wooden bench or kneeling on the dusty footboard, he would fix his steadfast, deep-set eyes on the vestmented celebrant and say his prayers slowly, or go into that strange trance, beyond dreams and visions, where the soul is almost at one with the unknowable.

But after a time, Shawn's eyes no longer fixed themselves on the celebrant. They went no farther than two seats ahead. A girl sat there.

Sunday after Sunday she sat in front of him, and Sunday after Sunday his first casual admiration grew warmer.

She had a white nape to her neck and short red hair above it, and Shawn liked the colour and wave of that flame. And he liked the set of her shoulders and the way the white neck had of leaning a little forward and she at prayers – or her dreams. And, the service over, Shawn used to stay in his seat so that he might get one quick but sure look at her face as she passed out. And he liked her face, too – the wide-set grey eyes, cheekbones firmly curved, clean moulded lips, austere yet sensitive. And he smiled pityingly that one of her name should make his pulses stir – for she was an O'Grady.

One person, only, in the crowded chapel noted Shawn's look and the thought behind the look. Not the girl. Her brother, Big Liam O'Grady of Moyvalla, the very man who as good as stole the Kelvin acres. And that man smiled to himself too - the ugly, contemptuous smile that was his by nature – and, after another habit he had, he tucked away his bit of knowledge in mind corner against a day when it might come in useful for his own purposes.

The girl's first name was Ellen – Ellen O'Grady. But in truth she was no longer a girl. She was past her first youth into that second one that has no definite ending. She might be thirty – she was no less – but there was not a lad in the countryside would say she was past her prime. The poise of her and the firm set of her bones below clean skin saved her from the fading of mere prettiness. Though she had been sought in marriage more than once, she had accepted no one, or, rather, had not been allowed to encourage anyone. Her brother saw to that.

Big Liam O'Grady was a great, raw-boned, sandy-haired man, with the strength of an ox and a heart no bigger than a sour apple. An overbearing man given to berserk rages. Though he was a churchgoer by habit, the true god of that man was Money – red gold, shining silver, dull copper – the trinity that he worshipped in degree. He and his sister Ellen lived on the big ranch farm of Moyvalla, and

Ellen was his housekeeper and maid of all work. She was a careful housekeeper, a good cook, a notable baker, and she demanded no wage. All that suited Big Liam splendidly, and so she remained single – a wasted woman.

Big Liam himself was not a marrying man. There were not many spinsters with a dowry big enough to tempt him, and the few there had acquired expensive tastes – a convent education, the deplorable art of hitting jazz out of a piano, the damnable vice of cigarette smoking, the purse-emptying craze for motor cars – such things.

But in due time, the dowry and the place – with a woman tied to them – came under his nose and Big Liam was no longer tardy. His neighbour, James Carey, died in March and left his fine farm and all on it to his widow, a youngish woman without children, a woman with a hard name for saving pennies. Big Liam looked once at Kathy Carey and looked many times at her broad acres. Both pleased him. He took the steps required by tradition. In the very first week of the following Shrovetide, he sent an accredited emissary to open formal negotiations, and that emissary came back within the hour.

"My soul," said he, "but she is the quick one! I hadn't ten words out of me when she was down my throat. 'I am in no hurry,' says she, 'to come wife into a house with another woman at the fire corner. When Ellen is in a place of her own, I will listen to what Liam O'Grady has to say.'"

"She will, by Jacus!" Big Liam stopped him. "She will so."

There, now, was the right time to recall Shawn Kelvin and the look in his eyes. Big Liam's mind corner promptly delivered up its memory. He smiled knowingly and contemptuously. Shawn Kelvin daring to cast sheep's eyes at an O'Grady! The undersized chicken-heart who took the loss of the Kelvin acres lying down! The little Yankee runt hidden away on the shelf of Knockanore! But what of it? The required dowry would be conveniently small, and the girl would never go hungry, anyway. There was Big Liam O'Grady, far descended from many chieftains.

The very next market day at Listowel he sought out Shawn Kelvin and placed a huge, sandy-haired hand on the shoulder that hunched to meet it.

"Shawn Kelvin, a word with you! Come and have a drink."

Shawn hesitated. "Very well," he said then. He did not care for O'Grady, but he would hurt no man's feelings.

They went across to Sullivan's bar and had a drink, and Shawn paid for it. And Big Liam came directly to his subject – almost patronisingly, as if he were conferring a favour.

"I want to see Ellen settled in a place of her own," said he.

Shawn's heart lifted into his throat and stayed there. But that steadfast face with the steadfast eyes gave no sign and, moreover, he could not say a word with his heart where it was.

"Your place is small," went on the big man, "but it is handy, and no load of debt on it, as I hear. Not much of a dowry ever came to Knockanore and not much of a dowry can I be giving with Ellen. Say two hundred pounds at the end of harvest, if prices improve. What do you say, Shawn Kelvin?"

Shawn swallowed his heart, and his voice came slow and cool: "What does Ellen say?"

"I haven't asked her," said Big Liam. "But what would she say, blast it?"

"Whatever she says, she will say it herself, not you, Big Liam."

But what could Ellen say? She looked within her own heart and found it empty; she looked at the granite crag of her brother's face and contemplated herself a slowly withering spinster at his fire corner; she looked up at the swell of Knockanore Hill and saw the white cottage among the green small fields below the warm brown of the heather. Oh, but the sun would shine up there in the lengthening spring day and pleasant breezes blow in sultry summer, and finally she looked at Shawn Kelvin, that firmly built, small man with the clean face and the lustrous eyes below steadfast brow. She said a prayer to her God and sank head and shoulders in a resignation more pitiful than tears, more proud than the pride of chieftains. Romance? Welladay!

Shawn was far from satisfied with that resigned acceptance, but then was not the time to press for a warmer one. He knew the brother's wizened soul, guessed at the girl's clean one and saw that she was doomed beyond hope to a fireside sordidly bought for her. Let it be his own fireside then. There were many worse ones – and God was good.

Ellen O'Grady married Shawn Kelvin. One small statement; and it holds the risk of tragedy, the chance of happiness, the probability of mere endurance – choices wide as the world.

But Big Liam O'Grady, for all his resolute promptness, did not win Kathy Carey to wife. She, foolishly enough, took to husband her own cattleman, a gay night-rambler, who gave her the devil's own time and a share of happiness in the bygoing. For the first time, Big Liam discovered how mordant the wit of his neighbours could be, and to contempt for Shawn Kelvin he now added an unreasoning dislike.

II

Shawn Kelvin had got his precious, red-haired woman under his own roof now. He had no illusions about her feelings for him. On himself, and on himself only, lay the task of moulding her into a wife and lover. Darkly, deeply, subtly, away out of sight, with gentleness, with restraint, with a consideration beyond kenning, that moulding must be done, and she that was being moulded must never know. He hardly knew, himself.

First he turned his attention to material things. He hired a small servant maid to help her with the housework. Then he acquired a rubber-tyred tub cart and a half-bred gelding with a reaching knee action. And on market days, husband and wife used to bowl down to Listowel, do their selling and their buying and bowl smoothly home again, their groceries in the well of the cart and a bundle of second-hand American magazines on the seat at Ellen's side. And in the nights, before the year turned, with the wind from the plains of the Atlantic keening above the chimney, they would sit at either side of the flaming peat fire and he would

read aloud strange and almost unbelievable things out of the high-coloured magazines. Stories, sometimes, wholly unbelievable.

Ellen would sit and listen and smile, and go on with her knitting or her sewing; and after a time it was sewing she was at, mostly small things. And when the reading was done, they would sit and talk quietly in their own quiet way. For they were both quiet. Woman though she was, she got Shawn to do most of the talking. It could be that she, too, was probing and seeking, unwrapping the man's soul to feel the texture thereof, surveying the marvel of his life as he spread it diffidently before her. He had a patient, slow, vivid way of picturing for her the things he had seen and felt. He made her see the glare of molten metal, lambent yet searing, made her feel the sucking heat, made her hear the clang; she could see the roped square under the dazzle of the hooded arcs with the curling smoke layer above it, understand the explosive restraint of the game, thrill when he showed her how to stiffen wrist for the final devastating right hook. And often enough the stories were humorous, and Ellen would chuckle, or stare, or throw back her red, lovely curls in laughter. It was grand to make her laugh.

Shawn's friends, in some hesitation at first, came in ones and twos up to the slope to see them. But Ellen welcomed them with her smile that was shy and, at the same time, frank, and her table was loaded for them with scones and crumpets and cream cakes and heather honey; and at the right time it was she herself brought forth the decanter of whiskey – no longer the half-empty stone jar – and the polished glasses. Shawn was as proud as sin of her. She would sit then and listen to their discussions and be forever surprised at the knowledgeable man her husband was - the way he would discuss war and politics and the making of songs, the turn of speech that summed up a man or a situation. And sometimes she would put in a word or two and be listened to, and they would look to see if her smile commended them, and be a little chastened by the wisdom of that smile – the age-old smile of the matriarch from whom they were all descended. In no time at all, Matt Tobin the thresher, who used to think, "Poor old Shawn! Lucky she was to get him," would whisper to the schoolmaster: "Herrin's alive! That fellow's luck would astonish nations."

Women, in the outside world, begin by loving their husbands; and then, if fate is kind, they grow to admire them; and if fate is not unkind, may descend no lower than liking and enduring. And there is the end of lawful romance. Look now at Ellen O'Grady. She came up to the shelf of Knockanore and in her heart was only a nucleus of fear in a great emptiness and that nucleus might grow into horror and disgust. But, glory of God, she, for reason piled on reason, presently found herself admiring Shawn Kelvin; and with or without reason, a quiet liking came to her for this quiet man who was so gentle and considerate; and then, one great heart-stirring dark o' night, she found herself fallen head and heels in love with her own husband. There is the sort of love that endures, but the road to it is a mighty chancy one.

A woman, loving her husband, may or may not be proud of him, but she will fight like a tiger if anyone, barring herself, belittles him. And there was one man that belittled Shawn Kelvin. Her brother, Big Liam O'Grady. At fair or market or chapel that dour giant deigned not to hide his contempt and dislike. Ellen knew why. He had lost a wife and farm; he had lost in herself a frugally cheap housekeeper; he had been made the butt of a sly humour; and for these mishaps, in some twisted way, he blamed Shawn. But – and there came in the contempt – the little Yankee runt, who dared say nothing about the lost Kelvin acres, would not now have the gall or guts to demand the dowry that was due. Lucky the hound to steal an O'Grady to hungry Knockanore! Let him be satisfied with that luck!

One evening before a market day, Ellen spoke to her husband: "Has Big Liam paid you my dowry yet, Shawn?"

"Sure there's no hurry, girl," said Shawn.

"Have you ever asked him?"

"I have not. I am not looking for your dowry, Ellen."

"And Big Liam could never understand that." Her voice firmed. "You will ask him tomorrow."

"Very well so, agrah," agreed Shawn easily.

And the next day, in that quiet diffident way of his, he asked Big Liam. But Big Liam was brusque and blunt. He had no loose money and Kelvin would have to wait till he had. "Ask me again, Shawneen," he finished, his face in a mocking smile, and turning on his heel, he ploughed his great shoulders through the crowded market.

His voice had been carelessly loud and people had heard. They laughed and talked amongst themselves. "Begobs! The devil's own boy, Big Liam! What a pup to sell! Stealing the land and keeping a grip on the fortune! Ay, and a dangerous fellow, mind you, the same Big Liam! He would smash little Shawn at the wind of a word. And devil the bit his Yankee sparring tricks would help him!"

A friend of Shawn's, Matt Tobin the thresher, heard that and lifted his voice: "I would like to be there the day Shawn Kelvin loses his temper."

"A bad day for poor Shawn!"

"It might be then," said Matt Tobin, "but I would come from the other end of Kerry to see the badness that would be in it for someone."

Shawn had moved away with his wife, not heeding or not hearing.

"You see, Ellen?" he said in some discomfort.

"The times are hard on the big ranchers, and we don't need the money, anyway."

"Do you think Big Liam does?" Her voice had a cut in it. "He could buy you and all Knockanore and be only on the fringe of his hoard. You will ask him again."

"But, girl dear, I never wanted a dowry with you."

She liked him to say that, but far better would she like to win for him the respect and admiration that was his due. She must do that now at all costs. Shawn, drawing back now, would be the butt of his fellowmen.

"You foolish lad! Big Liam would never understand your feelings, with money at stake." She smiled and a pang went through Shawn's breast. For the smile was the smile of an O'Grady, and he could not be sure whether the contempt in it was for himself or for her brother.

Shawn asked Big Liam again, unhappy in his asking, but also dimly comprehending his woman's object. And Shawn asked again a third time. The issue was become a famous one now. Men talked about it and women too. Bets were made on it. At fair or market, if Shawn was seen approaching Big Liam, men edged closer and women edged away. Some day the big fellow would grow tired of being asked, and in one of his terrible rages half-kill the little lad as he had half-killed other men. A great shame! Here and there, a man advised Sean to give up asking and put the matter in a lawyer's hands.

"I couldn't do that," was Shawn's only answer. Strangely enough, none of these prudent advisers were amongst Shawn's close friends. His friends frowned and said little, but they were always about, and always amongst them was Matt Tobin.

The day at last came when Big Liam grew tired of being asked. That was the big October cattle fair at Listowel, and he had sold twenty head of fat, polled-Angus beeves at a good price. He was a hard dealer and it was late in the day before he settled at his own figure, so that the banks were closed and he was not able to make a lodgement. He had, then, a great roll of bills in an inner vest pocket when he saw Shawn and Ellen coming across to where he was bargaining with Matt Tobin for a week's threshing. Besides, the day being dank, he had had a drink or two more than was good for him and the whiskey had loosened his tongue and whatever he had of discretion. By the powers! – it was time and past time to deal once and for all with this little gadfly of a fellow, to show him up before the whole market. He strode to meet Shawn, and people got out of his savage way and edged in behind to lose nothing of this dangerous game.

He caught Shawn by the hunched shoulder – a rending grip – and bent down to grin in his face.

"What is it, little fellow? Don't be ashamed to ask!"

Matt Tobin was probably the only one there to notice the ease with which Shawn wrenched his shoulder free, and Matt Tobin's eyes brightened. But Shawn did nothing further and said no word. His deep-set eyes gazed steadily at the big man.

The big man showed his teeth mockingly. "Go on, you whelp! What do you want?"

"You know, O'Grady."

"I do. Listen, Shawneen!" Again he brought his hand clap on the little man's shoulder. "Listen, Shawneen! If I had a dowry to give my sister, 'tis not a little shrimp like you would get her. Go to hell out o' that!"

His great hand gripped and he flung Shawn backwards as if he were only the image of a man filled with chaff.

Shawn went backwards, but he did not fall. He gathered himself like a spring, feet under him, arms half-raised, head forward into hunched shoulder. But as quickly as the spring coiled, as quickly it slackened, and he turned away to his wife. She was there facing him, tense and keen, her face pale and set, and a gleam of the race in her eyes.

"Woman, woman!" he said in his deep voice. "Why would you and I shame ourselves like this?"

"Shame!" she cried. "Will you let him shame you now?"

"But your own brother, Ellen – before them all?"

"And he cheating you – "

"Glory of God!" His voice was distressed. "What is his dirty money to me? Are you an O'Grady, after all?"

That stung her and she stung him back in one final effort. She placed a hand below her breast and looked close into his face. Her voice was low and bitter, and only he heard: "I am an O'Grady. It is a great pity that the father of this my son is a Kelvin and a coward."

The bosses of Shawn Kelvin's cheekbones were like hard marble, but his voice was as soft as a dove's.

"Is that the way of it? Let us be going home then, in the name of God!"

He took her arm, but she shook his hand off; nevertheless, she walked at his side, head up, through the people that made way for them. Her brother mocked them with his great laughing bellow.

"That fixes the pair of them!" he cried, brushed a man who laughed with him out of his way, and strode off through the fair.

There was talk then – plenty of it. "Murder, but Shawn had a narrow squeak that time! Did you see the way he flung him? I wager he'll give Big Liam a wide road after this. And he by way of being a boxer! That's a pound you owe me, Matt Tobin."

"I'll pay it," said Matt Tobin, and that is all he said. He stood wide-legged, looking at the ground, his hand ruefully rubbing the back of his head and dismay and gloom on his face. His friend had failed him in the face of the people.

III

Shawn and Ellen went home in their tub cart and had not a single word or glance for each other on the road. And all that evening, at table or fireside, a heart-sickening silence held them in its grip. And all that night they lay side by side, still and mute. There was only one subject that possessed them and on that they dared speak no longer. They slept little. Ellen, her heart desolate, lay on her side, staring into the dark, grieving for what she had said and unable to unsay it. Shawn, on his back, contemplated things with a cold clarity. He realized that he was at the fork of life and that a finger pointed unmistakably. He must risk the very shattering of all happiness, he must do a thing so final and decisive that, once done, it could never again be questioned. Before morning, he came to his decision, and it was bitter as gall. He cursed himself. "Oh, you fool! You might have known that you should never have taken an O'Grady without breaking the O'Gradys."

He got up early in the morning at his usual hour and went out, as usual, to his morning chores – rebedding and foddering the cattle, rubbing down the half-bred, helping the servant maid with the milk in the creaming pans – and as usual, he came in to his breakfast, and ate it unhungrily and silently, which was not usual. But, thereafter he went out again to the stable, harnessed his gelding and hitched him to the tub cart. Then he returned to the kitchen and spoke for the first time.

"Ellen, will you come with me down to see your brother?"

She hesitated, her hands thrown wide in a helpless, hopeless gesture. "Little use you going to see my brother, Shawn. 'Tis I should go and – not come back."

"Don't blame me now or later, Ellen. It has been put upon me, and the thing I am going to do is the only thing to be done. Will you come?"

"Very well," she agreed tonelessly, "I will be ready in a minute."

And they went the four miles down into the vale to the big farmhouse of Moyvalla. They drove into the great square of cobbled yard and found it empty.

On one side of the square was the long, low, lime-washed dwelling house; on the other, fifty yards away, the two-storeyed line of steadings with a wide arch in the middle and through the arch came the purr and zoom of a threshing machine. Shawn tied the half-bred to the wheel of a farm cart and, with Ellen, approached the house.

A slattern servant girl leaned over the kitchen half-door and pointed through the arch. The master was out beyond in the haggard – the rickyard – and would she run across for him?

"Never mind, achara," said Shawn, "I'll get him…Ellen, will you go in and wait?"

"No," said Ellen, "I'll come with you." She knew her brother.

As they went through the arch, the purr and zoom grew louder and, turning the corner, they walked into the midst of activity. A long double row of cone-pointed corn stacks stretched across the yard and, between them, Matt Tobin's portable threshing machine was busy. The smooth-flying, eight-foot driving wheel made a sleepy purr and the black driving belt ran with a sag and a heave to the red-painted thresher.

Up there on the platform, bare-armed men were feeding the flying drum with loosened sheaves, their hands moving in a rhythmic sway. As the toothed drum bit at the corn sheaves it made an angry snarl that changed and slowed into a satisfied zoom. The wide conveying belt was carrying the golden straw up a steep incline to where other men were building a long rick; still more men were attending to the corn shoots, shoulders bending under the weight of the sacks as they ambled across to the granary. Matt Tobin himself bent at the face of his engine, feeding the firebox with sods of hard black peat. There were not less than two score men about the place, for, as was the custom, all Big Liam's friends and neighbours were giving him a hand with the threshing – "the day in harvest".

Big Liam came round the flank of the engine and swore. He was in his shirtsleeves, and his great forearms were covered with sandy hair.

"Hell and damnation! Look who's here!"

He was in the worst of tempers this morning. The stale dregs of yesterday's whiskey were still with him and he was in the humour that, as they say, would make a dog bite its father. He took two slow strides and halted, feet apart and head truculently forward.

"What is it this time?" he shouted. That was the un-Irish welcome he gave his sister and her husband.

Shawn and Ellen came forward steadily and, as they came, Matt Tobin slowly throttled down his engine. Big Liam heard the change of pitch and looked angrily over his shoulder.

"What the hell do you mean, Tobin? Get on with the work!"

"To hell with yourself, Big Liam! This is my engine, and if you don't like it, you can leave it." And at that he drove the throttle shut and the purr of the flywheel slowly sank.

"We will see in a minute," threatened Big Liam, and turned to the two now near at hand. "What is it?" he growled.

"A private word with you. I won't keep you long." Shawn was calm and cold.

"You will not – on a busy morning," sneered the big man. "There is no need for private

words between me and Shawn Kelvin."

"There is need," urged Shawn. "It will be best for us all if you hear what I have to say in your own house."

"Or here on my own land. Out with it! I don't care who hears!"

Shawn looked round him. Up on the thresher, up on the straw rick, men leaned idle on fork handles and looked down at him; from here and there about the stockyard, men moved in to see, as it might be, what had caused the stoppage, but only really interested in the two brothers-in-law. He was in the midst of Clan O'Grady, for they were mostly O'Grady men – big, strong, blond men, rough, confident, proud of their breed. Matt Tobin was the only man he could call a friend. Many of the others were not unfriendly, but all had contempt in their eyes, or, what was worse, pity. Very well! Since he had to prove himself, it was fitting that he do it here amongst the O'Grady men.

Shawn brought his eyes back to Big Liam – deep, steadfast eyes that did not waver.

"O'Grady," said he – and he no longer hid his contempt – "you set a great store by money."

"No harm in that. You do it yourself, Shawneen."

"Take it so! I will play that game with you, till hell freezes. You would bargain your sister and cheat; I will sell my soul. Listen, you big brute! You owe me two hundred pounds. Will you pay it?" There was an iron quality in his voice that was somehow awesome. The big man, about to start forward overbearingly, restrained himself to a brutal playfulness.

"I will pay it when I am ready."

"Today."

"No; nor tomorrow."

"Right. If you break your bargain, I break mine."

"What's that?" shouted Big Liam.

"If you keep your two hundred pounds, you keep your sister."

"What is it?" shouted Big Liam again, his voice breaking in astonishment. "What is that you say?"

"You heard me. Here is your sister Ellen! Keep her!"

"Fires o' hell!" He was completely astounded out of his truculence. "You can't do that!"

"It is done," said Shawn.

Ellen O'Grady had been quiet as a statue at Shawn's side, but now, slow like doom, she faced him. She leaned forward and looked into his eyes and saw the pain behind the strength.

"To the mother of your son, Shawn Kelvin?" she whispered that gently to him.

His voice came cold as a stone out of a stone face: "In the face of God. Let Him judge me."

"I know – I know!" That was all she said, and walked quietly across to where Matt Tobin stood at the face of his engine.

Matt Tobin placed hand on her arm.

"Give him time, acolleen," he whispered urgently. "Give him his own time. He's slow, but he's deadly as a tiger when he moves."

Big Liam was no fool. He knew exactly how far he could go. There was no use, at this juncture, in crushing the runt under a great fist. There was some force in the little fellow that defied dragooning. Whatever people might think of Kelvin, public opinion would be dead against himself. Worse, his inward vision saw eyes leering in derision, mouths open in laughter. The scandal on his name would not be bounded by the four seas of Erin. He must change his stance while he had time. These thoughts passed through his mind while he thudded the ground three times with iron-shod heel. Now he threw up his head and bellowed his laugh.

"You fool! I was only making fun of you. What are your dirty few pounds to the likes of me? Stay where you are."

He turned, strode furiously away, and disappeared through the arch.

Shawn Kelvin was left alone in that wide ring of men. The hands had come down off the ricks and thresher to see closer. Now they moved back and aside, looked at one another, lifted eyebrows, looked at Shawn Kelvin, frowned and shook their heads. They knew Big Liam. They knew that, yielding up the money, his savagery would break out into something little short of killing. They waited, most of

them, to prevent that savagery going too far.

Shawn Kelvin did not look at anyone. He stood still as a rock, his hands deep in his pockets, one shoulder hunched forward, his eyes on the ground and his face strangely calm. He seemed the least perturbed man there. Matt Tobin held Ellen's arm in a steady grip and whispered in her ear: "God is good, I tell you."

Big Liam was back in two minutes. He strode straight to Shawn and halted within a pace of him.

"Look, Shawneen!" In his raised hand was a crumpled bundle of greasy banknotes. "Here is your money. Take it, and then see what will happen to you. Take it!" He thrust it into Shawn's hand. "Count it. Make sure you have it all, and then I will kick you out of this haggard, and look" – he thrust forward a hairy fist – "if ever I see your face again, I will drive that through it! Count it, you spawn."

Shawn did not count it. Instead, he crumpled it into a ball in his strong fingers. Then he turned on his heel and walked, with surprising slowness, to the face of the engine. He gestured with one hand to Matt Tobin, but it was Ellen, quick as a flash, who obeyed the gesture. Though the hot bar scorched her hand, she jerked open the door of the firebox and the leaping peat flames whispered out at her. And forthwith, Shawn Kelvin, with one easy sweep, threw the crumpled ball of notes into the heart of the flame. The whisper lifted one tone and one scrap of burned paper floated out of the funnel top. That was all the fuss the fire made of its work.

But there was fuss enough outside. Big Liam O'Grady gave one mighty shout. No, it was more an anguished scream than a shout:

"My money! My good money!"

He gave two furious bounds forward, his great arms raised to crush and kill. But his hands never touched the small man.

"You dumb ox!" said Shawn Kelvin between his teeth. That strong, hunched shoulder moved a little, but no one there could follow the terrific drive of that hooked right arm. The smack of bone on bone was sharp as whip crack, and Big Liam stopped dead, went back on his heels, swayed a moment and staggered back three paces.

"Now and forever! Man of the Kelvins!" roared Matt Tobin.

But Big Liam was a man of iron. That blow should have laid him on his back – blows like it had tied men to the ground for the full count. But Big Liam only shook his head, grunted like a boar, and drove in at the little man. And the little man, instead of circling away, drove in at him, compact of power.

The men of the O'Gradys saw then an exhibition that they had not knowledge enough to appreciate fully. Thousands had paid as much as ten dollars each to see the great Tiger Kelvin in action, his footwork, his timing, his hitting; and never was his action more devastating than now. He was a thunderbolt on two feet and the big man a glutton.

Big Liam never touched Shawn with clenched fist. He did not know how. Shawn, actually forty pounds lighter, drove him by sheer hitting across the yard.

Men for the first time saw a two-hundred-pound man knocked clean off his feet by a body blow. They saw for the first time the deadly restraint and explosion of skill.

Shawn set out to demolish his enemy in the briefest space of time, and it took him five minutes to do it. Five, six, eight times he knocked the big man down, and the big man came again staggering, slavering, raving, vainly trying to rend and smash. But at last he stood swaying and clawing helplessly, and Shawn finished him with his terrible double hit – left below the breastbone and right under the jaw.

Big Liam lifted on his toes and fell flat on his back. He did not even kick as he lay.

Shawn did not waste a glance at the fallen giant. He swung full circle on the O'Grady men and his voice of iron challenged them:

"I am Shawn Kelvin, of Knockanore Hill. Is there an O'Grady amongst you who thinks himself a better man? Come then."

His face was deep-carved stone, his great chest lifted, the air whistled through his nostrils; his deep-set flashing eyes dared them. No man came.

He swung around then and walked straight to his wife. He halted before her.

His face was still of stone, but his voice quivered and had in it all the dramatic force of the Celt:

"Mother of my son, will you come home with me?"

She lifted to the appeal, voice and eye:

"Is it so you ask me, Shawn Kelvin?"

His face of stone quivered at last. "As my wife only – Ellen Kelvin!"

"Very well, heart's treasure." She caught his arm in both of hers. "Let us be going home."

"In the name of God," he finished for her.

And she went with him, proud as the morning, out of that place. But a woman, she would have the last word.

"Mother of God!" she cried. "The trouble I had to make a man of him!"

"God Almighty did that for him before you were born," said Matt Tobin softly.

Chapter Three

The Plot Thickens

That then was the story about which John Ford got so excited when he first read it in 1933. By the time he obtained the film rights in 1936, he was probably even more excited, because by that time Walsh had expanded the story and included it as part three of the five-part novel *Green Rushes*. The publishers claimed that *Green Rushes* was not just a sheaf of disconnected short stories, but an ingeniously knit novel of original design. Walsh gathered about his arch-hero, Hugh Forbes ("The Small Dark Man") a company of kindred spirits whose lives were interwoven with his and one another's by the "cunning fingers of Destiny". The title had its origin in the old Irish love-saying:

I will spread green rushes under her feet that she may step softly.

The cynical, however, might justly claim that the *Quiet Man* story was a ready-made implant, perfect for insertion into *Green Rushes* and that the hero of *The Quiet Man* played only a very minor and non-essential part in the other chapters.

In fact, *Green Rushes* was inspired by the minor unnamed characters in the original *Quiet Man* story – the close friends who visited Shawn Kelvin in his cottage on the side of Knockanore. These were mentioned as "the school master, the young curate – men like that." Matt Tobin, the thresher, still appears in the new version of the story, but in a downgraded role. The *Quiet Man* chapter of *Green Rushes* became highly politicised and centred on the Irish Republican Army's struggle against the Black and Tans. Shawn Kelvin had to follow suit. Was this done to please Ford or maybe even requested by Ford? It is difficult to tell, though it is hard to imagine a writer of Maurice Walsh's ability and integrity

being swayed by what was then the rather remote prospect of his story becoming the screenplay of a movie. No, it is more likely that Walsh saw an artistic opportunity to paint a wider Irish canvas into which his original story fitted easily.

The central characters of *Green Rushes* who are relevant to our story are the following:

HUGH FORBES (allegedly modelled on Walsh himself) described as an ex-British officer and guerrilla commandant of an IRA Flying Column.

MICKEEN OGE FLYNN, his second-in-command and described as an unconditional republican, celibate by inclination and a "spoiled priest", i.e. one who had studied for the priesthood, but left the ministry before being ordained.

PADDY BAWN ENRIGHT, ex-boxer, known as "The Quiet Man" because he hoped to end his days in a quiet small place on a hillside, but was more likely to finish them in a Black and Tan ambush.

SEAN GLYNN, a gentleman farmer (possibly based on Walsh's own father) and area intelligence officer to the IRA.

Walsh had by now in the course of his job as Excise Officer spent many years in Scotland – several of the other major characters are Scottish and English people with military connections who were inadvertently caught up in the conflict between the Black and Tans and the IRA.

To accommodate the new military scenario of *Green Rushes*, many changes had to be made in the original *Quiet Man* story and many additional pieces of information emerge about the characters. Several aspects of the revised story made their way into the movie screenplay, if only as incidental details. Among these were:

(i) Castletown emerges as a place name.
(ii) Sean Glynn's housekeeper is called Johanna Dillane.
(iii) The name of the local bar is "Malouney's".

However, by far the most significant aspect of the *Quiet Man* chapter of *Green Rushes* is the huge number of changes from the story introduced to accommodate the wider plot and perhaps also to add more colour to the action. Some of the more important changes are as follows:

1. Shawn Kelvin had become Paddy Bawn Enright, which is precisely the name of the original inspiration. One wonders if Enright, who was still alive, was consulted – it is unlikely that he himself requested this change. Perhaps in his final years he enjoyed the fame the story brought him.

2. Shawn Kelvin went to the States at the age of twenty and returned at the age of thirty-five. Paddy Bawn Enright went at the age of seventeen and returned at the age of thirty-two. Perhaps Walsh felt these ages were more realistic and wanted younger characters for his romantic story.

3. Big Liam O'Grady has become Red Will O'Danaher. This is not as big a change as one might suspect, as "Liam" and "Will" are both short for "William" in Ireland. In addition, "Liam" is the word for William in the Irish language.

4. The word "ranch" has been retained to describe O'Danaher's farm. This would have been understood by American readers in their own sense, but few would have realised that the word "rancher" is used as a term of abuse in rural Ireland.

5. Paddy Bawn Enright joined an IRA Flying Column under the command of

Hugh Forbes and Mickeen Oge Flynn. He took an active part in the fight against the notorious British auxiliary force, the Black and Tans, until the Truce was declared.

6. After the War of Independence was over, under pressure from his IRA colleagues, Paddy Bawn took a job as land-steward to Sean Glynn at Leaccabuie, while Matt Tobin kept an eye on Paddy Bawn's own place, replacing the "middling imitation of a man, the ex-navy pensioner".

7. The Quiet Man's love of horses is introduced. He buys an old brood mare of hunter blood, hoping to breed a good class jumper. He hunts the hare with a black hound dog, shoots grouse with an old IRA gun, and catches trout in a nearby river. Walsh had turned Paddy Bawn Enright into a riding, hunting, shooting country gentleman.

8. The friends who visited Paddy Bawn in his cottage have been changed and are now named as specific IRA personnel. In addition, Major Archibald MacDonald of the British Army is introduced to link him with the other stories in *Green Rushes*.

9. Ellen O'Grady had become Ellen Roe O'Danaher. "Roe" is a corruption of "rua", the Irish word for "red-haired". Walsh's own wife, a beautiful Scottish lady named Caroline Isobel Thompson Begg (nicknamed "Toshon" from her childish pronunciation of Thompson), had lovely red hair.

10. Paddy Bawn Enright became a monthly sodality communicant so he could have the pleasure of seeing Ellen Roe at Mass every Sunday.

11. On their way to Moyvalla for the big fight, Paddy Bawn and Ellen Roe encounter Sean Glynn and Mickeen Oge Flynn chugging along in an ancient touring-car. They were additional friends of Paddy's at

the fight. Red Will O'Danaher asks if the IRA are in the fight too, but Mickeen Oge Flynn replies that they are not, because if they were, not even the desolation of desolation would be as desolate as Moyvalla – a thinly veiled threat.

12. The final comment – "God almighty did that for him before you were born" – is now spoken by Mickeen Oge Flynn, who has replaced Matt Tobin as the Quiet Man's spokesman and confidant.

Many other small but significant changes were made to the story – an adverb here, an adjective there, or a subtle change of phrase somewhere else. Ironically when the screenplay of *The Quiet Man* arrived at its final version, many of the major changes were reversed. The IRA references, for example, were either removed or completely sanitised. In fact, it would be fair to say that the movie screenplay is closer to the original story than it is to the *Green Rushes* version.

From the outset, Ford planned to turn the *Quiet Man* story into a movie, but there were many, many obstacles in his way, and it was almost twenty years after the appearance of the original story that his dream was to be realised. In 1937 he nearly pulled off a deal with a co-op company called Renowned Artists but it fell through at the last moment. Nobody, including Fox, RKO and Warner Brothers, was interested in producing what they thought was a silly, stupid Irish story that would never make a penny. Ford's previous Irish films *The Informer* and *The Plough and the Stars* had a serious political and psychological content, but *The Quiet Man* seemed to offer nothing more than a shallow love story and a brawl. Even Darryl Zanuck, who had so successfully produced Ford's Oscar-winning Welsh masterpiece, *How Green Was My Valley* in 1941, was not convinced

Duke Wayne and Maureen O'Hara in the grounds of Ashford Castle

of the merits of the venture and refused to be involved. The studios were showing very little faith in Ford's judgement and the acclaim for his previous Celtic movies seemed to account for nothing.

Ford, however, trusted his own feelings and continued for over ten years to seek a backer for what was now his passionate project. He proceeded with putting together the bones of a screenplay and assembling a suitable cast. In fact, the casting was the least of his problems. John Wayne was a natural for Shawn Kelvin/Paddy Bawn Enright, despite the fact that he was a tall man unlike the hero of the story that Maurice Walsh had written. The beautiful,

Victor McLaglen

and red-haired to boot, Maureen O'Hara was an equally natural choice for Ellen O'Grady/Ellen Roe Danaher, after her huge success as Angharad Morgan in *How Green Was My Valley*. There seems not to be a shred of evidence for Barbara Leaming's claim in her book *Katherine Hepburn* that Ford wanted the part to be played by Katherine Hepburn and that is why Ellen's name was changed to Mary Kate. In fact, in an interview with June Beck, Maureen O'Hara revealed how the name Mary Kate came about. The "Mary" was for John Ford's wife. "Kate" is the name that Maureen's father wanted to christen her when she was born but somehow she got called Maureen instead. So at least he got to see his daughter called Kate, even if it was only her middle name and on the big screen.

In fact, when Ford was back in Hollywood in 1944 on leave from the Navy, he and O'Hara had a handshake contract for her to play the female lead. She discussed the project with Ford many times and even typed early drafts of the screenplay to cut down on expenses. However, she too was worried by the passage of time and she used to say that if Ford didn't speed things up, she would have to play the part of the widow woman and Wayne the part of Red Will.

Other members of the Ford "Stock Company" such as Victor McLaglen, Ward Bond, Mildred Natwick and Arthur Shields, had handshake contracts also, but, surprisingly, Barry Fitzgerald was not the first choice for the part he was to make so famous. Denis O'Dea, who played the ballad singer in *The Informer* and was later to play the policeman in *The Rising of the Moon*, was originally intended for the part of Michaeleen Oge Flynn. Thus, fifteen years before he shot *The Quiet Man*, Ford had cast virtually all of the leading roles.

In March 1946 it seemed as if Ford's luck was turning. His old friend Merian C. Cooper, formerly deputy to David O. Selznick at RKO and best known for directing *King Kong* (1933), agreed to go into partnership with Ford to form their own production company. They named it Argosy Productions with Cooper as president and financial controller and Ford as chairman. Now that they had some control over the selection and making of movies, they resolved that *The Quiet Man* would be one of their immediate priorities. Immediately, there appeared on the horizon a potential financial backer – Alexander Korda, chairman of London Films Productions and one of Britain's most successful producers.

Ford at once wrote to his Irish friend, Michael Morris, Lord Killanin, telling him that he planned to shoot *The Quiet Man* in the following year, in Technicolor, "all over Ireland, but with stress laid on Spiddal". He commissioned Killanin's help in making the movie "a beautiful travelogue" as well as "a charming story". Kylemore Abbey, deep in the heart of Connemara, was mentioned as the setting for a possible scene and Killanin set about finding other beautiful locations in the West of Ireland to enhance the movie's visual appeal.

Soon, however, and perhaps inevitably, Cooper and Korda were at loggerheads about money, percentages, credits and like matters and found themselves deeper and deeper in conflict. Eventually, to Ford's despair, this deal, which seemed to promise so much, also fell through. However, Ford had one shot left in his locker – RKO Radio Productions, who had backed *The Informer* in 1935. RKO were very keen to sign a director of Ford's stature, but they too were suspicious about what they regarded as the slight plot of *The Quiet Man*. Eventually a deal was signed – Ford was to make three movies for RKO, and, if the first one made a profit, RKO would finance *The Quiet Man*.

Inexplicably, Ford chose as his first production for RKO *The Fugitive*, based on Graham Greene's novel *The Power and the Glory*. Rather predictably, *The Fugitive* was a flop at the box office and the moviegoing public stayed away in droves, although the critics liked it. RKO at once, as was their right, withdrew their support for the making of *The Quiet Man*. It looked as though this movie would never be made. In the meantime, between 1947 and 1950, Ford directed four classic Westerns for Argosy Productions, always hoping one of them would hit the financial jackpot that would allow him to make *The Quiet Man* in Ireland. The Argosy movies were *Fort Apache* (1948), *Three Godfathers* (1948), *She Wore a Yellow Ribbon* (1949) and *Wagon Master* (1950). All of these productions featured substantial numbers of cast members who would come together for *The Quiet Man*.

When the breakthrough finally came, it was from a most unlikely source. Like Ford and O'Hara, John "Duke" Wayne also had strong Irish roots. His great-great-grandfather Robert Morrison was born in County Antrim in 1782 and his grandmother Maggie Brown was an Irish Catholic born in County Cork in 1848. Wayne too desperately wanted to see *The Quiet Man* made so he "formed a little conspiracy" to ensure that it would come about!

Wayne had been contracted to churn out a number of B-Westerns for Republic Pictures Corporation which was controlled by Herbert J. Yates, a man who had made his fortune in the tobacco business and now fancied himself as a movie tycoon. Commercially, Yates was worried about the impact that television was having on his B-movie market, but he was also a movie snob who wanted to move his operations into the A-stream. Wayne rightly figured that Yates would not be able to resist the bait of having someone of Ford's calibre direct his productions, and he was right. He even persuaded Yates that other top directors would move to Republic in Ford's wake. All Yates had to do to attract Ford, Wayne told him, was to let him make a movie called *The Quiet Man* based on a story to which he already owned the rights.

Yates fell for the scheme – he agreed even to give Ford fifteen percent of the gross and not to check his budgets! Yet Yates was no fool – he made Ford sign a three-picture deal with the proviso that a profitable movie had to be made before *The Quiet Man* could be contemplated. He also insisted that the profit-making movie be a Western with largely the same cast and production crew as were being planned for *The Quiet Man* – more or less a dress rehearsal without risk. Yates had read the screenplay summary of *The Quiet Man* and thought very little of it. Basically, he felt that it was just a foolish Irish romantic tale that would do nothing except lose money, especially as it was to be shot in Ireland, in Technicolor and with a proposed budget of a million and three-quarter dollars – an unheard-of sum in those days. Yet this was the price that Yates seemed prepared to pay to acquire Ford's services, with Merian C.

Cooper thrown in as part of the deal. Ford, sensing that there was now a real possibility of having his beloved project realised, persuaded Wayne to waive his usual percentage deal with Republic and do *The Quiet Man* for a flat fee of $100,000.

Ford had obviously learned a thing or two from the flop of his earlier arty movie *The Fugitive* in similar circumstances for RKO. This time, in 1950, he went to Monument Valley and made *Rio Grande*, a classic Western, which became a solid if not spectacular box-office success. Actually, there were several complications. Ford was reluctant to do *Rio Grande* unless he was given a free hand with the casting, which of course included Wayne, but unfortunately Wayne and Yates had just had a major row and were barely on speaking terms. Duke was so anxious to do *The Quiet Man* that he ate humble pie and apologised to Yates in order that he be used in *Rio Grande*. The way was then clear for him to star in *The Quiet Man*. *Rio Grande* had many of the *Quiet Man* production crew though maybe not as many of the cast as Yates would have liked, but it did have Wayne and O'Hara playing opposite each other for the first time, and the chemistry was electrifying. Yates, though he still had many doubts, gave the financial go-ahead for *The Quiet Man* and the project was finally on. However, right up to the time when the movie appeared Yates was unhappy with the name of *The Quiet Man* and made desperate attempts to change it. Among the suggestions he made were *Uncharted Voyage*, *The Fabulous Yankee*, *Homeward Bound*, *Hearts Across the Sea*, *The Man Untamed*, *The Silent Man*, and famously, *The Prizefighter and the Colleen*, based presumably on the Wayne-produced *Torero*, whose title Yates changed to *The Bullfighter and the Lady*. Ford, however, stuck to his guns and the title remained *The Quiet Man*.

Ford was ecstatic about the long-wished-for project, although in his perverse way he seemed to resent Wayne's part in pulling off the deal which he himself had failed to deliver so many times. Late in 1950 Ford took off for a vacation in Ireland and liked what he saw, his enthusiasm growing by the minute for the forthcoming shooting. Again he called on his friend Lord Killanin and requested his help with briefing, the finding of locations and other production details. Killanin had an important role to play in the making of *The Quiet Man* so here may be a good place to discuss that role.

The Rt Hon. Sir Michael Morris, Baronet, 3rd Baron Killanin, to give him his full title, was born in Ireland on 30 July 1914 of an Irish military father and an Australian mother. He was educated at Eton, the Sorbonne and Cambridge University and in his youth he boxed, rowed and played rugby, as well as acting and editing a university journal. In 1935 he joined the *Daily Express* newspaper and afterwards the *Daily Mail*, where he was war correspondent as well as writing on diplomatic and political matters. In 1938 he volunteered for the army and was decorated for his part in the Normandy D-Day landings.

He was president of the Olympic Council of Ireland from 1950 to 1973 and president of the International Olympic Council from 1972 to 1980, where he became an internationally known figure, personally meeting many heads of state and emerging as a skilled diplomat in the difficult art of reconciling sporting bodies. Lord Killanin is the author of over a dozen books, mostly concerning Ireland and the Olympic movement. He was director of many Irish commercial companies and served as a member of numerous committees, particularly those concerned with films, horses, the sea and the environment. As Honorary Consul General for Monaco in Ireland, he welcomed the former movie star Princess Grace Kelly of Monaco on her visit to Ireland. Naturally, as befits a Renaissance Man, he had been showered throughout his life with awards, decorations and honorary degrees, literally from all over the world.

Michael Morris' family had been in Galway since the fourteenth century – one of Galway's fourteen tribes – and his grandfather, who was Lord Chief Justice of Ireland, was created Lord Killanin in 1900. On the death of his uncle,

Lord Killanin succeeded to the title which, among other things, means that he sat in the British parliamentary upper house, the House of Lords. Nevertheless, he was profoundly Irish in outlook and took a particular pride in his West of Ireland background from which his title is derived.

In 1945 Lord Killanin married Sheila Dunlop MBE, a distinguished lady who had worked as a code-breaker at Bletchley Park during World War Two. She was the daughter of Canon Douglas Dunlop, Rector of Oughterard, County Galway and Killanin claimed that Canon Dunlop was the model and inspiration for the Reverend Cyril Playfair in *The Quiet Man*. He recounted that Dunlop is supposed to have chosen Oughterard as his parish because it had "more fish than Protestants".

Killanin and Ford had family connections that went back a long way and Ford whimsically claimed that they might even have been blood relatives, because Killanin had a great-great-uncle who had freely populated the Spiddal area, inside and outside of marriage! In 1840, Killanin's great-grandmother died of cholera, having just given birth to a son, later to become Sir George Morris. The child was fostered to Ford's ancestors, the Feeney family, who occupied a cottage on the Morris estates. Ford and Killanin met for the first time in Los Angeles in the late thirties and even then Ford showed his "Irish cousin" a copy of Walsh's *Green Rushes* and told him that some day he would shoot it as a movie in Ireland.

In the official John Ford filmography, Michael Killanin is listed as an uncredited producer of *The Quiet Man* and by his own account he found all the locations for the movie. However, this is disputed by Maureen O'Hara, who claims that her brother Charlie

John Ford and Lord Killanin

Fitzsimons with Luke Lukather found most of the locations and that she herself found one or two also. She also suggests that Killanin's role in the making of the movie was confined to periodic attendances at the shooting, but this is surely an underestimation of the importance of his role.

Interestingly, a photograph in *The Galway Sentinel* dated 28 November 1950, the year before the filming, shows Lord Killanin, John Ford and Ward Bond at Ashford Castle Hotel and the caption reads – "Mr. Ford was on location in Connemara in preparation for the filming of Maurice Walsh's story *The Quiet Man*." Some accounts indicate that Yates accompanied Ford and Bond to Ireland. Ford was adamant that only Technicolor would do justice to the Irish scenery and countryside, but Yates, with an ever-anxious eye on the purse strings, was equally insistent that black and white would suffice. Legend has it that Ford had his way by showing Yates a randomly picked ruined cottage and bursting into tears as he related how all of his Feeney ancestors had been born there before being driven out by cruel oppressors.

There is no doubt, however, of the fact that in October 1951 after *The Quiet Man* was completed, Lord Killanin and Brian Desmond-Hearst began forming an Irish film company called Four Provinces Productions, with the intention of building up a native Irish film industry, concentrating on the classics of Irish literature, including works by Synge, O'Casey, Joyce and O'Flaherty. Ford was invited to serve on the board of the new company and he eagerly accepted, despite the misgivings of his wife Mary. Four Provinces planned to make its headquarters in Galway and to exploit the English-speaking movie world's desire for material of Irish interest. A few productions of some merit were actually made, for example, *The Playboy of the Western World* (1962) and *The Rising of the Moon* (1957), directed by Ford, but sadly none was a great commercial success, to put it mildly. Killanin was associated as producer or associate producer with two other Ford films – *Gideon's Day* (1958) and *Young Cassidy* (1965). Sadly, Lord Killanin died in 1998, deeply mourned in Ireland and worldwide.

Chapter Four

The Making of the Movie

Now that Ford was faced with the fact that his long-cherished dream of making *The Quiet Man* in Ireland was suddenly about to become a reality, there was a multitude of practical details to be worked out. The casting was not really a problem and we have already recounted how handshake contracts existed with many of the principals, and there were numerous Irish actors and actresses only too willing to take up the minor roles.

The screenplay was a different matter. Walsh's story contained some lovely ideas for a movie, but a short story and a movie are totally different media. Indeed, it is amusing to hear people complain that Ford "savaged" or "destroyed the essence" of Walsh's original story which centred on a little man taking on a big bully and transformed it into a scenario where an ex-professional boxer was more than a match for an ageing bully. Ford, however, very well understood the difference between a movie and the short story on which it was loosely based and we need offer no apology for the content or quality of his cinematic finished product, which millions of movie fans worldwide have acknowledged for nearly fifty years.

Ford's first inclination was to turn to Richard Llewellyn, the Welsh novelist who had written *How Green Was My Valley* on which Ford's Oscar-winning movie of the same name was based. Just before he flew to Korea in late December 1950 to film *This is Korea*, Ford asked Llewellyn to turn Walsh's short story into a novella, suitable for adaptation into a screenplay. The story was to be set, according to Ford's instructions, in the Ireland of 1921 at the height of "The Troubles", as the war against the Black and Tans was known. Clearly Ford wanted his movie to have a very strong political component even to the extent of having Shawn come home from the United States to do his bit in the fight for freedom.

However, when Ford arrived home from Korea and read Llewellyn's efforts, he began to have second thoughts. *The Quiet Man* was in essence a love story and a comedy, and intense violence and politics sat very uncomfortably on top of these themes. Indeed, Ford eventually described his movie as "a Western set in Ireland", showing that the fighting it contained was essentially comic in nature and more akin to a Tom and Jerry cartoon than to real violence. But a difficult decision now had to be made - was *The Quiet Man* to be a lighthearted movie or a serious one? A few of the more extreme extracts from Llewellyn's intended script may convey something of the mood of what *The Quiet Man* might have been like had the serious atmosphere prevailed. (Shawn, by the way, was to have yet another name - Sean Burke, and his lady-love was to be Breede Ruad.)

Denis O'Dea's side-car drives up to the Burke cottage. The young curate is seated in complete dejection. O'Dea hastily knocks at the door, which is opened by Sean Burke, already dressed with cap and trench coat.
"The time is here," says Denis.
"I am ready," says Sean quickly closing the door.
It quickly dissolves into daylight, and the roar of the Crossley lorries, and the coming of the "Terror".
A lonely cabin. A seventeen-year-old boy torn from his mother's arms. The family in the background, children, chickens and so forth.
They raid and search town street.
The men lined up, sixty or seventy.
Their hands and caps in the air.
Short close-ups of this action – women's faces at windows – the masked informer in nondescript mack, and the accusing finger (woman informer).

But no shooting (God Help Us)??
Perhaps pipe band music played in dirge.
This would be effective, and so on to our
story of Breede Ruad.
She is ploughing alone in the fields, her eyes
on the far-off hills.

Two extracts from the notes accompanying the
script, however, are significant.

1. Following our lengthy discussion with
Sean Nunan of External Affairs we thought
it would be better to show our phase of the
Anglo-Irish War of Liberation (the so-called
Troubles) in as briefly and as novel a form as
possible.

2. The "Terror" is used briefly for dramatic
purpose. The coming of the Armistice. We
should again try to get a gay mood into the
picture…
Activity in the fields. Characters that we
have seen in the ambush are now making
hay…
The blacksmith puts his rifle away and takes
down his fishing rod.

Ironically, many of these themes eventually
rejected as a part of The Quiet Man make their
appearance in David Lean's Ryan's Daughter,
another major film shot in County Kerry in
1970. Of that production scenarist Robert Bolt
said: "What I didn't want was a lot of Irish
whimsy." The success of The Quiet Man over
Ryan's Daughter with Academy Awards and at
the box office suggests that "Irish whimsy",
properly treated, wins over Irish violence and
seriousness no matter how well treated.

Several other incidental but significant details
also emerge from the production notes at this
stage. Denis O'Dea is to be cast as "Micaeleen
Joyce", Arthur Shields as the Parish Priest (not
his final role) and Eileen Crowe as the Church
of Ireland vicar's wife, the part she eventually
wound up with. As late as 19 May 1951, just a
month before shooting began, the part of
Feeney was to be played by the great Noel

Purcell and Jack MacGowran was a last minute,
but excellent, substitute. Sean Glynn was to be
played by "McCormick", surely not the great
Abbey Theatre actor F.J. McCormick, husband
of Eileen Crowe, who had died in 1947, and not
S. Barret McCormick, press agent for Ford's The
Informer. As we will see, Ford had a habit of
offering minor parts in The Quiet Man to
acquaintances and people he met, perhaps to
accentuate the natural atmosphere of his movie.
Actually, the proposed initial casting for the
character to be called Owen Glynn in the final
cut is little short of sensational – no less a
person than John McCormack, Papal Count
and Ireland's foremost tenor! Well, Owen
Glynn's was a singing part and one can imagine
Ford saying "Who's the top Irish singer? Let's
get McCormack!" McCormack had appeared
in several movies, notably The Colleen Bawn
(1911), Song O' My Heart (1930), the first sound
feature film shot in Ireland, in which he played
the lead part of Sean O'Carolan, and Wings Of
The Morning (1937), with Henry Fonda, the first
Technicolor feature film made in Britain or
Ireland. Sadly, John McCormack died as early as
1945, though Republic publicity material for
The Quiet Man listed his name as a cast member
as late as 1950.

Several minor parts such as Pat Cohan and
the Anglican Bishop remained uncast until the
very last minute, some indeed until Ford
returned to the United States in July 1951 to
shoot the interior scenes.

After reading Llewellyn's script, Ford
suddenly made an important decision – a
decision that every Irishman makes at some
stage during his lifetime. The decision is that
seriousness and trouble are not the really
important things in life but that comedy and
romance are. The politics and the violence
would have to go and the movie would have to
survive as a love story and a comedy – an Irish-
American cross between Romeo and Juliet and
The Taming of the Shrew. Conflict there would
be, but it would be an almost comic conflict,
easily resolved in a cathartic punch-up, the
longest in screen history. Undoubtedly, Ford

was more than a little worried that the love story might be too slight to carry a movie of over two hours' projected length, but he was prepared to take his chances.

Richard Llewellyn was uncredited for his contribution as a scriptwriter, but he was probably paid well enough for his troubles. Enter now the man who was a real genius behind *The Quiet Man* movie – Frank Stanley Nugent, half-Irish and half-Jewish, a man who had been for many years a highly respected film critic of *The New York Times*. Several books and articles suggest that Nugent was for a time married to Ford's daughter Barbara but this does not seem to have been the case. Nugent had already been the screenplay writer for a string of Ford-Cooper-Argosy successes, such as *Fort Apache* (1948), *Three Godfathers* (1948), *She Wore a Yellow Ribbon* (1949) and *Wagon Master* (1950), so he had worked with many of the Ford "Stock Company", and he knew well just what Ford wanted. Moreover, he had a very keen sense of humour and many of the comic moments in *The Quiet Man* screenplay originate from his lively mind.

Nugent was essentially a "method writer" who immersed himself totally in every screenplay he wrote. For every major character he worked on, he created a complete biography and background as much for his own benefit as for that of the actors and actresses. In ten short weeks, under the watchful eyes of Ford and Maureen O'Hara, who faithfully typed the final manuscript just to keep the expenses down, Nugent fleshed out the earlier plots and added several important characters that appeared in the final version. However, Ford seems to have had at all times the final say and by no means used all of Nugent's suggestions, but it is fair to say that the finished *Quiet Man* movie was the result of subtle changes and variations by Ford on Nugent's basic screenplay.

Nugent gave *The Quiet Man* its magic comic touch and lightened its whole tone. He quickly seemed to sense what Ford was really looking for and deliver it over a very short period of time, just when Ford needed his confidence boosted. Deep down, as an experienced film critic, perhaps Nugent sensed that when people go out for an evening to watch a movie, they prefer to be entertained and laugh rather than be confronted by serious issues.

It is also possible of course that Ford was worried by what might happen to a serious *Quiet Man* at the box office remembering one or two disasters he had had in the past – *The Fugitive*, for example. Irish-Americans would probably flock to see any Ford movie set in Ireland no matter what its theme, but there were also many millions of Americans who had no connections with Ireland. He also had to consider the British and Continental European markets where in those days Irish Republican sympathies were pretty thin on the ground.

With Nugent's inspired and light-hearted scriptwriting under Ford's guidance, *The Quiet Man* emerged in the way it is known and loved today. The hero becomes Sean Thornton, the surname being the name of one of Ford's Irish cousins, Martin Thornton, a well-known boxer who doubled for Victor McLaglen in the big fight scene. Suddenly Sean has become a heavyweight, afraid to fight his brother-in-law because he once killed a man in the ring. The heroine has become Mary Kate Danaher and her big bullying brother Red Will Danaher. These new polysyllabic names roll off the tongue much more easily than the previous ones and the double first names would certainly appeal more to American moviegoers. Michaeleen Oge Flynn emerges as a major character as do Father Peter Lonergan and his curate Father Paul, and the creation of Mister and Missus Playfair and their bishop give *The Quiet Man* a whole new religious dimension, perhaps to be expected of an Irish movie by foreign audiences. The comic aspects of the movie are greatly enhanced, from Danaher's yes-man Aloysius Feeney (bearing two of Ford's own names) to the stage-Irish railwaymen, pub inhabitants, and an eloquent fishwoman.

In the final version of *The Quiet Man* only Forbes and Glynn remain as token remnants of the IRA and they are obviously gentlemen soldiers who have given up all thought of armed rebellion. Ford did manage to slip

Michaeleen Oge Flynn a few clever political lines such as talking treason with his friends, but these are more comic than military. In fact, everybody in the movie eventually becomes comic – even Red Will Danaher gets to utter several priceless Irish bulls, those superb self-contradictory statements for which Ireland is justly famous.

Slowly the pieces of the jigsaw began to fall into place. All Ireland, and especially Dublin's Abbey Theatre, was scoured for "Irish Players" to play the minor parts, and all these people were personally interviewed by Ford himself. Maureen O'Hara tells how her brother, lawyer Charles Fitzsimons, who was to play Forbes in *The Quiet Man*, was also instrumental in vetting and choosing players for the minor parts from his intimate knowledge of the Irish theatre. Ideally, the filming should have taken place in North Kerry, where Walsh's story had been set, but Ford had no doubt that he wanted the location to be County Galway where his ancestors had come from. Spiddal, a village on the Atlantic coast nine miles due west of Galway City would have been his first choice of location but this proved to be unsatisfactory for several reasons, not least of which was the lack of suitable accommodation there for cast and crew. By a happy chance, the next choice was the beautiful village of Cong on the isthmus between two of Ireland's largest and loveliest lakes, Lough Mask and Lough Corrib. Cong lies entirely in County Mayo but the Cong river, which forms part of the boundary with County Galway, skirts right around the village and is seen many times in *The Quiet Man*, especially in the courting and fishing scenes.

The filming, which began early in June 1951, changed the face of Cong forever. For a start, the ESB, which is the Irish Electricity Supply Board, brought forward their plans to electrify the village to accommodate the film crew who were largely English. Indeed, the ESB management had great difficulty in holding on to their workmen hired to dig holes and erect the electricity poles. They deserted in droves to become film extras at five times the wages they were being paid by the ESB. Ford

saw to it that the cast and crew acknowledged the importance of the arrival of electric power in a rural community by attending the switch-on ceremony in force. In addition to hordes of local clergy and other dignitaries, Ford, Wayne, McLaglen and Lord Killanin were in attendance and there was a reception beforehand in Ashford Castle. The rocky nature of the Cong area necessitated the use of explosives to erect the electricity poles and in the words of a local newspaper, there was a worry that "the sound boom that registers the gasps and sighs of the film stars would pick up the sound of the blasts and reproduce it on the sound-track of the film!" Care was therefore taken that the blasts were confined to times when the cameras were not rolling. It was also realised that the sudden appearance of electricity poles in the main street halfway through a scene supposedly set in the 1920s would constitute an anachronism that could hardly fail to be noticed on the screen, so there was close consultation between the art director and ESB.

New technology also arrived around this time in Cong in the form of an expanded and extended telephone service. Normally the existing phone service closed its lines to all but emergency calls between the hours of 8 p.m. and 9 a.m., but the volume of calls between a film unit on location and its controllers in the United States meant that Cong was given additional lines and a 24-hour service for the duration of the filming.

Ford was most particular that the cast and crew of *The Quiet Man* would not appear to be elitist and would take part in as many local events as possible, mixing with "the common people" of Ireland. Parties, fêtes and social events were attended, but two occasions stand out as having special significance. A local newspaper, *The Western People*, advertised that on the night of Friday 6 July 1951 there would be a dance in Cong Hall, with dancing from 11 p.m. to 3 a.m., where local people could meet all the celebrities. Photographers and reporters were present and the *Connaught Telegraph* waxed eloquent about the event. The hall was virtually empty when the Hollywood celebrities arrived at 9.30, completely ignorant of Irish rural dancing habits, but by 10 p.m. the place was jammed to the rafters, even before the pubs were closed! Ford, O'Hara, Wayne, Crowe, Natwick, Francis Ford, Pat Ford, Charles Fitzsimons, James Lilburn, Jack MacGowran and Winton Hoch were all present, obviously under a three-line whip, and danced enthusiastically until the small hours. Only Barry Fitzgerald and Victor McLaglen were exempt because of their age and were allowed to retire to bed after dinner. Maureen O'Hara speculated on how she would feel when her make-up call arrived at 5.30 a.m. in the morning.

However, a theatrical event around this time probably had more significance. Ford agreed that he and the *Quiet Man* cast would take part in a concert and play to raise funds for the "County Galway Volunteer Memorial Fund", very probably organised by Irish Republican supporters. The production was arranged for Seapoint Ballroom in Salthill near Galway Bay for Tuesday 3 July 1951, and the performers were to include all the principal *Quiet Man* stars singing and performing. In addition, Barry Fitzgerald and Arthur Shields were to take part in some extracts from Lady Gregory's play *The Rising of the Moon* which Ford later filmed. Duke Wayne was to be master of ceremonies and the admission charge was a steep ten shillings.

Before the concert, Ford gave a lengthy interview to a local newspaper explaining the reasons for his involvement in what could be interpreted only as a political event. He claimed that in October 1920 when he was a boy on holidays in his father's old home in Spiddal near Galway, he had seen for himself the terror that his fellow countrymen were subjected to by the Black and Tans, the British soldiers. He spun the reporter a tale of IRA kidnappings, spies, and assaults on local civilians with rifle butts. This appears to have been a particularly vivid flight of fancy on Ford's part, aimed at the gullible Irish public, but for once the facts have caught him out. John Ford was born in 1894 so in 1920 he would have been

twenty-six, hardly a boy. In addition, Ford married Mary McBride Smith on 3 July 1920 and their first child Pat was born on 3 April 1921 so it is exceedingly unlikely that he would have been cavorting in Ireland in October 1920 when his wife was expecting their first child. But then Ford had too much respect for the truth than to be dragging it out on every trifling occasion! Incidentally, another report in *The Connacht Tribune* around this time reported the arrival of Francis and Eamonn Feeney, Ford's brothers, in Ireland for the first time. It appears they were all deeply moved when they visited their father's old home at Tourbeg, Spiddal and saw the room and even the very bed in which he was born!

In fact, it is documented that Ford made his first trip to Ireland via Liverpool late in the Autumn of 1921 long after Patrick was born. A truce had now been declared, but he did see the aftermath of the Black and Tan atrocities in Spiddal including the burned-out shell of Feeney's ancestral cottage, travelling from Galway by jaunting car. According to Ford himself, he was deported to England and told that if he ever returned to Ireland he would be imprisoned.

The concert did take place but not without incident. Thousands queued in the rain outside Seapoint only for the stars to arrive half an hour late and in the words of a local newspaper "dash from their cars to the fire escape and disappear into the theatre before many of the worshippers could identify them". Maureen O'Hara was confined to bed with a sore throat and did not appear but Wayne introduced all the other members of the cast to huge applause from an audience of about a thousand crammed into the ballroom. Ford "with his hand on his heart and the Irish language on his tongue" proposed a vote of thanks to all the performers.

Because of Maureen O'Hara's absence, the musical part of the proceedings was curtailed and after a restless hour watching unfortunate support acts the audience was treated to an extract from *The Rising of the Moon* with Barry Fitzgerald, Arthur Shields and the Fitzsimons brothers. Barry Fitzgerald, as the ballad singer, managed to forget many of his lines but Arthur Shields as the policeman carried the day and brought the evening to a fitting climax.

During the filming in Ireland, the principals of the *Quiet Man* cast gave many interviews to the press and what they said was widely quoted. Their comments were invariably complimentary but they were quite sincere because there is little doubt that they genuinely enjoyed the Irish experience. Duke Wayne was quoted as being full of praise for the West of Ireland and its people. "I have made many films in and out of Hollywood," he said, "but I have seldom enjoyed my work so well. In the odd spells I had free from the camera, I took stock of what the countryside provided in fishing and hunting. It's a sportsman's paradise. I do a lot of deep-sea fishing and I thought I was up in all the thrills of the game until I saw them after shark in Achill. That, I thought, was the highlight of my visit and I would like to come back some time and do a little of it." Wayne was also particularly kind to autograph hunters and amateur photographers, remarking significantly, "It's the day people will not want my signature that I dread."

Maureen O'Hara declared that Ireland was the real star of the movie because the country had never been in technicolour on the screen before. She told a *Connacht Sentinel* reporter that she had never experienced such good luck on location before – brilliant sunshine when needed and a little rain right on cue, surely an omen for the success of *The Quiet Man*. She was ecstatic about the little cottage with the stream and stepping stones in front. The newspaper in turn was exceedingly complimentary about her. It said:

Miss O'Hara is the very antithesis of the popular conception of the temperamental and sometimes neurotic type of film star. Dressed in a simple summer frock under a tweed jacket and a broadrimmed straw hat, she chatted easily about everything under the sun, from her relatives in Castlebar to her seven-year-old daughter Bronwyn who had just made her First Communion.

Victor McLaglen showed that the many Irish parts he had played had left their mark when he blarnied, "My wish for Ireland is that your people will be as happy as your countryside is pretty." McLaglen had taken a strong interest in Irish history since his role in *The Informer* (1935) and whenever he saw a ruined abbey or castle as he travelled through the countryside he could be heard to mutter under his breath, "Cromwell, the bastard!"

Ward Bond, last of the cast to arrive in Cong, breakfasted on the five-pound trout he had caught in the Cong River, remarking that he would leave the really big ones for later. Colonel Wingate Smith declared, "I have never seen better country for technicolour film work. Though I have only been in the West for the past week, I have never in my experience come across anything to better the variety and colour I have seen there during that brief time." With Ford roaming around the countryside dropping phrases in the Irish language, the *Quiet Man* cast became more stage-Irish than the Irish themselves.

Many, many stories, some of them true and others merely flights of fancy, are told about the filming of *The Quiet Man* in Ireland. This one has a homely touch and is probably true: In 1951 Ireland was still in the grips of post-war rationing and supplies were sometimes scarce. John Ford was very fond of Irish brown bread and made a special case to the powers-that-be for extra supplies. The team were issued with special ration books that allowed them to purchase fourteen pounds of brown flour per day and this was enough to keep the whole film crew supplied with brown bread. A local lady, Mrs Mullen, mother of the night porter at Ashford Castle, produced twelve home-baked Irish brown cakes every day for seven weeks and these were eagerly devoured by the cast and crew.

Today, over fifty years on, Cong is visited by thousands of *Quiet Man* fans from all over the world. Visitors from Northern Ireland, Britain, the United States, France, Italy and Japan seem to arrive in great numbers to this magic village which has, thankfully, changed very little since the 1950s. Almost every inch of Cong, which doubles as Inisfree and Castletown in *The Quiet Man*, either appears in the movie or has strong connections with it. The choice of Cong was carefully determined by the availability of superb accommodation at the Ashford Castle Hotel.

Since June 1996 Cong has been lucky enough to have a Quiet Man Heritage Centre run by Gerry and Margaret Collins and their daughter Lisa. This comprises an exact replica of the White O'Morn cottage with fittings and furniture exactly as they appear in the movie. The cottage is beautifully situated on a site easily recognisable in *The Quiet Man* and it is a Mecca for all that visit Cong to worship at one of the world's greatest movie shrines.

One of the reasons for *The Quiet Man*'s huge success was that the cast and production crew were one big happy family, figuratively and literally. In fact, it would not be an exaggeration to describe the whole affair as almost incestuous, so many were the blood relatives involved. There was Ford's brother Francis as Dan Tobin, brother Eddie O'Fearna as second assistant director, daughter Barbara as assistant editor, son-in-law-to-be Ken Curtis as Dermot Fahy, brother-in-law Wingate Smith as first assistant director, and son Pat as stuntman and horserider in the Inisfree Races. Duke Wayne had brought his soon-to-be-divorced Mexican wife Chata and his four children from his first marriage – Michael, Patrick, Antonia and Melinda, some of whom were John Ford's godchildren! Victor McLaglen's son Andrew was second assistant director and Maureen O'Hara managed to get parts for two of her brothers – Charles Fitzsimons (Forbes) and James Lilburn (Father Paul), and the fireman on the train, Kevin Lawless, just happened to be a car driver for Maureen O'Hara's parents! Ford regulars Barry Fitzgerald and Arthur Shields were brothers and Webb Overlander (Stationmaster Bailey) was Duke Wayne's long-serving make-up man. Add to this further members of Ford's stock company such as

Maureen O'Hara on set in Cong

Mildred Natwick, Ward Bond, Sean McClory, Major Sam Harris, Mae Marsh, Harry Tenbrook and Harry Tyler and the cast is almost complete.

The Quiet Man brought great prosperity to Cong for a six-week period in the summer sunshine of 1951. Hundreds of local men and women were employed as extras, stand-ins and doubles at rates of pay previously unheard of. Local shops did a roaring trade and local carpenters were employed to make mobile wooden Celtic crosses for inclusion in some scenes. Even the Parish Priest of Cong, Canon Carney, was engaged as a consultant for the correct behaviour of the clerics involved.

Then as suddenly as it all started, it finished, and early on 14 July 1951 the cast departed from Cong, many of them to Hollywood to film the interior scenes which surprisingly comprise about half of the movie. Cong and the rest of the West of Ireland were returned to their sleepy ways but now with a touch of magic that will remain forever.

Ashford Castle

Chapter Five

The Quiet Man - The Movie

This chapter forms the longest and the most important portion of this book. It contains a line-by-line analysis of the dialogue of the movie *The Quiet Man*; detailed commentary on the action; identification of almost all of the players involved; a complete description, with illustrative maps, of all the featured locations and identification of all the music and songs on the soundtrack. To the best of my knowledge, this level of description and analysis has never been attempted in a book about a motion picture, and it will make *The Quiet Man* the most deeply analysed and best-described movie in the history of cinema. It is the result of nearly twenty years of work on location in the West of Ireland and countless hours of research in libraries, film institutes, newspaper offices, bookshops and on the Internet. My research team and I have interviewed hundreds of people directly and indirectly connected with the movie and made many good friends in the process. A unique feature of this book is the inclusion of a selection of the many hundreds of original black-and-white photographs I have been given by kind individuals, mostly amateur photographers, who used their own cameras to capture the action in the West of Ireland in 1951. Naturally, I myself have taken literally thousands of colour photographs of locations and people involved and many of these are included also. It is to be hoped that what all of these photographs lack in professionalism, they will make up in interest.

Naturally, a few niggling questions still remain and a few bit players have defied all my efforts to identify them. I have included a number of outstanding questions throughout the book, and if you, the reader, can answer any of them, you will have made a genuine contribution to *Quiet Man* research. I expect a lot of feedback from movie buffs worldwide in the recognition of some minor characters, especially in the studio scenes and I hope that this information can be added and acknowledged in future editions of this book.

A word now about the timing of the movie sequence. As *The Quiet Man* is rarely seen on the big screen nowadays (even I have seen it only three times in the cinema) I have chosen to work from the video cassette version throughout. Indeed, this book would not have been possible without the miracle of the video machine and in particular its rewind and stilling facilities. As the video playback machine shows 25 frames per second as against the 24 frames per second of a movie projector, this means that the running time in the cinema becomes 129 x 24/25 = 124 minutes approximately of video time. It is the time taken from the video version that I have used throughout. These times appear in the text at thirty-second intervals so that scenes can easily be located.

Incidentally, I don't know if I can claim the all-time record for having watched *The Quiet Man* the greatest number of times, although I have watched it at least three hundred times from start to finish, but I do claim the record for having watched each of its 178,330 frames individually over the years! By examining all the individual frames, one gets to see many things that pass unnoticed in a normal viewing, such as a fly landing on Maureen O'Hara's cheek, a glimpse of her underwear and Barry Fitzgerald spitting on Jack MacGowran! Of course, this stilling technique should not be used if you want to believe that the fight sequences were real, because you can see just how much the punches miss by! Remember too that John Ford never intended *The Quiet Man* to be viewed frame by frame – it is a motion picture.

The opening of *The Quiet Man* movie is the logo of Republic Studios – an eagle on top of a volcanic mountain surrounded by a colourful cloudy sky. We see on the screen:

A
REPUBLIC
PRODUCTION

HERBERT J. YATES

Presents

JOHN FORD
and
MERIAN C. COOPER's

Argosy Production

0:30

The Quiet Man

The expectant strains of Vic Young's music set the scene and the first Irish tune we hear is the lively *Rakes of Mallow*, a popular dance tune commemorating the bucks of the town of Mallow in County Cork. It is a theme that recurs at several points during the movie especially when the action is hectic. In the background is Ashford Castle **(Location 1A)** swathed in golden darkness at sunset and surrounded by tall trees. Ashford Castle is never seen again in the movie or mentioned by any name, real or fictitious, despite the fact that much of the footage was shot there, and that Ashford proprietor/manager Noel Huggard, his assistant Charles Harold and their staff co-operated in every way with the production, as well as housing the most important members of the cast and crew.

The real reason why Ashford did not appear is that Ford wanted to convey an image of Ireland that Irish-Americans could readily identify with – thatched cottages, jaunting cars, churches, ruined abbeys and glorious mountains, beaches, rivers and lakes. He wanted to avoid images of aristocratic castles, luxurious hotels and country mansions, which he would have associated with

the Anglo-Irish landed gentry and "drive-on" Americans, so-called because when they saw the humble cabins where their ancestors were born, they never got out of their big cars but told their chauffeur to drive on. A later example of this in the movie is the omission of the exquisite Kylemore Abbey, despite the fact that two scenes were shot within a short distance of it.

Ashford is an English-sounding name scarcely in harmony with the surrounding Cong countryside. Its Gaelic name is "Ceapach-Corcog" which translates as "The Market Garden of the Beehives", a name that conjures up the drowsy summer activities of the monks in the nearby abbey. In 1750 a French chateau-style shooting lodge was built there by the Oranmore and Brown family, and in 1855 it was bought by the Guinness family, of stout and porter fame, who enlarged it considerably. But it was Lord Ardilaun, heir to Sir Benjamin Guinness, who was responsible for Ashford as it is today. He rebuilt it in 1884 as a castle which is nowadays Ireland's finest and best-known hotel with a world-famous cuisine. Its guests have included international movie stars, the Prince of Wales, who later became King Edward VII of England and for whom a billiard room was specially built, and Ronald Reagan, while President of the United States.

In the movie a little rowing boat forms the foreground of the opening scene and we see the reeds and ripples on Lough Corrib - a foretaste of the exquisite visual delights that are to follow. The music now changes to the haunting *Isle of Innisfree*, the main theme of the movie. The word "Innisfree" (or Inisfree) plays such an important part in *The Quiet Man* that its origin and role deserve a close examination and discussion.

First of all, the "free" part of the name has nothing to do with the word "freedom", at least in derivation. "Inis" is the Gaelic word for an island, closely linked with the Latin word "insula", and "free" is an anglicisation of "fraoigh" meaning heather. Thus "Innisfree"

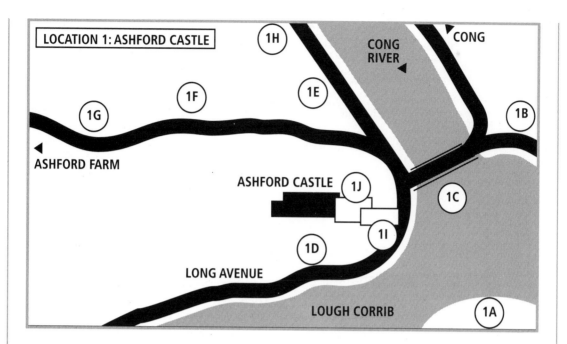

LOCATION 1: ASHFORD CASTLE

1H · CONG RIVER · CONG · 1E · 1F · 1B · 1G · ASHFORD FARM · ASHFORD CASTLE · 1J · 1C · 1I · 1D · LONG AVENUE · LOUGH CORRIB · 1A

means "Island of Heather". However, one of the aspects of the name that may have appealed to Ford was that the name sounded like "Island of Freedom", representing what Ireland offered to a weary American returning home to find peace and quiet and freedom from care.

From the production notes of *The Quiet Man* we see that there were two main sources for the word "Inisfree" as used in the movie:

(i) The famous Irish poet, Nobel prizewinner William Butler Yeats (1865-1939) was born in Dublin but had strong family connections with the West of Ireland, especially County Sligo and County Galway. Although Yeats was a Protestant Anglo-Irishman, he had a passionate interest in Celtic mythology and much of his poetry reflected this. While in exile in London, one afternoon he heard a faint trickling of water coming from a shop window where a little water-jet balanced a wooden ball on its point. Suddenly, he was overwhelmed by the memory of a little island called Innisfree in Sligo's exquisitely beautiful Lough Gill. Often in his youth when difficulties arose he had fantasised about escaping there, building a wooden hut and fishing in the bright lake for food.

There was a legend concerning Innisfree that particularly attracted Yeats to it. The legend concerned a tree that had once grown on the island – it had borne the food of the gods but was guarded by some terrible monster. A young girl pined for the fruit and asked her lover to kill the monster and bring her the fruit. (Shades of Sean Thornton and Red Will Danaher!) He did so, but as he returned he happened to taste it, and when he reached the mainland where she waited for him, he was dying of its powerful strength. And from sorrow and remorse she too ate of it and died.

What matter that the place in question was one of the most insignificant of Lough Gill's many islands, that it was only a stone's throw from the shore, and was known locally as "Cat Island". What matter that Yeats had probably never set foot on the place, that it had no glade, bee-loud or otherwise, and is covered in harsh scrub. In the poet's mind it suddenly represented Ireland and his lost youth. With an intense sense of longing and homesickness he wrote his poem "The Lake Isle of Innisfree" which has become one of the world's best-known and best-loved pieces of poetry.

I will arise and go now, and go to Innisfree,
And a small cabin build there of clay and
wattles made:
Nine bean-rows will I have there, a hive for
the honey-bee,
And live alone in the bee-loud glade.

And I shall have some peace there, for peace
comes dropping slow,
Dropping from the veils of the morning to
where the cricket sings;
There midnight's all a-glimmer, and noon a
purple glow,
And evening full of the linnet's wings.

I will arise and go now, for always night and
day
I hear lake water lapping with low sounds by
the shore;
While I stand on the roadway or on the
pavements grey,
I hear it in the deep heart's core.

The sentiments of the poem are certainly
similar to those Sean Thornton would have felt
as he viewed Ireland through the rosy tints of
his mother's description of the old country. A
clay-and-wattle cabin is not too far removed
from a thatched cottage, and the Inisfree of the
movie, while not an island, was certainly almost
surrounded by brooks and rivers. There is no
doubt that the Inisfree of *The Quiet Man* was
inspired by Yeats' Innisfree - all that is missing is
the roses.

(ii) In 1950, Richard Farrelly, a Dublin
policeman, had written the words and music of
a beautiful song which he called *The Isle of
Innisfree*. Ford heard the music sometime after
and was enchanted by it, so much so that he
made it the principal musical theme of the
movie. Certainly Farrelly was inspired by Yeats'
poem for his title and words, and it is quite
possible that Ford heard Farrelly's music and
words first and was then reminded of Yeats'
poem. It is Farrelly's music but not his words
that feature in the *Quiet Man* movie. The song
has been recorded by many singers – Connie
Foley in Ireland, but most notably Bing Crosby

for whom it was a huge international hit. The
lyrics had a strong relevance for the movie
because they concern the dreams of a man who
wanted to return home and find peace and
quiet in a humble shack. Perhaps it was the
word "isle" in the title that did not fit the
Inisfree of the movie. For the record, the words
of this song with a sublime melody are:

I've met some folks who say that I'm a
dreamer
And I've no doubt there's truth in what they
say
But sure a body's bound to be a dreamer
When all the things he loves are far away.

And precious things are dreams unto an exile
They take him o'er the land across the sea
Especially when it happens he's an exile
From that dear lovely Isle of Innisfree.

And when the moonlight peeps across the
rooftops
Of this great city wondrous tho' it be
I scarcely feel its wonder or its laughter
I'm once again back home in Innisfree.

I wander o'er green hills thro' dreamy valleys
And find a peace no other land could know
I hear the birds make music fit for angels
And watch the rivers laughing as they flow.

And then into a humble shack I wander
My dear old home and tenderly behold,
The folks I love around the turf fire gathered
On bended knees their rosary is told.

But dreams don't last tho' dreams are not
forgotten
And soon I'm back to stern reality
But tho' they paved the footways here with
gold dust
I still would choose the Isle of Innisfree.

I remember once standing transfixed in the
streets of Galway City as a blind musician played
The Isle of Innisfree on the accordion, endlessly
repeating the melody of the chorus and verse. I
was hypnotised and unable to move away for

Richard Farrelly

half an hour, so potent was the magic of the sound. Its lush tone is fairy music, released from another world by the genius of Richard Farrelly. Sadly, he received no mention in the screen credits for the vital contribution he made to the movie, but *The Quiet Man* wouldn't have been half the movie it was without *The Isle of Innisfree*. Of course, due credit must be given also to the superb orchestration and interpretation of the music by Vic Young who gave the melody a whole new dimension of beauty and grandeur.

The credits of *The Quiet Man* now begin to roll:

Starring

JOHN WAYNE
MAUREEN O'HARA
BARRY FITZGERALD

The rowing boat and reeds have now vanished with a change of camera position. An even darker Ashford Castle is now surrounded by a golden sunset reflected in the water, but the sombre pine trees reflect the dark mood of the conflict that is to come. The credits continue:

With

WARD BOND
VICTOR McLAGLEN
MILDRED NATWICK
FRANCIS FORD

Ford now saves himself a lot of bother about precedence by lumping together virtually all the Irish actors and actresses of importance:

And the
IRISH PLAYERS

EILEEN CROWE
MAY CRAIG
ARTHUR SHIELDS
CHARLES FitzSIMONS
JAMES LILBURN
SEAN McCLORY
JACK McGOWRAN
JOSEPH O'DEA
ERIC GORMAN
KEVIN LAWLESS
PADDY O'DONNELL

We notice that Charles Fitzsimons is given a rather grand font to his surname prefix and that Sean McClory could very well be read as Sean McGlory, which is perhaps easier to pronounce.

Screenplay by
FRANK S. NUGENT

From the story by
MAURICE WALSH

Music
VICTOR YOUNG

Color by TECHNICOLOR

Director of Photography
WINTON C. HOCH, A.S.C.
Technicolor Color Consultant
FRANCIS CUGAT
2nd Unit Photography
ARCHIE STOUT A.S.C.

Art Director
FRANK HOTALING

Film Editor
JACK MURRAY A.C.E.

Sound
T.A. CARMAN
HOWARD WILSON

Costumes
ADELE PALMER

Set Decorations
JOHN McCARTHY
CHARLES THOMPSON

APPROVED CERTIFICATE NO. 15529

1:00

Directed by
JOHN FORD

A fuller cast list (in alphabetical order) is the following:

Frank Baker	Man in bar
Ward Bond	Father Peter Lonergan
Tony Canzoneri	Boxing Second
Maureen Coyne	Dan Tobin's daughter (Ireland)
May Craig	Fishwoman with basket
Eileen Crowe	Mrs Elizabeth Playfair
Ken Curtis	Dermot Fahy
Mimi Doyle	Dan Tobin's daughter (USA)
Douglas Evans	Doctor in boxing ring
Barry Fitzgerald	Michaeleen Oge Flynn
Charles Fitzsimons	Hugh Forbes
Francis Ford	Dan Tobin
Robert Foy	Driver of cart across river
Eric Gorman	Costello, the engine driver

Major Sam Harris	General
Don Hatswell	Guppy
John Horan	Man at railway station
David H. Hughes	Police constable
Billy Jones	Bugler
Elizabeth Jones	Nell, Sarah Tillane's maid
Kevin Lawless	Fireman on train
James Lilburn	Father Paul
Jack MacGowran	Ignatius Feeney
Mae Marsh	Father Paul's mother
Sean McClory	Owen Glynn
Victor McLaglen	Red Will Danaher
Jim McVeigh	Man following cart across river
Jim Morrin	Thatcher on roof
Al Murphy	Boxing referee
Mildred Natwick	Sarah Tillane
Micheal Ó Bríain	Musha musha man
Frank O'Connor	Photographer at ringside
Joseph O'Dea	Molouney, guard on train
Paddy O'Donnell	Railway porter
Maureen O'Hara	Mary Kate Danaher
Pat O'Malley	Man in bar
Webb Overlander	Hugh Bailey, the stationmaster
Bob Perry	Trainer in Ring
Jack Roper	Tony Gardello, boxer
Arthur Shields	Reverend Cyril Playfair
Philip Stainton	Anglican bishop
Harry Tenbrook	Sergeant Hanan
Harry Tyler	Pat Cohan
John Wayne	Sean Thornton

Melinda Wayne	
Michael Wayne	
Patrick Wayne	
Toni Wayne	Children at the races
Ken Curtis	
Tommy Doss	
Hugh Farr	
Karl Farr	
Shug Fisher	
Lloyd Perryman	The Sons of the Pioneers (Singers)

The staff sheet of *The Quiet Man* contains many additional names which are listed here:

Director	John Ford
Producer	Merian C. Cooper
Unit Manager	Lee Lukather
1st Ass. Director	Wingate Smith
2nd Ass. Director	Andrew McLaglen
2nd Ass. Director	Albert Podlansky
2nd Ass.Director	Edward O'Fearna
Script Supervisor	Meta Sterne
Cameraman	Winton Hoch
Cameraman	Archie Stout
Film Editor	John Murray
Mixer	Tom Carman
Art Director	Frank Hotaling
Women's Wardrobe	Neva Bourne
Men's Wardrobe	Ted Towey
Accountant	Harry Williams
Make-up	Jim Barber
Hairdresser	Fay Smith
Technical Adviser	Don Hatswell
First Grip	Benny Bishop
Second Grip	Bob Harrison
First Prop	Ace Holmes
Gaffer	Bob Stafford
Best Boy	Ray Bensfield
Technical Adviser (Religion)	Father Stack SJ
Maureen O'Hara's make-up man	Jimmy Barker

There were many other personnel associated with the production, including:

Production	L.T. Rosso
	G.B. Forbes
(Morning Operations)	Mike Eason
Art Department	Ralph Oberg
Camera Department	Bill Wade
Camera Stills	Roman Freulich
Casting	Jack Grant
	H. Chiles
	H. Rossmore
Censorship	Steve Goodman
Chief Engineer	D.J. Bloomberg
Construction	F.B. Gibbs
	Gordon Lantz
Drapery	Francis Frank
Editorial	Al Horowitz

Electric	Paul Guerin
Film Library	E. Schroeder
Grip Department	Ben Moran
Hairdressing	Peggy Gray
Labour Department	Pete Matsk
Location Manager	J.T. Bourke
Make-up	Robert Mark
Miniature and Special Effects	Howard Lydecker
	Ted Lydecker
Music	Jerry Roberts
Paint Department	Lou Shields
Process	Bud Thackery
Projectionist	Hal Swanson
Property	John McCarthy
Purchasing	T.W. Yates
Publicity	Mort Goodman
Sound Department	W.O. Watson
Stock Room	Martin Horwitz
Transportation	Frenchie Valin
	Fred Manning
	Slim Metcalfe
Wardrobe (Men's)	Robert Ramsay
Wardrobe (Women's)	Adele Palmer
Irish Costumes	O'Máille's of Galway
Head Wrangler	Bill Jones
Hudkins Stables	Office Barn
Police Chief	Sandy Sanderson
Fire Chief	Leo Lotito
Studio First Aid	Fred Vinson
Studio Physician	Dr N.E. Gourson
Hospital Ambulance Service	Henry's Ambulance
Brittingham's Commissary	J. Lounsberry, Mgr
National Weather Service	L. Kolb and Gordon Wier
Weather Information	U.S. Weather Bureau

For the location shots in Ireland there were many doubles, stand-ins and extras, and dozens of other people involved in the making of The Quiet Man. Some of these were:

Double for John Wayne (rider)	Joe Fair

Double for John Wayne	Bill Maguire
Double for Maureen O'Hara	Etta Vaughan
Doubles for Barry Fitzgerald	Jim Morrin
	John Daly
Doubles for Victor McLaglen	Stephen Lydon
	Martin Thornton
	Pat Ford
	Steve Donoghue
Stand-in for Maureen O'Hara	Mary Maguire
Stand-in for John Wayne	Joe Mellotte
Stand-in for Ward Bond	Paddy Clarke
Stand-in for Eileen Crowe	Eileen Ryan
Train Crew:	
Driver	John Monaghan
Fireman	Gabriel Barrett
Guard	Joe Mullen
Ballyglunin Station House	Tom Niland
	Margaret Niland
Ashford Farmhouse	Peter Farragher
	Mary Farragher
Clerical Consultants	Reverend M. Canon Carney
	Reverend Father Lyons
Post Mistress	Mary Gibbons
Owners of White O'Morn	Walter Joyce
	Bridget Joyce
Driver of film crew	Jack Murphy
Irish locations	Charles Fitzsimons
	Luke Lukather
	Michael Killanin
Medical Consultant	Dr John McDarby
Supplier and trainer of horses	John Daly
Riders in Race	Joe Fair
	John Daly
	Willy Quinn
	Eamon Lydon
	Gibson Thornton
	Pat Ford
Owner and Trainer of "Jacko"	John Murphy

Owner of Mr Playfair's Car	Thomas O'Sullivan
Equipment Security at Lettergesh	Slippy Flaherty
Mole Richardson of London Technical Crew	Robert Rideout
	Albert Harrison
	Arthur Greene
	Dick Merrick
	Tommy O'Sullivan
	Jim Fletcher
	Jonathan MacDonald
Camera Operators	Arthur Grayham
	Harry Gillham
British Technicolour	Stanley Seger
	Ernest Day
	Dick Alloport
	George Lee
	Frank Turner
	Brian Stafford
Manager of Ashford Castle	Noel Huggard
Assistant Manager	Charles Harold
Owner of Pat Cohan's	John Murphy
Police Supervision	Sergeant P. Gallagher
IRA Consultant	Ernie O'Malley
Extras	Eddie Gibbons
	John Gibbons
	Joe Mellotte
	Martin Thornton
	Paddy Clarke
	Michael Hopkins
	Pakie Ryan
	Bertie Costello
	Bill Maguire
	Jackie Gibbons
	Robert Foy
	Jim Morrin
	John McGrath
	Stephen Lydon
	Paddy Hopkins
	Jim McVeigh
	John Luskin
	Pat Conroy
	Bridie Hopkins
	Eileen Ryan

Phyllis Joyce
Mary Maguire
Eileen Murphy
Phyllis Luskin
and many,
many others…

Technical Details:

Camera	Mitchell Cameras
Film negative format (mm/video inches)	35mm
Cinematographic process	Spherical
Printed film format	35mm
Aspect Ratio	1.37:1
Length of film	11,632 feet

Release Dates:

The Quiet Man was released in May 1952. It had its world premiere at the Adelphi Cinema, Dublin on 6 June 1952; it was first shown in the UK on 21 July 1952 and, in August 1952, it was released in the USA.

Meanwhile, back at the movie, as the name of the director is robustly credited, the music reverts to the strong theme of *The Rakes of Mallow*, to lead us into the start of the action.

This is the perfect tune to herald the arrival of a steam train into a station, its beat echoing the rhythm of the train. Ford used the arrival of a train to open several of his movies – *The Man Who Shot Liberty Valance* (1962) for example – and this ploy has been much imitated. It represents very successfully a transition from the new world to the old, and a train is always full of excitement and surprises both for the passengers and those waiting - who will emerge from the train and who will be there to meet them?

The railway station chosen for the opening scene was the picturesque Ballyglunin south of the town of Tuam in East Galway **(Location 2)** although for a while the station at Craughwell was in contention. The railway station here had already won a prize for being one of the best-kept stations in Ireland. Ballyglunin is a lovely spot, still visited by many thousands of movie fans every year who receive a warm welcome from the Niland family who occupied the station house during the filming. The location is still in a good state of preservation despite no longer being a main-line station with regular passenger services. As a tribute to the local people, Ballyglunin is mentioned by name later in the movie, when Owen Glynn says during the big fight:

"The people from Ballyglunin are coming over by bus - thousands of them."

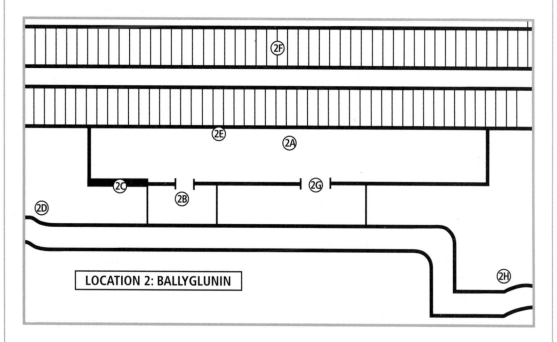

LOCATION 2: BALLYGLUNIN

Originally, Ford had intended this scene to be shot on the Galway-Clifden line through Connemara but so delayed was the movie that the line had been closed down in the meantime. Ballyglunin was an inspired alternative.

As *The Quiet Man* opens we see a Córas Iompair Éireann (Irish Transport System) train steaming into Castletown Station. Actually, this is something of an anachronism as the railway system in the Ireland of the twenties was operated by Great Southern Railways, and CIE did not come into existence until much later. Six sturdy pillars support a Victorian shelter over a platform peppered with puddles of rainwater from a recent shower.

The actual train crew were local men, John Monaghan (driver), Gabriel Barrett (fireman) and Joe Mullen (guard). However, the first person to be seen in the movie is Ballinrobe man Paddy O'Donnell playing the part of the railway porter in his uniform of cap and braces, strolling casually away from the camera with one hand behind his back. Although Paddy O'Donnell is listed in the credits as one of the Irish Players, he was not a professional actor at all. In fact, he was a "hackney man" or taxi driver who was frequently employed by Ashford Castle to ferry guests to and from trains at Ballinrobe and Galway. It is likely that one of his passengers at one stage was John Ford who offered him a part in the movie on the strength of his appearance and general demeanour. Years later he appeared as an extra in *A Minute's Wait*, the comic segment of *The Rising of the Moon*, also set in an Irish railway station. At the end of each day's filming in Cong, O'Donnell also had the important task of rushing the canisters of film to Shannon Airport where they were immediately dispatched to Hollywood for processing.

As engine No. 59 pulls the train further into the station with a hiss of steam, Abbey Theatre actress May Craig emerges from the waiting room onto the platform carrrying a basket. She is referred to throughout the movie as simply "a woman at the railroad", but it appears that she was originally intended to be a fishwoman - hence the basket. She is dressed in a traditional Irish shawl as she greets the passengers and crew of the incoming train.

May Craig featured in two of Ford's later Irish movies, *The Rising of the Moon* (1957) and *Young Cassidy* (1965). Originally, her part in *The Quiet Man* was confined to the opening scene, but according to her daughter, as time went on she pleaded her difficult family circumstances to Ford and several other short inserts were improvised for her throughout the movie, with great success. In particular, Ford gave her the much quoted line:

"Here's a good stick to beat the lovely lady."

In fact, May Craig's role in *The Quiet Man* is an important and deeply symbolic one. She represents the ghost of Sean Thornton's long-dead mother come to welcome him home to the Ireland of his dreams which her stories and tales had created in his imagination. The fact that she is nameless is significant and it is May Craig's voice that is used as the mother's voiceover when Sean first sees his ancestral home. We will examine this theory in more detail as the evidence for it arises in the movie.

As the train grinds to a halt, we get our first view of the returning American, Sean Thornton, played by John Wayne who was himself returning to his Irish roots. He is sitting in a third-class smoking carriage with an advertisement for Will's Gold Flake cigarettes as part of the smoking notice. He is dressed in what Ford imagines was the uniform of every returned Yank — a tweed cap, a tweed jacket, rust-coloured tie and pullover. As Sean leaps up excitedly to open the carriage window he places both hands in full view of the camera and we see the first "oops" of *The Quiet Man* — the supposedly unmarried Sean Thornton is clearly wearing a gold wedding ring on his left hand.

Now we hear the opening words of the movie spoken by Ward Bond, the narrator, who plays the part of Father Peter Lonergan, Parish Priest of St Anselm's. (He was also narrator in Ford's movie, *The Fugitive*.) Bond represents the most

Ward Bond

movies, he was of Red Indian extraction himself.

"Well, then," coughs Father Lonergan as narrator, "now I'll begin at the beginning. A fine soft day in the spring it was, when the train pulled into Castletown, three hours late as usual, and himself got off. He didn't have the look of an American tourist at all about him, not a camera on him, and what was worse, not even a fishing rod."

The Quiet Man follows the seasons of the year – the opening is in the spring, the development of the plot happens over the summer and the climax is at the harvest in the fall or autumn.

In the meantime, action at Castletown Station is hotting up. The guard of the train, Molouney, a name taken from the Maurice Walsh story, descends in full uniform from the back carriage and flag in hand proceeds to walk along the platform. So curious is he about the identity of the mysterious Yank disembarking at a small station that he fails to greet or acknowledge the presence of the porter standing by his side.

serious piece of miscasting in the entire movie and his mock Irish brogue immediately grates on the ear. Admittedly he had practised his Irish accent in several previous Ford movies, most notably as Sergeant Major O'Rourke in *Fort Apache* (1948) but he never got it right and no Irishman has ever spoken with Bond's "Oirish" accent. But Bond was a long-standing friend of Ford's and part of his "stock company", and a part had to be found for him. The part is crying out for a native Irish actor who had seen a parish priest in action and could portray him authentically. Noel Purcell would have been the obvious choice – he was an experienced Irish actor of the right stature, but it seems he was not available at the time.

Like Duke Wayne, Ward Bond also started out as a college football player and starred in over two hundred movies, playing the part of either a brutal heavy or a kind-hearted lawman. However, he did not achieve real stardom until the coming of television when he played the starring role of the wagon master in the popular TV series *Wagon Master*. Ironically, for somebody who killed so many Indians in

The part of the guard Molouney is played, rather well, by Joseph O'Dea, Abbey actor and step-brother of Jimmy O'Dea, Ireland's best-loved comedian. Both O'Dea brothers were to appear again in *The Rising of the Moon* (1957) and it is surprising that Jimmy O'Dea managed to avoid appearing in *The Quiet Man*.

Next we see the stationmaster Mr Bailey emerging alongside a large CASTLETOWN sign. This part was played by Webb Overlander, another American with a rather dreadful attempt at an Irish accent, and another unfortunate piece of miscasting. The story of Webb Overlander's involvement in *The Quiet Man* is a fascinating one. He had acted for many years as Duke Wayne's make-up man and was probably looking forward to a trip to Ireland to act in that capacity for *The Quiet Man*. However, he fell victim to Herb Yates' cost-cutting which decreed that all expenses must be cut to a minimum and it was decided that he should not travel to Ireland. Yates decreed that Jimmy Barker, Maureen O'Hara's make-up man, should act for Wayne also, but O'Hara and Wayne formed a little conspiracy. Barker was ordered to include certain caustic chemicals in Wayne's make-up which caused the main star's face to break out in a severe rash. Webb Overlander was immediately sent for, and perhaps as comic revenge, Ford offered him a part in the movie. However, he was an inexperienced actor and his part suffered accordingly.

"Castletown," says Hugh Bailey, rather quizzically as if he was a bit unsure of the name of his own station. His walk resembles that of the front part of a pantomime cow as he tiptoes to the train. There has been some discussion as to why Ballyglunin became Castletown. The name is fairly common in Ireland and features in the original Maurice Walsh story, but there is also a quaint village called Castletown not far from Cong on the shores of Lough Corrib.

Sean Thornton now alights from the train carrying a gaberdine over his left arm. He seems to be the only passenger for Castletown. Sean takes from the train his sleeping bag which features in several important scenes later in the movie and reaches into the carriage for his well-worn suitcase which he puts beside the sleeping bag on the platform. All the while, the woman with the basket keeps a motherly eye on the new arrival. Sean then reaches into his right-hand pocket and takes out an apple which he holds up to the occupants of the carriage and says "thanks".

This is one of the many scenes in the movie that are rather difficult to understand until one realises that *The Quiet Man* was very severely cut to its present length, mostly at the insistence of Herb Yates. Although the editing in general was very good, the seams show through in a few places. Frank Nugent's original screenplay called for an opening scene in the train where Sean Thornton shares a carriage with a mother accompanied by a boy of about five and a little

girl of about four. As they stare at the American stranger opposite in unembarrassed curiosity, they offer him an apple which he gratefully accepts. This is why he says "thanks" as he leaves the train - the proposed opening scene was anticipated and was shot in the studio. For the record, the parts of the little boy and girl were played by brother and sister Freddie and Darla Ridgeway, and the part of the mother was played by Ruth Clifford, who is to be seen is another Ford movie, *The Searchers* (1956), where she played the part of the deranged woman at the fort. In fact, Sean's "thanks" is difficult to hear and may have been deliberately covered up by Ford using Ward Bond's narration.

Nugent gives the following thumbnail description of the hero of the movie:

> Sean Thornton is in his late thirties, a big man with a light tread, an easy smile and the gift of silence. Born in Inisfree, he was fatherless at four. An uncle in America sent for the mother and himself – she died when he was twelve. From that time forward he had to fend for himself – newsboy, sweeper, labourer, stoker, steel puddler, boxer, contender, near-champion and then – killer of a man in the prize-ring. A different killing this than in the war in which Sean had served. So "Trooper" Thorn hung up his gloves, counted his ring earnings and bethought himself wistfully of his mother's somewhat idealised recollections of their native Inisfree. Now to Ireland he is returning, a Quiet Man seeking forgetfulness of all the wars of the human spirit.

The train driver, played by Eric Gorman, a member of the Abbey Theatre company and well-known Irish character actor, leaves his steaming engine behind to investigate the rare sight (in the 1920s) of a Yank disembarking at a rural Irish station. Eric Gorman was yet another member of the cast to appear in *The Rising of the Moon*. The fireman too cannot resist leaving his post in the general atmosphere of curiosity and following the engine driver onto the platform. The part of the fireman is played by Kevin Lawless, who, like Paddy O'Donnell, was not a professional actor, but got the part presumably because he worked as chauffeur to Maureen O'Hara's parents!

Sean Thornton closes the door of his carriage as the crowd converges on him. He is now surrounded by the porter, the lady with the basket, the guard and the stationmaster who in the space of ten yards seems to have lost his pipe, though he still retains a rather important-looking folder of documents under his arm. He again announces the name of the station "Castletown" rather hesitantly as if he was hoping that somebody would confirm the fact for him. Sean makes the fatal mistake of addressing a question to the stationmaster.

"Could you tell me the way to Inisfree?" he asks innocently.

(At this stage it was realised that the hissing sound of the steam engine was drowning the conversation, so it was moved a distance down the track.)

As is usual in Ireland, Sean's question is helpfully answered by someone to whom the question was not addressed. Molouney chips in, "Inisfree, ah five miles and maybe a half more. Do you see that road over there?" pointing southwards.

"Yeah," says Sean, looking helpfully in the indicated direction.

"Well, don't take that one," says Molouney in the best stage-Irish tradition, "it'll do you no good. No, the best road to Inisfree, and many's the walk I've walked in it..." (Here O'Dea seems to fluff his lines a little, rather surprisingly.)

He is rudely interrupted by Hugh Bailey and it is obvious that there is no love lost between the two men. In fact, there is a long-standing feud between them. Bailey launches into a cringe-making stream of speech spoken in what Irish-Americans fondly imagine is an Irish accent. In addition, the "Oirish" grammar employed is one never heard outside the United States.

"Ah, it's Inisfree you want," butts in Bailey, "be saving your breath, Mister Malouney, let me direct the gentleman."

While Malouney looks daggers at him, hating like most Irishmen to be upstaged, Bailey addresses Sean, "Happen you know the way to Knockanore?"

This place name, irrelevant to the main action, is mentioned as a tribute to the location

2:30

Fun on the platform at Ballyglunin station

of the original Maurice Walsh story.

Malouney now sees the opportunity to go centre stage again and seizes it eagerly.

"Knockanore," he says contemptuously and with irrefutable logic, "if he knew the way to Knockanore, would he be asking the way to Inisfree and it just beyond?"

"There's many knows Knockanore that doesn't know Inisfree," says Bailey defensively and then tries to pull intellectual rank on his lower colleague by continuing, "and if you took the time to study your country's history, Mister Malouney, you'd be the first to admit…"

While all this is going on, the woman with the basket looks curiously at Sean's sleeping bag and sidesteps his suitcase rather pointedly. This action will be interpreted in our analysis of the later part of the movie.

The train driver and the fireman now join the welcoming party on the platform. Mister Costello, convinced that nobody would come to Ireland for any other reason than to fish, now chips in and chides the entire company for not sensing the stranger's needs. "Ah now, don't be sending the poor man to Knockanore," he says, "sure the fishing is finished there entirely." Placing his hand on Sean's shoulder as if they were lifelong friends he continues, "Now tell me this, Yank, what is it you're after, is it trout or salmon?"

Sean is baffled and totally confused by his first adult confrontation with Irish logic, or the lack of it. He has stepped out of a straightforward, industrialised and relatively sane society into the leprechaun land of the Celtic Twilight. He hasn't stepped back just a generation – he has stepped back two thousand years into a never-never land where time and space don't seem to matter, as if he had fallen down the rabbit hole with Alice into Wonderland. He is like a man in a dream and the moment he stepped off the train into dreamland he totally lost control of his life.

"All I want is to get to Inisfree," he says helplessly, clinging to the one piece of information he can be sure of.

"Ah now you're talking sense," says Costello, restarting the nightmare, "the best fishing in the country."

"True for you there, Mister Costello," interjects the woman with the basket, but he continues: "Trout, trout as long as your arm, and salmon – the last one I got I was expecting Jonah to pop out of his mouth. Ah, Inisfree, I'd be bringing you there myself, only I've got to drive the train."

3:0●

This is a very Irish sentiment – an expression of regret that mundane duties must take precedence over hospitality because the railway authorities have an inverted sense of priorities.

Costello continues, now addressing his remarks to his fireman. "Hey, was I telling you about that trout I got two Sundays before last?"

"You did," says the fireman, but Costello goes on.

"At Inisfree?" asks Sean hopefully, sucked into the conversation against his wish, almost like a fish himself but still desperately trying to steer the topic towards his immediate needs.

"Ah, not at all, not at all," says Costello pouring scorn on the Yank's ignorance, "at Ballygar, over the other end of the country."

(Ballygar is about twenty miles away in north-east County Galway, near County Roscommon.)

Now the woman with the basket seems to offer Sean some real hope.

"Me sister's third young one," she interjects gently, smiling and curtsying in Sean's direction in a truly lovely frame with the porter and stationmaster on her right, "is living in Inisfree, and she'd be only too happy for to show you the road."

"Oh well, thanks," smiles a relieved Sean, but she continues, "No, no, if she was here."

Certainly, Sean's mother would show him the way back to Inisfree, if she were here; but she is not here, she is dead, and not even her body is here because she is buried in America.

3:3

At a lighter level, these lines spoken by the woman illustrate another Irish characteristic of wanting to help even if the information they have to offer is true but useless, or worse still, downright false. Even false information communicated in a friendly manner is better than an admission of ignorance which would reflect badly on the local population.

"It's Inisfree the man wants to go to," says the porter, adding absolutely nothing to the proceedings, apart from the fact that Paddy O'Donnell now has a speaking part, for which he was presumably paid at a higher rate.

"Do you see that signpost there with the long arms?" the guard asks Sean in a desperate attempt to direct him towards the right road.

"Well you know it's been turned about," says the stationmaster, referring to a favourite rural Irish pastime practised by rustic buffoons in the long winter evenings for the inconvenience of strangers - shure it's not walking they are!

"I know all about that and the long arm," retorts the guard and the stationmaster repeats,

"Well you know it's been turned about."

"I was coming to that, Mister Bailey," explains the guard, as if he was personally responsible for the rotation of the road signs, and maybe he was.

Here the conversation becomes incoherent, with the welcoming party all gesticulating and arguing with each other in mild chaos. Sean's nightmare is continuing and in his dream he cannot rely on the usual certainty of the signposts - they have all been turned about or maybe some haven't been and he has no way of knowing.

Now, for the first time, we see the scene from the reverse angle, perhaps an indication that there will soon be some semblance of sanity in the proceedings. We see too for the first time the pedestrian footbridge at Ballyglunin Station **(Location 2B –** see page 51**).** This bridge had actually done duty on the Galway–Clifden line where Ford had originally planned to shoot *The Quiet Man*. After that line closed, the bridge was moved to enhance passenger facilities at

May Craig and Paddy O'Donnell await the arrival of the train at Ballyglunin

Ballyglunin, sometime in the mid-1930s. After Ballyglunin closed as a main-line station, the bridge was moved to Ballinasloe in east County Galway where it now does duty on the main Dublin–Galway line. It was suggested to Ford that for the opening scene featuring the arrival of the train that he place the cameras on the footbridge. He gave the famous reply – "People waiting in a railway station see the arrival at eye-level, so that's where the cameras should be too." Incidentally, since the platform conversation now deserves to be covered by the hissing steam, the engine of the train is back in its rightful position.

The bridge today at Ballinasloe

The reverse angle shot heralds the arrival of one of the principal characters of the movie, Michaeleen Oge Flynn, played by Barry Fitzgerald, one of Ireland's and indeed the world's best-loved character actors. Even Maurice Walsh, who had severe reservations about Ford's adaptation of his story, had to admit "Barry Fitzgerald stole the show." His real name was William Shields (1888-1961) and he was already a veteran of Dublin's Abbey Theatre. Ford had lured him to Hollywood in 1936 to repeat his stage role in Sean O'Casey's *The Plough and the Stars*. A notorious scene stealer, he won an Academy Award as best supporting actor for his role as Father Fitzgibbon in Leo McCarey's *Going My Way* (1944). He had the distinction of being nominated as best actor and best supporting actor in that year. He was a regular member of Ford's stock company and three of his most notable performances were in *The Plough and the Stars* (1936), *The Long Voyage Home* (1940)

and *How Green Was My Valley* (1941). He was absolutely perfect for his part in *The Quiet Man* though he was not the first choice for the part – as we have seen, it was originally intended for another Irish favourite of Ford's, Denis O'Dea. Barry Fitzgerald became in many moviegoers' eyes the ultimate stage-Irishman playing whimsical characters with undeniable charm. By all accounts, he seems to have been one of the most lovable and gentle-mannered actors ever to grace the stage or screen.

The character of Michaeleen Oge Flynn is closely based on the Maurice Walsh character of the same name but the emphasis is now on his comic persona and, while he makes a few military or revolutionary remarks during the movie such as about "talking treason with my friends", these are more in jest than anything else. In fact, Michaeleen illustrates a truism often spoken about the Irish:

"All their wars are merry and all their songs are sad."

Nugent's screenplay describes Michaeleen as "an impish man, bibulous, contumacious, locquacious and imperturbable. He is master of all trades, none of which he follows. It can be said of him that he has his nose in everything, his heart in the right place and his mouth – by preference – in a large glass of potstill."

Ironically, Michaeleen is the one rock of sanity in the dreamworld that Sean now finds himself in – he is the chief leprechaun and Sean's guide throughout the movie, his mentor and maybe his only real friend. Michaeleen is also a no-nonsense man of action. Dressed in a bowler hat, black jacket and trousers, riding whip in his hand and characteristic pipe in his mouth, he strides purposefully down the platform and, without as much as by-your-leave, lifts both pieces of Sean's luggage in one movement and heads for the exit **(Location 2B)**. Sean at once takes notice and, glad to escape from the mayhem, follows him coat on arm with the characteristic crab-like sideways walk that only Wayne could do so well. The animated

Archie Stout and Barry Fitzgerald – two Oscar winners

discussion continues on the platform despite the fact that the Yank is no longer there, supporting the theory that the "helpers" are more intent on scoring points off each other than offering directions to the stranger.

Michaeleen stops at the open doorway of the Castletown waiting room and places the bags on the ground. The exit is clearly visible and through the large window we can see a hint of jaunting car **(Location 2B)**. Turning to Sean, Michaeleen, who always acts first and speaks afterwards, utters the immortal line: "Inisfree, this way," words forever associated with the character, and the title of at least one of the many videos made about *The Quiet Man*.

Now there is a masterly touch – the introduction of Vic Young's lively woodwind interpretation of *The Kerry Dances*, a main musical theme of the movie. This lovely lively tune is possibly a tribute to Maurice Walsh's home county. While the lyrics are not used in the movie, their sentiments are so in keeping with the plot - the too-quick passing of youth, memories of singing and dancing, pipers and merriment - that the lovely words of J.L. Molloy deserve to be reproduced in full.

THE KERRY DANCES
O the days of the Kerry dancing
O the ring of the piper's tune
O for one of those hours of gladness
Gone, alas! like our youth too soon:
When the boys began to gather in the glen
of a summer night,
And the Kerry piper's tuning made us long
with wild delight:
O to think of it,
O to dream of it, fills my heart with tears!
O the days of the Kerry dancing,
O the ring of the piper's tune!
O for one of those hours of gladness, gone,
alas! like our youth too soon.

Was there ever a sweeter colleen in the dance
than Eily More!
Or a prouder lad than Thady,
As he boldly took the floor:
"Lads and lasses, to your places, up the
middle and down again."
Ah! the merry-hearted laughter ringing
through the happy glen.
O to think of it,
O to dream of it, fills my heart with tears!
O the days of the Kerry dancing,
O the ring of the piper's tune!
O for one of those hours of gladness, gone,
alas! like our youth too soon.

Time goes on, and the happy years are dead,
And one by one the merry hearts are fled,
Silent now is the wild and lonely glen,
Where the bright glad laugh will echo ne'er
again,
Only dreaming of days gone by,
In my heart I hear.
Loving voices of old companions, stealing
out of the past once more,
And the sound of dear old music,
Soft and sweet as in days of yore:
When the boys began to gather in the glen
of a summer night,
And the Kerry piper's tuning made us long
with wild delight;
O to think of it,
O to dream of it, fills my heart with tears!
O the days of the Kerry dancing,
O the ring of the piper's tune!
O for one of those hours of gladness, gone,
alas! like our youth too soon!

Michaeleen, standing in the doorway showing
Sean the way, is surely something of a father
substitute inviting him to return to his past. *The
Quiet Man*, if one looks for it, is pleasantly
riddled with mythology and imagery and surely
here we have Open Sesame, the Pied Piper of
Hamelin and Yeats' "Come Away, O Human
Child" all rolled into one. Sean is now really
entering the world of his dreams, nurtured by
his mother's tales and stories, that his conscious
mind has forgotten. But with "Father

Michaeleen" (who was of course a spoiled
priest in the original story) to hold his hand he
need have no fears or worries about his ultimate
triumph. Along the way, however, he will have
to endure all the trials and pitfalls of his second
childhood, to replace the first childhood that
was stolen from him by emigration.

Michaeleen now exits and Sean follows him
even more eagerly with a quizzical look on his
face. Once through the doorway, he pauses, as
if unsure of what the future may bring, while in
the background we see the bemused passengers
still sitting in the train vainly hoping for their
journey to continue. No wonder the train is
behind time if this happens in every station!
Sean looks to the big waiting-room window
with a large crack in its right-hand pane,
perhaps symbolising how cracked everybody in
the station is. Ford loved separating characters
from what they sought using panes of window
glass, and uses it elsewhere in *The Quiet Man*.
On the other side of the window **(Location
2B)**, which is perhaps through the looking
glass, we see a lovely shot of a patient horse with
four white feet hitched to a traditional jaunting
car. This is a superb example of Ford's
cinematic artistry – turning a mundane scene
into a classic shot.

4:0

As Michaeleen is seen to
put the luggage on board,
a broad grin spreads over
Sean's face when he
observes his primitive but
magical mode of
transport and his
diminutive driver. Now
he understands what is
happening and he at least
knows where he is going
- he is going home. He
rushes eagerly to the
doorway to join
Michaeleen on the
sidecar. As they leave the
station they are watched
by half a dozen of the
platform party **(Location
2C)** standing behind a

*Waiting room and window
at Ballyglunin*

Outside Ballyglunin station house

high ivy-covered wall with a platform lamp in the background.

"I wonder now why a man would go to Inisfree?" (if not for the fishing?) asks Costello, and the porter, the stationmaster, the guard (still with flag in hand), the fishwoman and fireman, all in agreement for once, shake their heads in wonder. This short scene has a stagy ending with the platform party taking a bow as it were, a device repeated at the end of the movie.

The scene now shifts to the open countryside as the train makes its way across the plains of Galway **(Location 2D)**. There is a bit of camera trickery involved here as in the opening scene the train is facing southwards in the direction of County Clare. Now, supposedly a few minutes later, it is steaming northwards towards County Mayo. This was forcibly brought home to the author who examined half a dozen bridges south of Ballyglunin before discovering the correct location by accident about half a mile north of the station.

Railway bridge

This scene was filmed in isolation from the other Ballyglunin scenes on a Sunday morning. Doubling for John Wayne in this scene is Bill Maguire, now an engineer living in the United States. His father was a friend of Ford's and while Bill was home on vacation from his studies at University College Dublin, Ford pulled up his car near the Maguire's house at the village of Cross, just a few miles from Cong and said to him, "Young man, how would you like to be in the movies?" Bill was the right height and build for the part and doubled for Wayne in several of the long shots.

Doubling for Barry Fitzgerald in this scene is John Daly from Lough Mask House near Ballinrobe in County Mayo. This house had been the dwelling of Captain Boycott, Lord Erne's notorious agent, whose treatment by the locals in the nineteenth century gave a new word to the English language. *Captain Boycott* (1947) was another famous movie to be shot in the same area as *The Quiet Man* and, as we will see later, it had a very big influence on many of the scenes. It was actually proposed that *Captain Boycott* be shot at Lough Mask House, but John Daly's father, P.S. Daly, rather foolishly in retrospect, would not allow this, and a location in County Meath was used instead.

John Daly also made another very important contribution to *The Quiet Man* - he supplied, trained and managed many of the horses used in the scenes involving sidecars, ponytraps and the Inisfree Races. This was a massive undertaking for which he deserves a great deal of credit. Horses pervade the movie and a moviegoer is apt to forget the very complicated logistics, especially in the West of Ireland in the 1950s, of directing horses and having them behave in the right way, in the right place and at the right time. Many a day, during the shooting of the movie, John Daly left Lough Mask House before dawn with a fleet of horse boxes and sometimes stood around all day without being used, only to return home at night and repeat the process the following day. John Daly's contribution to *The Quiet Man* was immense and is here being acknowledged for the first time.

John Daly was himself a very accomplished rider and showjumper who had won innumerable cups and prizes all over rural Ireland and at the Dublin Horse Show. Later in *The Quiet Man* he was one of the riders in the Inisfree Races, doubling for Don Hatswell who played the part of Guppy, the Widow Tillane's steward.

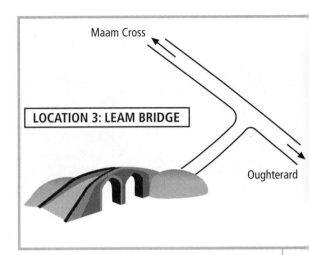

As Michaeleen and Sean pass under the railway bridge, the train passes overhead and whistles a farewell to the newly arrived Yank seeking his Irish roots. On the morning of the shoot, it was realised that "Sean" had no luggage with him and the second unit director had to look around for something to fill the gap. It was provided by Margaret Niland, wife of the Ballyglunin stationmaster, Tom Niland, who produced a red suitcase, still in her possession, which was used in the shot.

The next scene is shot in a Hollywood studio, and that fact is given away by the shadows cast by the studio lighting and the obvious back projection of the Irish scenery. The sidecar has no horse attached and is merely vibrated up and down to simulate the effect of driving along an Irish country road. Many moviegoers are surprised to learn that only about half of *The Quiet Man* was shot outdoors on location in Ireland and that the other half consists of interior shots taken in the studios in Hollywood. The many very obvious studio scenes with artificial lighting and blatant back projection are one of *The Quiet Man*'s major weaknesses commented on by many movie commentators over the years.

4:30

As the pair drive along together, supposedly through the Irish countryside, Michaeleen turns to his passenger who is smiling as he feasts his eyes on the beautiful scenery. Michaeleen tentatively opens the conversation in a rather unusual manner by questioning Sean about his height by means of a question totally devoid of a verb.

"Six foot six?" he asks him.

"Four and a half," replies Sean, equally laconically, to which Michaeleen reacts with an incoherent mumble.

(The soundtrack at this stage continues with the music of *The Kerry Dances* and a piercing blast from the train in a vain effort to preserve continuity from location to studio.)

Sean now lights one of the many cigarettes he smokes during the movie. Ironically Duke Wayne was to die many years later from smoking-induced lung cancer. Distress at seeing his father die in this painful and unnecessary way caused his son Michael to quit smoking on the spot. Of course, Sean lights his cigarette macho-style, striking the match on the sole of his shoe. As he does so, he appears to be wearing yet another ring, a signet ring this time, on his wedding-ring finger despite being still unmarried.

Michaeleen probes a little further into his passenger's origins as the director drags a few leaves and branches in front of the camera for added realism.

"Cincinnati?" he inquires tentatively.

"Nope, Pittsburgh," replies Sean equally tersely.

"Yeah, yeah, Pittsburgh, yeah," agrees Michaeleen, wondering how he could have ever doubted the fact.

5:0

They now arrive at the bridge over the brook. This is Leam Bridge **(Location 3)** situated a few hundred yards off the Galway-Clifden road just a few miles north-west of Oughterard. This

Leam Bridge

The view over Leam Bridge

lovely humpbacked bridge has been preserved by Galway County Council and is signposted for the benefit of *Quiet Man* enthusiasts. It looks just as good today as it did during the filming even down to the reeds in the water. This scene is one of the most beautiful in the whole movie, an absolute masterpiece of artistic composition. In the foreground is the gently rippling brook bordered by golden reeds. Through the eyes of the bridge we see the lake from which the stream flows and in the background are the pair of hills Lecknabragh Beag and Lecknabragh Mór, rising as many Irish hills do like a pair of maternal breasts. Fittingly, in real geography, it is between those two hills that White O'Morn, which Sean will soon pretend to be looking at, actually lies.

The sidecar stops at the north end of the bridge and Sean jumps off. Although the actors are seen only at a distance, it seems that Wayne and Fitzgerald actually appeared in this shot. Sean now walks slowly to the centre of the little bridge. Sadly, and inexplicably, Ford now chooses to continue this scene in the studio – the backdrop is certainly authentic but it is much too dark and static and the plastic stones of the bridge wouldn't fool a five-year-old child. Perhaps the location camera angle would have been difficult but it would have been vastly better to have a close-up of Sean against a clear blue Irish sky than an obviously phoney studio set. The foreground studio lighting too, with its dark shadows, grates on the eye.

Sean sits on the parapet of the bridge and looks left and right as if familiarising himself with his surroundings. The *Isle of Innisfree* theme is heard gently on the harp as the memories begin to flood back.

His mother's voice, spoken by May Craig, is heard in the background and Sean hears her say,

"Don't you remember it, Seánín, and how it was?"

We are suddenly shown a little Irish cottage under the shadow of a hill nestling by a little river and surrounded by trees **(Location 4)**. This is White O'Morn at Teernakill some fifteen miles west of Cong beside the tiny village of Maam Bridge on the extreme north-western shore of Lough Corrib. The cottage is almost encircled by the Failmore River and one of its minor tributaries. It was discovered by Lord Killanin and at the time it was owned by Walter and Bridget Joyce. It was an idyllic locality with a brook in front and stepping stones leading to the cottage. Killanin suggested that Republic Pictures pay the Joyces £25 a day but Ford, anxious to spend Yates' money, gave them £100 a day, a fortune in the Ireland of the 1950s.

Sean's mother says, "The road led up past the chapel and it wound and it wound."

Now we feast our eyes on a lovely shot of Clifden, the capital of Connemara with the twin spires of its churches **(Location 5A** – see page 65**)**. Clifden is about fifty miles north-west of Galway City on the coast. In the background of this splendid scene we see Connemara's majestic mountain chain The Twelve Pins. This shot is quite in keeping with

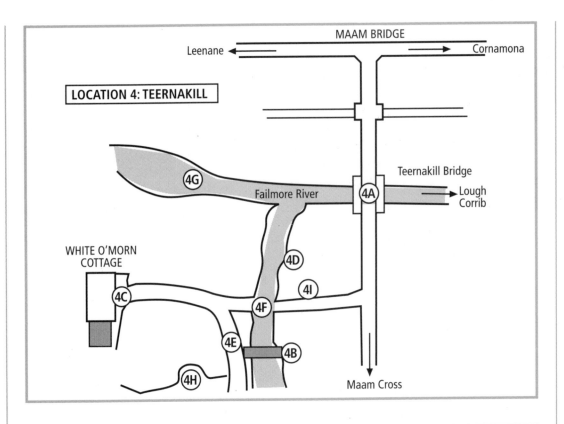

MAAM BRIDGE

Leenane ← → Cornamona

LOCATION 4: TEERNAKILL

4G

Failmore River

Teernakill Bridge

4A → Lough Corrib

WHITE O'MORN COTTAGE

4C

4D

4I

4F

4E

4B

4H

Maam Cross

5:30

Nugent's comment in the screenplay instructions – the director intends to take dramatic liberties and play the countryside for all it is worth.

Sean's mother continues: "And there was the field where Dan Tobin's bull chased you," and Sean looks in a suitable direction towards the studio field. In the background a church bell tolls as Sean looks at his ancestral home with a gentle smile on his face.

"It was a lovely little house, Seánín," she continues, "and the roses – your father used to tease me about them but he was that proud of them too."

Clifden, County Galway

Again we see a beautifully composed shot of the cottage as Sean drifts in and out of his childhood dreams to the sound of his mother's voice and *The Isle of Innisfree* played on a heavenly harp.

But dreams don't last though dreams are not forgotten. The spell is broken by man-of-the-world Michaeleen Oge Flynn who must feel that Sean's dreaming is eating into his drinking time and that if they don't get a move on, the pubs will be shut.

White O'Morn cottage at Teernakill

"Ah that's nothing but a wee humble cottage," he tells Sean, bringing him down to earth. Sean climbs down from the studio set and walks back to the jaunting car on Leam Bridge, six thousand miles away. Back in the studio again he climbs up beside Michaeleen and asks:

"That little place across the brook, that humble cottage, who owns it now?"

"The widow Tillane, not that she lives there," answers Michaeleen.

"Think she'd sell it?" asks Sean.

"I doubt it," says Michaeleen huskily.

"Don't bet on it, 'cos I'm buying it," grins Sean with the arrogance of an American who feels that money can buy everything.

"And why would a, why would a Yankee from Pittsburgh want to buy it?" asks Michaeleen in mock astonishment.

:00

Sean puts his arm around the little man and says in a very friendly manner:

"I'll tell you why, Michaeleen Oge Flynn, young small Michael Flynn, who used to wipe my runny nose when I was a kid, because I'm Sean Thornton and I was born in that little cottage over there" (pointing towards it) "and I've come home and home I'm gonna stay. Now does that answer your questions once and for all, you nosy little man?"

:30

Sean must have a very good memory if he remembers Michaeleen wiping his nose before he went to America at the age of four. Michaeleen's name by the way has been given a full literal translation for the benefit of non-Irish speakers.

The change in Michaeleen's demeanour is remarkable. His face breaks into a broad smile for the first time in the movie and he takes his hat off and buries his face in his hands. He replaces his hat on his head at a rakish angle, splutters the name "Seanín Thornton" and places his hand horizontally to indicate Sean's height last time he saw him.

"And look at you now," Michaeleen gushes.

"Saints preserve us what do they feed you Irishmen on in Pittsburg?"

"Steel, Michael Oge," answers Sean, "steel and pig-iron furnaces so hot a man forgets his fear of hell; when you're hard enough, tough enough, other things, other things, Michaeleen."

7:00

There is something going on here that perhaps needs a few words of explanation. Michaeleen knows very well who Sean is, and knows all about him. He knew all about him and his background, even his career as a boxer, from the

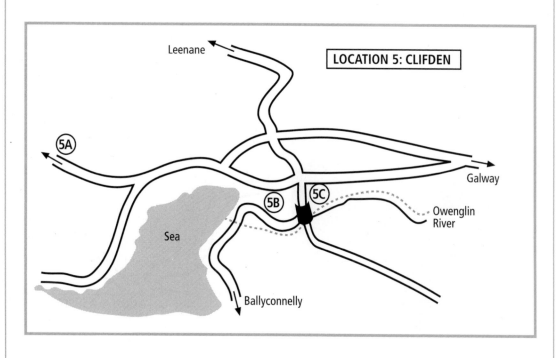

moment he picked him up at the station - in fact he probably even knew he was arriving on the Dublin train. Michaeleen is no ordinary mortal, he is part human being and part leprechaun and he knows the past, present and future. The trick is not to let Sean realise that he knows who he is and to feign surprise at the revelation. This is a well-known Irish tactic to make visitors feel superior and important and perhaps to increase the size of the tips also.

The scene now switches to the grounds of Ashford Castle, the Deerpark (**Location 6A**), nowadays a golf course for hotel residents. Sean and Michaeleen drive along the road linking the main Cong–Galway road with Ashford Castle. To their left on the roadside is a Celtic cross which is obviously a prop made by a local carpenter. Such crosses are fairly common in Ireland but rarely seen outside graveyards. Ford, however, missed no opportunity of embellishing the Irish scenery.

Now they see a tall dark figure approaching and they stop beside what is now the third fairway of the Ashford golf course (**Location 6B**).

"Now then," says the voiceover of Ward Bond, "here comes myself, that's me there, walking, that tall, saintly-looking man, Peter Lonergan, Parish Priest."

7:30

"Whoa," says Michaeleen to the horse, as he touches his hat to the priest and Sean likewise touches his cap.

"Good day, Father," he addresses him. "Sean, this is Father Lonergan. Father, would you believe it, this is Sean Thornton, born right here in Inisfree, home from America."

Third fairway, Ashford Deerpark

The Yank and the priest exchange handshakes and grins. We get our first grotesque full frontal of Father Lonergan, whose unctuous smile and limp handshake seem to be modelled on those of Uriah Heep.

"Hello, Father," drawls Sean.

"Ah yes," continues the priest in an excruciating brogue, "I noo your people, Sean. Your grandfather, he died in Australia, in a penal colony. And your father he was a good man too. Bad accident that."

8:0

For the uninitiated, Ford is having a little anti-English dig here – that the English deported all the best Irish men to Australia for trivial criminal offences such as stealing a handkerchief. The Parish Priest is expected to know all the details of the family history of all his parishioners.

He continues: "And your mother?"

"She's dead, America, when I was twelve," says Sean with an almost comic mournfulness.

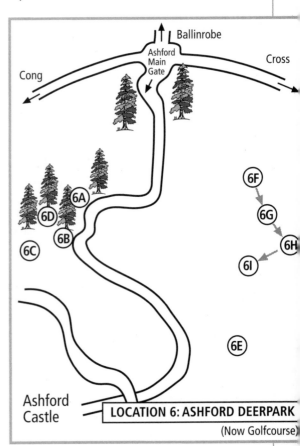

"I'll remember her in the Mass tomorrow, Sean," says the priest and then adds, "you'll be there, seven o'clock?" This is a preposterous demand of a weary traveller who has come all the way from the United States but Sean takes it on the chin like a trooper.

"Sure I will," he replies.

"Good," replies the priest, brandishing his blackthorn stick. "Sean, I'd like to have a little word with Michaeleen," he continues, quite happy to prevent the weary traveller from continuing his journey, "in reference to a…"

"Oh sure thing, Father," says Sean getting down from the sidecar.

"It'll only take a minute, it's a little matter of…" says the priest mysteriously.

Well, maybe Sean does need to stretch his legs and it is time for his second cigarette of the movie.

"Take your time, I'll be up ahead," says Sean agreeably as he saunters up the road, lighting his cigarette.

The movie does not record what business Father Lonergan wanted to transact with Michaeleen because this scene was cut from the final version - and small wonder. Thanks to the existence of the screenplay, the truth can now be told. Michaeleen is the local unofficial bookmaker and Father Lonergan, God forgive him, is one of his best clients. In this scene the priest is checking how his betting account stands in Michaeleen's tattered ledger. For the record, Father Lonergan has three pounds six and sixpence to his credit, having lost two shillings on Mad Hatter the previous Friday. He ventures half-a-crown (two shillings and sixpence) on Ard Rí (High King) in the day's steeplechase.

One of the reasons why this scene was cut was that Ford was afraid that it might not look right for a Catholic priest to be seen gambling at a time when Irish clergy were strictly forbidden by their bishop to attend even a horse-race meeting. However, the scene deserved to be cut because of its inherent dullness - just another piece of stage-Irishness that would have contributed very little to the movie.

However, the previous scene does give an excuse for Sean to observe what is not just one of the most beautiful scenes in *The Quiet Man* but, in the opinion of some, in all of cinema history. Suddenly, the screen is filled with fleecy sheep scrambling towards the tall trees with luxuriant furze bushes in the foreground. Actually, the flowers of the June furze in Cong are now past their best, but it is still supposed to be "a fine soft day in the Spring", so we will let this pass. A collie sheepdog rushes frantically over and back barking furiously **(Location 6C)**. For the record, the dog's name was Jacko and he was the property of local man John Murphy. At one stage, Ford thought he might have to abandon this lovely scene because it was proving impossible to direct the dog to do what was required, but John Murphy himself stood out of sight behind a tree in front of the cameras and the dog obeyed his master's voice and whistles to perfection.

The scene shifts to Sean standing under a massive beech tree **(Location 6D)** striking a match on the sole of his shoe to light his cigarette. He has just taken his first draw on the weed and is putting out the match when he stops suddenly and looks up like a man who has seen a vision, and indeed he has. From screen right there emerges a beautiful red-haired colleen dressed in a pale-blue blouse, a darker blue skirt with a sumptuous red petticoat underneath. Surrounded by the black-faced white sheep, the tall trees, the green grass and the yellow furze, she is truly a vision of loveliness. This is the dramatic entrance of Maureen O'Hara playing the part of Mary Kate Danaher.

Maureen O'Hara was born Maureen Fitzsimons in the Dublin suburb of Ranelagh in 1920. She trained with the Abbey Players before making her film debut in minor roles in London in 1938. In 1939 she went to Hollywood with Charles Laughton where she starred as Esmerelda in *The Hunchback of Notre Dame*. Ford gave her the lead female role as Angharad in *How Green Was My Valley* (1941) and afterwards she became a regular member of

Meeting Father Lonergan

Maureen O'Hara on set

his stock company. She appeared in many productions for RKO, Fox and other studios and her fiery temperament and splendid red hair were ideally suited to swashbuckling technicolour movies, of which she made many. She was an excellent swordswoman who liked to be part of the action, using doubles as little as possible. After her last movie with John Wayne, *Big Jake* (1971), it looked as if she had gone into retirement but luckily she returned to the screen with *Only The Lonely* (1991), *The Christmas Box* (1995) and *Cab To Canada* (1998). Astonishingly, she has never been even nominated for an Academy Award despite popular pressure.

Mary Kate suddenly looks up from tending her sheep and then looks down again modestly averting her eyes from the stranger's gaze. She is a barefoot colleen - exactly what American moviegoers expect an Irish girl to look like. The script describes her as a spinster of possibly twenty-seven (O'Hara was thirty-one at this time) and adds "unlikely as that must seem to American audiences, but somewhat more credible in rural Ireland, where marriage comes late and frequently depends on elements other than romance". As *The Isle of Innisfree* suddenly and sumptuously breaks out in the background, Mary Kate stops and looks slowly back over her shoulder at Sean, almost flirtatiously, as the script suggests. He blinks in astonishment that she is looking at him and then she slowly backs away from the camera and disappears from the bottom of the screen. Then she reappears in the

green valley where she looks back yet again at the quiet man who has just entered her life.

9:00

Sean is standing among the tall beech trees in a trance when the spell is broken by a shout of "Sean" from Michaeleen who has now finished his bookmaking business with Father Lonergan. He runs to the jaunting car and clambers up. Still looking back at the scene he drawls to the shocked Michaeleen, "Hey, is that real? She couldn't be."

9:30

"Ah, nonsense man," says Michaeleen suggestively, "it's only a mirage brought on by your terrible thirst," emphasising the dreamlike quality of the vision and strongly hinting that it is time to find a public house.

"Come up, Napoleon," he says to his horse, cracking his whip, and as the sidecar moves off Sean looks back goggle-eyed at his dream girl. The camera cuts to Mary Kate with her sheep on the hillside, hopping barefoot from fern to tree trunk and then on to the grass, all the time pausing to look back over her shoulder at the stranger. She is now so confused and excited that she is attempting to herd the flock of sheep from the centre, unorthodox to say the least - but the overall image of this beautiful sequence is one of love at first sight, a magic moment of mutual attraction and curiosity.

John Ford skilfully and surreptitiously introduced into *The Quiet Man* very many legends and folk-tales of ancient Irish origin. The scene we have just described is a perfect example of this. There is a tradition in poetry in the Irish language of the "aisling" or dream sequence, dating from the eighteenth century. While the poet sits sleeping under a tree, he is visited by a beautiful woman from the sky. She is a vision of loveliness in every respect – hair, teeth, eyes, face and figure. The poet realises that she is Ireland, soon to throw off her yoke of Anglo-Saxon oppression with the help of Bonnie Prince Charlie or the Stuart Kings. There will be religious, political and personal freedom and a future full of peace. The woman then vanishes and the poet wakes up, full of hope for a bright future. In many cases, such poems were a clever device for spreading the message of Irish nationalism under the nose of

Maureen herds sheep

the authorities who would have difficulty understanding poems written in the Irish language.

This may be an appropriate place to mention a possible influence on both Maurice Walsh's and Frank Nugent's version of *The Quiet Man*, which does not seem to have been noticed before. I am grateful to my good friend and colleague Dr Pádraigín Riggs for pointing this out to me and for her excellent translation of the original Irish short story.

In Eyre Square in Galway City there sits a statue of a little man which is visited by many thousands of people every year. It is a statue of Padraig O'Conaire, a writer of stories in the Irish language known to many generations of school children. He was a friend of Maurice Walsh and it is possible that he was the inspiration for one of the characters in some of Walsh's novels. In 1913 O'Conaire wrote a short story whose title translates as *The Woman in Torment*. One of the opening paragraphs of this story reads in translation as follows:

One day, shortly after his return from America, Burke was lounging by the wall, known in Galway as "Idlers' Corner", when who should he see coming along the road towards him but the prettiest, most light-footed damsel he had ever set eyes on. The young woman could scarcely have been more than eighteen years of age, but you would think she was a mere child of twelve when you saw her footprints in the mud, so tiny were her feet.
Burke took an instant fancy to the tiny-footed damsel as she tripped past him, humming a tune to herself. He had a lump of plug tobacco in his mouth which he shot out through the gap in his upper teeth, in such a way that it traced a loop in the air before it landed in the water.

Is this the true origin of this scene in *The Quiet Man*? The likeness is uncanny, right down to the barefoot colleen, one of only two times Mary Kate appeared so clad in the movie, and significantly, the name of the hero of this story is Burke, one of the surnames proposed by Llewellyn for Sean before Thornton was decided on. Even the name of the beautiful girl is Mary.

Filming the scene – Meta Sterne in charge!

There are further points of coincidence in the story. For his new wife Burke spends a thousand pounds on a piece of land in Knockmore. And she was not happy. His peculiar affection for her was the cause of her unhappiness. He was a bit rough. His life in the States had left its mark - the hardship he'd known and the strange things he had seen. Whatever the reason, a shiver would go through her whenever he approached her for fear he'd become too amorous. She'd feel her flesh freeze whenever he laid a hand on her…

… she burst out crying and rushed from the room. So he knocked on the door, intending to go in and apologise to her. But she refused to let him in.

"Open the door," he said.

"I won't," said she.

He was getting angry.

Later on Mary returns to her father but eventually went back to her husband and she whispered something in his ear that only the two of them heard.

While all of this evidence is circumstantial, it points very strongly to the conclusion that the story of *The Woman in Torment* by Padraig O'Conaire had a very strong influence on the screenplay of the movie rather than Walsh's short story.

Looking back even further in time, it seems clear that *The Quiet Man* owes more than a little to J.M. Synge's masterpiece *The Playboy of the Western World*. This wonderful play, set in Mayo with strong references to Kerry, concerns the Playboy, Christy Mahon, who arrives "from a far distance" at a little cottage sheebeen, with the reputation of having killed a man. He woos the heroine Pegeen Mike who dressed in a vivid red petticoat and is engaged to a man named Shawn. There is intrigue with the Widow Quin who has her eye on Christy - he wins the mule race on the sandy beach, coming from behind as the tide comes in. There is talk of "women in their shifts" (which caused a riot in Ireland at the time), the banns being read and stepping stones on the river. Lines of dialogue such as "God bless you kindly", "Woman of the house" and "Glory be to God", all have a

John Ford supervises the cleaning of Mary Kate's beautiful legs

girl, auburn-haired, scarlet-skirted, dressed in two shades of blue, driving her sheep down the rocky dell, yellow gorse in the foreground, the countryside opening out greener in the distance. Then her backward glancing at Sean, as she moves slowly out of frame. Such close-ups in *The Quiet Man*, and this was the most memorable, have an intense communication of mood which take the breath away and give the film's language a sustained dignity of direct statement.

Sean and Michaeleen have now arrived at the promised land - Inisfree, which is the village of Cong **(Location 7A)**. As the jaunting car makes its way down the little village street, a little cart heaped with peat (locally known as turf) is making its way in the other direction - a homely and authentic touch. To the left is the Market Cross of Cong around which a little crowd with a horse is gathered. To the right, dressed in knee-length breeches, is Charles Fitzsimons, who plays the part of Hugh Forbes, retired IRA commandant, sportsman and gentleman of leisure.

10:(

Charles Fitzsimons was a lawyer by profession and had been involved in some behind-the-scenes work for *The Quiet Man*, such as the recruitment of actors and the finding of props and locations. He was of course the brother of Maureen O'Hara and went on to appear in two further Ford movies – *What Price Glory* (1952) and *The Last Hurrah* (1958). Speaking to Forbes is Abbey Theatre actor Micheal Ó Bríain wearing a bobbled hat, and from the books under his arm he could well be the local schoolteacher, though this is not mentioned in the script. In fact, he was doubling for Sean McClory playing the part of Owen Glynn. (Sadly, Micheal Ó Bríain died in 1997 and Charles Fitzsimons passed away in 2001.)

The jaunting car now pulls up in front of The Sarsfield Arms, the local inn. This name was intended to play a major role in the movie but is never mentioned in the final cut although the sharp-eyed may just be able to read the name from the swinging sign over the door in the

familiar ring to them, and in the final climatic fight, Christy bites Shawn's leg. *The Playboy of the Western World* in turn is partly based on the sensational story of the Achill adventurer and fugitive from justice, James Lynchehaun, who escaped twice from jail and fled to America, but perhaps we have traced the ancestry of *The Quiet Man* far enough.

The overwhelming beauty of the scene in which Mary Kate and Sean first lay eyes on each other has been commented on by many movie critics. In particular, the English commentator Lindsay Anderson has written the following, which seems to encapsulate the feelings of many.

> Sean's first glimpse of Mary Kate is presented with a Pre-Raphaelite relish for sharp and varied colouring, as well as a kindred romanticism of view; a fairy-tale shepherd

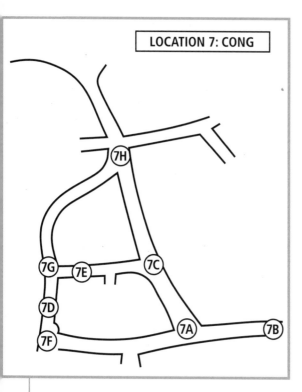

LOCATION 7: CONG

As Sean and Michaeleen enter Inisfree to the tune of *The Kerry Dances* there are many pairs of curious eyes anxious to identify the newly arrived stranger. A crowd of adults and children (no doubt containing some of the young Waynes) are clustered round the doorway of Pat Cohan's bar behind a ponytrap. Around the Market Cross is gathered a smaller crowd all of whom have been identified. To the left holding a horse is Joe Fair, a well-known horse owner and rider who doubled for John Wayne in many of the horse-riding scenes, especially in the Inisfree Races. The man in the dark suit is called Pakie Ryan, and the man with the hat is Bertie Costello, gamekeeper at Ashford Castle. The tall man with his hand on the cross is Paddy Clarke, a champion handballer who appears in several other scenes in the movie and the lady wearing the traditional Irish cloak is Phyllis Joyce.

As Michaeleen dismounts and Sean puts his coat over his arm preparing to dismount, he looks at the little crowds of villagers with a bemused smile. Now with his feet at long last on the sacred ground of Inisfree he eyes the village inn with some curiosity. We see the scene from the reverse angle and the premises of Clarke's (house of Paddy Clarke just mentioned) are clearly seen on the opposite side of the street.

10:30

Here we see one of the many breaks in continuity in *The Quiet Man* necessitated by Ford's trimming the footage right down to the bone to satisfy Herb Yates' demands. In the

close-up of Sean Thornton. Perhaps this is just another example of Ford's pruning all political and nationalistic elements from the movie, because Patrick Sarsfield was a legendary Irish patriot whose name would have been well known among Irish-Americans. In the movie the inn goes by the name of

PAT COHAN BAR

as the sign over the door indicates.

In reality, this was the corner grocery store of John Murphy, and never a bar, as many a thirsty traveller has found out to his cost, although even to this day the sign is over the door as a memorial to the movie. John Murphy, not to be confused with the owner of the sheepdog, was paid £600 by Republic Pictures for the use of his store over a four-week period and for putting up the Cohan sign. He used the money wisely and invested in a farm of land. His genial son Jack Murphy appeared as an extra in the movie and also used his station wagon or shooting brake to transport the second unit to Clifden and Tully Cross for some of the long shots.

Pat Cohan's pub

Market Cross of Cong

of humour. Feeney is Red Will Danaher's right-hand man, described as his shadow and Greek chorus, with all the independence of a chameleon. MacGowran gives a superb performance in the part and he must have been in contention for an Oscar nomination as best supporting actor.

Jack McGowran, more properly MacGowran, was born in 1918 in the Dublin suburb of Ranelagh, close to where Maureen O'Hara was born. He shared the same Christian Brothers' class in Synge Street School as Liam Cosgrave, a future Irish Taoiseach and Cornelius Ryan, author of *The Longest Day*. He made his theatrical debut with the Rathmines and Rathgar Musical Society in the chorus of a Gilbert and Sullivan operetta in Dublin's Gaiety Theatre in November 1940 and then progressed to the Peacock Theatre. Ultimately, he progressed to the highest theatrical level in Ireland – the Abbey Theatre, becoming a full-time actor after abandoning a safe job in the insurance business. Eventually he was to become one of the world's most sensitive and surrealist actors often personally chosen for roles by Samuel Beckett and Roman Polanski.

original screenplay there is a longish contribution at this stage from the narrator Father Lonergan, which we quote for interest's sake.

> And so Sean Thornton came home to Inisfree, a peaceful little village, drowsing under the sun, with nothing to disturb its quaint serenity. The old houses, the cobbled streets, the friendly faces, it was all as he had dreamed it. In the square is the centuries-old Celtic cross which has stood unchanged through wars and rebellions, and across from it a well-known hostelry – The Sarsfield Arms, owned and managed by Pat Cohan.

Michaeleen, pipe in hand, now says to Sean:

"Over here we pronounce it Co-*han!*" but he is actually answering the narrator in the previously intended version. Michaeleen has reached his promised land too – the bar – and he smilingly enters the hostelry. With a grin on his face, Sean follows him.

All through this little scene there stands on the right-hand side of the door one of the real stars of *The Quiet Man*, the weasel-faced Jack MacGowran, playing the part of Aloysius Feeney. Feeney is a prototype of a rural Irish character known as the corner boy – a lazy, unemployed propper-up of walls, with a strong eye for detail and a keen ear for gossip. The character's name is a splendid joke on Ford's own real name, a part of his self-effacing sense

Jack MacGowran

His first movie was *No Resting Place* shot in Ireland in 1950. In 1951 he stepped in for Noel Purcell to grab the role of Feeney in *The Quiet Man* and thereafter he went on to star in many movies notably *The Titfield Thunderbolt* (1953), *Darby O'Gill and the Little People* (1959), *Tom Jones* (1963) and *Doctor Zhivago* (1965). His success in *The Quiet Man* led Ford to employ his talents again as Mickey J., the poteen-maker, in *The Rising of the Moon* (1957).

MacGowran was fond of drink, and drink certainly contributed to his premature death in 1973 at the age of fifty-five. During *The Quiet Man* Ford had a strict rule that cast and crew should abstain from alcohol during the filming, but this rule was more honoured in the breach than the observance. Incredibly, Ford suspected MacGowran of leading those two notorious drinkers Wayne and McLaglen astray in this regard, so one night after the trio had been on a binge, Ford reprimanded MacGowran. The Irish Jack took off his coat and challenged the American Jack to a fight; verbal fireworks only followed, but Ford would not tolerate such disrespect and decided to make an example of MacGowran. The next morning, while filming the scene where Red Will's money was thrown into the firebox, Ford told MacGowran to stand with his back to the burning-hot engine. The actor had a king-sized hangover and the director knew that, but MacGowran gritted his teeth and stood upright near the searing heat for nearly three hours, all the time swearing under his breath and determined not to lose face. Eventually Ford, who could be surprisingly sadistic towards his actors, said: "You can move away now."

There were similar problems again with Ford during *The Rising of the Moon* (1957). Neither had forgotten their showdown during *The Quiet Man*, but when MacGowran arrived at the set in Galway clearly hungover from an all-night card-playing and drinking session Ford diplomatically adopted a humorous approach on this occasion. Total abstainers are called "pioneers" in Ireland, so Ford grabbed a teetotaller's pin from a crew member and stuck it into MacGowran saying, "From now on you're the pioneer on this picture - no more drinking!"

Back at the movie there is a total fade-out, rare in *The Quiet Man*, and used to denote the passage of time. Presumably Sean stayed at The Sarsfield Arms that night and slept soundly on his first night back in Inisfree.

In the next scene it is an early weekday morning in Inisfree as the small congregation make their way to seven o'clock Mass (**Location 7B**). In the background the church bell rings gently six times as the women in their traditional shawls pass by with their children, followed by some younger women in more modern headscarves. In the background is the little Protestant Church of Ireland which formed part of the Ashford grounds (**Location 8C**). Three children run across the field leading from Inisfree to the church. Reputedly they are three of Wayne's children who are placed in front of the camera at every possible opportunity in the movie.

11:00

Field by Church of Ireland church

In the next scene we are inside St Anselm's Chapel and Mass is already over, but there is some cinematic deception here. We saw the outside of the Protestant church but now we see the shabby interior of the Catholic church with the unmistakeable Stations of the Cross in the background (**Location 8B**). Late in 2000 there was a curious instance of life imitating art when it was announced that Saint Mary's, the

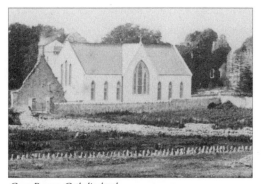

Cong Roman Catholic church

Cong Catholic Church, was closed for repairs and during its closure mass would be celebrated in the Protestant church. The small congregation tells us that it is a weekday morning, but maybe Sean, like Paddy Bawn Enright before him, did go to Mass just to catch a glimpse of his lady-love. Sean is kneeling up near the front on the right-hand side, while Mary Kate is kneeling on the left-hand side, her head bowed in prayer and her hair covered modestly with a black Galway shawl. Behind Sean is the gaffer Old Dan Tobin, played by Francis Ford, of whom more anon. The custom at the time in rural Ireland was strict gender segregation – men on one side of the church and women on the other, and even married couples separated when they entered the church to go to Mass. Sean looks around the church as if faintly remembering worshipping there as a child.

'Harry Clarke' window

This was one of only two indoor scenes of the movie shot in Ireland and soon we see the reason why – the church's magnificent stained-glass window which Ford wanted to show the world as an example of modern Irish art. It is often claimed that the window was the work of renowned Irish artist Harry Clarke (1889-1931) but this is not strictly true. The window was installed in Cong church some time around 1932, about two years after Clarke's death, but it was made in Clarke's studio which continued to produce works for a period after his death. The Cong window is not included in the official list of Clarke's work which does include church windows in nearby Ballinrobe and Tully Cross and a breathtaking "Last Judgement" in St Patrick's Church in Newport, County Mayo, his last work.

The church whose interior appears in the movie has long since been knocked down and a modern more functional building has been erected. Sadly, the window has been split in two to fit the smaller dimensions of the new church, but it is an essential part of a present-day *Quiet Man* tour.

As the altar boy, played by Michael Wayne, quenches the candles, he turns towards his father, and Duke emerges from his seat and genuflects. The Technicolor film used in 1951 was slow and the natural light levels in the church were low. The light could have been boosted, but that would have destroyed the spiritual atmosphere, so Ford instructed Winton Hoch to decrease the camera speed to half of normal (about twelve frames per second) and to allow more light into each frame. Then he directed Wayne to move down the aisle in slow motion. Ford had learned this trick from silent movies, so that when the film was projected at the usual speed everything appeared to be normal. As Duke passes by Mary Kate, he has a quick look in her direction, and she notices, because when he has gone by, she steals a glance at him behind his back. Dan Tobin now leaves his seat and genuflects and follows Sean down the aisle.

11:

There is a pleasant musical background to this scene played on the organ, and it is likely that this was added later in Hollywood. Unfortunately, part of the music being played seems to be an excerpt from *Abide With Me*, a hymn common in Protestant churches at the time but certainly never heard in a Catholic church during this period. John Horan told me that he and other members of the Galway Taibhdhearc company recorded several Latin hymns for this scene on the bus to Lettergesh, but these like many others, "died on the cutting-room floor".

Now the gaffer, Old Dan Tobin, leaves the church. The part is played by Ford's elder brother Francis Ford, originally Frank T. Feeney, whose early career we have described already. Tobin is never mentioned by name in the movie except when his bull is referred to as having chased Sean as a child. Francis was a regular member of John Ford's stock company but never rose above the level of playing bit parts in his brother's productions, typically a grizzly old-timer, barman, town fool, juggler or juror. He played the silent Judge Flynn in *The Informer* (1935), Billy Pickett in *Stagecoach* (1939) and Brother Finney in his last movie *The Sun Shines Bright* (1953).

Rumours abound that Francis and John were not on speaking terms for many years as a result of a rivalry over a girl's affections. Some stories have them communicating by written notes only during the shooting of *The Quiet Man*, but this seems to be a flight of fancy. In contrast, Ford pushed his elder brother in front of the camera at every available opportunity, often artificially and out of context. Perhaps it was Pappy's way of repaying the great debt he owed to his older brother who had introduced him to movies in the first place. However, quite an amount of *Quiet Man* footage featuring Dan Tobin was not included in the final cut, in particular, silly incidents involving him throwing clods at the police sergeant as he passed on his bicycle.

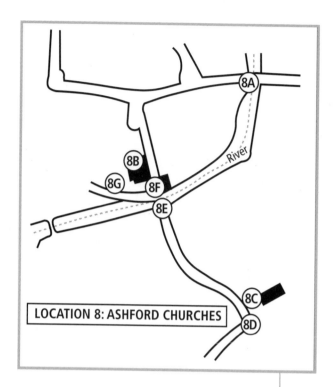

LOCATION 8: ASHFORD CHURCHES

Back at the action, Sean with a trilby hat on his head is pacing up and down outside the church (the other church again) waiting for the object of his affections to appear. On the sidecar Michaeleen is waiting patiently, and although he is meant to be an ex-clerical student, does not feel inclined to attend Mass.

To preserve the illusion that the church is a Catholic one, outside there is a holy-water font in which those leaving Mass bless themselves. The font was taken from the Cong Catholic church about half a mile away and it seems that after the filming it was accidentally left in its new location for a few days, much to the disgust of the local Protestant parishioners attending their Sunday service. Again, another story has the Church of Ireland Bishop of Tuam and his clergy petitioning Ford to cut this essential scene from the movie – one can imagine what the gruff director said to that request! Incidentally, the holy-water font in question seems to have vanished and despite extensive investigations by the author and his team of researchers, no trace of it has been found! Perhaps it was destroyed at the time of the demolition of the church.

As Sean looks anxiously towards the doorway of the church, Michaeleen sits alert on his perch, suspicious that something is afoot. First, six young women emerge, heads modestly covered with scarves and berets as was the custom at the time, but only one bothers to dip a hand in the holy water.

The young women were Bridie Hopkins, Eileen Ryan, Phyllis Joyce, Mary Maguire, Eileen Murphy and Phyllis Luskin. Bridie Hopkins, who had got married just a few weeks previously and welcomed the thirty shillings a day she earned as an extra, relates that the parents of the girls were very unhappy about their daughters even entering a Protestant church and suggested that they mention it next time they went to confessions!

Dan Tobin now emerges and stops to size up Sean before dipping his hand in the holy water, blessing himself and leaving the scene clear for the main players.

Now the bould Mary Kate emerges from the church, her eyes looking skyward as if to see what the weather is doing, but in reality she is merely trying to avoid Sean's gaze and pretending he isn't there. As she lowers her eyes to the ground and puts her Galway shawl over her shoulders, she heads for the holy-water font, still not having made any eye contact with the American. Sean is galvanised into action; doffing his hat he rushes over to the font and she looks up at him like a startled animal, and finally their eyes meet. "Good morning," he greets her as he scoops some holy water from the font and cups it in his hand with the practised ease of a movie cowboy who has scooped water from almost every stream in the Wild West.

On his sidecar, Michaeleen is so shocked that he removes his pipe from his mouth and can only stare in horror at the licentious carry-on at the church door. Mary Kate stares wide-eyed at Sean, almost unable to comprehend what is happening, but then she lowers her eyes again and delicately dips her fingers into his palm

before crossing herself quickly. She suddenly brushes by him almost running and Sean, hat in hand, turns to watch her depart, her mane of beautiful red hair flowing over her Galway shawl. As she reaches the gate she turns again to look at him and pulls her shawl over her head for protection, in a state of fear and excitement. Catching up with the shuffling Dan Tobin, she rushes out the gate to where her bicycle is waiting. She turns yet again and hides behind the pillar, the better to view the tall stranger.

This scene is typical of the veiled eroticism of many of John Ford's movies. The players are fully clothed, indeed well wrapped up for a cool Irish spring morning, yet one can easily sense the seething passion lurking underneath. Sean's presentation of his hand full of holy water and Mary Kate's dipping of her fingers therein, is both highly symbolic and suggestive of the act of conception, sanctioned by the holy water in front of the mother church, and made all the more exciting by its happening under the nose of the chaperon Michaeleen. What more excitement could any moviegoer ask for? Eat your heart out, Bo Derek!

But by now Michaeleen is beside himself with indignation and Barry Fitzgerald hams it up for all he is worth.

"None of that now, none of that now," he chides Sean. "It's a bold sinful man you are, Sean Thornton."

Here Sean replaces his hat, pleased with his morning's work.

"And who taught you to be playing patty fingers in the holy water?" he continues sternly.

"Just being polite, that's all," Sean defends himself, going round the back of the sidecar to climb up on the other side. Michaeleen is forced to rotate his neck almost a full revolution to follow him.

"Polite is it?" continues Michaeleen. "Maybe you don't know it's a privilege reserved for courting couples, and then only when the banns has been read."

Here Nugent and Ford are poking fun at the excessively regimented Irish courtship rituals as laid down by the Church - needless to say, no such patty fingers regulations ever existed, but given the spirit of the times, moviegoers might just believe they did! Michaeleen, who later on turns out to be the village matchmaker, knows very well what is going on, and continues with a mocking imitation of Mary Kate – "and Mary Kate Danaher, dipping her fingers in as neat as you please" – screwing up his face.

Gate of the Church of Ireland church.

There is a glorious cut to Mary Kate, hiding behind the gate **(Location 8D)** and listening to every word, her flame-red hair contrasting with the grey-green of the gate.

"What did you say her name was?" asks Sean huskily, almost in a trance.

"Mary Kate Danaher," replies Michaeleen, "and don't be getting any notions in your head," but of course this is precisely what Michaeleen wants to do to drum up some matchmaking business.

"Mary Kate," says the love-smitten Sean musically as if he were saying the most beautiful name in the world.

"Forget it, Sean, forget it, put it out of your mind entirely," says Michaeleen with impeccable reverse psychology.

"Why, what's the matter, she isn't married or anything is she?" asks Sean, with a worried look.

"Married? Married, that one?" answers Michaeleen indignantly. "Not likely and her with the freckles and her temper. Oh that red head of hers is no lie. Still, a man might put up with that, but not with her lack of a fortune."

All this is for Mary Kate's benefit because the wily Michaeleen realises that she is still listening near the gate and that he is speaking the opening lines in what he knows very well by now will be the matchmaking negotiations.

The camera cuts again to Mary Kate by the gate. Suddenly she leaps from her hiding place and jumps on her bicycle (a prop belonging to Maureen Glynn) before cycling down the laneway all the time looking back over her shoulder. She has overheard most of the men's conversation as indeed she was meant to, so she knows exactly what the situation is.

In the original screenplay there was another scene here, cut from the final version. In this scene, Michaeleen first explains that a fortune is a dowry payable on marriage, and briefs Sean on the Danaher family situation. He is reminding him not to delay because they have business with the Widow Tillane, when Father Lonergan emerges from the church door with a slouch hat in his hand – a hat with a few dozen assorted trout and salmon flies in its band. Father Lonergan thanks Sean for coming to Mass and chides Michaeleen for his irregular attendance. Michaeleen retaliates by telling the priest he has come from the house of the Protestant minister, who has just won a lot more on the horses than the priest has lost. The priest storms away as the pair continue their journey. With flawless editing, the scene switches to the road in front of the lovely thatched two-storey house of the Widow Tillane **(Location 1B)**. This house, now sadly demolished, stood in what is now the car park of the Ashford Castle estate. It was called Strandhill House and was originally the home of the Elwood family before being bought by the Guinness Family in the 1870s.

The ponytrap containing the Widow Tillane and her agent and right-hand man Captain Guppy is driven towards the camera and stops at the little path leading to the doorway, where a bicycle is parked. As the Widow Tillane dismounts from the trap, the narrator Father Lonergan informs us:

Widow Tillane's house

"The wealthiest woman in Inisfree was the widow Tillane. She had neither chick nor child poor soul" (an expression of pity and almost contempt in fertility-conscious rural Ireland) "but she was well-respected and good to the poor."

This last comment relates to the two categories into which Irish landowners were divided dating from famine times – those who evicted their tenants for non-payment of rent and those who fed them during food shortages. The Tillane house is meant to be an impressive residence, Georgian in architecture, rising gauntly out of a yard with scarcely a bush or plant to soften its severity. The Tillane demesne is extensive.

The part of the Widow Tillane is played by yet another member of Ford's stock company, Mildred Natwick. Born in 1908 in Baltimore, USA, of Norwegian ancestry, she was introduced to Ford by the great Henry Fonda and made her debut in Ford's *The Long Voyage Home* (1940). Ford had admired and used in many of his movies the Irish-born actress Una

O'Connor, but as she grew older he longed for a younger replacement. Mildred Natwick, whose sharp features projected dignity rather than classic beauty, suited his requirements exactly and she became a regular member of his stock company. She was a gifted character actress, often playing older women and appeared in several other Ford movies such as *Three Godfathers* (1949) and *She Wore a Yellow Ribbon* (1949). She was nominated for an Oscar as best supporting actress for *Barefoot in the Park* (1967) and made a comeback with a major part in *Dangerous Liaisons* (1988). She died in 1992. While in Ireland for the shooting of *The Quiet Man* she spent time with her friend Kate O'Brien, the Irish novelist, at her house near Roundstone.

The screenplay instructions describe Mrs Tillane (whose name sounds suspiciously like Johanna Dillane of the original Maurice Walsh story) as a handsome woman of about forty (Mildred Natwick was forty-three at the time). She is a woman of breeding with a slightly bitter humour, great practicality and a severe manner, but her apparent coldness is superficial.

Although she may not be "gat-toothed" like the Wife of Bath, she is essentially a highly-sexed woman and her four years of widowhood have set her teeth on edge. Her dress is severe but no less attractive for that, and in fact no less revealing a fine proud figure. She habitually wears a veil.

Her land agent and companion Captain Guppy (played by the English actor Don Hatswell) is a would-be gentleman. We may assume that he was a clerk's son in Bristol or Streatham who got as far as public school – where he unquestionably won the nickname of "Slimy". He is a wasp-waisted, brush-moustached little man who has great hopes of winning Mrs Tillane and her extensive estate. In the original screenplay Guppy has quite an extensive speaking part, but he wound up without saying a single word in the movie. However, his name survives because he is mentioned by one of the stewards in the race scene when he says "Foul Guppy". It is likely that Ford intended to use him to poke extensive fun at the sort of Englishman he would have depised and held in contempt, but in the end decided that it was just not worth the effort. Incidentally, Don Hatswell does not seem to have appeared in any film other than *The Quiet Man*. He is listed as being the wardrobe master on Ford's *She Wore A Yellow Ribbon* (1949) and interestingly he is listed also as a "technical adviser" on *The Quiet Man*. Perhaps it is just another example of Ford's rewarding a non-actor for services rendered. But in this case the wily director, under the guise of "Say mister, how would you like to come to Ireland to be a movie actor?", had no doubt that he had acquired the necessary English twit to play the part!

Back at the action, Guppy opens the back of the trap and Sarah Tillane dressed in her widow's weeds and carrying a shooting stick, a typical English country lady, steps down. She turns to face the camera and casts a quick glance over her estate as she closes the door of the trap. Then, veil fluttering in the breeze, she turns and walks up the path to her house.

The scene now switches to the interior of the Tillane house, which is of course a studio shot. The room is ornate, almost elaborate, and although the furniture is a mixture of Italian and English styles, the scene looks distinctly American.

Sean is standing hat in hand in front of Mrs Tillane's formidable desk, with his Sancho Panza Michaeleen by his side. Clearly, negotiations for the purchase of his ancestral home have already got underway and the lady of the manor is responding to his inquiries.

"So you were born there, is that it?" she asks him.

"Yes ma'am," replies Sean deferentially but proudly. "All the Thorntons were born there, seven generations of them."

13:30

"I see," she comments sarcastically, having a little fun with the upstart peasant. "And what is your thought, Mr Thornton, are you planning to turn White O'Morning into a national shrine?"

"What?" asks Sean incredulously, unable to understand that she is poking fun at him.

"Perhaps charge tuppence a visit for a guided tour through the little thatched cottage where all the Thorntons were born?" she continues with heavy sarcasm. "Are you a man of such eminence then?" "No, not exactly," says Sean defensively.

"My own family, Mr Thornton," says the widow, asserting her right to be considered Irish or perhaps more so than Sean because they didn't have to leave the country when times got hard, "has been in Ireland since the Normans came, some hundred of years ago (1169 to be exact), but we've seen no reason to establish monuments or memorials to that fact!"

This is one of Ford's many attempts in *The Quiet Man* to show that the Anglo-Irish are Irish too. As if to emphasise her point, the camera shows her in defiant close-up, nervously fingering the shooting stick across her desk.

14:00

Sean with his trilby hat held awkwardly against his stomach and Michaeleen still mute by his side (though taking everything in) interrupts her somewhat angrily.

"Look, Mrs Tillane, I'm not talking about

memorials or monuments," Sean tells her. "It's just that ever since I was a kid living in the shack near the slagheaps, my mother's told me about Inisfree and White O'Morn. Inisfree has become another word for heaven to me."

He continues: "When I quit the ri…" Oops, Sean almost gives his background away, but this is just a cinematic device to let the viewers know that he is an ex-boxer. Having given nothing away, however, to Mrs Tillane, he quickly catches himself and continues: "When I decided to come here it was with one thought in mind."

"Inisfree is far from being heaven, Mr Thornton," says the widow in a worldly-wise manner.

In the original screenplay the conversation continues with the widow asking Sean what he would do with the land if she sold it to him. He replies that he would farm it and plant some flowers. She smiles faintly and tells him that he is not a practical man. The widow rises as if to signal the end of the interview when Captain Guppy enters the room from another part of the house. Mrs Tillane attempts to introduce the two men to each other but they make no move even to shake hands. Guppy repairs to the fireplace, liking the extra inches of height the hearthstone gives him.

We learn from this cut scene that the widow tells Sean that she could not sell White O'Morn for less than seven hundred guineas, Guppy having suggested the figure. Guineas were wisely later changed to pounds for the benefit of American viewers, though they would probably have preferred the price in dollars. Sean quickly agrees to this price despite Michaeleen's horrified protests that the sum is way too much, but the widow rebukes him as one would a pup with "Quiet, Flynn." She then reminds Sean that the quoted price would apply only if she were selling the property and she is about to say "No" when the maid enters.

It seems as if Ford in his anxiety to cut the movie down to nearly two hours erased important explanatory parts of this scene. The editing is a little clumsy as Guppy suddenly appears at the fireplace out of nowhere and the initial negotiations between Sean and the widow have been omitted.

Back at the movie, the door of the widow Tillane's drawing room opens and the diminutive figure of Nell, her tiny maid, appears. The part is played by character actress Elizabeth Jones who appeared in several Ford productions including *Drums Along the Mohawk* (1939). Dressed in her mob cap and maid's outfit, feather duster in hand, she is clearly annoyed because her household work has been interrupted by so many callers.

"Ma'am," she shouts out, "Mister Red Will Danaher wishes to be announced." Then she adds: "I mean Squire Danaher," showing her contempt for the trumped-up landowner who is now a self-styled squire.

"Wipe your muddy boots," she says crossly to the huge Danaher who is twice her size, but there is no doubt he is terrified of her – she has enough to do than to be cleaning up the footmarks of a huge oaf. (The word "muddy" by the way is not used in this sense in the West of Ireland.) Under Guppy's contemptuous gaze Danaher retreats into the hallway and gives his boots a token cleaning on the mat.

According to the original screenplay instructions, Danaher is a giant of a man with a close-cropped bullet head, tremendous shoulders, arms like a gorilla and fists the size of catcher's mitts. He is a skinflint, a large farmer and – by some freak of biology – the brother of the lovely Mary Kate Danaher.

Now Danaher makes his entrance, his dignity dented a little by his encounter with the tiny maid, just as Ford intended. The part is played by Victor McLaglen and was written with him in mind. Born in 1886 in Tunbridge Wells, England, the son of an Anglican bishop, McLaglen was nearly sixty-five when *The Quiet Man* was shot, although Mary Kate was supposed to be under thirty. He had a very colourful career, first as a boy soldier during the Boer War and then as a vaudeville and circus performer. In Canada he worked as a farmer, a miner and a gold prospector, and in his spare time did a little wrestling and boxing. Indeed he very nearly reached the top of the tree in boxing when in 1909 he fought an exhibition bout against Jack Johnson, the first black heavyweight champion of the world. The result was reported as "no decision" after six rounds but Johnson claimed a victory.

After stints full of adventure in Fiji, Australia and Baghdad he turned his attention to movie-acting and having made twenty films in England, he moved to Hollywood. Here he was typically cast as a big, savage but soft-hearted man of action. He immediately attracted the attention of John Ford and starred as Terence O'Dowd, the Giant of Kilkenny, in Ford's *Mother Macree* (1928). He became a regular member of Ford's stock company where he invariably was cast in heavy Irish roles. Under Ford's direction, which often took the form of unorthodox taunts, goadings and even incidents of deliberately getting him drunk, McLaglen won an Academy Award for his magnificent portrayal of the traitor Gypo Nolan in Ford's *The Informer* (1935).

McLaglen, whose son Andrew V. McLaglen was an uncredited assistant director on *The Quiet Man*, was nominated for an Academy Award as best supporting actor for his portrayal of the gruff Squire Danaher. He certainly deserved an Oscar for his superb performance but the fact that he was a previous winner may have counted against him. In the event the award went to another actor of Irish ancestry, Anthony Quinn, for his part in *Viva Zapata!* The other contenders in 1952 were Richard Burton, Arthur Hunnicut and Jack Palance.

Danaher marches over to the widow's desk, blackthorn stick in hand and addresses her:

"Mrs Tillane," having first glanced at Sean.

She, however, attempts to observe the social niceties by introducing him to her guest, so she stops him in his tracks saying, "Mr Thornton from America."

Red Will merely expresses his disgust with a contemptuous "Aaah."

"Boo," says Sean by way of introducing himself.

"It's him I'm here about, Mrs Tillane," says Red Will, shaking his stick. "Is it true?"

"Is what true?" asks the widow.

"That behind me back," says Red Will, "he's trying to steal White O'Morn right from under me nose?"

(This is one of the many superb Irish bulls, seemingly contradictory statements that make perfect sense in Ireland, that Red Will utters throughout the movie.)

"And what concern of yours is this, Will Danaher?" asks the widow.

"Concern?" says Danaher indignantly. "Concern enough. Haven't I made you a good fair offer for that same piece of land, and mine lying right next to yours?"

15:00

"You may keep your offers," says the widow smugly with her eyes lowered.

"Ooh, so it's true," retorts Will, "you've sold it."

Here in the original screenplay Will grabs her by the arm in fury and spins her round but she pulls out of his grasp. This scene was very wisely dropped as it would have been totally out of character.

"No I have not," she tells him.

Relieved, Danaher now turns on the blarney, to his cost as it turns out. He relaxes, a great load off his mind and he attempts to mend broken fences. He smiles and gives a chesty laugh.

"Ho ho," he chuckles, "I knew it was a dirty lie the very minute I heard it," raising and lowering his shillelagh in triumph. "Shure," he continues, "I said to him, Packy MacFarlane, you'll never make me believe that Sarah Tillane would be selling White O'Morn."

15:30

The camera cuts to the widow obviously concerned that her business affairs should be a topic of conversation between two men. Packy MacFarlane is one of Red Will's farm workmen to be seen later in the movie.

Red Will opens his mouth wider and inserts his foot more deeply into it. His insensitivity is monumental and is equalled only by his inability to size up the situation in which he now finds himself. If Red Will Danaher were a house he would be a bungalow – nothing upstairs.

"Why it would be like building a fence between your land and mine," he goes on with an inanely childish smile on his face. "And for a stranger to move in, says I, and what would she to be doing that for, and us so close to an understanding as you might say?"

The last line is delivered with a silly lovelorn smile on his face – a superb piece of acting. However, McLaglen has fluffed his lines at least three times in that little speech, but the mistakes were pretty trivial and Ford let them stand - one wonders how many takes there had been previously.

As Danaher digs himself deeper and deeper into a hole of his own making the widow is furious but speaks in a dangerously calm voice.

"So you told him all that did you?" she asks like a skilful prosecuting counsel manipulating an easily led witness.

"That I did," says Danaher proudly, mug that he is.

"Down at the pub, I suppose," continues the widow as Danaher nods happily in agreement. "In front of all those big ears with pints in their fists and pipes in their mouths."

Danaher continues to nod and smile inanely agreeing with her and not seeing which way the wind is blowing.

"You may have the land, Mr Thornton, for six hundred pounds," says the widow defiantly, in revenge for having her private affairs discussed in public.

"Done," shouts Michaeleen triumphantly - Sean has been listening to the dialogue for several minutes in a state of increasing bewilderment.

Red Will is shocked and stunned but springs into action – he turns the proceedings into an impromptu auction.

"No you can't," he tells Michaeleen. "Six hundred and ten."

Sean calmly reminds her, "As I remember, Mrs Tillane, you said seven hundred pounds," referring back to the earlier scene that was cut.

"See here, little man," says Danaher, although both men are almost exactly the same height. "Seven hundred and ten," spoken with as much defiance as he can muster.

"How about an even thousand?" asks Sean casually. Money is no object to him in this matter and he rightly figures that this wildly extravagant sum in its day is well beyond even Danaher's profligacy.

"A thousand and…and…and…" stutters Danaher, before suddenly remembering himself. "And I'll be saying good day to you, Mrs Tillane and all here but one, and I've got you down in my book," the last remark a threatening one to Sean. With that he storms from the room slamming the door behind him.

The widow has clearly enjoyed herself having two fine single men competing for her favours. At this stage in the original screenplay she tells Sean that he is either a very rich man or a very foolish one and he replies that he is a very happy man and thanks her. She watches his departure with brooding interest.

The scene now switches to the interior of the Danaher house, again a Hollywood studio scene. The Danaher residence is not a small cottage but a well-built house. All life there during the waking hours centres in the one long room which is the kitchen, dining room and living room combined. There is a huge fireplace on which pots are boiling. The time is noon and Red Will's farmhands, five of them, including Aloysius Feeney, who has probably never done an honest day's work in his life, are seated at their midday meal of meat and potatoes. The lovely Mary Kate is bustling between the fire and the table, filling the plates when they are empty. She is hot from her work yet taking a woman's pleasure in satisfying the appetites of the men (writes Frank Nugent). In the absence of Red Will, talk is free, and about the newly-arrived Yank.

16:00

As we enter, Packy MacFarlane, a man of fifty, is talking at the table. (Despite intensive investigations, our team has not been able to identify the actor playing this role. Can any reader help? Recently this actor has been spotted in Ford's *The Long Gray Line* (1955) in a bit part as a soldier who falls off a bench when Donald Crisp arrives at the football match.)

"My dad remembers his dad well," he tells the others. "Mike Thornton, he had shoulders on him like an ox." As he speaks he extends his arms like a fisherman describing the one that got away.

"I saw him myself this morning," interjects Feeney, casting a sly teasing glance in Mary Kate's direction. "A tall handsome man, as I was passing the chapel."

News travels fast in Inisfree and clearly Feeney has heard about or maybe even witnessed the patty fingers scene. But Mary Kate is no slouch when it comes to verbal retaliation.

:30

"If you'd pass the pub as fast as you pass the chapel," she scolds him, "you'd be better off, you little squint," voicing her opinion of him at the same time.

Feeney was not originally meant to be part of this scene and here he speaks the line originally written for Dermot, another of the workers. Mary Kate even manages to put venom into serving Feeney's boiled potatoes, one of which rolls authentically onto the table. She places a cake for dessert on the table and then circles the diners putting potatoes on each man's plate without asking if anybody wants another portion – in Ireland it can always be safely assumed that everyone wants more potatoes. The tableware, cups, saucers and plates are willow pattern, very commonly found in the West of Ireland. The men have now fallen silent, afraid of a lashing from Mary Kate's tongue as she circles the table, still glowering at Feeney, who peeps at her to see if she is cooling down a little.

But another storm is about to break. Suddenly the back door of the house is thrown open and violently slammed as the angry Red Will, having crossed the fields after his unsatisfactory encounter with the widow, comes charging in. He is red-faced with anger which he is about to vent on his unfortunate employees. Hanging up his hat and throwing his stick roughly aside, he suddenly explodes:

"Just look at them," he shouts to nobody in particular, "eating me out of house and home. Get back to the fields. Come on, all of you, there's work to be done."

17:00

The workmen jump up at once but some of them manage to grab a few pieces of food from the table and take it with them. Feeney must feel that "all of you" does not apply to him, because he merely heaps up his plate and restarts his dinner from a standing position, but Red Will marches to the kitchen dresser and takes down the bottle of whiskey and a glass before sitting on his fireside chair. Even though Mary Kate is clearing up the dinner table, she at once begins to scold him – clearly there is no love lost between the two of them.

"Isn't it a bit early in the day for the bottle," she asks, "even for you?"

Red Will ignores her and pours himself a glass of whiskey.

"Feeney," he says, "get your book out."

Feeney puts his plate down and takes out his famous book, wetting his miserable pencil stub between his lips.

Feeney's book is one of the great underestimated comic devices of *The Quiet Man*, a device whereby Danaher in an almost voodoo-fashion feels that if a name is put in the book and then crossed out, an evil end will come to the person involved. This is the very essence of superstition and the hallmark of a man desperate for control when he feels that power is slipping away from him. The fact that the book is Feeney's and is kept in Feeney's possession makes it even more interesting - Danaher is able to avoid the consequences of calling down evil on another by acting through a third party, especially when the third party is totally expendable!

"Set down the name of one Sean Thornton," says Red Will vehemently and as he speaks the hated name he spits forcefully on the floor. This enrages Mary Kate who squeals: "Ooh, look at me clean floor. Ya dirty little…where do you think you are, in your barns?"

"Oh shut your gob," says Red Will wittily, raising his hand in defiance.

"Ah shut you, me little man," says Mary Kate, somewhat inappropriately, but maybe the "little" refers to Red Will's mind. "Here, clean it up yourself or there won't be any dinner in this house tonight," she adds as she throws a dishcloth in her brother's face, a type of action that is repeated several times in the movie.

Red Will throws the cloth on the floor but Feeney averts the crisis by going on his hands and knees and vigorously mopping up the offending wet patch. As he works he attempts to placate Mary Kate in his most toadying manner saying, "There now, there now, isn't that grand, isn't that grand now, what? Look it, you mustn't mind himself this day, Mary Kate."

"Ah, that's all the work you're good for, you little tattletale," says Mary Kate contemptuously as she continues to clear the table.

"Feeney," says Red Will, "have you written the name I gave you?"

"I have," says the barely literate Feeney.

"Well then, strike a line through it," says Red Will with a childish laugh. "Ha, ha, that's for him, Sean Thornton," he says contemptuously, adding a note of disgust. Now all he has to do is to sit back and wait for the curse to take effect.

Mary Kate suddenly gets the picture and says knowingly, "So he bought White O'Morn in spite of you." She goes to the window and looks out, and her eyesight must be very powerful because she sees a little cottage in the West of Ireland over six thousand miles away from the Hollywood studio in which Danaher's house interior is set (**Location 4A**).

"Good for Widow Tillane," she shouts defiantly at her brother who nearly chokes on his whiskey. So shocked is Red Will at this lack of family solidarity that he furiously switches his drink to his left hand and reaches for the poker with which to attack her, or given Mary Kate's temper, with which to defend himself maybe.

The ever-vigilant Feeney, however, restrains him saying diplomatically, "Pay no attention to her at all, Squire darlin', take no notice of her, take no notice." This is known in Ireland as "Hold me back, let me at him," type of fighting where the combatant wishes to go through the motions of battle but wishes more to be held back by the bystanders.

Mary Kate grabs the pot (a light prop by the look of it) from the window sill to protect herself and lashes verbally at her brother.

"You do and there'll be a fine wake in this house tonight," she threatens him, brandishing the pot. "After all, he's got more right to that land than you have," she says with a fine sense of fairness and family and perhaps with an eye to a future family of her own. Then she slams the pot down on the table rattling the crockery in the process. Finally, turning on her heel and grabbing a scarf, she runs out the back door of the house, slamming it behind her.

Red Will stays sitting on his chair, a lonely abandoned figure, his only friend the next drink he is about to consume from the bottle in his hand. He then utters one of the best lines in the movie – a superb Irish bull, perfectly delivered. In reference to Sean Thornton he says: "He'll regret it to his dying day, if ever he lives that long!"

Of course, the line makes perfect sense to Irish ears as most Irish bulls do – it is only foreigners who find it funny. Sean's dying day refers to his naturally allotted lifespan but this may be shortened if Red Will has his way. By the way, the circle you now see in the corner of your video screen indicates that the first reel of the movie is now completed!

Several other scenes cut from the final print were now meant to follow. A brief description of these may help to throw some light on a few further puzzling breaks in continuity in *The Quiet Man*.

Mary Kate stands looking at White O'Morning from a distant rise of ground as Sean and Michaeleen are viewing the new property. The cottage is surrounded by weeds, and the thatch is ragged and covered in grass. Again Sean hears his mother's voice giving the second part of the monologue on roses already heard. As Sean goes into the cottage through the cobwebs and dust in the pantry and bedroom, his mother's voice continues:

"Everything inside was as neat as a pin – you could have eaten your supper off my floors… and at night with a good turf fire burning and your father with his pipe, and you in your cradle beside the big bed – the happy days."

This is essentially a description of idyllic Irish family life as Ford's parents would have described it to him. But Sean's mother had a complaint – she never had a casement on her house from which to view the brook as she worked!

Sean tells Michaeleen that he has lots of plans for the cottage and from time to time a flash of red is seen as Mary Kate dodges through the bushes spying on the pair of them. Sean's smile as he sees her emphasises to Michaeleen that he has lots of plans. Seeing them drive away in the sidecar she cautiously peeps out and convinces herself that it would be a good Christian gesture to clean the cottage. The prospect fills her with a strange pleasure.

With hindsight, it was perhaps fortunate that these scenes were not included in the final cut. As well as being over-sentimental, they give perhaps too much away about the couple's feelings and intentions. Perhaps Ford decided that there are times when the viewers should be allowed to use their imagination and be left to guess a little.

The scene now shifts to the lobby of Cohan's, The Sarsfield Arms, which is the Inisfree Inn. It is obviously the hotel where Sean has been staying the previous night. This again is a studio scene, but one cannot help feeling that the decor is just a little fancy and elaborate for an Irish country inn.

As Sean comes down the stairs from his room he is carrying his leather suitcase, his sleeping bag and his coat over his arm. It is late evening

and he is checking out of the hotel and, as he bends his huge frame to avoid the rafters, he spies in the lobby two Irish country gentlemen. These are Hugh Forbes, played by Charles Fitzsimons, already described, and pipe-smoking Owen Glynn, played by Sean McClory.

From a technical point of view, McClory is a very important player in the movie because he appears only in the Hollywood studio scenes and ironically never visited his native Ireland during the shooting of *The Quiet Man*. He therefore acts as a "marker" in that any scene in which he appears was not shot in Ireland.

Sean McClory was born in Dublin in 1924 and grew up in Galway City, spending three years there as a medical student. He made his theatrical debut at the age of eight at the Galway Gaelic Theatre (An Taibhdhearc) and afterwards he had a two-year stint at Dublin's Abbey Theatre. He then went to the United States where he had a distinguished career in Hollywood, starring in over seventy movies. He too became a member of Ford's stock company and appeared in *What Price Glory* (1952), *The Long Gray Line* (1955) and *Cheyenne Autumn* (1964). In more recent times he turned to television and appeared in literally hundreds of episodes of various series. He made a spectacular return to the big screen with a fine performance in John Huston's final movie *The Dead* (1987), based on the James Joyce short story.

The screenplay describes Hugh Forbes and Owen Glynn as typical upper-class Irishmen, well-dressed in country style, with good tweed jackets, riding breeches and handsewn boots. The fact that Forbes was a Commandant of the IRA and Glynn his former right-hand man is described as "not important to this story, but is noted for the record". However, perhaps a better description of Forbes and Glynn in *The Quiet Man* be a pair of upper-class layabouts. As has been already described, their revolutionary roles have been completely sanitised and reduced to just a few fleeting references.

As Sean crosses to the open turf fire the two men watch him with interest and in his informal American way he addresses them without introduction.

"Think it'll be all right if I leave my bags in here?" he asks, more or less assuming their permission.

Glynn deliberately misunderstands and answers sarcastically as he continues to light his pipe, "I imagine they'll be safe enough," as if to say this is not lawless America, it is well-behaved Ireland.

Sean deposits his luggage by the fire and continues: "Oh, and if you see a little guy named Michaeleen Flynn, will ya tell him I'm waiting for him in the bar?"

Hinting at Michaeleen's drinking habits, Forbes answers, "It'll be a pleasure, especially for Michaeleen Flynn," with a bit of Irish doublespeak.

This is the first time we hear the voice of Forbes in the movie. It is perhaps a bit high-pitched for that of a former IRA commandant.

Sean says, "Thanks" and turns to go but Owen Glynn, throwing away his spent match with a fine sweep, says with heavy sarcasm, "Is there anything else you'd like now, Yank?" What he is really saying of course is: "Do you think that two important Irishmen like us have nothing better to do than to act as unpaid luggage minders and messenger boys for a returned American?" However, Sean suddenly realises that he is being taken for a ride but reacts with characteristic good humour and goes along with the game by replying, "If I think of anything, I'll let you know."

As Sean leaves the room, Forbes and Glynn rise from their seats and stand looking after him and at each other wondering what sort of man has come among them. In his quest to be re-accepted in his native Inisfree, Sean has now met the upper echelons of society – the Widow Tillane, Red Will Danaher, Forbes and Glynn, with varying degrees of success. Now in the sombre surroundings of Cohan's Sarsfield Arms he passes the door marked "BAR" to meet the lower classes, the ordinary people of Inisfree. Curiously he is more nervous and less confident

and aggressive as he confronts the very people from whom he sprang.

As he shuts the door behind him, he greets the nearest customer, a man with a tweed cap, pipe, and coat over his arm (this is obviously Ford and Nugent's idea of a typical rural Irish uniform!)

The part is played by Frank Baker, yet another stalwart of Ford's stock company, who appeared in dozens of Ford movies back as far as 1923, including *Men Without Women* (1930), *Stagecoach* (1939), *How Green Was My Valley* (1941) and *Donovan's Reef* (1963), but almost always as a bit player.

"Good evening," says Sean cordially, but except for a curt nod of the head the man ignores him and turns away. Outsiders, whose credentials have not been established, were treated with suspicion in 1920s Ireland and given its history this is perhaps no surprise.

"Pleasant night," continues Sean to the seated old gaffer Dan Tobin, but again he receives no reply.

Sean then advances to the bar, behind which stands the bowler-hatted proprietor of the premises, the bould Pat Cohan.

This part is well played by yet another Ford stalwart, Harry Tyler, a veteran of such Ford movies as *The Grapes of Wrath* (1940), *Young Mr Lincoln* (1939) and *Tobacco Road* (1941). He is described in *The Quiet Man* as trying to run a nice quiet place and every so often he does.

Pointing at a bottle, Sean addresses Pat Cohan, "I'll try one of those black beers."

"Ah, the porter, yes sir," replies Pat politely.

Sean then leans forward and lights his cigarette in the globe of the oil lamp, one of the many he smokes in the movie. He is now desperate to make contact with the villagers, so, noticing that Dan Tobin's glass is empty, he asks him, "Sir, will you join me?" As Pat Cohan places his drink in front of him, Sean says loudly, "Matter of fact, I'd like to buy everybody a drink."

Suddenly Sean is talking the locals' language. Dan Tobin sits up straight and says, "I do not believe I heard your name, tall man."

"Thornton, Sean Thornton," answers Sean hopefully as a smile of recognition crosses Pat Cohan's face.

"And ah, your father's name?" asks Dan Tobin, getting more interested by the minute and even standing up in his excitement.

"Mike, Michael Thornton," says Sean more confidently now, "he used to live here, White O'Mornin', I just bought the place back – that's why I'm here."

As this piece of information is being disclosed, Pat Cohan slowly doffs his hat in reverence at the name – perhaps Mike Thornton was Cohan's best customer!

"Then your grandfather would be," continues Dan Tobin, pointing his finger and advancing towards Sean, "Old Sean Thornton."

"Right," nods Sean smiling now that he is at last being listened to.

:00

"Bless his memory," says Dan Tobin, "so it's himself you're named after. Well, now, that being the case, it is a pleasant evening and we will have a drink." So saying, he bangs his blackthorn stick on the counter several times as a signal for the celebrations to begin.

Here Ford is making the point that Sean cannot be accepted back into the Inisfree community until at least two generations of bona-fide ancestors have been checked out, but that on acceptance he is very warmly welcomed indeed. The irony is that Dan Tobin knew all along who he was and that he had bought White O'Morning, but Sean had to be put through this public initiation ritual.

At Dan Tobin's signal, the other customers in the bar rush to the counter in a rather contrived manner to claim the round of drinks that Sean is standing them. We notice they are all male – no woman worthy of the name would have been seen dead in a bar of an Irish pub in the 1920s and ladies like the Widow Tillane objected strongly to having even their names mentioned in such places.

The accordion player Dermot Fahy now appears from nowhere dressed in his traditional Aran outfit and cap and begins to sing and play his "box". The part is played by Ken Curtis, Ford's son-in-law to-be, who married Barbara Ford in 1952. Inevitably, Curtis became a Ford veteran, appearing in *Rio Grande* (1950), *Mister Roberts* (1955) and *The Wings of Eagles* (1957). His greatest triumph, however, was his performance as the wimpish Charlie McCorry in *The Searchers* (1956).

Curtis had a fine singing voice and was a member of the group The Sons of the Pioneers with Hugh Farr, Karl Farr, Lloyd Perryman, Shug Fisher and Tommy Doss, who had first performed for Ford as regimental singers in *Rio Grande* (1950). Most of the pub songs for *The Quiet Man* were originally recorded in the waiting room of Ballyglunin railway station and a few on a pier in Lough Corrib by the Galway Taibhdhearc players but, according to Maureen O'Hara, they were all re-recorded by The Sons of the Pioneers in Hollywood and it is those versions that appear in the movie.

Actually, while Ford quite liked The Sons of the Pioneers, he didn't feel they were very suitable for *The Quiet Man*. However, Herb Yates could not conceive of any movie that didn't include singing cowboys and that seems to be the reason why they were included!

The song now sung is *The Wild Colonial Boy*, a lovely singalong Irish ballad which was a great favourite of John Ford's. It concerns an Australian bushranger and outlaw of Irish extraction called Jack Duggan (originally Doolin). There is some dispute as to whether the Castlemaine in question is the Kerry village or a little Australian goldmining town, but *The Quiet Man* clearly opts for the Irish location! The most popular version of the song goes as follows:

> There was a wild colonial boy, Jack Duggan was his name.
> He was born and bred in Ireland in a town called Castlemaine.
> He was his father's only son, his mother's pride and joy
> And dearly did his parents love their wild

colonial boy.
At the early age of sixteen years he left his
native home,
And to Australia's sunny shore he was
inclined to roam.
He robbed the rich to feed the poor, he
stabbed James McEvoy
A terror to Australia was the wild colonial boy.
One morning on the prairie as Jack Duggan
rode along
Listening to the mockingbird singing a
cheerful song
Out stepped three troopers fierce and grim,
Kelly, Davis and Fitzroy
They all set out to capture him, the wild
colonial boy.
Surrender now, Jack Duggan, for you see
we're three to one
Surrender in the Queen's high name, for
you're a plundering son.
Jack drew two pistols from his belt and glared
upon Fitzroy,
"I'll fight, but not surrender," said the wild
colonial boy.
He fired a shot at Kelly which brought him
to the ground
And turning then to Davis he received a fatal
wound,
A bullet pierced his proud young heart from
the rifle of Fitzroy,
And that was how they captured him, the
wild colonial boy.

We note that one of the lines has been skilfully
doctored to fit the plot of *The Quiet Man* – "He
robbed the rich to feed the poor, he stabbed
James McEvoy" – has become "He robbed the
wealthy Squireen, all arms he did destroy" just
as Red Will Danaher enters the pub!

A smiling Sean places a pint of porter in front
of the ballad singer Dermot Fahy, just to keep
his throat lubricated. As he hands around the
drinks, Sean is happy and smiling – he has come
back to Inisfree and has been accepted by his
own people.

The scene now shifts back to the hotel lobby
where Forbes and Glynn are examining Sean
Thornton's sleeping bag with some interest.
They stand and turn as Father Lonergan,
accompanied by Father Paul, described as a

Father Paul (James Lilburn) takes a break

young dark-eyed athletic curate, enter and
interrupt them.

The part of Father Paul was played by James
Lilburn, alias James Fitzsimons, another brother
of Maureen O'Hara's. He took his stage name
of Lilburn from his mother's maiden name, but
later in his career he changed his name to James
O'Hara. This was his first Ford movie but he
went on to play a young soldier in *What Price
Glory* (1952) also directed by Ford and also
starring Lilburn's brother Charles Fitzsimons
and Sean McClory. Earlier, in 1937, Ford had
already used a character called Father Paul in
the Samuel Goldwyn production *The Hurricane*.

"Good evening, Father," says Glynn to
Father Lonergan.

"Is the rest of the committee here?" asks the
parish priest curtly, putting the stress in the first
syllable of the word "committee", a common
pronunciation in rural Ireland and a nice
authentic touch to the dialogue.

"They're waiting," says Forbes, signalling in
the direction of the meeting room.

At times Forbes and Glynn remind us of
Tweedledum and Tweedledee in *Alice in
Wonderland* or Rosencrantz and Guildenstern in

20:30

Hamlet. Their roles are almost interchangeable and they have alternate lines of dialogue in almost equal amounts. Maurice Walsh must have cringed at the fate of his two military heroes about whom he had written such stirring tales. What the committee is for we are not told – perhaps it was the Inisfree Races Committee.

"I'm sorry we're late," says Father Lonergan.

"Ah, the fishing was bad, was it?" says Glynn sarcastically but Father Lonergan is in no mood to exchange light-hearted banter.

"Ah, fishing is it?" he retorts. "Fine lot of time we have for that." He then adds, "Come along," motioning to Father Paul.
As the priests hurry off, Forbes and Glynn are about to follow them when they spot Michaeleen Oge Flynn ambling towards them – in the background we can still hear the strains of *The Wild Colonial Boy* wafting in from the bar.

"Oh Michaeleen," says Forbes.

Out of force of habit, Michaeleen stands to attention and gives Forbes, his former commander in the IRA, a military salute.

"Commandant Forbes," he addresses him, perhaps just a little sarcastically.

"Ah, you can forget about the commandant," says Forbes, "we're at peace now, man."

"True," says Michaeleen, "but I haven't given up hope."

Glynn laughs in a stagy manner as he puffs on his pipe.

This sequence is typical of the way in which the Irish fight for freedom is treated in *The Quiet Man*. It has been reduced almost to a joke so that box-office sensibilities will not be affected and yet one wonders why any mention of it is allowed to remain in the movie at all.

"Your Yankee friend is waiting for you in the bar," continues Forbes, and Michaeleen, sensing either business or a free drink says, "O bedad, is he here already?" But Forbes stops him by asking, "Wait a minute now, Michaeleen, who is he anyway?"

As usual, Michaeleen is not short of an answer.

"Well, he's a nice quiet peace-loving man come home to Ireland to forget his troubles," he replies.

This is the closest we get to the words "quiet man" in the screenplay, but the implication is that the magic leprechaun Michaeleen knows all about Sean and why he has returned to Ireland.

"Troubles?" asks Forbes quizzically, having just come through what he regarded as Ireland's real "troubles".

"Sure yes, yes," says Michaeleen, "he's a millionaire you know, like all the Yanks."

(Here Nugent and Ford are poking fun at the common rural Irish belief that all returning Americans are rolling in dollars, a theme well portrayed in John Murphy's play *The Country Boy*.)

"But eccentric, oh ho ho, yes, eccentric," continues Michaeleen, "wait till I show you," and so saying he picks up Sean's sleeping bag as the ultimate example of eccentricity.

"What is it?" asks Forbes.

"It's a bag to sleep in," chuckles Michaeleen, "a sleeping bag he called it. Did you ever hear the like of that? A sleeping bag! Here, wait until I show you how it operates."

All three of them bend down to unfasten the sleeping bag, but Forbes and Glynn are laughing more at Michaeleen than at the bag.

"Where does it open?" asks Forbes.

"Well, hurry it up now because I have a very important appointment," says Michaeleen.

"Well, open up now, man," says Glynn (for it is his turn to speak).

"Here, here, here is a button here," says Forbes and the light-hearted banter continues.

Meanwhile back in the bar of the hotel the singing of *The Wild Colonial Boy* is continuing in full flight. The words of the song are of course not without a certain amount of irony in the circumstances. Jack Duggan went to Australia from Ireland as a young boy and killed

21:30

a man as a result of his exploits; Sean Thornton went to America from Ireland as a young boy and he too killed a man as a result of his activities.

There is a nice shot of Frank Baker as one of the men in the bar, and Dermot Fahy as he continues to sing lustily and play his accordion.

"At the early age of sixteen years, he left his native home," sings Fahy.

The scene cuts to the bowler-hatted Pat Cohan singing and smiling as he serves a pint of porter at the bar.

"And to Australia's sunny shore he was inclined to roam," the singing continues, but now there is trouble brewing, even as Sean raises his glass in celebration.

Enter stage left Red Will Danaher, formally dressed in his tweed suit and hat, and brandishing a blackthorn stick. He is accompanied by his shadow Feeney, and Red Will has a very nasty look indeed on his face. As he ambles up to the bar, he sizes up the cosy scene that he is about to shatter.

"He robbed the wealthy Squireen," continues the song, the words cleverly adapted to refer to Red Will just as he enters. "All arms he did destroy, a terror to Australia was the wild colonial boy."

22:00

By this time Red Will and Feeney have reached the bar as the locals pull aside. Red Will pushes the oil lamp to one side as Feeney, perhaps modelling himself on Harpo Marx, slyly drinks up the dregs of a glass of stout on the counter.

Meanwhile Sean's initiation ceremony is reaching its climax. Dan Tobin, drink in hand, is saying, "Sean Thornton, the men of Inisfree bid you welcome home!" (The women of Inisfree have yet to express their feelings.)

"Thank you," says Sean, as their glasses touch in a toast.

From the other side of the bar there is a prolonged cackle, and Red Will mimics the toast in mincing tones.

"And the men of Inisfree bid you welcome home," he mocks. "What's wrong with that little speech, Feeney?"

"Ah, you'd be knowing what, Squire," answers Feeney diplomatically.

Danaher now swaggers over to the counter to confront Sean and Dan Tobin as two locals wisely give way to his huge bulk. Sean looks apprehensive as he and the gaffer stare at Red Will who puts his stick on the counter, opens his jacket and puts his hands on his hips in the manner of a lawyer opening the case for the prosecution.

"I'm a man from Inisfree," he bellows, "and the best man, and I'll bid no welcome to any man fool enough to pay a thousand pounds for a bit o' land that isn't worth two hundred."

"Ah, true for you, Squire," says a triumphantly smiling Feeney.

Sean and Dan Tobin take in all this in silence – Dan Tobin horrified that the traditional welcome ceremony has been violated, and Sean knows that he must not get involved, either verbally or physically.

Help, however, comes from Dermot Fahy, the ballad singer, described as a long, lean, loose-jointed impertinent rascal with an indolent air and the immunity that the ages have conceded to all troubadours and minstrels. With quite a passable Irish accent for an American, he interjects: "Didn't I hear of someone named Danaher, bidding to eight hundred and ten? Hah?"

It is truly amazing the effect that giving a free drink to a musician can induce and obviously Michaeleen has given a full account of the transactions in the widow's house, no doubt lubricated by free drinks.

Actually, in the earlier part of the movie, Danaher had bid only as far as seven hundred and ten pounds, so Dermot Fahy appears to be a hundred pounds out. This is due not to Michaeleen's exaggeration, but to the fact that Danaher's final bid of eight hundred and ten pounds was cut from the movie to shorten its length.

Danaher reacts in the only way he knows. "Get your book out," he says to Feeney, "put his name down," and Feeney obliges.

"Dermot Fahy," says Danaher, pointing his stick at the singer's nose and giving the name its

American pronunciation FAYEE, instead of the more usual Irish FAHEE.

To show he is not afraid of the bully, Dermot helps them out with spelling of his name.

"F-A-H-Y, no E, Squireen Danaher."

"And if you were half the man you think you are," says one of the customers to Danaher, "you wouldn't begrudge a Thornton the right to his own birthplace." (We have not been able to identify the actor who speaks these lines – help, readers, please!)

"And that's my opinion too," adds the customer, played by Frank Baker.

Danaher, realising that public opinion in Inisfree is not behind him, cuts the previous speaker short, though maybe this was just over-eagerness on McLaglen's part.

"What right has he to land that he's never worked," asks Danaher aggressively, showing that he can make a logical point when he is cornered.

"It's Thornton land, isn't it?" says Dan Tobin, speaking from many years of experience.

"You've too much of your own as it is," adds Dermot Fahy.

Feeney, who is taking an inordinately long time to write two words in his book, suddenly realises that the tide is turning against his lord and master so he falls back on the old trick of protocol.

"Quiet, if you please," he interjects suddenly. "Parliamentary procedure, Squire Danaher has the floor."

"If I had the floor," says Dan Tobin to Sean, brandishing his stick, spitting on his hands and thumping on the ground, "I'd hit that big ape with it," but Sean restrains him by holding back the stick. The time has come for him to intervene to prevent a violent clash.

"Hold on," he says, "I don't blame Mister Danaher for getting on his ear," but Sean's choice of words is unfortunate and Red Will chooses to misunderstand the Americanism.

"Who's on his ear?" he thunders. "Why, you and ten Thorntons like you couldn't put a Danaher on his ear."

"It's just a way of speaking," says Sean, "I didn't…"

"Well, mind your ways then," retorts Red

Will, giving us an unscripted "then" free and for nothing.

At this stage and perhaps for devilment, Dermot Fahy begins to play a slow air on the accordion. The tune is one of Thomas Moore's most beautiful melodies, *The Meeting of the Waters*, also known as *Sweet Vale of Avoca*. Ford chose several other melodies of Moore's in *The Quiet Man* and it is likely that he would have learned many of them at his mother's knee, because they were enormously popular in Victorian Ireland at all levels of society. For the record, the words of the accompanying lyric are:

There is not in the wide world a valley so sweet
As that vale in whose bosom the bright waters meet;
Oh! The last rays of feeling and life must depart,
Ere the bloom of that valley shall fade from my heart.

Yet it was not that Nature had shed o'er the scene
Her purest of crystal and brightest of green;
'Twas not her soft magic of streamlet or hill,
Oh! No, - it was something more exquisite still

'Twas that friends, the belov'd of my bosom, were near
Who made every dear scene of enchantment more dear,
And who felt how the best charms of nature improve,
When we see them reflected from looks that we love.
Sweet vale of Avoca! How calm could I rest
In thy bosom of shade, with the friends I love best,
Where the storms that we feel in this cold world should cease,
And our hearts, like thy waters, be mingled in peace.

"The point is," continues Sean, "it's already

done, I own the property now and as long as we're going to be neighbours…"

"Neighbours, ho, ho, ho, neighbours," interrupts Danaher, turning round and looking for popular support as to how ridiculous this notion is - of course he receives none except for a smile and a shake of the head from the ever-reliable Feeney.

"Never," says Red Will, "and if I so much as catch you putting a wet foot on my property I'll, I'll…"

Lowering the finger he has been pointing at Sean and raising his blackthorn stick, Red Will pauses as if remembering another piece of ammunition in his locker.

"Oh, and another thing, you keep away from my sister Mary Kate," he adds, "she's not for the likes of you."

Clearly he regards Mary Kate like a heifer or a piece of land to be disposed of as he wishes.

Sean's patience is now exhausted and he decides, like a boxer, to attack with a smart little counter-punch.

"Where I come from," he jabs, "we don't talk about our womenfolk in saloons. You sort of make a habit of it. This morning it was Widow Tillane…"

"What's that?" asks Red Will, unable to believe his ears.

"It's true," interjects Dan Tobin in an outburst of stage-Irishism, "it's ashamed you should be."

(The original screenplay had "Be shamed for yourself," which is even worse. What he should have said is – "You should be ashamed of yourself.")

"I'm not accusing Mary Kate," says Danaher, very angry now and trying to bluff his way, "it's him," pointing at Sean. "Why, this very morn, let him deny it if he can, at the back of the chapel, he took liberties that he shouldn't have."

Sean replies half-laughingly, "I said good morning to her." (Not quite true, Sean, how about all that patty fingers business?)

"Good morning," repeats Red Will. "Yes, but it was good night you had on your mind."

(In Ireland "good night" is used as a greeting at night time, whereas elsewhere in the English-speaking world it is used as a farewell at night.)

"That's a lie," says Sean firmly but angrily.

Pat Cohan immediately grabs an oil lamp and a glass from the counter knowing from bitter experience that a major fight could break out at any minute.

Red Will can hardly believe his ears, so he asks for confirmation of the insult.

"That's a what?" he asks Sean.

"I said 'that's a lie'," repeats Sean.

Red Will now has, in the manner of all bullies, the excuse for aggression that he was looking for all along. He throws his hat and stick on the floor shouting: "That's a word I take from no man, put up your fists!"

In mid-sentence the door of the bar opens and, their meeting disturbed by the commotion, in rush Father Lonergan, Father Paul, Michaeleen and the other members of the committee.

"I'm not going to fight you, Danaher," says Sean quietly, his arms still folded.

"Well, I'm going to fight you then," shouts Danaher, rushing forward and throwing punches wildly, great ox that he is. Sean neatly steps aside and throws his trench coat over Danaher's head, blinding him temporarily.

Dan Tobin throws his head back at this event and laughs uproariously and, as a reward for his overacting, has his face covered by the same coat as Danaher throws it roughly aside.

Turning to make a quick getaway from the trouble, Sean puts some money on the counter and says "thank you" to Pat Cohan, but Danaher launches himself at Sean in another bout of "hold me back, let me at him" fighting. This time he almost strangles Frank Baker who is holding him back.

"Take it easy, Danaher," says Baker, but now Danaher finds himself face to face with the ultimate authority in Inisfree – Father Lonergan.

"Danaher, Danaher, what's the matter with you?" shouts the parish priest.

"Ah, he's drunk," says Glynn. "Hey, Feeney, Feeney, take him home."

In Ireland, drink is used to excuse all forms of behaviour, but it is obvious that Danaher is not drunk.

"Come, Squire, don't soil your knuckles on the man," says Feeney, in the best tradition of making the best of a bad lot.

"Are you all right, Sean?" Michaeleen asks with concern in his voice.

Sean, however, is anxious to pour oil on troubled waters and extends his hand in a gesture of friendship.

"Come on, Danaher, what do you say?" he asks.

"Never," says Danaher predictably.

"You'll take the man's hand," says Father Lonergan sternly, "or I'll read your name in the Mass on Sunday."

This was the ultimate threat in the rural Ireland of the 1920s – there was no greater shame than to have your name read out from the altar at Sunday Mass. Red Will is now threatened with being put in Father Lonergan's book.

Feeney, by no means a religious man, is absolutely terrified at the prospect of this social stigma.

"Oh take it, Squire, take it, take it, take it," he implores his master, but Danaher is not moved.

"Ah, I'll join the Church of Ireland first," he retorts, invoking his ultimate threat of becoming a Protestant, which was equivalent to going over to the opposition.

"As if they'd have you," says Father Lonergan realistically. "Now go on, take his hand, shake hands with him like I tell you."

Incidentally, the grey-haired man with the cap who is standing by the doorway all through this scene has been identified as Pat O'Malley, veteran Irish-American character actor, starring in *The Virginian* (1923) and *Invasion of the Body Snatchers* (1956).

Now Danaher is completely on his own – even Feeney has gone over to the other side, but wily old bird that he is, a new thought occurs to him. He will take Sean's hand and crush it in a show of strength, tantamount to a bout of arm-wrestling. He turns to Feeney smiling and cackling, "Shake hands, shake hands," as the terrified Feeney encourages him with "go on, go on, go on".

Danaher feels that he can shake Sean's hand without losing face and inflict some pain on him into the bargain, so he rolls up his sleeve

and, grabbing Sean's hand, grips it with all his might. Sean grits his teeth as Danaher's giant hand crushes his, and the onlookers, especially Father Lonergan, look from man to man, knowing full well what is going on.

Danaher's cackle soon turns to a grimace of pain as Sean matches his grip saying, "That's a good grip you have there, Danaher, I always hated a flabby handshake myself."

The onlookers now begin to smile as they realise that the bully of Inisfree has at last met his match.

Danaher disentangles and Feeney picks up his hat and stick and without a further word the pair of them leave the bar, the servant pushing his master, hands on his back.

"Father Paul," says Father Lonergan and they too leave, but actually in the rural Ireland of the time a priest in clerical uniform would not have been seen in a public bar, especially in the presence of his parishioners.

Forbes and Glynn, previously suspicious of the Yank, now turn enthusiastically towards him with hands outstretched.

"Michaeleen," says Forbes, "introduce me to this quiet peace-loving man of yours," as Sean recovers his coat.

"I've a strange notion we're going to be friends, Yank," says Glynn, extending his hand. Sean grins and starts to extend his hand but then winces in pain.

"Well, give me a minute just to let some blood run back into this hand," he jokes and there is laughter all round as he shakes hands enthusiastically with the two men.

The tension is broken, and Michaeleen can now revert to his usual humorous self. "Sean Thornton," he intones, "his grandfather, oh, a grand man he was, was hung in Australia." Taking off his hat reverently he continues, "Oh, I could tell you blood-curdling stories if I was…but me throat, me throat is gone dry."

This is the cue for Michaeleen to be propelled to the bar for another bout of drinking in the company of Sean, Forbes and Glynn, with shouts of "All right, Michaeleen, come on." In the background the accordion once again strikes up *The Wild Colonial Boy*:

He was born and bred in Ireland

In a town called Castlemaine

He was his father's only son,

His mother's pride and joy

And dearly did his parents love

This wild colonial boy.

White O'Morn bridge

The assembled company all sing lustily and raise their glasses to toast the returned Yank as Pat Cohan works overtime to keep the glasses filled. Sean hands round the glasses, but as he reaches for his own drink, Michaeleen, with perfect timing, beats him to the draw for the next pint. Sean Thornton has finally arrived and been accepted by the people of Inisfree, bar one.

26:30

This drinking and singing scene is not in the original screenplay but was skilfully inserted afterwards.

The last thirteen minutes of action in *The Quiet Man* have taken place indoors, filmed in rather gloomy Hollywood interior sets. The scene now shifts outdoors to the beautiful Irish countryside. As Sean and Michaeleen walk along the bank of the brook, which is a little tributary to the Failmore River **(Location 4B)**, it appears to be night time, but this scene was shot during daylight hours and suitably darkened afterwards. This technique is known as "day-for-night" and Winton Hoch was one of the most skilful practitioners of this technique in the history of cinema. It occurs in several

other sequences in *The Quiet Man*. The stepping stones on the little river in the foreground have a magical look as Sean strides out towards his ancestral home, sleeping bag in hand. In the background is the 2012-foot peak of Corcogemore or Leckavrea Mountain with a little cap of cloud. In the distance a dog gives a welcoming bark and Vic Young plays a lovely orchestral arrangement of *The Wild Colonial Boy*. However, as Sean and Michaeleen reach the little concrete bridge over the river there is a break in continuity and all of a sudden the mountain in the background has a large cloud obscuring its eastern slope – a minor flaw and one visible only on a stop-start video copy of the movie.

27:

Overall, this is a scene of stunning visual beauty, a gentle contrast with the raucous conflict in the hotel bar. Sean and Michaeleen pause at the end of the concrete bridge (still happily standing) **(Location 4B)** while Sean surveys his ancestral home, White O'Morning, with his sleeping bag under one arm and case in the other. The cottage itself is surrounded by tall trees swaying in the real freshening wind. Sean, filled with emotion and nostalgia for his mother, his father and his vanished childhood, is shown in close-up, contrasted against the night sky.

Michaeleen, who is leaning against the parapet of the bridge calmly puffing on his pipe, allows Sean to wallow in his emotions for a few moments and then breaks the spell with a practical suggestion.

"Are you sure you won't change your mind, Sean," he asks, "and come along home with me?" knowing full well that there is no possibility of his doing so.

"Don't worry about it," answers Sean laconically, "I have my sleeping bag, haven't I?"

It is tempting to speculate on the symbolic role of the sleeping bag in *The Quiet Man*. Firstly, it is given somewhat undue prominence in the earlier scene where it is a source of amusement for Michaeleen and his friends. Now it is all Sean says he needs for a night in the cottage and, later on, when Sean is forced out of Mary

Kate's bedroom on the first night of their honeymoon, he spends it in the sleeping bag. Freudian psychologists might suggest that the sleeping bag represents Sean's mother's womb, a safe haven from Danaher, Mary Kate, the boxing ring and all the other troubles and worries of his life. In the sleeping bag Sean is isolated, but warm and safe and immune from attack by the outside world.

Michaeleen smiles at Sean's reply, obviously not relishing spending a night in a sleeping bag. Putting out his hand to test the weather he observes: "Well, it's a nice soft night, so I think I'll join me comrades and talk a little treason," with a sly wink at Sean. This is IRA talk and, although tradition has it that John Ford wrote these lines, they do appear in Nugent's original screenplay.

"Good night, Sean," says Michaeleen, with a wave of the hand.

"Good night, Michaeleen," answers Sean.

As Michaeleen departs back over the bridge he says to Sean "God bless you", a line not in the original script.

Sean walks up the laneway through the trees in the bright moonlight towards White O'Morn. The cottage is thatched in traditional Irish style with straw from the surrounding fields and on its southern-facing gable is a thatched barn. Consistent with the story of the movie, White O'Morn is in a somewhat dilapidated and run-down condition when Sean arrives **(Location 4C)**.

As Sean approaches the cottage, the music is ominous, almost like that of a horror movie, and he senses that something is amiss. Smoke is coming from the chimney across the thatch of a supposedly empty cottage. A close-up of the chimney shows a surprisingly weak stream of smoke from that source. In reality, it is Cong man Jim Morrin who is inside fanning the smoky flames in the old fireplace.

Sean surveys the scene and his suspicions are aroused. He goes up to the front door, which is unlocked, and opens it suddenly. The action just as suddenly switches back to a studio set and, although the scene is flawlessly edited in typical Ford fashion, the change in the texture of the light is quite apparent. However, the skilful back projection of the Irish trees blowing in the wind helps to preserve the illusion.

Many moviegoers are surprised to learn that two cottages were used for White O'Morning in *The Quiet Man*. The first is the one at

The sad ruins of White O'Morn today

Teernakill near Maam, which features in exterior scenes only. The second is a much bigger studio mock-up of the cottage, which features in both exterior and interior scenes.

When Sean opens the door of the cottage he is amazed to see a fire burning brightly in the hearth and a broom, obviously hurriedly dropped beside a pile of leaves and debris on the floor. Dropping his bags he slams the door behind him, as the howling wind continues to play with the leaves on the floor.

The scene now cuts to the bedroom where the beautiful Mary Kate is cowering in fear with a pretty blue scarf covering her head and shoulders. As Sean enters the cottage, she stands up against the bedroom wall in the moonlight, her right hand holding her scarf protectively around her neck. The back door of the cottage is banging in the wind and the torn curtains on the window are blowing furiously on account of a broken pane. Sean quickly slams the back door shut and the sound of his action further alarms Mary Kate. He knows now that some thing, human or animal, is in the bedroom, but how is he to scare it out? Taking a stone from the floor, he hurls it through a pane of the window of the room that he is in, shouting a blood-curdling "Yaaaow" as he does so.

Terrified at herself and the situation she now finds herself in, Mary Kate is really scared out of her wits. As she turns even more towards the corner of the bedroom for protection, she unexpectedly catches sight of her own reflection in a mirror on the wall and screams "Oh I" or words to that effect. Here we have two very primitive mating calls – a veritable Tarzan and Jane; me Sean, you Mary Kate!

As Sean stands his ground beside the beam that is supporting the front wall of the dilapidated White O'Morning, Mary Kate decides to make a bolt for the front door of the cottage. With a symbolic leap over the sleeping bag, she nearly makes her escape, with Sean looking on more amused than amazed. She opens the door and gets out, her white apron flying in the wind, but

Sean follows and grabs her, pulling her back in through the doorway – real caveman stuff! This overpowering scene now becomes almost like a filmed ballet dance, as Mary Kate is swept back into the cottage, her red skirt and white apron again flying in the wind. She twists and resists the pull of Sean's outstretched arm – just a couple of hours previously he has twisted the arm of her big brother in very different circumstances.

Sean now draws her to him with his left arm around her waist and her resistance is merely token as she raises her face to meet his. Sean's right arm goes over her shoulder as they kiss passionately and for a moment it appears as if her left arm is going to go around his waist. All the time during this beautiful scene the wind is howling through the open front door and broken window pane causing their garments to flutter like the sails of a Galway hooker. The wind machine too works overtime on Mary Kate's lovely red hair.

Silently, they disengage and Sean slams the front door shut and they face each other again. Mary Kate brushes the hair from her face with her left hand and pulls back her right hand to strike him, but she telegraphs her intention to the ex-boxer and he blocks the blow with his open right. Rumour has it that Wayne and O'Hara were in open conflict at this stage of the shooting and that she hit him so hard that she broke a bone in her hand but the slow motion reveals that they did not actually make contact here – the sound of smacking hands gives rise to the cinematic illusion.

"It's a bold one you are," she accuses him, "and who gave you leave to be kissing me?"

(In Ireland "bold" has connotations of naughty rather than brave, a translation of the Irish *dána*, but what is really interesting is Mary Kate's attitude that the permission of a third party, Red Will or Father Lonergan perhaps, is necessary before somebody can kiss her.)

"So you can talk," says Sean, a peculiar remark in the circumstances, which will be explained later.

"Yes I can, I will and I do," Mary Kate retorts

28:30

29:00

29:

angrily as she strides towards the door. "And it's more than talk you'll be getting if you step a step closer to me," she continues defiantly as she turns towards him again from the safety of the doorway.

"Don't worry, you got a wallop," smiles Sean, holding up his injured hand. (Wayne's wedding ring is very clearly visible in this scene, as it has been in several earlier scenes.)

"You'll get over it, I'm thinking," says Mary Kate as she turns to leave.

"Some things a man doesn't get over so easy," says Sean and this line represents the opening of his courtship overtures.

"Like what supposin'?" asks Mary Kate, softening a little and leaning back against the wall, her mood completely changed and all thoughts of escape gone from her mind.

Sean follows up the verbal advantage he has gained with a load of blarney.

"Like the sight of a girl coming through the fields with the sun on her hair," he says, placing his hands on the wall on either side of the door, trapping her willingly as she looks into his eyes, "kneeling in church with a face like a saint."

"Saint indeed," says Mary Kate; she has never heard such talk from a man before and she secretly likes it, but she mustn't let Sean know that.

"And now coming into a man's house to clean it for him," continues Sean.

"But that was just by way of being a good Christian act," explains Mary Kate politely.

"I know it was, Mary Kate Danaher, and it was nice of you," adds Sean, reminding her that she still bears a surname he has come to hate and perhaps hinting that she might like to change it.

"Not at all," she says very sexily and Sean is strongly tempted to kiss her again as the sensuous *Isle of Innisfree* once again is heard in the background.

Mary Kate opens the door and turns to go, but just to let him know where he stands, she lunges forward and plants a quick kiss on his cheek. Suddenly she is gone, leaving him standing there wryly smiling to himself, anticipating the joys that are to come.

Stream in front of White O'Morn

Mary Kate plunges from the studio into the wild Irish night, which in reality was a darkened day shot. However, the storm was real and since it came up suddenly Ford decided to use it. As the trees blow lustily in the strong wind Mary Kate splashes across the little river and the foam is whipped up from the water downstream **(Location 4D)**. The Innisfree music is still being played, but in a much harsher tone.

Mary Kate turns to look back at the cottage and then falls due to the wind, her speed and the rough terrain. According to Maureen O'Hara, this was a real, accidental fall, but Ford decided to leave it in, perhaps as a symbol of Mary Kate's fall from grace. However, she gets up and continues her run, her clothes billowing in the wind like those of a woman in a state of extreme passion.

The scenes just described constitute one of the most moving and powerful sequences in the movie; indeed they constitute one of the most memorable sequences in movie history. Steven Spielberg in his movie *ET – The Extra Terrestrial* (1982), one of the best grossing movies of all time, pays tribute to *The Quiet Man*, one of his favourite movies, by including a short extract from this part of the action. ET, left to his own devices in his host Elliott's house, amuses himself by rigging up a remote control to change the channels on the TV set. One of the movies which appears on the screen is *The Quiet Man* and the scenes shown are: Sean entering the cottage, Mary Kate's fright and

31:00

attempt to escape, and the couple's first kiss. While all this is going on, Elliott is liberating all the frogs in his biology class just because they remind him of his alien friend. In the chaos that ensues, somebody places a frog on the shoe of a pretty blonde girl – she screams and attempts to run out the door. She is of course dressed like Mary Kate with a blue top and red skirt. Elliot pulls her back by the hand into the classroom exactly as in *The Quiet Man* and attempts to kiss her. However, he is too short and can kiss her only when a classmate allows him to stand on his back – shades of Alan Ladd. All of the time, the action is interspersed with appropriate *Quiet Man* scenes while an orchestral version of *The Isle of Innisfree* plays lustily in the background. ET is absolutely captivated by *The Quiet Man* and stares at the screen as if hypnotised – perhaps Mary Kate reminds him of the mother he hasn't rung yet. This is yet another proof of the literally universal appeal of *The Quiet Man* and a very deliberate tribute on Spielberg's part. Spielberg also used music from *The Quiet Man* in his earlier movie *1941* (1979), when *The Rakes of Mallow* is played frenetically during several of the fight scenes.

Surprisingly, however, these scenes bear very little resemblance to the ones envisaged in Nugent's original screenplay. In this version, Mary Kate speaks mostly in Gaelic, hence Sean's line "So you can talk," when she speaks in English. Most of their confrontation takes place outdoors near the shrubbery where she has been hiding. The dialogue is positively corny with lines like:

"So you're the leprechaun that's cleaned my house!"

"Why did you have to come in so soon?"

"I know one thing about leprechauns, you're supposed to hang onto them till they've told you where the pot of gold is buried."

"Ah, you big silly man."

"Well, if you won't tell me, there's only one thing to do," and with that he gives her a very firm and very well-planted kiss.

As we have observed several times before, the filmed version is vastly superior to the one proposed in the screenplay and provides us with yet another example of the creative way in which *The Quiet Man* was enriched at every possible opportunity during its production. We note that at one period in these scenes hardly a word of dialogue was spoken for nearly two minutes of running time, but one hardly notices. Ford cut his cinematic teeth on silent movies and knew very well how to hold the viewers' attention without dialogue.

Time has now passed. It is a "week or three later" according to the screenplay and the scene is White O'Morning on a radiantly sunny summer's day. Sean and the craftsmen of Inisfree have been hard at work and the cottage has been lavishly restored to its former glory. On the roof is a thatcher finishing what appears to be a complete re-thatching of the cottage. This part is played by Jim Morrin, who had earlier made the smoke signals, and who had several other roles in the movie, notably as a double for Barry Fitzgerald and even as a hooked fish in another scene. The actual thatching job was done by a Cong craftsman, Joe Varley. However, it is also said that only the front of the cottage was re-thatched – yet another example of cinematic illusion.

New diamond-paned windows have been added to the cottage. These were made by John Gibbons of Cong, carpenter at Ashford Castle, who appears in some later scenes of the movie as an extra. The cottage has been brightly whitewashed with slaked lime and the traditional half-doors have been added. There are flowers and plants growing in the flower beds in front of the cottage and window boxes on all the windows. Two ladders lie against the cottage and the barn which also seems to have been re-thatched. White O'Morning and its surrounds are spick and span and it has become the enchanted cottage of Sean's dreams. If Hansel and Gretel had passed by they would have thought it looked good enough to eat, and maybe this is what Sean wanted to recreate – all the oral satisfaction that he missed out on in childhood.

Wayne, Ford and Arthur Shields at Ashford

The Quiet Man, Ford pokes fun at the Anglo-Irish characters in a gentle tongue-in-cheek fashion, and his treatment of the Playfairs is no exception. Even the very surname seems to suggest a sportsman rather than a clergyman, someone to whom the notion of playing fair was more important than everything else in life.

The part of the Reverend Cyril Playfair is played by yet another of the Ford stock company, Arthur Shields, the brother of Barry Fitzgerald (William Shields). He had already appeared as a supporting actor in several Ford productions – as rebel leader Padraig Pearse in *The Plough and the Stars* (1936) for example and appropriately so, for Shields had himself taken part in the fight for Irish freedom and had during the Rising been an occupant of the world's most elastic building, Dublin's General Post Office. He also appeared in other Ford movies such as *Drums along the Mohawk* (1939), *The Long Voyage Home* (1940), *How Green Was My Valley* (1941) and *She Wore a Yellow Ribbon* (1949). Indeed, the part of Mister Playfair seems to have been written into *The Quiet Man* specifically with him in mind – Nugent writes: "Mister Playfair bears an uncanny resemblance to 'Boss' Shields." However, although he had considerable international experience, he is still listed in the credits as one of the "Irish Players".

The part of Missus Playfair is played by the accomplished Abbey Theatre actress, Eileen Crowe. She had already starred as Bessie Burgess opposite Arthur Shields in Ford's 1936 production of the Sean O'Casey play *The Plough and the Stars* and went on to star in Ford's *The Rising of the Moon* (1957). Her character in *The Quiet Man* is that of "a rangy woman, with an extravagant taste for flowered bonnets, the brighest eye in the world, a rattling tongue, the kindest of hearts, a vast joy in living and an entirely maternal solicitude for the moral sensibilities of that very proper man, her husband."

At the end of the patch is a new gate and, behind a lone rowan tree, Corcogemore Mountain provides a magnificent backdrop to this splendidly colourful scene. The yard has been weeded and cleaned and has obviously been given tender loving care. Sean Thornton is seen with paint brush in one hand and a pot of paint in the other, putting the finishing touches to an outhouse, possibly a hen house or a shed for winter fuel. He is dressed, most inappropriately, in a white waistcoat, black shirt and trousers. In the foreground is a pony cart with the collar thrown carelessly on the front and as the background music plays softly, Sean turns to admire his handiwork. The implication is that he has done a lot of work himself, but in the original screenplay it is suggested that the site should be bustling with several workmen doing all the work while Sean merely planted roses.

Suddenly Sean looks up and a strange sight meets his eyes. Along the path by the brook there comes a tandem, briskly propelled by a man in front and a woman behind, and they ride up to the front of the cottage.

The couple are the Reverend Mister and Missus Playfair, the local Church of Ireland Protestant clergyman and his wife. Throughout

Mister Playfair on the other hand is depicted as a man whose clerical collar is the only stamp of the cloth on him, and the small book in which he keeps his notes is a sporting guide rather than the King James Bible. Originally it was intended that he take the rear seat of the tandem while his wife steered (as she did in most things anyway) but this was not how they finished up in the final cut.

The eagle-eyed viewer will here notice that as the Playfairs enter the cottage yard there is a large dog sleeping peacefully by the wall in the sunshine. We do not know whose dog it is but it is one of the many such to be counted in the movie as unpaid extras.

"Hello," Sean greets them with his paintbrush as they dismount from the tandem in front of the cottage.

"Good morning, Mister Thornton," they reply in unison, adopting a rather ridiculous pose.

In the wicker carrier clipped to the handlebars of the tandem sits a potted plant, a gift for the newcomer.

Sean, like many an Irish Catholic before and since, is confused and doesn't know by what title to address the reverend gentleman.

"How are ya, Father, Doctor…" he splutters.

"No, no, 'Mister'," says Playfair, "and on formal occasions 'The Reverend Mister Playfair'. And this is Missus Playfair," he adds rather unnecessarily.

From the rooftop, the thatcher Jim Morrin looks in disbelief at the alien social ritual that is taking place beneath him – of course the Playfairs totally ignore his existence.

"Well, Mister Thornton, you are a wonder," says Missus Playfair, inspecting the cottage. "It looks the way all Irish cottages should – and so seldom do."

This is perhaps a little dig at the Irish peasantry who in previous generations, if they showed any signs of prosperity around their holdings, immediately had their rents raised by the landlord.

32:00

"And only an American," she continues, "would have thought of emerald green," admiring Sean's paintwork.

"Red is more durable," interjects her husband.

This is clearly a reference to the national colours – the green of the recently declared Irish Free State and the red of England where the Playfairs' sympathies might be expected to lie.

"And the roses, how nice," says Missus Playfair, turning towards the rose garden, implied but not shown. "You'll be needing lots and lots of horse manure," she says. "Fertiliser I mean," she adds in case her husband is shocked, "horse is the best."

Suddenly she remembers the purpose of her visit. "Oh, I've brought you a plant," she coos, fetching it from the tandem basket. "You know 'a primrose by a river's brink'."

"Brim," snaps her pedantic husband rudely. "The next line ends in 'him'."

Extensive research has revealed that these lines are from William Wordsworth's *Prologue to Peter Bell* (line 248):

A primrose by a river's brim
A yellow primrose was to him
And it was nothing more.

The poetic sentiments are quite appropriate but perhaps the real reason why Frank Nugent chooses them here is that line 166 of the same poem reads:

There sits the Vicar and his Dame.

As Missus Playfair hands over the plant, which looks nothing like a primrose, she remarks to Sean, "Poets are so silly, aren't they?" and adds anxiously, "Oh I hope you're not one, Mr Thornton."

"Oh no, ma'am, I…" grins Sean, turning his head away in embarrassment.

But Mister Playfair is suddenly suspicious.

"Thornton," he muses, "it has a familiar ring to it."

Sean looks up anxiously, afraid his true identity will be revealed.

"Ring to it…Thornton…" continues Playfair, for the moment unable to make the connection.

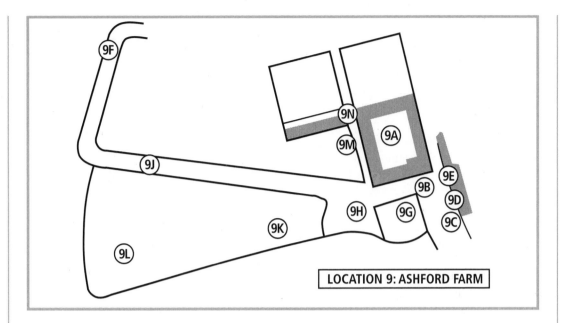

LOCATION 9: ASHFORD FARM

2:30

"It's a common name," says Sean and then wisely changes the subject.

"Thank you for the plant, Missus Playfair," he says uncomfortably. "This is dash, darn, awfully nice of you."

Missus Playfair smiles, but suddenly her expression becomes all serious as her attention is attracted to something happening at the stream **(Location 4F)**.

"Oh," she exclaims with an air of curiosity and maybe she is even anxious to pick up a bit of gossip.

A horse and cart loaded with furniture are being driven across the stream near the stepping stones. Prominent among the furniture is a large four-poster bed securely tied on.

The driver of the cart was Cong villager Robert Foy, descended from a long line of stonemasons and craftsmen. The holy-water font seen earlier, for example, was the work of his uncle. Robert Foy recalls that this particular scene was shot sixteen times before the crew was satisfied about the light and cloud cover. In general, the extraordinarily bright light of Connemara, thought by some to be accentuated by reflections from the sea, caused the camera crew many problems throughout the shooting. Things were frequently so critical

that Winton Hoch doubled the accuracy of his instruments and often shot each scene for three light settings just in case.

Incidentally, Lord Killanin relates that the bed used in this scene was given to him by John Ford as a gift after it was finished with, but that it disappeared when he was moving house and nobody knows where it is now. The eagle-eyed may see the name of the owner of the cart, P.S. Daly of Ballinrobe, written on the side; he was father of John Daly who supplied many of the horses for the movie. For the record, the horse pulling the cart belonged to Tim Kelly, Killower, The Neale.

As the cart crosses the river, the Playfairs and Sean Thornton are not the only interested spectators. In the Danaher house nearby, Mary Kate is also keeping a close eye on the action as she runs to the dividing wall between her brother's holding and Sean's. This scene is set on the Ashford Farm **(Location 9)** attached to Ashford Castle, in reality over ten miles away from where White O'Morning is situated. Surrounded by ox-eye daisies, Mary Kate looks over the wall and experiences a strange feeling of excitement when she sees the big bed.

The wall at which Mary Kate is standing was

one of the most difficult *Quiet Man* locations to find as it has for many years now been enclosed by other buildings **(Location 9A)**. Through the kindness and generosity of Mrs Mary Farragher and her family, however, we were allowed to inspect and photograph the wall.

The cart has now safely negotiated the stream and is heading up the little laneway to the cottage. Sean smiles as the Playfairs look on in astonishment. In the original screenplay, Mister Playfair, appalled at what he sees, says, "My word, what can the man be thinking of?" but this line does not appear in the final version.

"It's a bed," Sean informs the Playfairs rather unnecessarily and says, "Excuse me," before heading off towards the cart to lend a hand, still carrying his potted plant and pot of paint.

"Good morning," he greets the man with the cap who is guiding the cart from behind.

(This part is played by local man Jim McVeigh from the village of Dringean, one of the few extras to have a speaking part.)

"That's a fine big bed you have, Mister Thornton," he says flawlessly as he climbs up on the cart to untie the load.

"Biggest one I could find," says Sean, putting down his two pots. It is just his luck to have his double bed arrive in broad daylight in front of so many prying eyes.

Again we see a beautiful close-up of the very interested Mary Kate, peeping up through the daisies on the wall with her shawl wrapped protectively around her shoulders.

Ox-eye daisy wall

Michaeleen consults his book

Meanwhile, Sean lifts part of the bed from the cart and struggles up the pathway with it. We must assume that it is Wayne himself that is doing all this heavy lifting, for at no time can we see his face.

Again, Mary Kate, crouching now, watches the scene intently, so intently that she does not notice the arrival of Feeney, full of sarcasm.

"Is that a bed or a parade ground?" he asks, smiling slyly and suggestively at Mary Kate. "Aw, a man would have to be a sprinter to catch his wife in a bed like that!"

Mary Kate gives him a withering look and pulling her shawl over her head departs towards the Danaher household without speaking even a single word to this unpleasant sneak.

As Mary Kate stands in front of the Danaher house **(Location 9B)**, still angry at Feeney and still blushing at the sight of the bed, she sees Michaeleen Oge Flynn alighting from his sidecar with great difficulty. He is dressed in a black suit and a top hat with a black cockade, and has primed himself for his visit with a drop or six of Pat Cohan's best brew so that his voice is not always under perfect control and wobbles a bit from time to time. He groans and, as his feet hit the ground, he lets out a little whoop, before walking towards Mary Kate in as dignified a manner as he can manage and raising his hat to her, whip in hand and daisy buttonhole prominent.

To the air of *The Kerry Dances*, Mary Kate puts her hands on her hips and walks condescendingly towards him. He takes from his pocket a little black filofax which contains all his business transactions, turf accountancy and matrimony, but on this occasion also his script. (In fact, this may have been a device used by Barry Fitzgerald who was notorious for having difficulty with learning his lines.) He clears his throat as Mary Kate comes alongside him.

:00

"Well, Mister Flynn," she says sarcastically, "and what are you all dressed up for, Michaeleen Oge?"

Michaeleen wets his thumb in his mouth, turning the pages to find the right place in his little book. "I have…" he says in falsetto and coughs. He tries again. "I have come," he says in a deeper voice.

"I can see that," says Mary Kate haughtily. "But from whose pub was it?"

He gives her a scathing look.

:30

"Pub, pub!" he says, "you have a tongue like an adder. I've a good mind to go about me own business and tell Thean Shornton he's well off without you."

Here is yet another humour form which Ford added to the script (Nugent had had "Sean Thornton"). It is the spoonerism, or slip of the tongue, where the initial sounds of two words are transposed – for example, saying "every crook and nanny" instead of "every nook and cranny". It is called after the Reverend Canon Spooner (1844–1930), Warden of New College, Oxford, who is reputed to have called Queen Victoria "our queer old dean".

"Wait a minute," says Mary Kate, her interest suddenly aroused. "What was that?"

Michaeleen now knows he has the upper hand.

"Will ya listen then," he chides her, "and not be interruptin' the shaughran, the matchmaker."

The translation is for the benefit of non Irish-speaking moviegoers.

The matchmaker, marriage broker, or arranger of marriages between couples, often to form an alliance between wealthy families, was a common feature of Irish life in previous generations. The name was made famous in a play called *The Shaughran* by Dion Boucicault

and this is not the only influence of Boucicault on *The Quiet Man* – the later deathbed revival of Dan Tobin is lifted from another of his plays. Interestingly, Maureen O'Hara, as Angharad Morgan in *How Green Was My Valley* (1941), was the unhappy victim of an arranged marriage with the son of the pit boss.

Mary Kate's heart is now in her mouth. She is as excited and nervous as a teenager facing her first date. She pulls her shawl protectively around her and folds her arms around her waist. For a change, she is speechless and we can see the whites of her eyes. Michaeleen is now in complete control as he reads from his prepared script.

"I have come," he repeats in a deep voice, "at the request of Thean Shornton…"

"Sean Thornton," Mary Kate corrects him.

35:00

"Shut up," he retorts rudely, knowing that he can offend her as much as he likes.

"Bachelor and party of the first part," he continues legalistically, "to ask if you, strictly informally, mind ye," (here she nods in agreement) "eeh, Mary Kate Danaher, spinster, and party to the second part."

Michaeleen enunciates the word "spinster" with a little laugh and through closed eyes while raising his head. He manages in one word to convey all the contempt of a rural Irish community towards an unmarried woman - a woman who had failed to attract a man and start a family unit of her own. Mary Kate feels the insult deeply but she lets it go.

Michaeleen, master of drama, now pauses.

"Well," she says, "go on, you were saying."

35:30

"Ah, sure me mouth is like a dry crust," says Michaeleen, licking his lips and wiping his hand across his mouth, "and the sun is that hot on me pate, I…"

Mary Kate finally takes the hint that such important negotiations should be conducted in the privacy of an indoor location and, more importantly, that Michaeleen is in need of further lubrication.

"Would you be steppin' into the parlour?" she asks in her best stage-Irish voice, and with a smile she proudly continues, "The house may belong to my brother, but what's in the parlour belongs to me."

"I will then," says Michaeleen, reacting with feigned surprise, as if the suggestion had not come from him in the first place, and for safety he adds, "and I hope there is a bottle there whoever it belongs to."

"It could be," says Mary Kate, curtsying and taking his arm as he takes off his hat. To the cackling of the farmyard chickens, they proceed arm in arm to the Danaher house.

The action now moves to the interior of the Danaher house, which is a studio scene. Michaeleen sits in the little parlour as Mary Kate fetches the bottle of whiskey and the glass. The room is well furnished, admittedly in a rather American style, and there is a blazing open fire. Mary Kate puts the glass in Michaeleen's hand, pours a little drop, stops and steps back, but he looks at her condescendingly and says, "You've a fine steady hand," a roundabout Irish way of telling her to continue. She pours a little more, puts the stopper in the bottle and wisely places it by his side as he looks down approvingly. Mary Kate then turns around to pull up, of all things, a wicker fuel basket full of turf as a seat for herself.

In the meantime, Michaeleen puts down his glass, takes the cork from the bottle and throws it contemptuously in the direction of the fire without looking at where it is going (actually it strikes Mary Kate lightly on the shoulder as she sits on the basket). Having disposed of the cork and made sure that it will never again be employed for the purpose of stopping the bottle, Michaeleen then proceeds to pour himself a generous measure of whiskey.

Throughout this performance, Mary Kate looks on in amazement with her mouth hanging open – clearly she is not *au fait* with the finer points of whiskey drinking.

"To a good bargaining," toasts Michaeleen as he lowers almost the entire contents of the glass in a single gulp. Mary Kate folds her arms with a mixture of amazement and impatience.

"To resume," says Michaeleen at last, "the party of the first part…"

"That's him," interrupts Mary Kate excitedly.

"Has instructed me to inquire," continues Michaeleen, "before entering into formal negotiations," (this word is spoken in a drunken falsetto) "whether the party to the second part…"

"That's me," again smiles Mary Kate, hands clasped to her breast.

"…thinks kindly of the general idea," continues Michaeleen, now in full flight, "or in his own words, ah American, ah ya yes, he wants to know if ya go for it."

(Here Barry Fitzgerald is having his customary difficulty in remembering his lines.)

"Go for it?" asks Mary Kate quizzically, not understanding the transatlantic idiom.

"And if you do," adds Michaeleen, "I'll speak to your brother."

This is the crux and they both know it.

"Oh, that won't be easy," replies Mary Kate, coming down to earth with a bang.

"Oho, it's well I know it," agrees Michaeleen, "he'd as soon put his clog of a fist in me teeth as bid me the time of day."

Michaeleen, of course, has an aversion to physical violence except when bookmaking is involved.

"Aah," sighs Mary Kate and then, turning to more practical matters, asks him, "Oh now tell me, what did Sean, I mean, the party of the first part, say about my fortune?"

(The party of the first part is probably based on the famous comic sequence in one of the greatest of the Marx Brothers' movies *A Night at the Opera* (1935).)

"He says he doesn't give a d…" replies Michaeleen, almost but not quite resorting to unparliamentary language. Then coughing and reverting to legal terminology he adds, "He says it's a matter of complete indifference to him."

"He did?" says Mary Kate indignantly.

"He says he doesn't give a…" repeats Michaeleen, "he says it is all the one to him if you come in the clothes on your back, or without them for that matter."

Mary Kate is so excited by this last remark that she gets up and faces the camera, her hand protectively covering her breast and throat. However, she suddenly realises that she mustn't appear too eager and that a girl must at least pretend to play hard to get. In addition, she is very annoyed about Sean's indifference to her fortune which is obviously very important to her. So she attacks the messenger, the hapless Michaeleen.

"Oh, he did, did he?" she says to him, hands on hips. "Well, a fine opinion he must have of me if he thinks I'd go to any man without a proper fortune," and wagging her finger at him she continues, "and this you may tell your party of the first part, that when I wed, whatever is my own goes with me."

Mary Kate is now in full flight, reminding one of the female spider devouring the male after mating. She grabs the terrified Michaeleen by the shoulders saying, "Get up little man," and lifts him to his feet. Michaeleen struggles to retain his dignity, but she senses this and rushes away. However, Michaeleen is an experienced matchmaker well used to the erratic behaviour of young women in love and pays very little attention to her. Actually, he is much more concerned for his drink and turns to rescue his bottle and glass which he takes, one in each hand, as he follows her into the adjoining room as perpendicularly as he can manage under the circumstances.

The finely carpeted parlour is crammed with furniture — tables and armchairs covered by linen dust covers which must have solved quite a few problems with regard to props. Obviously the room is rarely used, Red Will not being the sociable type. Now Mary Kate tells Michaeleen just how well off she is.

"And all this furniture is mine," she boasts to him as he follows her into her Aladdin's cave, where she rearranges a big book on the table. "And I have that china and linen," she continues, "and fifty pounds in gold my father left me, and my mother's wedding rings and brooches, and my grandmother's wedding veil, and her silver combs and buckles, and thirty pounds-odd in notes and silver I've earned the past fifteen years. That's all."

This last amount is mentioned defiantly as a measure of her worth through money earned and not inherited, but throughout this little speech Mary Kate sounds more like an insecure little girl boasting about her toys and trinkets rather than a mature woman.

Suddenly Michaeleen perks up. Perhaps he senses a bigger fee for his matchmaking services to a richer woman, but whatever the reason, he

Courtyard of Ashford/Danaher Farm

actually puts his bottle and glass on the floor and takes out a notebook and pencil with which to make an inventory of the lady's estate.

"Heh, heh," he jokes to her, "ye're a well-propertied woman, I wouldn't mind marrying you myself."

(This last remark was probably added by Ford to Nugent's original script.)

Mary Kate smiles, knowing that he is not serious, but then Michaeleen suddenly comes to his senses.

"Where did ya leave the bottle?" he asks her in confusion, as he heads back into the little sitting room.

"And I'd have you tell him," she calls after him, "that I'm no pauper to be going to him in my shift," wagging her finger provocatively to emphasise her point.

At this stage one notices an uncanny resemblance between Maureen O'Hara and another beautiful Irish-American movie star of later years – Grace Kelly – both in tone of voice and appearance. One wonders if Grace Kelly, later to be Princess Grace of Monaco, modelled herself on Maureen O'Hara. Incidentally, Grace Kelly once named *The Quiet Man* as her all-time favourite movie.

Mary Kate is now like an excited teenager again. She pirouettes, rushes to the spinet and pulls off the dust cover. Then she sits down and begins to play and sing. Maureen O'Hara had a fine singing voice and in fact at one stage had a record in the Irish charts, an old ballad called *I Wish I Had a Kerry Cow*, appropriately about a young woman bemoaning her lack of a fortune and consequently her poor marriage prospects.

The song she sings now is one of the most beautiful of Thomas Moore's Irish melodies *The Young May Moon*, based on the old Irish air *The Dandy O!* Again, Ford probably heard this tune at his mother's knee and it is one of several of Moore's melodies included in *The Quiet Man*. This scene with its light-hearted banter does not appear in Nugent's original script – it was inserted afterwards to ease the tension, and the witticisms have a distinctly Fordean flavour. For

the record the words of the song are as follows:

The young May moon is beaming love,
The glow worm's lamp is gleaming love.
How sweet to rove
Through Morna's grove
When the drowsy world is dreaming love.

Then awake!   The heavens look bright my dear
'Tis never too late for delight my dear
And the best of all ways
To lengthen our days
Is to steal a few hours from the night my dear!

Now all the world is sleeping love
But the Sage, his star-watch keeping love,
And I whose star
More glorious far,
Is the eye from the casement peeping love.

Then awake! 'Till rise of the sun my dear,
The Sage's glass we'll shun my dear
Or in watching the flight
Of bodies of light
He might happen to take thee for one, my dear.

Midway through Mary Kate's song, Michaeleen appears by her side, having recovered his bottle and glass.

"Do you know *The Peeler and the Goat*?" he interrupts her.

"I do not," she replies.

"Neither do I," he adds, with typical Irish logic.

(This is a dig at a very standard and very boring old Irish ballad, much sung and much revered by traditionalists and one which probably got on John Ford's nerves.)

"Could you use a little water in your whiskey?" Mary Kate asks Michaeleen, again in a pantomime tone.

"When I drink whiskey, I drink whiskey," he replies, "and when I drink water, I drink water."

This echoes the famous line of James Joyce who reported that the Widow Grogan used to say, "When I makes tea, I makes tea, and when I makes water, I makes water."

During the banter, Mary Kate continues to play and hum *The Young May Moon*, but the pantomime is over when Michaeleen says:

"But back to business now, what answer will I give Sean Thornton, Mary Kate Danaher?"

The names are said in full to emphasise that nothing is yet definite and to remind Mary Kate of her status of dependent spinster.

"Well, you can tell him from me that…" she replies defiantly, hands on hips, and then changing her tone she adds smilingly, "that I go for it."

Michaeleen's face bursts into a wide grin because he has carried out this part of the operation successfully. With that she again sings the line: "Is to steal a few hours from the night my dear" and Michaeleen joins in on the last two words.

Together they laugh loudly and Michaeleen leaves down his bottle, spits on his right hand and extends it to Mary Kate. She in turn spits on her right hand and they shake hands vigorously in the time-honoured way of sealing a bargain in rural Ireland.

In the next scene we are back again in the Ashford Farm **(Location 9C)** outside the Danaher house. It is after dark as Sean and Michaeleen make their way slowly but purposefully to meet Sean's prospective brother-in-law. Michaeleen is still wearing his official matchmaking outfit while Sean is dressed in his Sunday-best dark suit and wears a bowler hat on his head. Michaeleen carries a riding whip from the sidecar supposedly parked nearby and Sean carries a fertility symbol in the

form of a large bunch of roses.

"How do I look?" he asks Michaeleen as they approach the doorway.

"You look fine," replies Michaeleen as he dances up to the front door to the tune of *The Kerry Dances* and rattles the door knocker. The windows on either side of the door are beautifully lit and the Danaher house has all the appearance of a cosy homestead. Symbolically, Sean turns his back to the house and smiles ruefully at his bunch of roses. He is as nervous as most men would be under the circumstances and he would possibly be happier to be entering the boxing ring rather than the Danaher house.

Mary Kate's face now appears at the window – one of the very few interior shots of the movie shot in Ireland. This is Maureen O'Hara at her most exquisitely beautiful, taken aback at Sean's sudden arrival but excited nevertheless. This is a favourite Ford shot of the object of desire seen through a window pane and he used it in several of his movies.

In the background the lively *Kerry Dances* gives way to the more romantic *Isle of Innisfree* as Mary Kate stares through the gloom at the pair of visitors. Michaeleen hums casually and smiles as he observes his client's nervousness and Sean looks to high heaven wondering how he has managed to get himself into this situation in the first place. Like a fussy mother hen, Michaeleen preens him as Sean asks: "Hey, what do I say?"

"Nothing," says Michaeleen, "I'll do all the talking."

"And I'm supposed to stand here like a dummy?" retorts Sean as Michaeleen says: "Ssh, now," with a raised finger.

Inside the Danaher house, back in the Hollywood studio, Mary Kate frantically tidies herself up and jumps down the little staircase. Her brother Will is seated at the table in his shirtsleeves and tweed waistcoat devouring his evening meal. The china is willow pattern and there is a big jug of buttermilk on the table in front of him.

"Will, there's someone coming to call," says Mary Kate as she nervously buttons her cuffs,

Courting at Ashford Farm

just to make his sister even more nervous. Finally Mary Kate loses her temper with him.

41:

"Will Danaher, they're coming to the front door," she shouts in exasperation.

"Well, since when has the back door been not good enough?" he retorts, fluffing his lines once again. As he stuffs another great forkful of meat into his mouth, Mary Kate gives up the struggle to civilise him and, grabbing her oil lamp, rushes towards the front door.

Back outside in the Ashford Farm, Mary Kate opens the door and looks straight into Sean's face as both men respectfully doff their hats.

"God bless all in this house," says Michaeleen using an authentic and lovely Irish greeting upon entering a house, a line not in the original script.

"Good evening," says Sean, stepping forward rather eagerly, before Michaeleen takes over again.

"Miss Danaher," he says, "we would like a word with your brother."

Mary Kate is as pale as a ghost. "Come on in so," she says nervously, "and welcome," but she has eyes only for Sean.

Sean now prematurely offers her his bunch of roses, and Michaeleen, slightly shocked at this breach of protocol says, "Easy now."

They go into the studio set but with the skilful editing it is hard to notice; however, sharp observers will at once see that the bunch of flowers inside is not the same as the one Sean had outside. The blooms are fuller and there are fewer of them. The use of roses is highly symbolic as the flowers that Sean's mother grew round White O'Morn.

41:

Mary Kate closes the door but she and Sean still have eyes only for each other. Now it is time for the formal introduction – remembering that the couple have met at least three times, played patty fingers and even kissed twice.

"Mister Sean Thornton, bachelor," intones Michaeleen, "meet Miss Mary Kate Danaher, spinster."

Mary Kate still finds the word "spinster" offensive and glares at him.

"Miss Danaher," he continues as Mary Kate

Duke waits at Ashford Farm

but his only reaction is to stuff another big forkful of food into his mouth.

"Who?" he asks eventually, speaking with his mouth full, unmannerly lout that he is.

"It's a… well, it's Michaeleen Oge Flynn and there's a gentleman with him," replies Mary Kate as casually as she can manage in the circumstances, but Will is not to be distracted from his dinner.

"Ah here, Will, put on your coat," she says gently, holding up his jacket, but again he just slurps his tea and shows no interest. The half-smile on his face suggests that he knows very well what is going on but is feigning ignorance curtsies to her suitor, "meet Mister Sean Thornton from Pittsburgh, Massachusetts, USA."

This line, inserted at the last minute by Ford himself, is designed to reveal Michaeleen's sketchy knowledge of American geography and to raise a laugh from American audiences. One can hear them shouting "Pittsburgh, Pennsylvania" at the screen, a nice example of Ford at his manipulative best.

All the time Sean and Mary Kate are smiling at each other – Sean bows and says, "Good evening, Miss Danaher." Mary Kate bows in return and echoing Michaeleen's earlier falsetto says, "This way," in an unnaturally squeaky voice. She then corrects herself with a baritone "This way, please," as the procession of three heads for the kitchen to beard the lion in his den. Mary Kate is "the lady with the lamp", sandwiched in between Michaeleen and Sean.

In the dining room, Red Will is calmly pouring himself another cup of tea with his eyes lowered. He is pretending not to know who is calling and why, but he is well aware of what is going on and letting the tension build up so that he can refuse his sister's hand with maximum ferocity. Sean and Michaeleen stand nervously on the right-hand side of the table while Mary Kate on the left-hand side attempts to introduce the visitors. We remember that Red Will has already refused an introduction to Sean at the Widow Tillane's house.

"This is my brother," Mary Kate tells the pair, but her next words are lost in a mumble as Red Will says rudely to her, "Leave the room."

"But this is…" she tries to continue, shocked at his bad manners in the presence of guests, but Will repeats equally rudely, "I said, leave the room."

"Yes, Will," she says meekly, obedient Irish younger sister that she is, and departs, lamp in hand, without another word of protest.

"Sit down, sit down, that's what chairs are for," says Red Will with mock geniality. "If ye've come for supper, ye're late!"

"A gracious invitation," says Michaeleen, with thinly disguised sarcasm, "but thank you no," and then with his usual alcoholic cough inquires, "I don't suppose there's a drop of anything wet in the house?" Some chance, the whiskey is for Red Will's personal use only.

"Help yourself to the buttermilk," says Red Will equally sarcastically, pointing to

Fitzgerald, Wayne and O'Hara – no to marriage

the jug on the table.

"Buttermilk," says Michaeleen with a shudder, "the Borgias would do better," referring to the notorious Italian family who were accused of poisoning their guests with spiked drinks.

42:30

All the time Sean is standing like a dummy smiling at the quaint Irish customs he is observing for the first time. By now he has moved to the left of the table, giving us a more balanced frame from the point of view of the camera.

"We'll come with your permission," says Michaeleen in his formal manner, "to the object of this visit. You've noticed I presume that I'm, ah, wearing my official, ah, black coat?"

"I have," says Red Will. "For your dead friend here?" pointing a forked hand towards Sean but as yet making no eye contact with him.

This last comment is yet another example of Red Will's sparkling wit. Sean of course winces, raises his eyes to heaven and says a silent prayer for patience, but just about manages to restrain himself.

"I need no shuaghran to arrange any marriages for me," says Red Will.

"I see," says Michaeleen, hitting at his weak spot. "You've been making fine progress with the Widow Tillane then in the last ten years?" (This period of time conflicts with the widow's stated four years of widowhood in an earlier part of the script.)

"Oh, is that what you've come to talk about?" asks Red Will.

"I have not," says Michaeleen sharply. "I've come to talk about your sister Mary Kate and 43:00 him," nodding in Sean's direction but afraid to speak his surname in case Danaher explodes.

"Oh, get out," says Red Will looking at Sean for the first time. "Why, if he was the last man on the face of the earth and my sister the last woman, I'd still say no."

This is another pregnant Irish bull – if Sean was the last man on the face of the earth, then Red Will wouldn't be there to say "no", but again we all know very well what he is getting at.

Red Will, by the way, does not consider the purpose of Michaeleen's visit serious enough to interrupt his meal – he chews happily on his food throughout and frequently speaks with his mouth full, often swallowing his words in the process.

"Now just a minute," intervenes Sean, but Michaeleen cuts him short saying, "If it's a question of the girl's fortune we'd…"

"Fortune, fortune," scoffs Red Will. "If it was but a shilling piece he wanted with her, I'd still say no."

"Oh, come on, Michaeleen," says Sean leaving the table and taking the law into his own hands. "I told you it would do no good. I'll explain it to her myself."

Clearly he regards asking Red Will's consent to marry his sister as a mere formality. However, Red Will is enraged that Sean would propose to Mary Kate without his permission. Rising from the table to his full height he barks, "Hey, Yank, I'll count three, and if you're not out of the house by then, I'll loose the dogs on ye."

"If you say three, mister," says Sean in a deadly serious voice, "you'll never hear the man count ten."

This chilling threat is followed by some of the most sombre music in the movie.

In the original screenplay, Danaher does actually begin to count one, two and this is why Sean threatens him about what will happen if he continues. Danaher chickens out, however, by counting two and a half, a silly device that was wisely dropped in the final version.

Sean then remarks that a fight wouldn't settle anything or prove anything.

"It would prove the best man," says Danaher. "And you can tell the rest of yer friends who that is, Michael Flynn." Thus almost from the beginning Sean knows that the only way to settle things with Danaher is to fight him, man to man. However, cuts in the script meant that the movie audience is denied this information.

As Sean leaves, quickly followed by Michaeleen, Mary Kate comes down the stairs straightening her tweed jacket and smilingly hoping against hope that all will be well. As the romantic strains of *Innisfree* are heard in the background a simple shake of the head from Michaeleen is all that is needed to fill her with despair. Sean overcomes his anger long enough to return and explain his position to Mary Kate. Meeting her at the bottom of the stairs he looks her in the eye, the bunch of roses still in his hand.

"Well, Mary Kate, he..." he stumbles, "we tried."

"We'll see him again some other time," says the downcast Michaeleen trying to soften the blow, knowing full well that, short of a miracle, no amount of time or persuasion will change Red Will's mind.

"I thank you anyway, Sean Thornton, for the asking," says Mary Kate in a voice close to tears.

Sean is mesmerised – having grown up in a different culture he cannot understand what is going on.

"You don't think this changes anything," he says desperately to Mary Kate. "It's what you say that counts, not him," gesturing towards the gloating Red Will.

"Now, now, Sean," says Michaeleen, "you've gone too far, that's enough," intimating that traditions are much more important than the feelings of individuals - perhaps he also feels that if people take courtship rituals into their own hands, he will be out of a job.

"Say, what is this?" asks Sean now even more bewildered since Michaeleen appears to have joined in the conspiracy against him. "We're going to be married, aren't we?" He turns to Mary Kate for confirmation, but even she turns sadly away from him, unable to face the prospect of breaking tradition and defying social convention. She quickly runs up the stairs and away from him.

Flowers still in hand, and now more mesmerised than ever, he turns to Michaeleen and says, "I don't get it." (The wedding ring on Sean's finger is incongruously obvious here.)

"This is Ireland, Sean, not America," explains Michaeleen solemnly. "Without her brother's permission she couldn't and wouldn't. I'm sorry for both of you," he adds, indicating that there is nothing further that can be done.

Sean has had enough. Back at the Ashford Farm he rushes for the door and storms out putting his hat on. Outside it is raining heavily – a judiciously placed hosepipe out of sight on the roof is used to give this effect. Ford liked to utilise the "pathetic fallacy", the notion that the behaviour of nature is in harmony with the feelings of man.

Sean hurries off, angrily throwing aside his unused bunch of flowers and Michaeleen follows him with a resigned look on his face. At the side door of the house Red Will comes to watch the two men depart. He leans against the door frame smirking, obviously satisfied at a good night's work **(Location 9E)**. Not alone has he demonstrated his control over Mary Kate, but he has also humiliated Sean into the bargain.

Sean leaves in disgust

At the upstairs window Mary Kate appears red-eyed with tears to watch her true love disappear into the night, maybe forever. The large raindrops outside on the window pane are echoes of Mary Kate's freely flowing tears inside, and once again Ford cleverly uses a window to symbolise the barrier between the couple. The pane of glass separates Mary Kate from her object of desire as it did Angharad Morgan in *How Green Was My Valley* (1941).

44:30

Mary Kate weeping at the window

The lovely shot of Mary Kate weeping at the upstairs window **(Location 9D)** looks like a studio shot but according the Etta Vaughan it was shot at the Danaher house on the Ashford Farm, with a wallpaper background inserted. This makes it one of the three indoor scenes of the movie shot in Ireland.

As the scene fades, we are treated again to the strains of *Innisfree*, of which we never tire. This is a transitional point in *The Quiet Man*, a move from soft femininity to rough masculinity. It is now time for action, for the expenditure of vast quantities of energy and what better way to do this than to bring on the horses! Horses play a huge part in *The Quiet Man* and in fact have provided Sean with his principal mode of transport up to this stage of the movie, but from now on horses predominate in almost every part of the action, justifying Ford's description that *The Quiet Man* was "a Western shot in Ireland"!

From the unfilmed screenplay we learn that Hugh Forbes has just made a present of a black hunter to Sean Thornton and that the horse and rider are a fine black-tempered pair. Mary Kate and the others are terrified that Sean will do himself a damage riding dangerously through the countryside on Blackjack, as the hunter is called, although its real name was Canadian Stream.

In real life the hunter actually belonged to Lord Killanin and it seems he was a very quiet animal. However, when Wayne rode it later in the racing scene he complained that he had been given a really wild horse. Killanin suddenly realised that Duke had never ridden on a hunting saddle before and if the action of the race to come is watched very closely, it will be seen that Wayne's double uses a hunting saddle while Wayne is on a cowboy saddle which had to be specially flown over from the United States at very short notice.

Failmore river ford

Carrowgarrif walls in jumping sequence

There now follows just a little over thirty seconds of daredevil riding and jumping through some of the most spectacular scenery in the West of Ireland, indeed in the world, as Sean attempts to work off his anger. These scenes are of course just another excuse to show off Ireland's beauty at its greenest and they did more for Irish tourism worldwide than any advertising campaign ever could have done.

The first of these riding scenes is through a ford in Failmore river **(Location 4G)** a hundred yards or so north of White O'Morning, although the cottage is not seen in the shot. The rider is not Duke Wayne but Joe Fair of Headford, County Galway, a brilliant local horseman who appeared holding a horse near the beginning of the movie as Sean Thornton is arriving at Inisfree. Throughout this scene, Joe Fair's face is covered by the shadow of his white cap and he rides in a crouched position to disguise the fact that he was shorter than Wayne was. Towards the end of the scene he rides towards Teernakill Bridge which, however, is not seen in the shot. The voiceover here is Wayne's as he encourages the horse with a series of "Yeah, yeah-yeah, yeah" shouts.

People interested in finding *Quiet Man* locations might bear in mind the following: one, Ford filmed almost the entire movie close to good roads which his trucks and equipment could easily follow; two, several scenes were shot with the camera in exactly the same position but merely rotated – later they appeared as if in entirely different locations.

That elusive cottage

In the next scene Fair is again seen riding and jumping across the countryside in another spectacular location **(Location 10A)** at Carrowgarriff on the hillside about two miles from Maam Bridge on the Cornamona road. This location is on the northern side of the main road overlooking the inlet of Lough Corrib. In the background is Leckavrea Mountain to the left as the horse ploughs through ferns before jumping a stone wall and riding up the hillside at an angle exaggerated by the camera.

The voiceover is Father Lonergan's and the accent hasn't improved much from the beginning of the movie: "Ah, those were the bad days," he brogues, "Sean with a face as dark as the black hunter he rode. A fine ill-tempered pair they were, it was only a matter of time before one or other of them broke his neck. We knew things couldn't go on this way." Ford liked the previous scene so much that he has Fair jump again, just a few yards down the road **(Location 10B)** over what appears to be the roadside wall, or perhaps the same wall again from a different angle.

In the next scene, Fair rides in front of a traditional Irish cottage, not unlike White O'Morn, but situated on the roadside about a mile and a half east of the village of Cornamona **(Location 11)**. This beautiful cottage has smoke gently billowing from its chimney as it nestles under Benlevy Mountain. This was the last of the *Quiet Man* locations to be found by the author – it involved a three-year search and an astonishing coincidence that is worth

45.00

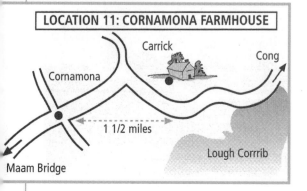

LOCATION 11: CORNAMONA FARMHOUSE

Carrick

Cong

Cornamona

1 1/2 miles

Lough Corrrib

Maam Bridge

relating. With my two indefatigable research assistants, Charles Harold and Liam O'Raghallaigh, I searched the West of Ireland for over three years for this cottage and the red-roofed barn beside it. We consulted hundreds of people, local and foreign, the Irish Tourist Board, Bord Fáilte, local historians, mapmakers, extras in the movie, the men who supplied the horses and rode in the racing scenes, and, of course, the surviving members of the cast, but to no avail. The geometry of the mountain outline in the background should have been a giveaway, but it wasn't. We scanned the shape of every hill and mountain in the West of Ireland, in particular the region between Clifden and Cong, with increasing frustration, time and time again, without success.

Then on the weekend of 21-23 June 1997 Charles Harold and the author spent three days in the West of Ireland with the single task of finding this elusive location. For three whole days we searched, probed and asked everybody we met and, despite what looked like a few promising leads, at 10 p.m. on the night of Monday 23 June, as darkness fell we were no nearer to finding the location than when we began. At this stage I reluctantly decided to abandon the search as it was holding up several other tasks and to accept that there would be one unknown location for others to find – a bitter pill to swallow for researchers.

At about 11 p.m. on that night we decided to pay a courtesy visit to another "Quiet Maniac", Eddie Gibbons, a native of Cong who now lives in the United States but has a house near the village of Cornamona. Eddie appeared in the movie as an extra in many scenes and possesses one of the world's finest collection of *Quiet Man* memorabilia, photographs and posters, with which he has been very generous to the author over the years.

As we sat drinking our tea, Eddie went to another room in his house to fetch the latest *Quiet Man* stills he had acquired. I was making conversation with Eddie's wife, Mary Gibbons, and just happened to show her a photograph of

the elusive cottage taken from the movie with a video printer.

"I know where that is," said Mary Gibbons casually.

"You couldn't possibly," I gasped. "Where is it then?"

"About two miles from here," she replied, "on the road from Cornamona to Cong."

Even though it was now midnight and quite dark, I insisted that she take us to the location in case it was all just a pleasant dream. With her husband's consent, Mary Gibbons accompanied me down a country lane to the location – I afterwards remarked to Eddie that she gave me more pleasure there than any woman could! She told me that she herself had nearly been present at the filming of this scene, arriving too late for the action just as the horses were being returned to their boxes.

In the midsummer moonlight we could just discern the outline of the mountain and it seemed to fit. The cottage was in ruins and the barn had vanished, but it was the correct location all right, easily verified by the distinctly long and narrow fields leading up to the mountain. Next morning at first light, about 5 a.m., we returned to the site and photographed it from every angle, happy that we had found it at last. It was bliss and we felt that, for a change, the gods were on our side **(Location 11)**.

The location of the ruins of the cottage and its barn and walled fields is the village of Carrick

Joyce's Tower, Ashford Farm

about a mile and a half from the village of Cornamona on the road to Cong. The cottage belonged to a family named Conroy who later moved in a land resettlement scheme to County Meath and the cottage fell into ruins. Thank goodness that the other locations were a little easier to find! It is quite possible that this cottage had originally been chosen as White O'Morn and lost favour when the other cottage at Maam was discovered. However, Ford would have seen to it that the Conroy family received a fee for their trouble and a fleeting appearance in the movie.

Back at the movie, Fair jumps the wall alongside Conroy's cottage and rides away eastwards into the Carrick countryside as Wayne's voiceover is heard going "Yeah, yeah, yeah," encouraging his horse. In the next scene the ride continues as Fair jumps a wooden gateway in the woods near the Ashford Farm **(Location 9F)**. This shot was an excuse to show Joyce's Tower (or Leonard's Tower) which is seen in the background. This magnificently preserved folly is nowadays sadly almost completely obscured by the surrounding wood which has grown up to smother it, but in 1951 it was a magnificent site.

In fact, Joyce's Tower plays a part in *Quiet Man* folklore and gave rise to a good story. Duke Wayne, staying in Ashford Hotel with his four children and soon-to-be-divorced wife Chata, hated the producer Herb Yates and his penny-pinching attitude to the movie, and made no secret of the fact. One day Ward Bond climbed Joyce's Tower and on the inside of the wall at the very top carved the words

★ ★ ★ ★ Herb Yates

but of course Bond didn't use asterisks! He then craftily persuaded someone to tell the Duke about the spectacular view of the surrounding countryside that was to be seen from the top of Joyce's Tower. Good fisherman that he was, Ward Bond caused Wayne to swallow the story – hook, line and sinker. He

of course saw the writing on the wall and came back to the hotel bursting with laughter.

There then follows a spirited ride through the Deerpark at Ashford **(Location 6A)**, with Fair again in the saddle, past a Celtic cross made from plaster of Paris by local man Mick Conroy. Three bystanders are concerned for Sean's safety: Dan Tobin holding a chequered rug, Hugh Forbes, cap in hand and wearing plus fours; the third person is Abbey Theatre actor Micheal Ó Bríain who related that he was meant to double for Sean McClory in the Irish location scenes. He later played a leading role in *The Playboy of the Western World* (1962), a movie produced by Four Provinces Productions, the company set up by Ford and Killanin, among others, to promote the Irish film industry.

"Easy, Sean," says Forbes.

"O musha, musha," says Micheal Ó Bríain, which loosely translated means "Dear, oh dear." We come now to a major aspect of *The Quiet Man* which does not seem to have been noticed before. Ever since the time of ancient Greece, dramatists, scriptwriters and moviemakers have used the device of the echo in various forms to enhance their productions. Using the echo, the director repeats an action, a situation or perhaps a location, that has already appeared in the production, but frequently from a different and ironic viewpoint. This clever technique has the advantage of appealing to the viewers' existing knowledge so that less explanation is necessary and it gives productions a satisfying symmetry and balance. In *The Quiet Man* there are literally dozens of such ironic echoes which we shall be commenting on as they arise. They are so frequent that it is impossible to believe that they are anything else but deliberate on the part of Nugent and Ford, but, on the other hand, they are so skilfully inserted that it is only when one's attention is called to them that they begin to stand out.

One of the first of these echoes is the next meeting of Sean and Mary Kate, right on the spot **(Location 6A)** where they first met as Sean was being driven to Inisfree. Then they didn't know each other and their meeting was full of mystery and expectation – now they know only too well that their feelings for each other are futile, for the moment anyway. In this scene, not in the original script, Mary Kate is riding her bicycle towards home, dressed in a skirt and a fetching tweed jacket and *bubalín* hat, commonly worn in the Aran Islands. Sean is riding towards her on his black hunter, and a close-up reveals that it is now Wayne in the saddle. They pass each other by and then stop and look back, Mary Kate dismounting from her bicycle. To the strains of *Innisfree* they look briefly at each other eyeball to eyeball. As she looks at him wistfully he breaks the silence.

"Hello, Mary Kate, Danaher," he says harshly putting as much venom as he can manage in to saying her surname, implying that although he cares for her he cannot forget the fact that she bears a hated name.

45:30   Her reply is infinitely more tender, gentle and feminine.

"Good morning, Sean Thornton," she says slowly and softly, speaking his surname as if she desperately wants to acquire it for herself.

Sean's bitter enunciation of Mary Kate's name is a perfect echo of the warm gentle way he first pronounced it outside the church when Michaeleen told him what her name was.

If you, dear reader, really want to establish yourself as an expert on *The Quiet Man*, watch very carefully what happens during Mary Kate's reply, using the frame-by-frame device on your video playback machine. Just after she says the word "Thornton" there is a silence for a few seconds and a large fly lands on her cheek! It is visible for just about seventeen frames, which is only just over half a second, and although when you are told about it, it is clearly visible at normal speed, if you blink you will miss it. Clearly it was missed at the editing stage and was probably not felt or sensed by Maureen O'Hara because she was concentrating so hard on her lines and body language.

Duke Wayne now rides out of shot to the right and his double Joe Fair takes over the riding again, jumping a gate in a fence specially constructed for the scene. It appears that the horse refused several times until the rider put extra pressure on him by approaching the fence at an angle.

As the broken-hearted Mary Kate looks sadly after the departing Sean and goes her despairing way, the voiceover of Father Lonergan is heard:

"So we formed a little conspiracy, the Reverend Mister and Missus Playfair, Michaeleen Oge and, saints forgive us, myself. And, on the day of the Inisfree Races we sprung the trap on Red Will Danaher."

Two posters, one of them torn and flapping in the wind, are now shown, bearing in red and black the words:

INISFREE RACES

and three black horses striving for victory.

In the original screenplay there are now twelve typewritten pages which do not appear in the movie. It is possible that they were never filmed, because they would almost all have been studio shots, but as their content has a good deal of bearing on the plot and fills in quite a few gaps, they are worth describing and commenting on.

Sean comes at a canter down the main street of Inisfree and reins in before The Sarsfield Arms, which is Cohan's pub. On the hotel there is bunting and a tattered poster which says:

INISFREE RACE MEET
PONY RACES   FLAT RACES
GRAND STEEPLECHASE
PRIZES - PRIZES - PRIZES

In the bar Michaeleen is engaging in his bookmaking activities and entering bets in his ledger, which is perhaps a benign echo of Red Will's notorious book. Michaeleen orders a pint of porter for Sean who quickly changes the order to whiskey.

Michaeleen comments, "When a man starts drinking himself into an early grave, the least his friends can do is to keep him company. I'll have the same."

The men at the bar, including Dan Tobin, sympathise with Sean on his disappointment in love, and one of them goes so far as to say that he's lucky not to have Red Will Danaher for a brother-in-law. Sean is annoyed that his personal affairs are being talked about in the pub (he should be grateful – it was the fact that the Widow Tillane's affairs were talked about in the pub that allowed him to buy White O'Morn in the first place!)

"A man can't brush his teeth in this town without everybody knowing it!" he declares angrily. Farcically, Dan Tobin retorts with, "I never brushed my teeth since the day I was born – look!" opening his mouth into which Sean peers in spite of himself.

"Not a one left," smiles Dan proudly, as Sean leaves in disgust only to have his unfinished drink gulped down by Michaeleen before following.

In not including this scene, Ford may have decided *The Quiet Man* had quite enough stage-Irishry already. The next proposed scene is in the lobby of the hotel which has been decorated for a meeting of the race committee. The race secretary is in position and his assistant is chalking the following information on a blackboard:

ENTRY	OWNER	RIDER
Minotaur	J. Connell	T. O'Dair
Shining Posy	P. Flynn	P. Flynn
Danny Boy	W. Danaher	A. Feeney
Fingal	Mrs S. Tillane	B.G.D. Guppy

Around the table are Mrs Tillane, Guppy, Red Will Danaher and Mister and Missus Playfair, and hovering nearby is Father Lonergan. They are all drinking cups of tea. As Guppy hands over the widow's entry fee of a guinea, Danaher asks Mrs Tillane if she is putting up her bonnet for the big race, but Missus Playfair interrupts and launches into a long and rather pointless anecdote about how her husband Cyril once

put up his hat for her in a race. The race turns out to be a three-legged race in which Cyril hopped and skipped like a man possessed to win his wife's hand. Father Lonergan is amused to hear of a hitherto unsuspected romantic side to the Reverend Playfair.

Missus Playfair then encourages Sarah Tillane ("a woman with your figure has no right to go on wearing widow's weeds") to put up her bonnet for the race, and of course Danaher concurs – "My very words," he says. "It's unnatural, that's what. Ah, put up your bonnet, give me something to ride for."

But Guppy, who of course has designs on the widow himself, says to Red Will, "I like that! Give you something to ride for, when your man Feeney is doing the riding for you. At least I am still capable of taking my own fences."

As Danaher counter-insults Guppy and Father Lonergan intervenes, there is a diversion as Sean elbows his way between Guppy and Danaher. He does not acknowledge their presence but he does return Missus Playfair's greeting.

"Horse's name is Blackjack, owner S. Thornton, and I'm ridin' him. How much?" he asks the secretary curtly. The secretary indicates that the fee is a guinea and tells him that since the race is not a handicap, there is no allowance for weight. "Mr Danaher, for example," he says, "has his own rider."

Sean suddenly sees his chance to score a point over Red Will. "I thought this was a gentleman's race," he says for all to hear. "I didn't know they allowed jockeys. But here's your fee; if a man can't ride, he can't ride."

Danaher is furious and says to the secretary, "Change my entry! I'm ridin' Danny Boy myself, and five pounds says he beats Blackjack."

"I'll take it," says Sean and with a face as dark as his speech warns, "just don't anyone get in my way tomorrow," as he quickly leaves the hotel. Mrs Tillane's pulse quickens and before leaving with Guppy decides that she will after all put up her bonnet.

Now the conspiracy is decided upon and Missus Playfair is seen to be the prime mover in the plot. "If Sarah Tillane knew what is in my mind," she says thoughtfully, "she'd never speak to me again as long as she lives."

Mister Playfair reminds the plotters that the services of that arch-rascal Michaeleen Flynn will be needed and both clerical gentlemen agree that some little white lies will have to be told, so they forgive each other in advance. Each declares that his bishop wouldn't like what is going on and this jokingly becomes their main reason for taking part.

Still discussing relevant unfilmed screenplay, we move now to the race meeting on the strand. The first race was meant to be for "shaggy little Connemara ponies, ridden by excited youngsters between nine and thirteen, some barefoot".

Mrs Tillane has cast off her widow's weeds and is "radiant as a girl at her first prom". Guppy is wearing a "gentleman rider's outfit" and even Danaher is an example of sartorial elegance. Missus Playfair points out Sean Thornton and suggests that she and Mrs Tillane examine Blackjack, a suggestion to which Sarah willingly agrees.

Mary Kate sits on a rough farm cart surrounded by a group of children. She stares at Sean as much as she can without appearing too obvious about it, and he in turn is casting longing glances in her direction.

Missus Playfair declares, "Oh, he is a handsome animal," referring ambiguously to Sean's horse and Mrs Tillane bluntly asks him whose bonnet he will be riding for. Confused, and seemingly not part of the conspiracy, Sean answers that he doesn't know whose bonnet he is riding for, but diplomatically he goes on to admire the widow's bonnet. As they exchange friendly banter about backing Sean's horse and proceed arm in arm to the betting booth, they are followed by two jealous men, Guppy and the furious Danaher. Mischievously, Missus Playfair takes Danaher's arm and on a signal from his wife Mister Playfair says, "They do make a handsome couple."

"Absolutely made for each other," agrees Missus Playfair.

Danaher is flabbergasted. "What are ye talking about?" he splutters. "Ye know full well that Sarah and I…"

"I admit I thought so once…" says the scheming vicar's wife. "You don't think Sean is too young for her, Cyril?"

"No," says Mister Playfair on cue, "although a younger woman might be…"

"And how is your sister these days, Mr Danaher?" she asks him coyly as the scene finishes.

It is a pity that this last scene was not included in the movie. It shows the strength of Missus Playfair's determination to see the plot through and would have explained in a short time a great deal about the conspiracy that is left too much to the viewer's imagination.

Father Paul now leads out the parish horse Kilrua and Father Lonergan tells him that despite the novena he has made, he doesn't expect him to win and that he would settle for second or even third place with its £10 prize money. The prize money would be used to buy a fiddle for Dermot Fahy and a new suit for Father Paul. As Father Lonergan is about to bless Father Paul, the Playfairs accompanied by Danaher arrive on the scene, and Mister Playfair makes uncharacteristically derogatory comments about the Catholic parish's horse. Missus Playfair, however, continues to make pointed remarks as part of her plotting.

"Father," she says to the parish priest, gushingly, "isn't it grand about Mrs Tillane?"

Father Lonergan agrees and says to Danaher, "And to think it might not have happened if you'd given him permission to court Mary Kate."

Danaher pulls his arm loose from Missus Playfair and goes stamping away. As he does so, Father Lonergan looks as guilty as hell.

One of the more ridiculous aspects of this suggested scene is Danaher's taking any lady on his arm for the sake of courtesy – this is totally inconsistent with his overall behaviour.

In a final short scene, Sean wants to place a bet of £10 on Blackjack, but Michaeleen refuses to accept his money as he doesn't want to have Sean's losses on his conscience. However, he immediately lays off a £5 bet on Blackjack with another bookmaker, feeling that the horse will win and that he himself will be the overall winner in the transaction.

As at last the screenplay and the action once again coincide, it thus appears that the conspiracy was very much the idea of Missus Playfair, aided and abetted by her husband and Father Lonergan. However, because of the deleted portions of screenplay this fact is almost totally lost to the viewers who get the impression that Michaeleen is the driving force behind the deception. In fact, it is more likely that Michaeleen's script in the plot was written by Missus Playfair. It is a major flaw of *The Quiet Man* that nearly a dozen pages of screenplay, fairly vital to the development of the action, have been compressed into a single sentence uttered by Father Lonergan.

Nevertheless, a short pre-race episode is introduced to set the scene. This scene is very obviously shot in a studio and little or no effort seems to have been made to conceal this fact. The lighting is clearly artificial, coming from several different directions at the same time, and the shadows are unnaturally dark. The colours of the costumes are rather lurid in the artificial light. The actual race scene was Lettergesh Beach **(Location 12)**, a spectacularly beautiful stretch of coastline about ten miles south-west of Leenane and about twenty miles north of Clifden, the capital of Connemara. In fairness, however, it must be admitted that the studio shots of the race use many beautiful backdrops of the sea and mountains, including the 2686-foot-high Mweelrea, the highest peak in the West of Ireland. At times also we see that back projections are used and we see moving waves and cloud. Almost inevitably, however, despite the fact that the studio race scenes have been cited as major flaws in *The Quiet Man*, Ford does manage to achieve a certain grandeur, especially with the magnificent West of Ireland clouds, reminiscent of the work of the artist Paul Henry.

Meanwhile, back at the movie, the scene opens with what appears to be two Scottish pipers (actors not identified) playing *The Wearing of the Green*, a patriotic Irish tune. They are wearing outfits associated with the Aran Islands, where some of Ford's ancestors were born.

On the beach where the race for the Inisfree Cup is to be run, the local gentry have gathered. On the podium are Hugh Forbes in a splendid red hunting outfit and black top hat, and Owen Glynn in a similar outfit, without a hat but with his trusty pipe. The Widow Tillane with a stylish bonnet and a smart outfit is being helped onto the podium by Forbes, while Mister and Missus Playfair follow. Guppy, who is to ride for Mrs Tillane, walks by touching his cap to the party. The bystanders include many of the American bit players who appeared in the pub scenes such as Pat O'Malley and Frank Baker.

Incongruously, Father Lonergan now appears leading the white Kilrua, the parish horse who is dragging the parish cart on which are seated Father Paul, the curate of St Anselm's and his mother. The part of Father Paul's mother is played by Mae Marsh, a very regular small-part player in Ford movies, appearing in such productions as *Drums Along the Mohawk* (1939), *My Darling Clementine* (1946) and *Fort Apache* (1948). *Donovan's Reef* (1963) seems to have been the last Ford movie she appeared in before her death in 1968.

Kilrua is clearly a dual-purpose horse, pulling the cart before he takes part in the race. Father Paul and his mother dismount and she takes his hat as he doffs his jacket in preparation for riding in the race. As the pipers continue to play *The Wearing of the Green*, Feeney walks ponderously by leading Danaher's horse Danny Boy who is protected by a check blanket.

Now Mary Kate arrives to view the race from her personal cart. She is accompanied by four "children" dressed in kilts and traditional Irish costumes but in truth they look more like renegades from the Scottish Highland Games. As the ubiquitous Dan Tobin passes by leading one of the horses and the young people climb up on the cart beside Mary Kate, we see that they are none other than Duke Wayne's four children from his first marriage to Josephine

Saenz in 1933. Reading from left on the screen they are Mary Antonia "Toni" (1936), Patrick (1939), Melinda (1940) and Michael (1934). Both Michael and Patrick went on to become movie personalities in their own right, both in acting and production. However, their insertion in this studio scene of *The Quiet Man* was an afterthought which is not in the original screenplay. But then John Ford is said to have been the godfather of several of Wayne's children, so perhaps a little nepotism is in order here. Ford skilfully inserts the Wayne children into several other scenes, some of which we have already noted. After Ford's death the tradition was continued, notably in *McLintock* (1964) which starred John Wayne, Maureen O'Hara and Patrick Wayne with production by Michael Wayne and direction by Andrew V. McLaglen, son of Victor McLaglen.

46:30

By 1951, Wayne and Josephine had divorced with Josephine having custody of the four children, so the trip to Ireland was a special treat for them. Wayne was now married to a Mexican actress Esperanza Baur ("Chata") by whom he had no children. In fact, Chata came to Ireland for the filming of *The Quiet Man* but by this time the second marriage also was on the rocks and ended in an acrimonious divorce in 1953. Duke finally married Pilar Palette in 1954 and they had three children, Aissa, Ethan and Marisa.

Back at the movie, Father Lonergan is saddling up Kilrua for the race while Father Paul's mother fusses over her son. Putting on the riding saddle, Father Lonergan hands out a piece of rather meaningless advice to his curate.

"And you remember what I told you," he tells him, "you make your speed when you hit the water." (The attempted Irish pronunciation of the word "water" is excruciating.)

"Yes, Father," says Father Paul meekly as his fussy mother takes an Irish *crios* from around her neck and ties it to his arm as his colours for the race.

"And ride carefully, my son," she warns him and he replies, "Yes, mum," very quietly.

Sean with Blackjack now approaches the race judges dressed in hats, tweeds and rosettes. The judge on the left is played by Major Sam Harris, yet another veteran of Ford's stock company. He appeared, always in very minor parts, in *When Willie Comes Marching Home* (1950), *The Wings of Eagles* (1957), *The Horse Soldiers* (1959) and *Donovan's Reef* (1963). He always played very dignified parts, and looked for the world like a retired military man – his character's name in *The Quiet Man* is "General". The other race judge still awaits identification.

"Thornton, no silks?" says Sam Harris to Sean while the other judge ties Sean's colours to his arm saying, "Your colours, Thornton."

"Thank you," says Sean.

Scintillating dialogue indeed!

A little man with a cap, also awaiting identification, holds Sean's horse during this exciting scene.

As the pipers strike up *The Rakes of Mallow*, echoing the music played as the train first pulled into the station, Mary Kate, wearing a fine bonnet, is seen sitting on her cart opposite Melinda Wayne. She is very conscious of the fact that Sean is nearby so she looks all around her and even over her shoulder, trying to be noticed and not noticed at the same time. Suddenly she sees her beloved and he, seeing her, smiles wryly. Clearly Mary Kate is wondering if she should put up her bonnet for the race.

"Good luck," say the judges to Sean as his horse is led away. Mary Kate suddenly takes off her bonnet as if she has made a decision but perhaps this is just a cinematic device to give us a close-up of her lovely red hair tied up with a ribbon.

47:

The backdrop now changes to the 1800-foot mountain Benchoona on the south-eastern side of Lettergesh beach. Forbes armed with a megaphone is making the race announcements. Flanked by Owen Glynn and Missus Playfair and accompanied by mock studio echoes from the surrounding mountains, he yells: "Ladies, gentlemen, your attention please!"

The camera cuts to the studio race crowd with the Widow Tillane and Sean face to face eyeing each other curiously. It is not clear how much Sean knows about the conspiracy, but his wry smile from time to time lets us know that he suspects that something is going on. The widow too must suspect that she is being used as a pawn in the game but it is possible that she is using the situation to make Red Will jealous.

As the crowd all turn towards Forbes, he continues, "Will all the lovely ladies who are putting up their bonnets for the Inisfree Cup, please place their bonnets on the finishing line."

7.30

Owen Glynn now hands the Inisfree Cup to Missus Playfair tapping her on the shoulder to attract her attention.

"Ladies, your bonnets please," says Forbes as the scene cuts to a crowd of principals. Michaeleen is still taking bets while the widow very pointedly removes her bonnet in front of Sean with what is almost a smirk on her face.

The scene switches to a beautifully framed shot of Mary Kate, all red hair and ribbons, flanked by Patrick and Melinda Wayne – the "children" but whose children is not made clear. Mary Kate is looking down sadly at her bonnet on her lap, feeling sorry for herself with a wistful look on her face.

Patrick Wayne tenderly puts his hand on her arm, and says in his best stage-Irish accent, "Will you not be putting up your bonnet, Mary Kate?"

"Indeed I will not," answers Mary Kate indignantly.

"No?" queries Melinda Wayne – just one word presumably to show that she could talk, and to give her a speaking part.

"No," says Mary Kate emphatically, and with that she puts her bonnet back on her head. The wind machine immediately blows it off again and Patrick Wayne scuttles off to rescue it. The pipers now strike up a well-known march, known in Ireland as *Garryowen*.

The widow is now helped down from the little platform beside the rowing boat by Sean and one of the judges while Michaeleen smiles benevolently on them, happy in the knowledge that the plot is proceeding smoothly.

At this stage several further scenes have been cut, leading to a bit of confusion. Originally, it was intended to have the scene (soon to follow), where Red Will unsuccessfully tries to force Mary Kate to put up her bonnet, inserted here, and when Michaeleen sees this he runs to Sean and says, "Sean, don't put a finger on Mary Kate's bonnet; if you win, grab Mrs Tillane's instead."

Thunderstruck, Sean replies, "What? Are you crazy?"

Michaeleen pleads desperately, "Do as I say, boy, or we'll be ruined."

However, as Sean rides out to the starting line, neither Michaeleen nor anyone else can tell if he is going to play ball or not.

All that remains of that scene in the final version is Sean saying, "OK, Michaeleen," aiming a mock blow with his riding whip which the little man skilfully avoids, "the widow's bonnet." In contrast with the earlier suggested script, Sean's mood is now flippant and he goes along with Michaeleen's suggestion almost as if it were a joke.

Back at the race officials' platform, Missus Playfair is proudly displaying the Inisfree Cup while Forbes is still droning on through his megaphone.

"Will all the gentlemen riders please go to the starting line, all riders please."

48.00

Next we see Father Paul's mother giving him a good-luck kiss before the race, after which he replaces his black cap as she smiles on him maternally. In the background Father Lonergan is still saddling the parish horse and making all the necessary last-minute preparations.

At his open-air betting office, Michaeleen is doing business. "Yes sir, a crown at twenty to one on the Yank," he says as he takes a bet from a punter and enters it in his little book.

"I'm giving twenty to one on the Yank," he announces loudly for all to hear.

These seem like extraordinarily generous odds in a six-horse race, especially as Sean can hardly be regarded as a rank outsider.

"Twenty to one," he continues but the sudden appearance of Red Will Danaher in full racing regalia consisting of a red-and-blue cap and tunic and creamy trousers causes him to stop short.

"I'm giving thirty to one," he says raising his hands tick-tack style. "Forty to one on Danaher, forty to one," as much as to say twice the odds on Thornton in a well-timed taunt.

"Flynn," says Danaher bluntly changing the subject to what really concerns him, "if you've been doing any matchmaking between Thornton and me widow, I'll put you in my book," waving an accusing finger at Michaeleen.

Danaher's calling the good lady "me widow" is a splendid joke that passes over most moviegoers' heads – she can be his widow only after he dies – but it does reflect the notion of a woman as a man's property prevalent in Ireland at the time. Incidentally, the threat to put Michaeleen in his book is a last-minute substitution for "I'll break you in two", hardly in keeping with this essentially comic scene.

"Ah, so you've heard," says Michaeleen to Red Will like an expert angler playing a fish on his line until the hook sinks in deeply. Red Will has indeed been hooked but he must be slowly and gently drawn in to the bank. Luckily, Father Peter Lonergan, fisher of men, is hovering near the scene, and in an addition to the original script, joins in the conversation.

48:30

"Father Lonergan," says Red Will, "what sort of a scoundrel is this Yank? One minute it's me sister and the next minute it's herself," pointing in the ladies' direction.

"Well, blame no one but yourself," says Michaeleen leading him on nicely. "If ye retained me as your matchmaker, you and the widow would have been married long since."

As Red Will swallows the bait, Father Lonergan adds, "True, Will, true," with clerical weight.

"And mind you, I'm not saying that it's too late yet," says Michaeleen impiously.

"What do you mean?" asks the sucker, suspicious but nevertheless interested.

"Why do you suppose the Widow Tillane has stood you off so long, huh?" Michaeleen asks Danaher who is now eating out of his

hand. This is perfect comedy – a classic example of a small intelligent man making a total fool out of a big slow-witted man.

"You're a fine-looking man, aren't you?" he asks Will.

"I am," says Will putting out the chest that Michaeleen has just tapped with his pencil to emphasise his point.

"A rich propertied man?" continues Michaeleen.

"And well she knows it," emphasises Will.

"Father, will I tell him?" Michaeleen asks the priest who is looking more and more embarrassed and guilty by the minute. They say that as every fisherman hauls in a big fish he feels a little bit of sadness for the deception he has perpetrated and at this stage even Michaeleen feels a little sorry for the big fish he is dangling.

"Go ahead, Michaeleen," says Father Lonergan, feigning reluctance.

"What woman," asks Michaeleen, poking the big man with his pencil, "would come into the house with another woman in it? If you got rid of Mary Kate, the widow would have been in like a shot."

"No," says Red Will incredulously. He is far too stupid to realise that the widow's house is much grander that his and that even if they were to marry, he would probably have been moving into her house.

"Yeees," says Michaeleen gleefully. "You had your chance and you flubbed it. You refused Sean Thornton and he reneged on ye. Now I doubt if he'd take your sister if you put a thousand pounds on her."

Red Will turns to the Church for confirmation. "Father Lonergan?" he asks trustingly.

The priest is incapable of telling a direct lie face to face, but he does his best to prevaricate in the best Irish tradition.

"Well, I can't say it's true and I won't say it's not, but there's been talk," he splutters, shaking his stick to emphasise his point.

"Oh, a lot of talk," echoes Michaeleen in his deepest voice.

"A lot of talk, eh," says Red Will, now truly

49:0

49:

hooked and slowly being pulled ashore of his own volition.

"Two women in the house and one of them a redhead," says Michaeleen, hauling the big fellow up on the bank.

There follows one of the most exquisite moments in the whole movie – just a tiny but significant indication of Barry Fitzgerald's immense acting ability. Still facing the camera, and without moving his head, he turns his eyes towards his prey, just to check that the big fish is still on the hook. To have moved his head would have given the game away and displayed eagerness, but he had to check what the position was.

"Two women," mutters Danaher as he departs, victim of a master con man who has led him to believe that all he is about to do has come from his own will.

Michaeleen now sits beside a smirking Father Lonergan who is clearly very pleased at the success of phase one of the conspiracy. However, he is soon brought down to earth by one of the best lines in *The Quiet Man*, not in the original screenplay and with all the hallmarks of a Ford ad lib. To show his total control of the situation and to remind the priest that he really should not be taking part in such deception, he says simply, poker-faced, "Three Our Fathers and three Hail Marys," which is the traditional penance handed out by the priest in the confessional for venial sins. The smile on Father Lonergan's face is replaced by a look of horrified guilt. Looking suitably chastened he joins his hands together as if in repentance. Michaeleen gives him a stern look – no doubt he is filing the incident away in his memory so that he can use it to his advantage next time he needs a favour from the Church.

The pipers now strike up another one of Moore's melodies – *Believe Me If All Those Endearing Young Charms*. The lyrics speak of undying love – perhaps appropriate in the cases of Sean and Mary Kate and maybe even Red

Will and the widow. The exquisite words are worthy of reproduction:

Believe me, if all those endearing young charms,
Which I gaze on so fondly today,
Were to change by tomorrow and fleet in my arms
Like fairy gifts fading away!
Thou wouldst still be ador'd, as this moment thou art,
Let thy loveliness fade as it will,
And around the dear ruin each wish of my heart
Would entwine itself verdantly still.

It is not while beauty and youth are thine own,
And thy cheeks unprofan'd by a tear
That the fervour and faith of a soul can be known,
To which time will but make thee more dear;
No, the heart that has truly lov'd never forgets,
But as truly loves on to the close,
As the sunflower turns on her god, when he sets
The same look which she turn'd when he rose.

Back at the race meeting, Mary Kate is sitting smiling on her cart surrounded by the Wayne children as nearby Feeney is sheepishly holding Danaher's horse. The effervescent Missus Playfair swaggers by, bonnet in hand and says breezily, "Good morning, Mary Kate, good morning, children."
(What is this? A race meeting in the morning? A thing unheard of in Ireland as people attempt to recover from the alcoholic excesses of the night before.)

Kilrua is once again paraded past, as is Father Paul, receiving a final good-luck kiss from his mother as some of the party depart for the start of the race. But before the race can begin we must have the all-important scene of the placing of the bonnets. In a rather beautiful studio shot with a still background of clouds in a Connemara sky we see four of the stakes with their pointed tops ready to receive their trophies. The two judges suitably bedecked

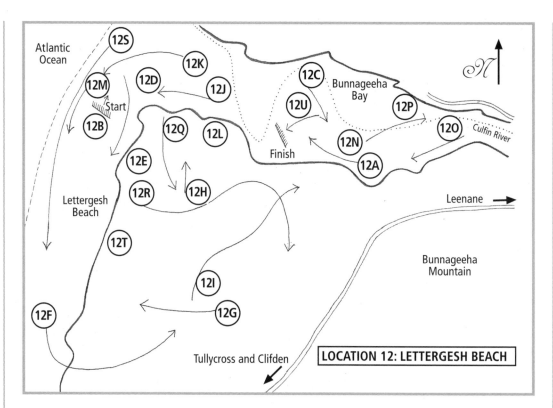

with official papers in their hands watch carefully as the Widow Tillane with a nervous glance in Mary Kate's direction places her bonnet on one of the stakes and curtsies to the judges. She is followed by a smiling Missus Playfair who places her bonnet on another stake as she curtsies too.

Mary Kate is now sitting sulkily between two of the children with her bonnet on her lap when Red Will comes over and scolds her saying:

"Don't sit there gawking, you're going to put up your bonnet." Clearly he has decided to sacrifice his sister to Sean as a result of Michaeleen's machinations.

"I will do no such shameless thing," answers Mary Kate defiantly.

"You will," he tries to bully her.

50:30

"I will not," she shouts at him and he realises that there is no point arguing with a redhead in a fiery temper. Instead he grabs his horse from Feeney and stomps away. Feeney with a horse blanket over his arm casts a withering look at Mary Kate before following his master.

Next, Dan Tobin's (unnamed) daughter places her pretty light-blue bonnet on a stake at the second attempt and smilingly curtsies to the judges. This part in the studio scenes is played by Mimi Doyle, although the same part in the Irish locations is played by a different actress. Mimi Doyle appeared in at least two other Ford movies – *Mister Roberts* (1955) and *The Last Hurrah* (1958) and she was sister to Murph Doyle who was a very close friend of John Ford's. Dan Tobin himself, always eager to hog the camera, exchanges banter with the judges before being dragged away by his daughter.

Now, Sean Thornton, cigarette in hand, marches Blackjack past Mary Kate's party. Without looking her in the face, he takes a cigarette from his mouth and stubs it on the ground, pretending not to notice her, while all the while she looks at him longingly. As he departs, she looks after him biting her lower lip to hold back the tears.

Mrs Tillane approaches the bench and taunts Mary Kate with the words "No bonnet, Mary Kate? What a pity!" spoken rather condescendingly. In an echo of the widow's own decisive action in selling White O'Morn when she learned that her affairs were being discussed in the pub, Mary Kate is stung into action by this taunt from her imagined rival. She springs up, throws the rug from her knees and heads for the stakes, one of which is conveniently still vacant. She places her bonnet on it and then adds her white headscarf for effect while pulling a face at the widow's bonnet. Finally, she pays her respects to the judges, her red hair billowing in the wind.

1:00

We come now to one of the most complicated sequences in *The Quiet Man* – the Inisfree Races. These scenes, which took over two weeks to shoot, occupy less than three and a half minutes of screen time but nevertheless constitute one of the most dramatic and colourful scenes in the movie. There is a story that Ford was ill for the shooting of the entire sequence and that the race scenes were directed by John Wayne, but Maureen O'Hara says that this is not the case and that Ford missed only half a day's shooting because of illness. Ford had already made several movies with a strong horse-racing element, notably *The Shamrock Handicap* (1926), so it was perhaps inevitable that *The Quiet Man* would have a lusty horse-racing sequence.

It is now time for the race to start on the glittering white sands of Lettergesh beach **(Location 12)**. In the first shot **(Location 12A)** the six riders walk their horses slowly through a soft part of the beach from where the tide has just receded. They move gingerly because at this stage the real actors are on board, and Ford didn't want to risk any accidents to his stars. Back in the studio, Owen Glynn now gets to make an announcement over the megaphone while his sidekick Forbes stands behind him in his Galway Blazer's outfit holding the Inisfree Cup.

"Betting will now stop," Owen Glynn announces, "and the sale of all intoxicating and alcoholic drinks will cease." Taking the megaphone from his mouth he quickly replaces it and adds, "I mean that now," to the shocked race-goers.

51:30

In the intended original screenplay there now followed a rather nauseatingly twee sequence where the ladies who put up their bonnets parade in single file in front of the riders and Forbes is meant to say, "The gentlemen salute the fair," as the riders doff their hats and make a

Riders line up for the race

gallant bow. Forbes then formally announces: "The fair thank the gentlemen and stake their bonnets and their favours." The girls then make a formal curtsy and parade between the stakes, now placing their bonnets in position. Thank heavens this totally alien scene was cut.

Back at Lettergesh, the riders on their horses have lined up. On the extreme left of the screen is Mrs Tillane's agent Guppy, played by Don Hatswell. He wears a black-and-white cap and his colours are a large black-and-white check. He is riding Mrs Tillane's grey Fingal who can be distinguished from the other grey in the race by the fact that his legs are black below the knees. Presumably Guppy is riding for the widow's bonnet.

Next in line is a local horseman named Willie Quinn riding a brown horse with a white spot on his forehead. The horse's name is meant to be Minotaur and the rider in real life was a bachelor farmer from Headford, County Galway where he lived in a picturesque 200-year-old thatched cottage. He was a renowned showjumper and won many prizes riding both for himself and Joe Fair. For identification in the race he is wearing the pinkish outfit and is the only rider without a cap. In the script the rider's name is given as T. O'Dair and the owner's is J. Connell.

The next bespectacled rider in line, wearing a black-and-white cap with a black diagonal stripe on his white top is meant to be the owner-rider of Shining Posy – P. Flynn. The part is played in this scene by a man who deserves a book all to himself – Pat Ford, the only son of director John Ford.

Pat Ford was a honeymoon baby, born exactly nine months after his parents' marriage on 3 July 1920, and named Patrick after his father's brother. Spending much of his childhood in the care of a nanny, Maude Stevenson, he had a difficult relationship all his life with his father who treated him with stern discipline. Pat developed as an outstanding athlete, swimmer and footballer during his schooldays in Honolulu. However, his talents were not appreciated by his father and he spent a great part of his life unsuccessfully trying to impress the old man on the sportsfield, in the Navy and finally in the movies. Although Pat Ford worked as a producer, writer, assistant and even stuntman in his father's movies, his efforts never seemed to satisfy the crusty old perfectionist and the son in turn developed problems with money and alcohol.

Pat Ford worked as associate producer on *The Searchers* (1956). He was co-producer of *Sergeant Rutledge* (1960) and co-wrote *Cheyenne Autumn* (1964). Around this time conflict between father and son came to a head and Ford excluded Pat from any future movie projects. Despite possessing a great deal of talent and flair, he never did succeed in impressing his famous father and the final ignominy was when he was cut out of his father's will and they saw little of each other in the final years, when Pat drifted out of the movie business.

Some accounts of *The Quiet Man* name Pat Ford as co-director with Wayne of many of the racing scenes during John Ford's illness, but this seems unlikely.

Next in the line-up for the Inisfree Cup is Kilrua ridden by Father Paul who is rather ludicrously wearing his full clerical outfit. Under the strict clerical rules of the time, priests were not allowed even to attend race meetings, let alone ride in one, and if a priest had the audacity to flout the laws of the Church, he would certainly have disguised himself a little better. To distinguish Kilrua from the other lighter-coloured horse in the race, we note that Kilrua has a black noseband and white legs that go all the way down to his hooves.

Fifth in line is Red Will Danaher in his colours of navy and red on the brown Danny Boy. The sixty-five-year-old McLaglen is very much overweight to be a jockey and the keen-eyed will notice Danny Boy buckling under the

Maureen O'Hara

The original Quiet Man – Paddy Bawn Enright

Quiet Man stalwarts, left to right, Robert Foy, Jack Murphy, Joe Mellotte

Leam Bridge

Sean's wall

White O'Morn, painted by E.J. Gryce

Trotting to the fair, painted by E.J. Gryce

Lettergesh Beach

The end of the race

Let the courting commence

Researcher Liam O'Raghallaigh with Maureen O'Hara

Left to right: Maureen O'Hara, Francis Ford, John Wayne, Barry Fitzgerald, Micheal Ó Briain, Charles Fitzsimons, Jack MacGowran, James Lilburn

Horses at vaulted gate

Tandem scene

Gabriel Barrett, fireman on the train

The tracks at Ballyglunin

Bill Maguire, double for John Wayne

Riding scene through the river

Quiet Man Heritage Cottage, Cong

Footbridge to White O'Morn

Same field, two different angles – hole in the wall

Sean breaks a stick

Charles Harold, Bill Maguire, the author

Maureen O'Hara with the author

Near Lettergesh (cottage and road)

Castle Kirke

Hayfield

Fight scene

Fight scene by the river

Front of Playfair house

Riders' doubles in the race

Father Paul's double blesses Sean's double

Willie Quinn, rider in race

strain. The line-up is completed by Sean Thornton in his black-and-white colours on Blackjack.

For the record, the real names of the horses in the race and the riders who doubled for the stars were as follows:

1. Don Hatswell on Fingal =
John Daly on Silvertail

2. Willie Quinn on Minotaur =
Willie Quinn on Erin Go Bragh

3. Pat Ford on Shining Posie =
Tom Monaghan on The Blackbird

4. James Lilburn on Kilrua =
Eamon Lydon on Peggy

5. Victor McLaglen on Danny Boy =
Charlie Hernon and Gibson Thornton
on John's Olive
6. John Wayne on Blackjack =
Joe Fair on Canadian Stream

Of course, Wayne is seen in several of the race scenes especially when the camera is close up. The riders for the race and their horses were recruited by Lord Killanin, a noted horseman himself, who knew many of the local riders personally. During the two weeks or so it took to film the race scene there was considerable switching around of the riders and horses depending on availability of men and their mounts. One extraordinary story about a horse used in some scenes has become part of *Quiet Man* folklore, but unlike a lot of Irish folklore, it has the advantage of being true. The story is as follows:

On the first day of the shooting at Lettergesh, Pat Ford was riding one of Joe Fair's horses through the water in rehearsal when it suffered a rather severely gashed leg. The duty veterinarian advised that the horse be put down and Fair was well compensated for his loss.

John Daly in full flight on the Quiet Man

Starting location for the race

However, he sought a second opinion from his own vet who recommended a stay of execution for a year while the horse was put out to grass to see how it progressed. The horse made a complete recovery and was promptly renamed "The Quiet Man" to celebrate its lucky escape. Ridden by John Daly it enjoyed considerable success at horse shows throughout Ireland and collected numerous prizes.

When The Quiet Man won a prestigious jumping competition at the Royal Dublin Society, Joe Fair was approached by Colonel Hugo Dudgeon on behalf of the Italian Equestrian Federation and the horse was sold to the Italian team. In 1955 at the Dublin Horse Show, Great Britain was seeking to win the Aga Khan trophy for the fifth successive time with only the Italian team left to jump. Great Britain had twenty faults, and Italy with sixteen needed a clear final round to take the trophy for the first time in its history. The last horse was ridden by Captain S. Oppes and although it was making its international debut, it glided over the fences without fault to take the trophy. That horse was The Quiet Man - John Ford would have been pleased.

Back at the movie race in a studio shot, Owen Glynn uses his megaphone to alert the starter that he wants the race to begin, saying,

"Sergeant Major, in your good time please." The suitably dressed sergeant major, played by Billy Jones bedecked in his medals, sounds a goodly blast on his bugle and the race for the Inisfree Cup is underway.

Sean's horse, perhaps startled by the starter's bugle, turns the wrong way and he is left at the start, but this is all for a purpose. We see a close-up of Sean adjusting his horse's direction while the other riders supposedly gallop away, but in reality this is just a device to have the horses stopped while the actors dismount and are replaced by their doubles. Wayne seems quite amused by the fact that he has been left behind which shows how confident he must have been of winning the race.

The race actually starts about two hundred metres to the north of the line-up position **(Location 12C)**. In the close-ups we see that Wayne is using the special high cowboy saddle flown in from the United States at the last minute.

Sean, now played by Joe Fair, rides furiously after the other riders, through a huge crowd of extras. In the foreground are a ponytrap and horsecart with shadowy doubles covering for Mary Kate and the children in the earlier studio shots. As Sean chases after the field, Glynn, pipe in hand, remarks to Forbes, "The Yank's holding back."

52:

The extras follow the race, one of them falling in the sand, whether deliberately or not, we cannot tell.

The race now proceeds southwards **(Location 12D)** past the spectators arranged in a long thin curved line, while women in brightly coloured shawls watch from the hill **(Location 12E)** where the camera is positioned. Guppy, riding furiously for the widow's hand, takes an early lead in the chequered colours but the other riders are close behind and by now Sean has caught up with the pack. Under the director's orders the spectators are shouting furiously and there is frenzied cap-waving.

In a studio shot with the appropriate backdrop, the Playfairs and Widow Tillane follow the race enthusiastically from behind a thick wooden fence with smiles on their faces. The Widow uses rather genteel opera glasses to follow the action and Vic Young adds to the general excitement with a thumpingly good musical gallop as accompaniment.

Over the stream

The riders then head inland over a little stream **(Location 12F)** to the south of a large rocky hillock with a smaller crowd now cheering them on either side and as Guppy, still leading, goes around the corner, we see that the hillock is dotted with onlookers. Sean has moved up into third place as they ride furiously through the sand dunes, but it is still anybody's race. A stone wall is visible to the right and this site is now occupied by several caravan parks.

As the crowds cheer, the scene cuts to a studio shot of a worried Mary Kate flanked by Patrick and Melinda Wayne, their hair blowing in the freshening breeze.

The next scene at Lettergesh **(Location 12G)** involves some breathtaking shots showing the horses climbing at almost impossible angles up a steep hill – but these effects were almost certainly helped by tilting the angle of the cameras. Guppy, his lead now considerably diminished, approaches the hill first, just ahead of Danaher who has come from nowhere. Next comes Sean (certainly Fair and not Wayne in this dangerous shot), followed by Shining Posy and Willie Quinn on Minotaur. Last of all is Father Paul, and his double, Eamon Lydon, a qualified medical doctor, has great difficulty in staying on. John Daly relates that there were seven takes of this spectacular scene before the final result was achieved.

The scene cuts to a studio shot with Father Lonergan and Father Paul's mother praying furiously as a result of her son's near fall. It is said that D.W. Griffith once had a shotgun fired behind Mae Marsh to induce a really startled and worried look on her face and that the effect lasted over thirty years. This shot in *The Quiet Man* is a perfect illustration of that wisecrack.

52:30

The horses now go over the top of the sand-hills **(Location 12H)** and descend back on to the beach – Guppy is still leading by a head from Willie Quinn who has suddenly sneaked up into second place, and Sean is a close third. Danaher, Shining Posy and Father Paul bring up the rear.

The riders now wind their way through the sand dunes **(Location 12I)**. Actually, there is a little trickery here – the northern end of Location 12I is first run by the horses, followed by the southern end – but what the hell. These sand dunes have unfortunately been levelled and filled in for caravan park development so that they are now green fields, but their position can be fixed by reference to the sea and the Tully Mountain in the background. For the moment, Duke Wayne is back in the saddle and we are allowed to see him in close-up.

The field is now well spread out, and away from the eyes of the judges, the riders try to take advantage of each other by taking little shortcuts through the sand dunes. Guppy actually loses his lead to such a ploy but retaliates by cutting across the line of Sean's path and inhibiting his progress. Sean's horse loses his stride and in the confusion Willie Quinn takes the lead. John Daly relates that there were at least three takes on this scene before a convincing foul could be recorded at high speed.

Racing through the sandhills

However, the judges with high-powered binoculars are on the ball and spot the incident. The binoculars must be very high-powered as the judges are six thousand miles away in a studio.

"Foul, Guppy," shouts Major Sam Harris, one of the judges, and the other judge does not disagree. This is the only place in *The Quiet Man* where Guppy's name survives – perhaps this was a deliberate decision on Ford's part to compensate for his relegation to a non-speaking part.

The horses swing round Bunnageeha Bay again **(Location 12J)** and they are now well strung out. The tide has come in, so now the scene looks totally different from where the race started, but then this scene was shot at a different time and on a different day. A stray dog follows the riders, one of the many dogs that wandered unscripted into the movie that Ford left in for atmosphere.

Now the riders splash spectacularly through the rising tide **(Location 12K)** with the camera on a higher hill **(Location 12L)** on which there stand a few hardy race-goers, waving their caps in encouragement. The horses are in very close order now as the water slows them all up and each rider must feel he still has a chance of winning.

Racing through the sea

As they continue along the beach **(Location 12M)** now partially covered by the tide, Guppy is still in the lead, but Sean is making a late run on the shore side – again Wayne is back on board so we are treated to a close-up of him as he passes the camera.

Back in the studio, we see Glynn and Forbes flanking the Inisfree Cup and observing the race keenly. It is clearly time for a further piece of stage-Irish drollery.

"Will you look at that crazy Danaher," (geddit, Will?) says Glynn pointing a finger nowhere in particular.

"Wouldn't it be wonderful now," says Forbes in his best accent, "if he broke his blasted neck."

"Maybe he will now," says Glynn putting his pipe back in his mouth, "God willing."

This is a bit reminiscent of the story of the two Irish tenants waiting to ambush their hated landlord. After they had hidden in a bog for over three hours there was no sign of him, so one of them said to the other, "He's very late, I hope to God nothing has happened to the poor fellow."

53:0

Clearly much of the race scene was improvised on the spot and on the day, but what was meant to happen was that after Guppy's foul on Sean,

Guppy becomes unseated and falls into a ditch whereupon Sean dismounts full of concern for his welfare. In the confusion, Danaher charges by with a triumphant laugh and Sean is forced to remount, dig his spurs into Blackjack and give chase. There is a suggestion of collusion here between Guppy and Danaher, but why should there be? After all, they are both rivals for the widow's hand, but there is the possibility that Danaher has bribed Guppy to foul Sean — clearly there should be a steward's inquiry into the running of the Inisfree Cup.

Next the horses gallop through the little Culfin river **(Location 12N)** which flows into Bunnageeha Bay from Lough Fee and Lough Muck, surely two of the most beautiful lakes in the whole world. Miraculously, Guppy is still in front followed by Sean and Danaher and the other three riders in close order. The darkened profiles of the horses and riders indicate that doubles are being used throughout this scene.

With the camera in the same position **(Location 12O)** the race once again changes direction along the sands **(Location 12P)** with Bunnageeha Mountain in the background. Now Danaher has hit the front, with Sean a close second while Father Paul brings up the rear a long way back. But where is Guppy?? He was leading a moment ago and now he has vanished from the race! Perhaps this is just another example of how enforced cuts have led to inconsistencies in the storyline but then on the big screen moviegoers were never meant to count the fast-moving horses. Another possibility is that Guppy's horse or rider may not have been available for action on the particular day that scene was shot.

Meanwhile, back in the studio, the Playfairs and the Widow Tillane are cheering the riders with lusty abandon. Suddenly the widow loses her Anglo-Irish reserve and control for a moment. She takes the binoculars from her eyes, stands up and shouts loudly, "Will, Will, come on," thereby betraying her true feelings.

However, she quickly realises who she is with and, resuming her seat, continues to watch the race through the binoculars with which she covers her embarrassed face. The Playfairs smile and exchange knowing glances feeling that the conspiracy is going according to plan.

As the music begins a frenzied crescendo, the riders now climb the grassy sand-hill **(Location 12Q)**. Danaher is in the lead, but what's this — Guppy is back in the race, large as life and a close second too! Where has he come from and where has he been? Yes, definitely a steward's inquiry is called for, even fifty years on from the running of the race.

However, Guppy accidentally lands in a bunker and loses several places but his rider, ace horseman John Daly, recovers well and follows at pace. The horses now pass over the flat ledge of the sand-hill **(Location 12H)** in the opposite direction to which they jumped earlier in the race. Father Paul now sees his chance and challenges for the lead, but back in the studios Major Sam Harris shouts out, "Foul, Father Paul." The other judge, perhaps scared of divine retribution, answers equally loudly, "I didn't see it," and they continue to watch the race through their field-glasses. The video evidence confirms that there was no foul.

Dear, oh dear, there is another visual contradiction here — Danaher's horse which is only two lengths in the lead has disappeared from the frame and is nowhere to be seen as the horses go over the top of the sand-hill — he couldn't possibly have climbed the hill and vanished from view in that space of time. So where is Danaher? Yet another suspicious incident for the stewards to investigate, I fear. In reality it is likely that Danaher's horse just veered off to the left out of shot for some reason.

Now the horses cross the lower part of the hillock leading inland **(Location 12R)**. The spectators are still wildly enthusiastic and have been joined by a horse and a horse and cart which have moved up from the beach. Danaher is back in the lead despite his earlier disappearance from the screen but now his lead over Sean has been cut to a length. Father Paul is fourth and this time Guppy seems to have vanished from the race again, but we are well used to such extraordinary phenomena at this stage. As Sean rides by the camera it is clearly Joe Fair on board from the shadow on his face.

54:00

In a studio shot we see Father Lonergan and Father Paul's mother. The good lady is praying furiously, her lips moving just as quickly as the horses. Like Mrs Tillane, the parish priest loses control of himself for a moment and in great excitement shouts, "Come on, Sean, Sean," and as the horrified mother looks at him aghast he changes his shout to "I mean Paul, Father Paul," a likely story. For Mae Marsh to look more surprised than she normally does takes some doing, but she manages it. She then redoubles her prayers and the music suggests that she is saying something like:

> Hail Mary full of grace
> Help my son to win the race

as she nods her head from side to side and raises her eyes imploringly to heaven. Father Lonergan grimaces and shakes his stick as much with embarrassment at his gaffe as with excitement about the race.

The race is now approaching its finish with a splendid run along Lettergesh's magnificent beach **(Location 12S)** with the camera located at **Location 12T**. The long shot suggests there may be only five horses still in the race, but at this stage, who's counting? By the time we go close up, however, there are definitely six riders with Guppy in the lead, Danaher by a short head from Sean who is gaining all the time, and the rest, including Father Paul, despite his mother's prayers, nowhere.

In the studio, Patrick Wayne, Mary Kate and Melinda Wayne look on anxiously as Mary Kate puts a protective arm around the young girl. It will be noted that Maureen O'Hara's splendid red hair is billowing in the wind blown in to her face from behind. When she suggested to Ford that it would be more appropriate for the wind machine to be activated from the other direction and have her hair blow back from her face, he scoffed at her directorial idea. Finally she lost her temper with him and shouted, "What would a bald-headed old son of a bitch like you know about hair in your face, anyway?"

There was a stunned silence in the studio as the crew waited for Ford's reaction. Maureen O'Hara thought, "I've blown it now, that's the end of my movie career."

Ford was silent for a moment, pragmatic Irishman that he was, as he looked around at all the faces on the set and then suddenly he burst into laughter in which everybody joined and the tension was dissipated. That's the sort of guy John Ford was, but it could just as easily have gone the other way.

Finishing run of the race

Lettergesh racecourse today

Now the stakes on the finishing line with their bonnets in place are seen (**Location 12U**) on the white sands of Bunnageeha. There is a big crowd of spectators on either side of the finish and they are cheering and furiously waving their handkerchiefs. As the horses thunder towards the finish we see that Sean Thornton (now clearly Wayne) has mysteriously taken the lead and is coasting to an easy victory by several lengths. As he passes through the stakes he grabs the widow's bonnet and smilingly holds it high for all to see. Danaher is a surprisingly close second, and in what is clearly a re-run of the finish, Father Paul comes from nowhere on Kilrua to snatch third place, verifying once again the power of prayer. Willy Quinn on Minotaur is fourth, and fifth is Tom Monaghan on Shining Posy, knocking down one of the stakes in their excitement. Last of all is poor Guppy who promised so much earlier on, but such is racing.

A studio shot now shows Mister Playfair raising his arm in the air and shouting, "Thornton," as the party all stand. As Playfair rushes away to congratulate the victor, Missus Playfair says, "He took your bonnet, Sarah," and the mesmerised Mrs Tillane can't decide whether to be flattered at Sean's attention or annoyed because her hero has not won the race. Each of the other riders awkwardly grabs a bonnet from the stakes – only Mary Kate's bonnet is left!

We now see a studio shot of Mary Kate surrounded by the four Wayne children – they run to the finish leaving her to stare in consternation and almost horror at her bonnet all alone on the stake. In a really beautiful shot she moves forward to the camera and looks wide-eyed – Maureen O'Hara at her most beautiful.

The villagers of Inisfree, men, women and children, rush forward shouting themselves hoarse to greet the winner of the race, but Mary Kate continues to stare with disbelief at her bonnet still on the stake. Now we see a studio shot, rather beautifully composed, of five of the stakes and the ribbons of the bonnet fluttering gently in the breeze. What matter if the studio stakes and the stakes on Lettergesh beach differ in shape; what matter if the keen-eyed protest that the colours of the ribbons and scarf are quite different from the bonnet on the beach and that the scarf seems to have shortened in length. The central message is all that is important – Sean has left her bonnet behind and taken the widow's. She bites her lower lip to hold back the tears, and then turns and runs away defiantly.

Meanwhile, and still in the studio, the delighted winner Sean dismounts from his horse with a backdrop of West of Ireland clouds all above him.

4:30

"Bless my soul," says a stray American accent in the background.

First to greet Sean is the Reverend Mister Playfair, who holds the reins of his horse. Still in the studio he exclaims shaking his hand, "A fine race, you rode like a trooper." And then it hits him – "Trooper, Trooper Thorn, of course, I knew I'd seen you somewhere before." Then, as now, there is no escape from the past in Ireland – someone is bound to find you out.

55:00

Sean knows the game is up but he tries a bit of damage limitation. "Well, now that you know it," he says to Playfair, "I wish you'd keep it under your hat, I mean forget it," in case the Reverend does not understand the idiom. He glances around nervously in case anyone has overheard.

"I understand," replies Playfair nodding his head, "it will be our secret."

"Thanks," says Sean as the judges lead him away for the presentation.

We note that the American Blackjack has a white triangular spot on his forehead but it is an inverted triangle whereas the Irish Blackjack has a triangle which is the right way up.

Playfair stands proudly holding the winning horse, smiling with pleasure because he has uncovered the Yank's true identity.

The presentation of the Inisfree Cup is also a studio shot with a smaller crowd of Hollywood extras, among whom the grey-haired Pat O'Malley is prominent. On the platform are Missus Playfair, Mrs Tillane, Forbes and Glynn. There is much cheering as Sean jumps up on the podium waving the bonnet in the air. Smiling and doffing his cap he says, "Your bonnet, Mrs Tillane." She takes the bonnet and hands it to Missus Playfair and then smiles graciously saying, "The cup for the winner," as she hands over the trophy to him. There are smiles all round as Sean says, "Oh thank you." (It would be interesting to count the number of times Sean says "thank you" throughout the movie – The Polite Man.)

55:30

Another studio shot shows Father Lonergan and Michaeleen Oge Flynn standing by a mock boat as Feeney leads away Danaher's horse now lathered in sweat after a hard race. Michaeleen is totting up his undoubted winnings from the race so much so that he is not aware of the company he is keeping. Father Lonergan turns smilingly to see a thoughtful Danaher approaching them. The background is yet another Paul Henry-type West of Ireland sky.

Back on the platform the widow, with mixed feelings, gives Sean a large bouquet of flowers and for the benefit of the watching Danaher, a lengthy and enthusiastic kiss. As the pipes strike up The Kerry Dances, Forbes signals to the crowd that they should applaud and they do so enthusiastically.

All this is too much for Red Will. Michaeleen, now well aware of Danaher's presence, looks up from his book to acknowledge him, as Father Lonergan raises his eyes to heaven for support. "Flynn," asks Danaher meekly but bluntly, "does your offer still stand?"

The wily Michaeleen does not want to appear too keen. "Well, now that, that depends," he replies coyly, still scribbling away in his notebook. "You were mentioning five hundred pounds?"

"Three hundred and fifty pounds, and not another penny," says Danaher who hasn't quite taken leave of his senses. This line is an echo of the much bigger sum he was prepared to pay for a piece of land earlier on in the movie.

"Well, I'll speak to me principal of the first part," says Michaeleen cryptically, turning his back on Danaher and looking tongue-in-cheek at Father Lonergan. The priest, afraid to make a sound in case he upsets the bargain, looks Danaher in the eye and merely nods at him. Danaher puts on his cap and walks away with as much dignity as he can muster in the circumstances.

56:0

Thus as the first half of the movie draws to a close, it looks as if the conspiracy has succeeded. However, in the original screenplay further action was intended. Sean was meant to follow Mary Kate on his horse across the sand dunes as she tries to escape on her cart while Danaher looks at Michaeleen and wonders if he has been hoodwinked.

"Mary Kate, wait," shouts Sean but she flees all the faster. He catches up with her and tosses the bouquet into her lap. This is the ultimate outrage – getting another woman's flowers. With an indignant exclamation, she dramatically takes the bouquet and throws it away. Sean stands despondently as the little cart goes bumping and bouncing over the dunes. This scene was not included in the final version, but it was filmed, as the accompanying photographs indicate.

Anyone who ever takes part in a movie should be aware that their contribution, no matter how important it seems to them, can easily wind up on the cutting-room floor. Cormac O'Malley, son of Ernie O'Malley, relates how he enjoyed immensely his part as a little boy of ten on the runaway cart as it trundled over the sand-hills. When he first saw the movie on the big screen he was faced with the agonising choice of going to the bathroom or watching his big moment in the movie. In the event, the bathroom won out and he always assumed that he had missed his film debut. In 1966, while on duty with the army in Vietnam, when the weekly movie turned out to be *The Quiet Man*, he excitedly called his fellow officers to come and watch. To his great embarrassment, however, there was no sign of him in the movie!

So we move into the second half of *The Quiet Man* which is in many ways a mirror image of the first half abounding as it does in many visual and situational echoes. The opening scene of the beginning of the courtship of Sean and Mary Kate is among the loveliest in the movie. The screenplay tells us that it is a radiant Sunday morning just after Mass. Sean is dressed in his Sunday best, a bowler hat on his head and gloves in his hand. He is pacing up and down nervously in front of the Danaher house **(Location 9B)** waiting for his beloved to emerge. On the right-angled walls of the Danaher garden sit many of the villagers of Inisfree, a lady with a vivid red coat sitting on the cornerstone being particularly prominent. Pipe smoke rises from the idyllic scene and we see that the potato stalks in the garden are in full bloom fixing the time of year as high summer.

Mary Kate runs away

Mary Kate and Sean

In the middle of the farmyard at Ashford Castle Michaeleen's ever-present horse and sidecar are waiting to convey the happy couple on their first official trip together, echoing its wait outside Castletown Station when Sean first arrived. Then, however, he was a stranger to Inisfree – now he is accepted as a member of the community.

In the background the church bell rings continuously and lush Irish melodies are played. It is hard to identify these, but there is more than a hint of *Kitty of Coleraine* most appropriately.

Red Will and Mary Kate emerge through the doorway flanked by Father Lonergan and Father Paul. There is a strong echo of the last time Sean fled through that very door dressed in the same outfit, as Mary Kate walks quickly out into the farmyard in a pretty dress and bonnet and carrying a bouquet like the one Sean threw away in disgust on that wet night. Red Will Danaher seems to be a changed man – he is now depending on Sean to take his sister off his hands, so he can get those very hands on the widow and more especially on her lands and money.

"Good morning, good morning," says Red Will curtly to the clergy and "Come on, come on," equally curtly to Mary Kate who runs forward at his beckoning. Each priest is carrying what looks like a fat prayer book and the two of them follow Red Will with Father Lonergan holding his walking stick under his arm military-style. The music and the church bells stop suddenly as Red Will looks up and down at Sean rather contemptuously before taking a handkerchief from his pocket, putting it to his mouth and clearing his throat. This appears to be a ploy on the director's part to prevent McLaglen from fluffing his lines as the camera goes close up.

"Well, now," he tells the assembled gathering, "the banns having been read" (he turns to Father Lonergan for confirmation of this fact and the priest solemnly nods his head in affirmation) "and no man objecting, I'm permitting this man to court me sister." Red Will glares around for possible objectors but

finds none.

Sean smiles broadly at Mary Kate and she smiles back at him shyly, modestly lowering her eyes at the same time.

"But under the usual conditions," adds Red Will to Sean's complete mystification, as Red Will nods questioningly, expecting Sean's assent. Red Will then looks to Michaeleen who is sitting high on his sidecar in his bowler hat, tweed jacket and magnificent rose in his buttonhole.

"Mister Flynn," he asks him, "do you assume the full responsibility?"

"I do, I do," answers Michaeleen, almost as if he is affirming the marriage vows himself, "and from now on they'll do their walking and their talking under me own eyes," he adds with a vehement nod of his head.

"Well, then, let the courting commence," pontificates Red Will putting his pipe in his mouth.

Sean puts his bowler hat on and gallantly attempts to help Mary Kate up on the sidecar, but he gets his first taste of Irish courting conventions when Michaeleen brandishes his whip saying, "Hey, none of that now, none of that, hands to yourself on your own side of the

road." Father Lonergan too appears rather shocked and shakes his head in disapproval as he beckons to Sean to move around the back of the sidecar to the other side. Then, ludicrously, Father Lonergan helps Mary Kate up, saying, "Up you go," as Sean meekly obeys Michaeleen's order, "Get on the other side of the car."

"Thank you," says Mary Kate quietly. One gets the distinct impression that the members of the Ford stock company are enjoying themselves enormously and having great difficulty keeping straight faces.

Where the courtship began

The whole scene is of course quite farcical. In the original screenplay it was intended to locate the scene outside St Anselm's Chapel as the local Catholic church was meant to be called after Sunday Mass – hence the reference to the banns and the presence of the clergy. There was meant to be another patty fingers scene, this time a legitimate one, but perhaps the local Protestant clergy had endured quite enough water sports outside their church and the scene was wisely relocated outside Danaher's house. In fact, Ford has let his imagination run riot in this scene – the clergy were not present in the original screenplay and historically would not have been there to launch a courtship officially or unofficially. Finally, a parish priest would certainly not be expected to give a leg up to a young lady, nor would he have been seen to do such a thing.

Anyway, Michaeleen having checked that both his passengers are safely on board says, "Come on," to his horse Napoleon and off they go to the cheers and waves of the villagers who follow lustily. In fact, they take off at such a pace that Mary Kate almost falls backwards off her perch, but Father Lonergan raises his hat and cheers, feeling that he has helped to carry out a successful conspiracy. The scene contains the by now almost obligatory dog barking loudly.

Standing nearby is the Widow Tillane and her party, and as Mary Kate passes by she throws her bouquet rather pointedly in the Widow's direction. Guppy bends down to retrieve it, dusts it and hands it to the widow, but by now Red Will has arrived on the scene and beams a most inane grin on his beloved. She looks him in the eye and then, full of embarrassment, looks at Guppy and finally down at the flowers. Guppy looks at Danaher in wonder − the land agent still has designs on the widow and her estate but Red Will thinks that the game is in the bag.

The courtship travels of Sean and Mary Kate are of course just an excuse to show as much delicious Irish scenery as possible. First the sidecar, obviously driven by Barry Fitzgerald's double, Jim Morrin, is trotted up the main street of Inisfree past the Market Cross (**Location 7A**) echoing Sean's arrival in the village. It appears to be Wayne and O'Hara on board though we do not see Mary Kate's face so it could very well be Etta Vaughan. The two Inisfree policemen are taking a leisurely stroll and wave to the happy couple. The police sergeant and his constable had quite meaty parts in the original screenplay but most of their scenes were deleted − they did survive in one short scene towards the end however. It is not known who played their parts at the Irish end, but the name of Abbey actor Bryan O'Higgins is mentioned in one newspaper report as having played the part of Sergeant Hanan.

8:00

To the air of *The Kerry Dances*, the couple are next driven over the bridge which is the entrance to Ashford Castle (**Location 1C**). This bridge over the Cong River actually marks the county boundary between Mayo and Galway and this time all three major stars are actually on board the sidecar, with Michaeleen merrily cracking his whip in time to the music.

There now follows a skilfully edited studio shot of the (horseless) sidecar in motion with back projection of the Irish countryside. Mary Kate and Sean sit back-to-back without a word being spoken, though in the original screenplay Michaeleen had to warn him several times about keeping his hands to himself. On screen Sean turns and smiles ruefully at his lady-love and then turns away again. Michaeleen, pipe in mouth, looks like a man who is merely doing a job of work, while Mary Kate just sits there haughtily playing hard-to-get. Glancing at Michaeleen, Sean says:

"I don't get this. Why do we have to have you along? Back in the States, I'd drive up, honk the horn, a gal would come running out."

This is one of the many in-jokes in *The Quiet Man*, based on an incident in Ford's own life. When his wife Mary threatened to leave him, he would go outside, start the car and begin honking loudly offering to drive her wherever she wanted to go. She did not "come a-running" and declined his offer.

"Come a-running," says Mary Kate turning towards him furiously and suddenly stung into speech. "I'm no woman to be honked at and come a-running" − that red head of hers is no lie right enough.

"America, huh," says Michaeleen with a shudder as if somebody had just walked on his grave, and continues, "Pro-hib-ition," as he urges his horse on with a "Come up."

This is one of the cleverest and best-known lines in *The Quiet Man* and represents a typical Irish technique of argument by understated abuse. The originally intended line was: "Ah, they're barbarians in America! Barbarians! Pro-hib-ition!" and this was wisely changed to avoid offending American sensibilities.

58:30

The camera now switches to the other side of the sidecar to face Sean. It is difficult to identify all of the Irish scenery featuring in the back

Ashford bridge – the courting

projection of these studio shots, but this one can be identified by virtue of a house appearing in the background **(Location 13)**. It is situated near the shores of Lough Corrib less than a mile south-east of the village of Cornamona overlooking one of the most splendid views in the West of Ireland. Undoubtedly the other back projection scenes were filmed in this locality also.

As they jog along merrily to the air of *The Kerry Dances*, Michaeleen suddenly nudges Sean on the shoulder and points to an old ruined building with his whip. Without taking the pipe out of mouth, he says, "Do you see that over there? That's the ancestral home of the ancient Flynns; it was taken from us by… by… by… the Druids."

The Druids were ancient Irish priests who were in no position to take property from anybody and here Michaeleen is merely retelling the popular legend that all Irishmen are descended from kings who have wrongfully been dispossessed of their estates.

The screenplay instructions call for a towering stone ruin, relic of some great castle or abbey. The ruined abbey chosen by Lord Killanin, Lee Lukather or Charlie Fitzsimons depending on what story you believe, was that of Ross Errily about a mile and a half north-west of the town of Headford in County Galway **(Location 14)**. It is west of the Headford–Cong road, just a few yards from the Mayo–Galway county boundary. Ross Errily is the site of a Franciscan monastery founded in

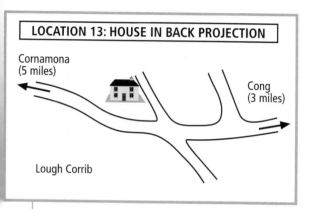

Cornamona
(5 miles)

Cong
(3 miles)

Lough Corrib

Ross Errily Abbey

Back projection house

the fourteenth century. Also known as Ross Abbey, it is among the best-preserved ancient monastic sites in Ireland and it has recently been partially restored to its former glory. Although it was sacked by the notorious Oliver Cromwell in 1656, it remained occupied until 1753 and the roof collapsed in 1812. It is the traditional burial place of the Burke, Browne, Kirwan and Lynch families.

Although this scene lasts a mere five seconds it forms a memorable vignette in *The Quiet Man* – a link with Ireland's former glory which is all part of Sean's ancestry. It is beautifully filmed and from a lovely angle, the ancient tree on the left (still standing) providing a perfect counterpoise to the abbey tower on the right. In this pastoral scene a few sheep walk lazily towards the entrance and the four young people advancing towards the abbey from the right are of course Michael, Melinda, Patrick and Antonia Wayne.

Sean looks suspiciously at Michaeleen not knowing whether to believe his claims of noble ancestry or not, but Mary Kate smiles to herself realising that the courier is indulging in a bit of blarney. Michaeleen hums a few bars of *The Rakes of Mallow*, a tune that even he can manage, and says, "Come up" to his horse. Sean shrugs his shoulders at the funny customs of the Irish.

One interesting and informative scene was intended around here in the original screenplay but did not make it to the final version. From photographic evidence shot by G.A. Duncan, we know that this scene was in fact filmed. As the sidecar is passing Mister Playfair's church, the reverend gentleman stands there wearing his clerical surplice. (On reflection one might ask where this scene should have been shot – the exterior of the Protestant church had already been used as the exterior of the Catholic church – Duncan's photograph indicates that it

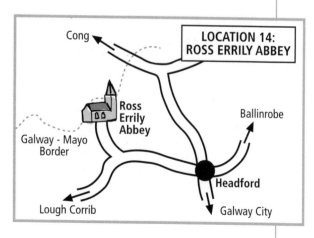

LOCATION 14: ROSS ERRILY ABBEY

Cong

Ross Errily Abbey

Galway - Mayo Border

Ballinrobe

Headford

Lough Corrib

Galway City

was shot outside the Playfair house.) Mister and Missus Playfair are looking mournfully at their tiny Sunday congregation, and on an inquiry from Michaeleen as to how clerical business was this Sunday morning, Playfair replies that he had just preached a brilliant sermon, profound, eloquent, dripping with literary and classical allusions, to a congregation consisting of just five people – his wife, Mr and Mrs Smyth – Smith and the sisters Abernathy, one of them quite deaf. He hints that the Bishop, not due to visit for a while yet, may consider moving him to another more populated parish. Michaeleen jokingly tells him not to despair, that there may be some (Catholic) backsliders before the Bishop comes, and as the sidecar is driven away, Missus Playfair congratulates the couple and wishes them the best of luck.

The movie here is rather clumsily trying to draw attention to the perilous state (now much worse) of the Church of Ireland in rural areas, but if scenes had to be cut, this was perhaps a prime candidate. However, in the later long scene between Sean and Mister Playfair, the same point is made in a somewhat more natural scenario.

Back at the action, the sidecar pulls up on the walk just between Ashford Castle and Lough Corrib **(Location 1D)**. Michaeleen is now concerned by the lack of action between the couple.

"Well, you're the quietest couple I ever courted," he tells them. "We'll get nowhere at this rate." Now we have a quiet man and a quiet woman!

Michaeleen's use of the words "I courted" is interesting – he feels that the entire operation is under his direction and that Sean and Mary Kate are merely players in his drama.

Courtship encounter

Lakeside of Ashford courting scene, Lough Corrib

"Off with ye," he decides suddenly, "I'll let ye do a healthy mile or so just to get used to walking correctly together."

We notice that although Michaeleen always observes the proprieties he is not above bending the rules a little in the interests of common sense. In fact, he frequently seems more intent on carrying out the ritual itself rather than ensuring that the ritual achieves its intended purpose.

Mary Kate smiles happily and Sean is down from the sidecar in a flash, anxious to help her alight. He gets his hands quickly around her waist and she puts her hands on his shoulders in response, but Michaeleen quickly reminds them that he is the one in control.

"Now, now, now," he reprimands Sean, "she's a fine healthy girl, no patty fingers if you please," echoing Sean's daring exploits outside the chapel. In fact, here Michaeleen is contradicting himself, because he is on record as stating that patty fingers is a privilege reserved for courting couples and then only when the banns have been read!

Sean gently helps Mary Kate down just by holding her hand in a courtly manner and the courtship walk commences, but this time to a slower rendition of *The Kerry Dances*, played on the harp. They walk silently side by side with no physical contact whatsoever as Michaeleen looks on approvingly.

The scene now switches to the western side of Ashford Castle **(Location 1E)** on the right bank of the lovely Cong river. They stroll along, still in silence, hands behind their backs and Sean looks hopefully over his shoulder just to check that Michaeleen and his sidecar have not drifted into the river! Further along the river bank they reach the trees and we see the arches of the Ashford bridge in the background.

Cong river courting scene

This is a perfect example of Ford's technique of shooting two scenes in almost the same spot and making them look as if they were completely different locations.

The scene switches once again to the road from Ashford Castle to the Ashford Farm **(Location 1F)**. As the couple amble along in silence, walking correctly together, Mary Kate steals a glance at Sean and he in turn steals a glance at her.

"Nice day," says Sean, choosing his words carefully and Mary Kate answers demurely, "It is that, Mr Thornton," with more than a hint of stage-Irish language.

"That's a pretty bonnet you have on," continues Sean more daringly, but he has no inkling of the effect this will have on Mary Kate – she remembers what happened to her bonnet at the end of the race even if Sean attaches very little significance to the incident.

"Bonnet?" she says furiously. "Don't you be talking to me about bonnets, after leaving mine stuck up there like a…" She turns towards him aggressively, pointing her arm towards the race course on the beach which in reality is over thirty miles away. As Sean attempts to take her arm in apology, she aims a swipe at him, which as a boxer he deftly dodges – an echo of the cottage scene.

1:00:00

:30

"Easy now, easy now," says Michaeleen from his perch on the sidecar, "is this a courting or a Donnybrook?"

Donnybrook is a suburb to the south of Dublin City in the upper-class Dublin 4 area. *The Parliamentary Gazetteer* describes the annual Donnybrook Fair thus:

> During the week beginning on the 26th of August is held the notorious Donnybrook Fair, professedly for the sale of horses and black cattle but really for vulgar dissipation and formerly for criminal outrage and the most revolting debauchery. It far surpassed all other fairs in the multitude and grossness of its disgusting incidents of vice, and, in general, it exhibited such continuous scenes of riot, bloodshed, debauchery and brutality as only the coarsest taste and the most hardened heart could witness without painful emotion.

Appropriately, Donnybrook is now the headquarters of the Irish national radio and television station – Radio Telefís Éireann.

On 18 May 1961, a musical version of *The Quiet Man* entitled *Donnybrook* opened in New York at the 46th Street Theatre. Music and lyrics were by Johnny Burke and among the stars were Eddie Foy Jr, Art Lund and Joan Fagan. It ran for sixty-eight performances and received several favourable reviews, including one rave review.

"Have the good manners not to hit the man until he's your husband and entitled to hit you back," continues the politically incorrect Michaeleen.

Sean grins as Mary Kate suddenly comes to her senses and realises that her behaviour is jeopardising the courtship.

"I am sorry," she says to her amused boyfriend, "I have a fearful temper. You might as well know about it now, instead of finding out about it later." However, she adds with not a little pride in her voice, "We Danahers are a fighting people."

1:00:30

But Sean obviously likes a girl with a spirited temper and says to her rather suggestively, "I can think of a lot of things I'd rather do to one of the Danahers – Miss Danaher."

Mary Kate scolds him in a mock fashion, "Ssh, Mister Thornton, what will Mister Flynn be thinking?"

Again Sean looks over his shoulder to check where their chaperon is, but Michaeleen is in a world of his own, puffing on his pipe and dreaming of opening time. He is more than happy with the way the courting is progressing and is probably being paid by the hour for his services.

The scene changes to another part of the same little road from the castle to the farm (**Location 1G**) a few yards to the east of the previous location, so that the couple have yet to come to the place they have just been. The foreground is covered with ox-eye daisies gently moved by the breeze, an echo of the previous time that the flowers were seen on the wall separating the couple as Sean carried the bed to the cottage. As *The Kerry Dances* still plays drowsily in the background, all is peaceful as the couple ramble along, looking at each other and over their shoulders at Michaeleen in turn.

In the original screenplay, the couple now sneakily hold hands, but Michaeleen spots the move and announces, "We'll be turning back now… ye've had enough excitement for one day." If you run the video frame by frame you will see that they do actually hold hands for a few seconds, but Michaeleen does not react to this lascivious behaviour. Anyway, the couple now have had quite enough of being chaperoned and, as they reach the little bridge before the Playfair house (**Location 8E**), they see the reverend couple's tandem leaning against the front window. In reality this was the house of Stephen Lydon, stand-in for Victor McLaglen in the movie.

"Can you ride a bike?" Sean asks Mary Kate and she nods approvingly. He must have a short memory because she rode away from the chapel

1:0

on a bicycle and that was again her mode of transport when they met when he was horse-riding.

"Well, what are we waiting for?" he asks her and holding hands they run together towards the tandem leaping exuberantly over a rain puddle as they go, but Mary Kate is careful to hold on to her bonnet.

The shocked Michaeleen is stung into action and rises from his seat. He fears the wrath of Red Will and the reputation of his matchmaking business is at stake.

"Mary Kate Danaher, Sean," he shouts to no avail – Mary Kate's surname is shouted to remind her that she is still a spinster lady and her behaviour is incompatible with that status. The couple do look back smilingly, almost

tauntingly, but they pay no attention and they are soon off on the tandem. Words fail Michaeleen but he, or rather his double Jim Morrin, quickly follows in hot pursuit and we hear Barry Fitzgerald shouting, "Come up," to his horse and a despairing "Come back here, come back here at once, ye shameless hussy, ye," to his charge Mary Kate. From the upstairs window of the vicarage Missus Playfair smilingly observes the whole scene and it is obvious that everyone in Inisfree will know all about the details before long.

During the couple's escape from the shackles of their chaperon, *The Kerry Dances* is played at a lively liberating tempo. We next see them careering down the main street of Inisfree on the tandem – no doubles used here and Maureen O'Hara's screams of terror and delight

1:01:30

Sean and Mary Kate make a dash for freedom

Escaping on the tandem

are quite real **(Location 7A)**. As they round the corner in front of Cohan's where Danagher's Hotel is now located we see on the left the Catholic church and part of the remains of Cong Abbey. Mary Kate holds on to her bonnet, just about, and a Freudian psychologist would have a field day interpreting this scene.

Meanwhile, Michaeleen's double gives hopeless chase, futilely repeating "Come back here, come back here at once, ye shameless hussy ya," to a Mary Kate who can no longer hear him.

There is a rather spectacular break in continuity here but one has to look for it. As Sean and Mary Kate ride down the street, there is a man sitting on a doorstep and a woman in a shawl with her back to the street. It is early morning and the long shadows go from right to left. As Michaeleen follows, presumably a few seconds later, the man and woman have vanished and it is much later in the day because the dark shadows are now coming from the other side!

The next scene is a studio shot so as not to have Barry Fitzgerald risking life and limb. In the background is a still of Cohan's pub and we see Michaeleen sitting high up holding the reins and still shouting, "Come back here when I order you to at once, come back." Now we see the studio mock-up of Cohan's, easily distinguished from the real thing by its blue-green colours, but the horse (which isn't really there!) stops very suddenly throwing Michaeleen on the flat of his back. This is in contravention of the laws of physics which state that a body would be thrown forwards – else why seat belts? But clearly *The Quiet Man* is not subject to the laws of physics or any other laws for that matter!

Michaeleen suddenly realises that his horse has stopped outside The Sarsfield Arms out of sheer force of habit, never having passed it in his life. Michaeleen of course has alcoholic constipation – he cannot pass a pub! As the horse turns round to survey the scene, Michaeleen says to him, "Bedad, I think you have more sense than I have meself," and the horse whinnies and nods vigorously in agreement.

1:0

Playfair/Lydon House

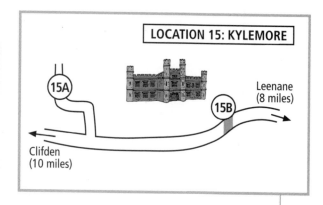

Michaeleen alights from the sidecar to enter the pub, forgetting that it is Sunday and that by law Cohan's is closed.

In the original screenplay there now follows a bit of dialogue between Pat Cohan and Michaeleen, with Michaeleen imploring him to open the door of the pub like a good Christian, followed by a rather confusing instruction to run into the pub and then run out slamming the door before realising that it is too late – the couple have escaped from his clutches and he might as well give up. In the movie, however, he simply marches into the pub (the Hollywood version) telling his horse, "Whoa there, Freddy." Freddy is presumably an American cousin of Napoleon's.

Meanwhile, Sean and Mary Kate are revelling in their freedom. Now they are seen pedalling madly down the hill towards the Danaher house on the Ashford Farm **(Location 9J)**. The house itself is wisely not shown, as it would have been the height of folly for the couple to have returned unchaperoned to where Red Will might have seen them. O'Hara and Wayne

certainly seem to be entering into the spirit of things and appear to be enjoying themselves enormously as they disappear down the little roadway.

Next they are seen in another of Ireland's most beautiful places **(Location 15A)**. This is a minor road from the exquisite Kylemore Abbey to Tully Cross, just a few miles from Lettergesh Beach where the race scenes were shot. It is just round the corner from Tullywee Bridge. Several people claim credit for discovering this location – Lord Killanin, Luke Lukather and Charlie Fitzsimons – but Maureen O'Hara herself claims to have discovered this site while walking near Kylemore Abbey, which is now an essential stopping place for all visitors to Ireland.

As the couple pedal gently down the hill towards Kylemore, the tandem represents the

Tandem ride towards Ashford farm

On the road to Kylemore

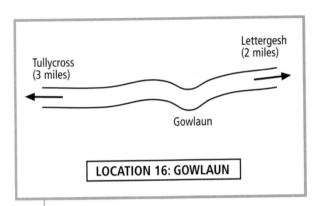

LOCATION 16: GOWLAUN

Tullycross
(3 miles)

Lettergesh
(2 miles)

Gowlaun

Dropping the tandem

their bike during the filming of *The Quiet Man* in 1951; I'm tired telling people that but they won't listen to me." It was a local farmer named Paddy Keane and he was a child during the shooting. He had to watch the action from inside the window because of illness and had never forgiven his mother for not letting him out. The field full of bog cotton or ceannabhán beside which the couple park the tandem now actually belongs to my informant and right proud he is too of the fact.

1:0

Sean and Mary Kate ride gracefully around the corner of the mountain road and stop by the roadside overlooking the magnificent Killary Harbour – the view is quite different nowadays because of extensive house-building. They dismount and Sean draws her attention to something out to sea by raising his arm and pointing his finger but Mary Kate is attracted by something on the other side of the road and runs out of shot. Sean turns to find himself suddenly alone and as he makes to follow her, the tandem is dropped unceremoniously on the roadside by the debris blocking the entrance to the field. One wonders what the Playfairs would have thought of their beloved tandem being abused so and it appears that Sean abandoned it here in the wilds of Connemara because it is not seen again during the courting scene. However, we can be assured that it was recovered to play an important role in the final part of the movie.

harmony of their actions and their state of union – the man leading the way of course. Ford gives us two lovely camera angles – one directly along the road as they approach and a second panned from a roadside track as they pass by. On either side of the road stand tall stately trees to guard them as the inevitable *Kerry Dances* plays in the background – a magnificent and memorable scene that lasts a mere twelve seconds.

Next we find the couple some six miles away **(Location 16)** on the road from Lettergesh to Tully Cross in the village of Gowlaun. This was a rather difficult location to find and in July 1996 the author had narrowed it down to three bends of the right orientation on the road from Lettergesh to Tully Cross. The towering mass of Mweelrea and the hill in the background give a pretty good geometric fix on the spot but I was not so sure I had found the correct location. I was examining it from various angles and as usual exposing roll upon roll of film when a voice behind me said, "That's the spot where John Wayne and Maureen O'Hara dropped

The site that has attracted Mary Kate's attention is Thoor Ballylee, a castle situated some four miles north-east of the town of Gort in the south of County Galway **(Location 17)**. In reality the scene is located nearly seventy miles away from where the couple abandoned the tandem, and geographically it is the most southerly location of *The Quiet Man*.

Thoor Ballylee is a Norman square tower, dating from the thirteenth century and was originally the home of Richard de Burgo in the sixteenth century. It fell into disrepair but in 1917 it was bought by the poet William Butler Yeats at the bargain price of £35 and over the

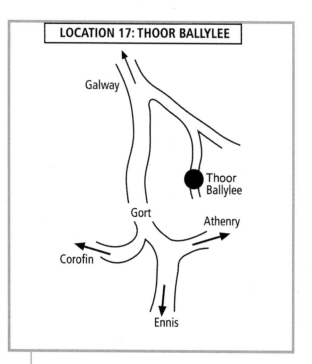

LOCATION 17: THOOR BALLYLEE

Galway

Thoor Ballylee

Gort

Athenry

Corofin

Ennis

Thoor Ballylee

next three years he fully restored it. He lived there on and off over the next ten years using it as his ivory tower to escape from city life. It was situated just a few miles from Lady Gregory's house at Coole Park, which was the centre of the Irish literary revival and nearby too is Kiltartan, often mentioned in the poetry of Yeats.

When Yeats moved back to Dublin in 1929 the castle, as the locals called it, once again fell into disrepair and in the movie in 1951 we see it as just a shell with darkened windows. Happily, since then it has been beautifully restored again by Bord Fáilte (the Irish Tourist Board) and it opened to the public in 1965. Today it is an essential stopping place for all visitors to Ireland – it houses an audio-visual theatre illustrating the life of Yeats and the history of the tower house, a craft giftshop, a bookshop specialising in Anglo-Irish literature and a delightful tearoom. In addition, it houses the original oak furniture designed by W.A. Scott, the china, some first editions of Yeats' works and paintings by Yeats' artist brother, Jack B. Yeats. Yeats' poetic description of the place, "Winding stair, a chamber arched with stone, A grey stone fireplace with an open hearth," are still there in

situ and there is a pleasing view of the surrounding countryside from the flat roof of the tower. Sadly, there is no recognition of the fact that a *Quiet Man* scene was shot there, despite the obvious connection with W.B. Yeats and Innisfree.

Nugent's screenplay instructions for this scene are as follows:

> At a brook with stepping stones across it. In a flash Mary Kate is off the bike, letting Sean trundle it aside and lean it against a stile. Meanwhile, she is kicking off her shoes and peeling down her stockings. Sean turns from the bike to find her splashing across the stream. He has to make his own best way over the stepping stones in belated pursuit. She taunts him from the other side.

The scene is pure Constable – the dried-up river with the abandoned horse-cart left casually in the middle and the ruined tower in the background. Mary Kate runs down to the river entering by the back of the tower with Sean in hot pursuit. A change of camera angle brings the cart to the right-hand bank at the

Stream at Thoor Ballylee

north-western shore of Lough Corrib at Carrowgarriff **(Location 10)**. This location is just over three miles from White O'Morn and very close to the place where the horse-jumping scenes were shot. The screenplay instructions were as follows:

Mary Kate then goes off on the run through the fields. She is running like a wild thing with her red hair flying behind her and Sean chasing after. As she races on out of shot, Sean comes in puffing a little. He looks after her with new respect – as he shucks his coat, loosens his tie and resumes the race.

The scene opens with Mary Kate sitting in a

Gap in wall

edge of the water. Mary Kate takes off her shoes and begins to take off her stockings but now there is a bit of camera trickery – suddenly she is taking off her stockings and showing her beautiful legs on the other side of the river without apparently having crossed over! Perhaps Ford could not do this close-up flesh shot at a distance, but the location of the wall and the bridge in the background give the game away.

Having exposed her legs, Mary Kate looks up to see if she has offended Sean's modesty (of course she looks in the opposite direction to preserve the illusion that she is still on the other bank of the river). He turns away and then looks up to the sky, pretending not to be affected in the least by what he has seen, while she coyly removes her other stocking complete with black garter. Again she eyes him suspiciously, holding her stockings in her hand. Suddenly she is back again on the other side of the river and, carrying her shoes and stockings in one hand and holding her bonnet securely with the other, she runs across splashing merrily as she goes. She emerges on a grassy bank (right beside where she has just been!) and skips smilingly past the camera enticing Sean to follow her. Mary Kate believes that a courtship should include a ritualised chase.

Sean raises his arms in exasperation and, still clutching his gloves, he tightens his bowler hat and follows her, splashing through the water in his shoes. During this beautiful scene, which lasts a mere forty-three seconds, not a word is spoken and we hear only *The Kerry Dances* with variations, as background music.

The scene now shifts some fifty miles to the

gap in a wall on the hilltop – she is putting her shoes back on after her run through the stream but in reality just giving us another chance to view her shapely legs **(Location 10C)**. The place is chosen so that Ford can show some more of the mouth-watering scenery of the West of Ireland to best advantage – in the background we see some of the Twelve Pins (or Twelve Bens) which are the mountains of Connemara. The wall and its gap look almost exactly the same today as they did in 1951 and it was a great thrill finding the location.

Mary Kate looks back into field B to see if Sean is coming and seeing that he is, she scampers off to field A feeling that it is nice to be chased but that it is nicer to be caught.

The next few scenes show considerable camera trickery, mostly because field A has a steep downhill slope and was not suitable for filming or larking across the countryside. We next see Mary Kate in field B **(Location 10D)** running eastwards towards the wall – in the background are the exotically named hills of Knockagussy, Lugacurry and Maumcloghaloon. As Mary Kate runs along she jumps over the rocks and boggy tufts of grass in her exuberance, stopping only to look back to see if Sean is following her. By now Sean has reached the gap in the wall and is in reality in front of her at Location 10C.

He runs into field A and Mary Kate now at **Location 10E** looks westward to see someone who is actually standing behind her back. Stockings draped over her arm, she takes the pin from her bonnet and takes it off her head, symbolising the throwing away of inhibitions.

Sean is now standing at **Location 10D** facing in the opposite direction. At last he gets the message she is signalling so he puts his gloves in his bowler hat and throws the whole lot frisbee-style over the wall bordering the main road **(Location 10F)**, which has been cleverly concealed throughout the scene to give the impression that the couple are miles away from any vestige of civilisation. Sean too has thrown away the trappings of polite society and the couple can now face each other bareheaded if nothing else. Sean is now back at Location 10F and he follows Mary Kate towards the gap

in the wall which of course is not shown. The three rocks in the foreground which fix the location of this scene are clearly identifiable today **(Location 10G)**.

Mary Kate, while going through the motions of accepting the rural Irish conventions of courtship, has shown what she really thinks about them and has conveyed her feelings to Sean. It is interesting to note that over five minutes have elapsed without a single word being spoken and yet viewers never seem to notice or mind this. This is surely a great tribute to the director and cinematographers but on the other hand perhaps people do not realise that they are watching the greatest-ever free commercial for Irish tourism. Incidentally, the old building seen in the top right-hand corner of this scene is Clement's Mine, a productive pit which in the nineteenth century produced considerable quantities of iron, lead, copper, zinc and silver and even today a visit to its spoil tip, also clearly seen in the movie, will prove rewarding to the mineral collector. Other rare metals which occur nearby are tungsten, barium, molybdenum, arsenic and even gold. Of course the area is also famous for its green Connemara marble.

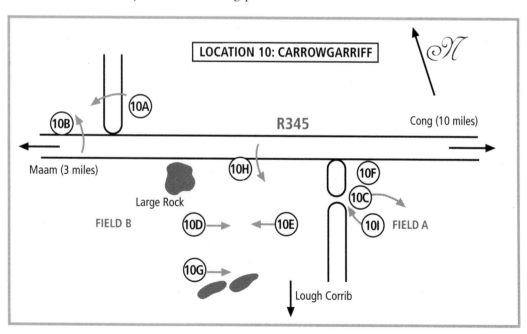

Rocks in the field

Sadly, the scene which now follows is one of the most stagy and least attractive in the movie — the graveyard scene. It could have been so different. The original intention was to shoot it on the famous Cliffs of Moher in County Clare. The original screen instructions read:

Ext. The Cliffs of Moher: Long (and a series of pictures). As Sean comes running up, overtakes her, and they start walking — hand in hand — along the cliff-tops. They come at last to a halt. (Close-up). Mary Kate drops to her knees, then swings her weight back on her haunches, both arms braced behind her and head thrown back to breathe the liquid air. Sean drops beside her, lost in wonder at her beauty.

The unit did go to the Cliffs of Moher and spent a whole day there shooting but the lighting was never satisfactory and the sea mist rolled relentlessly in from the Atlantic Ocean. Etta Vaughan, Maureen O'Hara's stand-in, describes how she ran over and back on the cliff-top time and time again until eventually it was decided to abandon this location because of the poor lighting conditions. The footage that was shot was never used, but interestingly Ford did use the Cliffs of Moher as background for the title sequence of another of his Irish movies *The Rising of the Moon* (1957), released in the United States as *Three Leaves of a Shamrock*.

What a scene this might have made but instead Ford went for a patently artificial studio scene, where the artificial lighting and plastic props are blatantly obvious. The scene is every Irish-

American's idea of an Irish graveyard — the ruined half-gate hanging like a giant angel's harp, three obviously plastic Celtic crosses serving as gravestones and a general atmosphere of doom and gloom. Why young lovers would want to go there is a mystery, except perhaps to find a flat tombstone on which to lie down together, or maybe to echo the humorous Irish marriage proposal — "How would you like to be buried with my people?" It is unlikely, however, that Ford is pursuing the Freudian suggestion of the link between sex and death and that the scene is more of a joke about the Irish being the only race on earth who would consider a cemetery a suitable place to conduct a courtship!

Mary Kate leads Sean by the hand into the graveyard, which is in fact an old churchyard, in a feeble attempt to preserve continuity from the previous scene. Looking back at him, she sees that he is grinning broadly and she is smiling too. In her left hand she is still holding her stockings and bonnet, highly symbolic of her openness and availability. Suddenly, she turns around and is confronted by the Celtic cross gravestone. She shudders with the spine-chilling sensation sometimes explained by the fact that someone has walked over your grave. Perhaps she is reminded that marriage and children are the first indications that she is mortal and will someday have to be replaced in society.

Sean, however, takes it all in his stride and clearly has other things on his mind. In the first dialogue for several minutes he says to Mary Kate, "If anyone had told me six months ago that today I'd be in a graveyard in Inisfree with a girl like you that I'm just about to kiss, I'd have told them…"

Suddenly Mary Kate's smile turns to a mock look of fear and she turns her back to him as he attempts to put his arms around her.

"But the kissing is a long way off yet," she tells him, despite the fact that they have already kissed twice in the cottage. Incidentally, the word "kissing" is a substitute for the originally intended "marriage".

"What?" asks Sean in a puzzled voice as she

The courting couple

proceeds to explain to him the complicated further stages of the rural Irish courtship rituals which she now begins to hide behind a little to cover up her fear of confronting him.

"Well, we've just started the coortin'," she explains, "and next month we…we start the walking out together, and the month after that, there'll be the threshing parties and the month after that there'll be…"

"Nope," says Sean with typical American firmness.

"Well, maybe we won't have to wait that month," she concedes and now his arms are around her waist without protest.

"Yep," he agrees laconically.

"Or for the threshing parties," she continues hopefully, knowing all the time he will agree.

"No," he agrees again.

Now she turns towards him person to person and says, "Or for the walking out together," as he takes her in his arms.

"No," he smiles gently and for the first time there is real tenderness between them.

Now she puts her arms, including bonnet and stockings, around his shoulders and says as all women since Eve have done, "Then so much the worse for you, Sean Thornton, for I feel the same way about it myself." Then she throws her arms back and suddenly embraces him smilingly.

The Isle of Innisfree now fittingly becomes the background music as the wind rises and the trees are blown about; lightning flashes and a clap of thunder is heard. Mary Kate blesses herself with the sign of the cross and silently mouths a prayer for God to protect her against the elements before running for shelter in the ruined abbey. Sean is mesmerised, because thunderstorms are common in America and he takes them in his stride, but they are much rarer in Ireland because summer temperatures are rarely high enough to spark them off. In any event the thunderstorm depicted is very much an American continental landmass one and totally unlike the kind that occurs in Ireland, but one must not forget that the American box-office was always a major consideration in the making of *The Quiet Man*.

They shelter from the thunderstorm under

1:05:00

one of the ornate windows of the ruined abbey, a very artificial-looking set modelled perhaps on the windows of Ross Errily already seen, but it could be any of a thousand ruined Irish abbeys. The couple are probably more at risk where they are now than they were out in the open, but as the lightning continues to flash, the terrified Mary Kate clings to Sean like a child for protection.

1:05:30 Finally she retreats to the shelter of the big ruined window itself as big raindrops begin to fall and Sean gallantly takes off his jacket to protect her.

1:06:00 Just after he has placed it around her shoulders and is looking up to see if there is any sign of the storm clearing, a huge flash of lightning causes her to put her arms around him once again. By now Sean is definitely in the wet T-shirt category and they kiss very passionately as the big raindrops pitter-patter on the ruins. Then they embrace tenderly and quietly, but echoing their first kiss in the cottage, Mary Kate steals a second kiss to give Sean's actions her seal of approval. Again it is noteworthy that a full two minutes of screen time have passed without a word being spoken.

1:06:30 Despite the artificiality of the scenery, the defects of the lighting and other studio giveaways, this scene has been described as one of the most erotic ever filmed and the closest Ford ever came to shooting a nude scene. Cynics have claimed that the director merely asked Wayne to do all the things to O'Hara that he would have liked to do to her himself, but perhaps this is a little unkind.

In the closing moments of this scene a very wet Sean looks pensively at the ground as he holds Mary Kate in his arms. The die is cast and he knows that he is about to take on the responsibility of being a husband and maybe a father, and that he has pledged his future to Inisfree and Ireland. The prize has been won but there is a certain sadness and maybe even fear in his eyes as he surveys the future. As we well know, his apprehension was very well justified. The scene fades with the delicious combination of raindrops and *Innisfree*, as good

a taste of Ireland as one could ask for.

And so to the wedding scene, supposedly held in the Danaher house. This seems to have suddenly acquired a lot of extra reception rooms, but of course the entire sequence was shot in the studios. Nugent's original screenplay located it first outside St Anselm's Chapel after the marriage ceremony and then in the open outside the Danaher house. He advises:

> It is a scene as gay as Breughel's wedding feast [after the famous painting]. Trestle tables with their long benches; a cleared central area with long planks laid for the dancing; carts and horses in the surround – and every able-bodied man, woman and child in the place to celebrate the wedding of Sean and Mary Kate.

There were to be pipers playing *The Walls of Limerick*, dancers – Michaeleen dancing with a woman twice his size, Father Paul stepping it out with Missus Playfair, clerical dignity overboard – and drinking, Father Lonergan and Mister Playfair with pints of porter in their hands. There was to be a suggestion of ribald banter between Sean and Mary Kate, with him proposing that they skip the reception and escape on the tandem to begin the honeymoon! These "taming of the shrew" scenes were never filmed. Indeed, a comparison between Ford's finished product and Nugent's overall script shows that many of his elaborate and trivially comic scenes were not used, almost as if Ford wanted to preserve an undercurrent of seriousness while Nugent would have preferred more of a farce.

The reception therefore begins indoors and is attended only by the local gentry with the common villagers inappropriately ignored. This is largely because the price to be paid for shooting the wedding reception in Hollywood is that only the principal players could be taken across the Atlantic, there to be joined by others such as Sean McClory and Harry Tyler. This is a pity, because the tradition in the Irish countryside was that everybody shared in the festivities, and that would have included Danaher's workmen, the railway employees and the villagers in general.

The scene opens with Sean (seated) and Mary Kate posing rigidly for a time-exposure photograph which was to be the official wedding portrait.

"And so they were married," intones Father Lonergan.

This is of course the title of another movie *And So They Were Married* (1935), a romantic farce directed by Elliot Nugent about a widow and a widower who marry despite the objections of their children.

"In the same little chapel I gave them their baptism," continues Father Lonergan.

This is a ludicrous line, not in Nugent's script. Father Lonergan is not much older than Sean if the actors' ages are anything to go by and Mary Kate is not a great deal younger than the two of them. So he could not possibly have baptized them, which would have been the correct phrase to use. Furthermore, a priest in the West of Ireland would have been transferred every ten years or so and would not have spent thirty years in Inisfree unless perhaps sent back there by his bishop as parish priest, which would have been unlikely.

"And later," continues our clerical narrator, "there was a nice quiet little celebration," as the primitive camera flash explodes ironically into action. The startled couple jump with surprise and can only stand dumbfounded as the celebrations begin. As the quality of Inisfree parade into the reception – a smiling Hugh Forbes, a grinning Mister and Missus Playfair, a sombre Mrs Tillane on the arm of Guppy, and a downcast Dan Tobin (who let him in – he's a commoner!) – we see Feeney, Owen Glynn and Michaeleen Oge Flynn standing round the piano at which Father Paul is seated and playing. They are lustily singing an old Irish ballad *The Humour is on me Now*, obviously a favourite of Ford's.

Oh, as I went out one morning, it being the month of May,
A farmer and his daughter I spied upon me way,
And the girl sat down quite calmly to the milking of her cow
Saying I will and I must get married for the humour is on me now
        Oh the humour is on me now
        Oh the humour is on me now
Saying I will and I must get married for the humour is on me now.

For the uninitiated, "the humour is on me now" means roughly "I am in the mood".

Several things happen during the singing of this first verse. Feeney, who is hanging back from the action as befits a hired man, is motioned to come forward by Father Paul and only then begins to join in the singing, a subtle touch and easily missed. Michaeleen inadvertently takes a glass of champagne from a passing waitress and begins to drink it without realising what it is. It is clearly not his usual beverage, because he spits is out in disgust immediately, but Owen Glynn quickly sizes up the situation and hands him a half-consumed glass of porter.

The role of the clergy at an Irish country wedding is, even still, somewhat ambiguous. Celibate themselves, they often gave the impression of disapproving of the whole business which was barely legitimised by the marriage ceremony, though this attitude has changed in recent years. Indeed, at many wedding ceremonies, the real celebrations did not begin until the parish clergy had departed. In this scene, even the curate is worried that his merrymaking is not going to be approved of, as the stern Father Lonergan arrives on the scene all grim-faced. The music suddenly stops and Father Paul stands up, but it is all an act on the part of the parish priest. As usual, Ward Bond just wants to steal the scene and because he is an old friend of Ford's, he is allowed to get away with it, so he sits down to play and begins to sing in an excruciating parody of an Irish accent. All the other four actors are native Irishmen and good singers to boot, so this ludicrous intrusion is one of the flaws of the movie, albeit designed to show how grateful the parish priest is to have the matchmaking problem off his hands. Father Lonergan sings, for want of a better word, as follows:

So at last the daughter married and she
married well-to-do
And loved her darling husband for a month
a year or two
But Sean was all a tyrant and she quickly
rued her vow
Saying I'm sorry I ever got married for the
humour is off me now
 Oh the humour is off me now
 Oh the humour is off me now
Saying I'm sorry I ever got married for the
humour is off me now.

The bystanders, once they realise what is happening, enthusiastically join in with the parish priest on the second line of the second verse but Michaeleen takes little part because it cuts into his drinking time. Pat Cohan suddenly appears and joins in, as does Hugh Forbes, while Owen Glynn seats Father Paul back at his rightful place at the piano.

Now it is time for the happy couple to receive the formal congratulations from members of the wedding party. Sean and Mary Kate stand stiffly together near the doorway but throughout this scene, Mary Kate, carrying her bouquet, looks extremely nervous as if she feared the worst and knew that something disastrous was about to happen. At first it might be thought that this was just a bad case of script anticipation by Maureen O'Hara, but this is not the case. In a very warm and friendly interview with the author in October 1996 she explained that the director insisted that she appear extremely nervous and unhappy throughout the reception. Mary Kate knew her bully of a brother only too well and that he would never part with the promised dowry and would find some reason to hold on to it. Now that he had got rid of her and the marriage was legally completed, he had no reason whatsoever to hand over the money – he could have both the

widow and Mary Kate's dowry. Mary Kate sensed all this and is waiting for the inevitable storm to break.

As the singing of *The Humour is on me Now* continues with its lyrics mangled a little to suit the circumstances, the Widow Tillane, with a huge flowery hat, and Guppy in close attendance, are the first to shake hands with the couple. Next, the ever-present Dan Tobin shuffles along the line and pays his respects and by now Mary Kate is wide-eyed with fear and anticipation, but the innocent foreigner Sean is still grinning inanely, anticipating actions of a totally different kind. The song finishes and there is raucous and forced laughter from the singers.

The scene now cuts to three of the plotters – Michaeleen and the Playfairs. Michaeleen has brought two glasses of champagne and a pint of porter and the three of them drink a toast to the plot that brought the couple together in marriage. As they raise their glasses looking towards their co-conspirator Father Lonergan, Missus Playfair whispers, "To a successful conspiracy." Michaeleen grins as innocently as a new-born baby and even Mister Playfair smiles and raises his glass in the priest's direction. Over at the piano, Father Lonergan grabs a glass from a rather mesmerised-looking Owen Glynn, winks broadly at the trio, before taking a drink from the glass and handing it back. The smile on his face resembles that painted on a balloon. The ever-nervous Father Paul has begun to play another melody of Thomas Moore's *Believe Me If All Those Endearing Young Charms*, already heard in the movie.

All looks rosy as Owen Glynn advances to the middle of the floor and raising his glass in the air announces, "A toast to the bride and groom." But that stickler for convention, Michaeleen Oge Flynn, rules him out of order.

"One moment, one moment," he interrupts, glass in hand as usual. "As shaughran, I say there'll be no toasts until we've seen the bride's fortune."

Dan Tobin nods his head in agreement – he

too appreciates the protocol.

Here the scriptwriter missed an opportunity to insert a line of the great Irish storyteller Eamon Kelly – "And there'll be no one half now and the other half at the first christening," which would have put the marriage in its true context of the couple's proving their fertility.

8:00

All this time Red Will, who has not been seen to congratulate the couple, is standing by the fireplace talking sweetly to the seated Widow Tillane. At the mention of the word "fortune" he springs to life and puts his glass on the mantelpiece advancing with a huge grin on his face to the table in the middle of the floor where he stands framed between the two candlesticks. Mary Kate smiles at Sean but he looks at her quite blankly, not quite comprehending the significance of what is about to take place.

"The bride's fortune," laughs Red Will, "you'll see it, never fear."

"I'll see it now, if you please," retorts the cautious Michaeleen, whom experience has taught to be extra careful where money is concerned.

"Now then, the proprieties must be observed," says Michaeleen, shepherding Mary Kate and Sean into their statutory places for the ceremony.

8:30

Michaeleen calls Father Lonergan as his witness and Red Will asks Feeney to hand him the bride's fortune which he is carrying on his person. Red Will takes the bag of gold coins and throws them dramatically on the polished table accompanied by the lovely sound of metal on hard wood.

"Three hundred and fifty pounds gold," says Red Will proudly, as we see a close-up of Mary Kate smiling at her husband as if to say, "Look what a fine, well-propertied wife you have acquired." Sean, however, merely cringes with embarrassment because he has no interest whatsoever in her material possessions.

"A car load" (he was meant to say "cart load") "of furnishings, linen and pewter, goes with the sister of William Danaher," continues the great man.

As Father Lonergan dips his pen into the ink before Red Will signs away his sister, Red Will himself wastes no time in turning suggestively towards the bemused Widow Tillane who is still sitting by the fireplace. Then he signs the book as Hugh Forbes (for it is his turn) steps forward to propose the official toast.

"Then a toast," says Forbes. "May their days be long and full of happiness; may their children be many and full of health; and may they live in peace and freedom."

1:09:00

Towards the end of this toast, it appears as if Charles Fitzsimons has fluffed his lines – not so. The original script has "And may they live in freedom and in peace". Ford changed this to "And may they live in peace and national freedom" and this is what was on the original soundtrack. At the editing stage, however, the word "national" was crudely cut, leaving a clearly discernible gap which sounds as if the emotional Forbes had a lump in his throat, carried away by the intensity of the situation. The truth is that Ford was strongly pressurised, for political reasons, to make this change by Republic boss and producer Herbert J. Yates. In a memorandum to Ford, dated October 16th, 1951, Yates writes:

> Also, I believe I called your attention to the dialogue when a toast is given after the wedding sequence, and the words "national freedom". I am sure this dialogue will be objected to, as it is indicative of propaganda, and surely Great Britain and the Sterling territories will not like it and the censors will probably remove it. I think "freedom" alone is just as good as "national freedom".

One imagines that Ford made this cut with the greatest reluctance, not least because it left an ugly technical blot on his final cut.

1:09:30

Sean and Mary Kate are clearly moved by the toast, during which they clasp hands as the strains of *Believe Me If All Those Endearing Young Charms* continue in the background. All the party raises their glasses and Missus Playfair gives her glass to Father Lonergan. He takes a sip and gives it back to her – after all, it would not be proper for a parish priest to be seen holding his own glass.

Now comes Feeney's big moment and clearly he has rehearsed his little speech many times. He coughs and begins, "Reverend Fathers," (though Father Paul is not visible in this shot) "ladies and gentlemen, attention, attention please, Squire, Squire Danaher has the floor; in other words he's got something to say to yez all."

So saying, he points a finger to his lord and master as if there were any doubt as to who and where he was.

Feeney is here echoing a line he spoke earlier in Cohan's pub, but he may have ad-libbed this line which is not in the original script. In addition, his use of "yez" for "you" (plural) is not authentic West of Ireland usage and betrays Jack MacGowran's Dublin background.

There now follows the most cringingly embarrassing scene in *The Quiet Man*. It illustrates both Danaher's crass ignorance and childish simplicity. When Mrs Tillane took offence at having her name merely mentioned in Cohan's, surely even Red Will cannot imagine that he can propose to her in public and be accepted, all the more so when her affections are just heresay, and yet he does propose to her in front of the whole village.

"Thank you," says Red Will gushingly to Feeney, standing by the fireplace with his glass raised. The seated Mrs Tillane in her fine bonnet and Captain Guppy stare at him intently, not knowing what is to come next.

"I've got a little announcement to make," smiles Red Will as the widow glances towards Guppy. "Cohan, fill up the glasses; go on all of them," he continues, motioning to Pat Cohan and his staff to do their duty – two elegant waitresses (of unknown identity) pass through the crowd of guests. Hand in pocket, Red Will advances towards centre stage and coughing nervously he takes a glass from the barman and places it on the table. Coughing again, he adjusts his jacket, meets the defiant stare of Father Lonergan and launches into his proposal speech.

"Ah today, I've given my sister in marriage,"

he begins, gesturing in Mary Kate's direction. "My only sister, and now she's gone from the house of Danaher."

Sean is grinning but Mary Kate is again wide-eyed and fearful that something is about to happen – things have been just too good to be true.

"But what's in a house without a woman?" asks Red Will rhetorically, fluffing his lines with an intrusive "in", as he spreads his arms out to appeal to the sense of logic in his listeners. (This line is possibly inspired by a line from *The Spanish Tragedy* by the English playwright Thomas Kyd (1558–1594): "For what's a play without a woman in it?")

"That's true," nods Dan Tobin.

"Ah, that's right," echoes Feeney. "What's a house without a woman in it?"

"Yah, what's a house without a woman in it?" re-echoes Red Will, now increasingly nervous and in fact having lost his place in the script. Throughout this scene the Widow Tillane is seen smiling benignly at the proceedings and the other cast members are positioned so as not to obscure our view of her at any time.

"Where would any man of us be without a woman?" continues Red Will triumphantly with a flamboyant sweep of his arm. "Why even Father Lonergan had a mother." This seems like a rather heavy-handed comment directed towards the clergy's denial of the connection between sex and reproduction, but the priest answers gruffly and defensively, "What do you expect?" and there is laughter and nodding of heads all round.

Danaher is now completely confused and says, "What do you expect?" as if it is part of his prepared speech. He raises his glass, says "So," stops, says "So, ah," and then turns to his prompter for inspiration.

"So without further eloquence," says Feeney, which of course falsely assumes that there has been previous eloquence.

"Without further eloquence," repeats Dan Tobin totally unnecessarily.

"Without further eloquence," says Red Will having picked up the line at last, "I will give you a toast, to myself, who is soon to be wed."

The great man seems to be unaware that it is not usual to toast oneself. He then turns to the shocked widow and there is a stunned silence. Red Will puts his glass down and shakes hands very enthusiastically with a rather subdued Father Lonergan, in the manner of a man who has bought a cow and is sealing the bargain.

"All she has to do is say that little word," he adds and walking towards his beloved he says, "When's the happy day, Sarah darling?"

To say that the widow is flabbergasted would be a profound understatement. Her mouth opens in genuine horror and she is lost for words, but not for long. Spluttering as she rises from her chair, she attacks him furiously.

:00

"Have you lost the little sense you were born with?" she explodes. "Happy day indeed."

"But Sarah darling," interjects Red Will, but now she is in full flight.

"And don't 'darling' me, you cad," she continues. "Who gave you the right to make such an announcement?"

"Cad" was a last-minute substitution for "left-footed oaf" which might have had religious implications, although Danaher is certainly an oaf. Advancing menacingly, the widow gives Father Lonergan and the Playfairs an accusing look, perhaps suspecting a plot, and the priest has the good grace to turn away from her.

Red Will is like a beached whale, unable to take in what is happening and for the first time in the movie we begin to feel sorry for the big lout. The widow slams down her glass and breaks it with great force. The Cossacks broke their glasses when they had drunk the wedding toast so they would never be drunk from again, but that is not quite what is involved here.

"But, Sarah, but they all, they all said..." splutters Danaher. "Why, the Reverend Mister Playfair, Missus Playfair, Father Lonergan, little Flynn," as Sarah darling storms from the room, accompanied by Guppy, who must now fancy his chances of landing the big prize. Father Lonergan looks very grim and turns to the Playfairs as if it were another Protestant plot, while the reverend couple lower their eyes, unable to speak for shame.

Danaher, however, is still hoping against hope that what he is hearing is not true.

"Michaeleen," he says desperately, homing in on the obvious target when deception has been involved, "didn't you tell me all I had to do was...?" Characteristically, Red Will lowers himself to the little man's level as he says this.

1:11:30

"Well, now, I did and I didn't," Michaeleen defends himself in classic Irish doublespeak. But now the full realisation of the plot dawns on Danaher and he blows his top – given his level of intelligence and awareness it has taken quite some time. Now he gives vent to his rage on the conspirators from the high moral ground. First of all he takes Michaeleen's drink and splashes it violently all over the floor, narrowly missing Mary Kate's wedding dress. If Danaher is not going to enjoy himself, then nobody is, and throwing away Michaeleen's drink is just about the greatest punishment he can inflict on the little matchmaker. However, the big man is careful to replace Michaeleen's glass on the table without breaking it – after all, he has to pay for any damages himself!

Then he turns on them verbally, starting with Michaeleen.

"Oh, oh, oh, you lied, didn't you, you lied, didn't you? Ye all lied," he continues, turning to the clerical trio. "It's bad enough for you people, but my own priest."

There is a nasty little dig here – lying is perhaps to be expected from the Protestant clergy, but not from a Catholic priest! Nugent's script here shows a decided lack of familiarity with the English language as used in Ireland – "you lied" would never be used by a native Irishman, not even nowadays. Danaher would have been more likely to say, "You told me lies" or "You deceived me".

Here another line has been cut by Ford who seems to have become so politically correct at the editing stage. Perhaps Yates intervened in this instance also, but there is no written evidence that he did. Danaher was meant to say with a sob, "And worst of all, the Irish Republican Army," a reference to the fact that he thought Forbes and Glynn were part of the plot. Although Danaher's back is to the camera, one can see his jaws move during the silent gap, a silence unnatural in the context of a man in the full torrent of anger, so it is likely that the line was recorded, but cut from the soundtrack.

Now Danaher turns his wrath towards the newly-weds, especially Sean.

"You got her by fraud and falsity," he accuses him. "You put them up to this," pointing an accusing arm.

"I don't know what you're talking about," protests Sean quite truthfully.

"Ah, don't deny it," snaps Danaher.

Mary Kate, now genuinely concerned at the turn of events, interposes, "Oh Will, for heaven's sake," as she puts down her glass.

"Ah Danaher, you're crazy, man," says Owen Glynn, so moved with emotion that he removes his pipe from his mouth.

"Crazy am I?" retorts Danaher, now beginning to move about like an enraged bull.

"Will, Will," pleads Father Lonergan but it is too late.

1:12:00

"This is something you won't get, now or ever," he shouts, brushing the gold sovereigns roughly onto the floor, and knocking over a candlestick in the process.

The sight of the glittering coins on the wooden floor immediately brings to mind a similar scene in Ford's *The Informer* (1935), when the traitor Gypo Nolan, also played by Victor McLaglen, accidentally drops on the floor all the blood money he has received for the betrayal of his friend Frankie McPhillip, during the wake. The allegory of betrayal and the thirty pieces of silver is never far from Ford's mind.

Andrew McLagen recalls that Ford was not satisfied with Victor McLaglen's intensity in rehearsals for this scene. On the day previous to shooting the scene, Ford goaded McLaglen by demanding five interrupted takes on another scene and then wrapping up proceedings for the day at one o'clock in the afternoon. Naturally, McLaglen was furious and vented his anger on the wily Ford with a storming

performance when he swept the coins off the table. This, of course, was exactly what the sadistic director intended.

"Now get out of here, all of you," bellows Red Will. Mary Kate's worst nightmare has come true and all of her anxiety was justified. Feeling that her life's ambition is slipping away from her, she is at once on her knees to retrieve her fortune of gold coins, picking them up in her hands. Sean kneels gently beside her and says tenderly, "Mary Kate, come on, let's go home." But Sean has underestimated the depth of feeling that a dowry gives rise to in a peasant society where women are so financially vulnerable and dependent on their menfolk. Like the American "mad money", Mary Kate's dowry is her one guarantee of independence, her pride, her honour and a concrete sign of her worth.

"No," she says defiantly, "not without my fortune; it's mine and my mother's before me, and I'm not going to…"

To her amazement, the forceful Sean slaps her heavily on the arm, knocking some of the coins to the floor. This is an echo of her slapping him in the cottage.

Meanwhile, Danaher is ranting on. "The reverend sirs," he jeers sarcastically, "ladies and gentlemen, get out, get out with you the whole of you, get out, geeet out." (Presumably McLaglen has lost a "lot" here somewhere.) As Sean rises from his knees, holding Mary Kate by the hand, he is now vulnerable to Danaher's sudden attack, but surely an experienced boxer would have seen the punch coming. Danaher has sneaked up behind him and, taking a full swing, hits Sean squarely on the jaw, knocking him flat on the floorboards as Mary Kate shrieks in horror.

McLaglen, whose career as a professional boxer has already been described, acquits himself well here in throwing what looks like a real punch, but of course slow motion reveals that it misses by a mile. However, in the original version Danaher is meant to have scooped the gold coins back into their bag and, instead of punching Sean, he swings a flailing backhand with the heavy purse dangling from it and catches Sean across his unguarded temple. Perhaps this would have been a more symbolic action which would have found an immediate echo in Sean's knocking out a man on account of a purse also.

Now we have the famous flashback scene showing Sean's last fight in the ring. Although it is of surprisingly short duration, it is among the most powerful and dramatic scenes in the movie. As Sean lies on the floor, he instinctively tries to get up and beat the count, further confused perhaps by Danaher's shouting "Out, out, out" to the other guests. However, he fails and sinks back into unconsciousness and immediately we see and hear what he is dreaming about – the sound of the ringside bell and the roar of the bloodthirsty crowd. With a bright light behind him, he is reliving the nightmare of killing a man in the ring. He stares in horror at the opponent he has just knocked out, although how he could know at this stage that the man is dead is a mystery – perhaps he just suspects.

:30

The referee, played by Al Murphy, rather roughly turns the fallen boxer, Tony Gardello, played by Jack Roper, over on the canvas to lie face up in the corner of the ring, as Sean retreats to a neutral corner. Roper was one of Ford's wife's family names and it is possible that this part was played by yet another member of the extended family; Pat Ford's full name was Patrick Roper Ford. In real life, Jack Roper was an accomplished boxer who had fought Joe Louis for the World Heavyweight Championship in 1939, although he was knocked-out in round one. At the time of the filming of *The Quiet Man* studio scenes, he was working as an electrician for the Republic Studios. He worked most of the night to rig the boxing ring for the next day's fight sequence, and in the morning he donned his boxing kit and gloves for the big bout scene with Duke Wayne. Roper also acted in several film musicals, notably *The Fabulous Dorseys* (1947) with Arthur Shields. Verily a man of many parts!

Back at the movie Gardello's limbs move momentarily but then he lies still, and as the referee is about to begin the count he becomes suspicious that something is wrong. He leans forward and examines Gardello closely, fearing the worst. As the camera bulbs flash, Trooper Thorn's trainer, played by Bob Perry (kindly identified by John Cocchi), puts a towel around his charge's shoulder and ushers him back to his corner. Most accounts of *The Quiet Man* identify the trainer as Ford veteran Hank Worden but although the actor does look a bit like Worden it does not appear to be him; in addition, Worden actually denied that he ever appeared in *The Quiet Man*. A policeman, played by an unidentified actor, sticks his head in to stare at the body, but no attempt is made to revive or resuscitate the unfortunate boxer. The grim-faced Sean is seen sitting in his corner with his trainer standing behind him. In front is Sean's second, played by Tony Canzoneri wearing a shirt with TROOPER THORN on the back with a large four-leaved shamrock in between the two words. This logo was originally intended to be shown on Trooper Thorn's shorts depicting him as a fighting Irishman. Another policeman played by an unidentified actor arrives in the ring and stands behind Sean.

At last, a doctor, played by Douglas Evans, is called and steps into the ring. He must be a doctor because he is carrying a big black bag; however, he is smoking a cigarette, which might have been acceptable in 1952, but he wouldn't get away with it nowadays. The helpful referee takes the bag and lays it down at the fallen boxer's feet, and then moves back as the doctor kneels down. Sean grimaces and covers his eyes as the doctor, after a very perfunctory examination, declares the victim dead in truly cinematic style by placing a white towel over his face. Again, no effort is made to revive him – nowadays he would he rushed to hospital for an emergency brain transplant and be fit for the return fight in just a few months.

The scene is accompanied by sombre music and even some booing from the fickle crowd, and at

1:13:00

one stage Vic Young even sounds a musical bell for the end of the round. There is much flashing of bulbs as a dozen or so photographers record the scene for the newspapers. Why so many? Well, Nugent's screenplay economically suggests that if there were enough bulbs flashing then there would be no need for an arena or spectators at all! As the photographers now turn to Sean, he stands up and stares pitifully at the body of the man he has killed, flanked by his trainer and second restraining him. As the bulbs continue to flash, we see close-ups of the trainer and second individually, and finally we see Sean himself, his face beaded in perspiration – no words can express how he feels and he doesn't even try.

1:13:30   The boxing-ring scene, which lasts just over a minute, is central to an understanding of the whole movie. Several times already Sean has nearly let slip that he was a boxer who quit the ring – now we know exactly why. He has come to Ireland to return to the idyllic land of his mother and his youth to leave fighting for money behind him. Ironically he has just been knocked out by one of his in-laws in a fight over money – in the original version, actually with the money. The original version too had Mary Kate saying, "He's dead, he's dead," another phrase that brought death in the ring back to Sean.

Slowly consciousness returns and Sean finds himself lying on the floor, his head being supported by Michaeleen and his wife gently wiping his chin with a handkerchief. As his boxer's instinct to get up and fight causes him to sit up suddenly, he is restrained by Mister Playfair who is holding a glass of water, with a reassuring "Steady, Trooper, steady." After all he is the only one who knows his secret, but Mary Kate and Michaeleen look a bit mystified. Realising now where he is, Sean stands up and steadies himself, looking silently at Mary Kate and Mister Playfair in turn. Picking up her bouquet he hands it to her and says quietly but firmly, "Let's go home." She meekly complies.

1:14:00   Next we see the newly-weds sitting by the

fireside of their traditional Irish cottage, custom-built in the Hollywood studio. The old-fashioned kettle is hanging over a blazing fire, and in the background a harp is playing rather ironically an Irish-American ballad *I'll Take You Home Again, Kathleen.* The lyrics are as follows:

I'll take you home again, Kathleen
Across the sea and ocean wild and wide.
To where your heart has ever been,
Since first you were my bonny bride.
The roses all have left your cheek,
I've watched them fade away and die.
Your voice is sad whene'er you speak,
And tears bedim your eyes.

I'll take you home again, Kathleen
To where your heart will feel no pain.
And when the fields are fresh and green,
I'll take you to your home again.

I know you love me, Kathleen dear,
Your heart was ever fond and true;
I'll always feel when you are near,
That life holds nothing dear but you.
The smiles that once you gave to me,
I scarcely ever see them now,
Though many, many times I see
A darkening on your brow.

To that dear land beyond the sea,
My Kathleen shall again return.
And when thy old friends welcome thee,
Thy loving heart will cease to yearn.
Where laughs the little silver stream,
Beside your mother's humble cot,
And brightest rays of sunshine gleam,
There all your grief will be forgot.

The song was composed by an American, Thomas P. Westendorf, and some believe it has no connection with Ireland at all, but the lyrics are very much in keeping with the theme of *The Quiet Man* and Kathleen is, of course, the Irish version of the name Kate.

The couple then face each other across the fireplace as Sean smokes another of the many cigarettes he consumes during the movie. Mary Kate sits sadly in silence, still wearing her wedding dress and clinging to her bouquet as a symbol of her married status. Sean stares moodily into the fire, and Mary Kate is close to tears as she tries to explain her feelings about her belongings and fortune to her husband who has little understanding or appreciation of Irish marriage customs.

"Ever since I was a little girl," she tells him sadly, "I've dreamed of having my own things about me; my spinet over there" – she points with her bouquet – "and a table here, and my own chairs to rest upon." Mary Kate is now more emotional and raises her voice to emphasise her point. She stands up and continues, "And a dresser over there in that corner, and my own china and pewter shining about me"; now she is almost crying with emotion. "And now…" she breaks off in despair.

Sean, who might just as well have landed from another planet, suddenly realises that he has a lot to learn about the ways of the Irish and the nature of his wife too.

"I didn't know you felt that way about it," he says with typical masculine reasonableness, "but it seems like a lot of fuss and grief over a little furniture and stuff." Oops, this is not the right thing to say just now, Sean. Mary Kate is shocked by his lack of understanding and sympathy – she throws aside her veil and walks out the front door of the cottage not knowing what to do next.

Now we see for the first time the outside of the studio White O'Morn – it is a passable reproduction of the original but it does look a little stagy. The fact that it is meant to be night time merely heightens this effect. Recorded birds are heard chirping in the background – but surely they would be tucked away in their nests at that time of night?
Sean follows Mary Kate as she runs forward but now, for the first time, she is afraid of him. As he approaches her, to distract him she turns towards their love nest and he turns too.

"It is a pretty cottage, isn't it?" she says to

him, acknowledging the home he has restored for the two of them. This is of course an attempt to distract him, as he replies, "Yeah, I think so." However, he mistakes her small talk for something else as he approaches her amorously, but as he moves to put his arms around her she suddenly freezes and pointedly turns around to face away from him.

"Don't touch me," she tells him frostily. "You have no right."

"What do you mean, no right?" he asks in angry amazement.

Mary Kate turns towards him in defiance, her angry temper fully aroused.

"I'll wear your ring," she tells him, "I'll cook and I'll wash and I'll keep the land, but that is all; until I've got my dowry safe about me, I'm no married woman. I'm the servant I have always been, without anything of my own."

This sad little summary of the rights and duties of an Irish married woman at the time leaves Sean in no doubt about what the situation is – the marriage will not be consummated until Mary Kate receives every penny of her dowry and every article of furniture that she is entitled to.

Naturally, he protests. "That's ridiculous," he tells her. "You're my wife and fortune or no fortune…"

He attempts to embrace her but she runs away from him into the cottage and slams the lower part of the half-door against him.

The half-door was a clever device in Irish cottages whereby the upper half of the door could be left open to let in fresh air while the lower half could be kept closed to prevent farm animals and chickens from entering the house. Here it forms a very effective partial barrier between the couple – it keeps them physically apart and yet they can engage in a passionate argument.

Sean follows her to the door and asks in genuine puzzlement, "What is this?" He is now more than a little scared at Mary Kate's depth of feeling.

"Haven't I been trying to tell you," she explains spiritedly, "that until you have my dowry, you haven't got any bit of me – me myself?" These last words are spoken passionately as she physically prods her breast and heart with her finger as if to emphasise the fact that she is a real flesh-and-blood human being and not an animal to be traded between men at their convenience. Mary Kate is here expressing the feelings of women everywhere since the beginning of time concerning their material dependence on men and their lack of identity associated with their lack of property. And like all women in this position she uses the only powerful weapon at her disposal – sexual blackmail. To put it crudely, she is saying to her bewildered husband, no dowry, no sex.

But she does attempt to justify her stance, as tenderly as she can manage under the circumstances. "I'll still be dreaming," she tells him, "amongst the things that are my own, as if I had never met you. There's three hundred years of happy dreaming in those things of mine – I want them, I want my dream; I'll have it and I know it." Here she thumps the half-door with intense feeling and her voice is raised. "I'll say no other word to you," she finishes.

1:16:30

"All right, you'll have your dowry or dot or fortune or whatever you call it," answers Sean quietly.

"Well, get it then," she says unrepentantly, and storms off to the bedroom. He follows her into the cottage but she has already vanished into the bedroom and slammed the door. Sean seems prepared to accept this and turns to the inevitable movie prop by striking a match on the roof beam and lighting yet another cigarette.

In the original screenplay as envisaged by Nugent there now follows a scene of extraordinary naivety and sentimentality. After Mary Kate had gone to the bedroom, Sean was meant to stand there and then with reluctant decision cross to a chest and open his original battered leather bag. He takes from it a silk boxer's robe, a pair of boxer's trunks and finally a pair of boxing gloves. Having tried on a glove and tenderly fingered the robe with its shamrock design and TROOPER THORN written on the back, he experiences a sudden wave of revulsion and throws the trunks and the robe into the fire. Then he strips off the glove – he has decided not to fight again – even for Mary Kate and her dowry. Wimpishly, he goes to the bedroom door and begs her to let him in, but she refuses. He asks again, but there is no reply.

Now his patience snaps and he raises a foot and drives it hard against the catch. The door splinters at the lock and caves in. In the bedroom Mary Kate cowers and falls back on the bed – she has never seen Sean in such a fighting mood before. Towering over her, he says lamely, "When I say something, I mean it. Keep it on your mind! And remember! There's no lock or door between you and me, except the one that's in your own heart." He stomps out, leaving her staring after him.

Back in the kitchen, by the fire, he picks up his gloves and tries them on. He has a look in his eye that does not bode well for Squire Danaher, and the scene fades.

This proposed scene pales in comparison with the one actually filmed – one of the most powerful in the history of cinema. Admittedly, it does bear a curious resemblance to a scene from *The Foxes of Harrow* (1947), starring Maureen O'Hara, Rex Harrison and Victor McLaglen and featuring a strong Irish storyline. We will explore this connection further in our later chapter devoted to influences on *The Quiet Man*.

Duke Wayne too had a big say in how this important scene was shot. In the Irish location shots he felt he had been upstaged time and time again by virtually everybody on the set, especially the Irish Players. He claimed the script had him kowtowing and saying "Yes, Ma'am" and "No, Ma'am" all the time and not displaying any of the rugged masculinity for which he was famous. He brought this up with Ford but got only a dirty look. Later, however, Pappy relented and changed Wayne's role saying to him, "Duke, I'm going to let you do what you always do when a broad locks you out. I'm going to let you kick the ∗∗∗∗∗∗∗ door down."

Back at the action, Sean is prepared to accept

Mary Kate's closing the door in his face, but when with a dramatic and unmistakable sound she bolts the door creating a real barrier between them, this is the last straw. Now there is a betrayal of trust – Mary Kate does not believe that Sean will leave her alone unless she locks him out. To dramatic music, he hurls his spent match into the fire, and in one stride kicks down the door as he enters the bedroom. Incongruously, Mary Kate is still carrying her bouquet, as if clinging to the romantic illusion of her marriage. Rumour has it that at one stage Ford suggested that Wayne break the door down with an axe, but maybe this smacked too much of an axe-murderer, and Wayne was allowed to do it the direct way.

7:00

Mary Kate runs in terror to the corner of the bedroom, echoing the time she hid there during their first encounter in the cottage. Sean throws away his cigarette to free his hands for action – how he didn't burn down the cottage, we will never know. He throws back the covers of the bed, but why? Just to scare her into believing that he is going to force his will on her perhaps. She stands near the wall with her back defiantly towards him, but he rotates her roughly towards him. She gasps as they make contact and is close to tears. He says dramatically, and this is one of the most memorable lines from *The Quiet Man*, "There'll be no locks or bolts between us, Mary Kate, except those in your own mercenary little heart." This is in fine contrast to his previous appreciation of her "good Christian act" on their first encounter in the cottage.

He kisses her passionately and she responds by placing her bouquet-filled arm around his shoulder. He picks her up bodily and carries her to the bed – by now she fears the worst and perhaps she is actually looking forward to a torrid session of lovemaking. However, he has a surprise in store for her – he dumps her unceremoniously on the bed and it collapses under the impact. As he stomps out of the bedroom she lies crying miserably on the bed and feeling very sorry for herself, with more than just her dignity hurt. Still in her wedding dress, she waves her bouquet about in despair.

The marriage has got off to the worst possible start, but wow, what a scene.

Now we see a black screen for a couple of seconds to denote the passage of time. By the morning, tempers have cooled considerably and passions have subsided. Mary Kate, dressed in her day clothes, is seen emerging from the bedroom brushing her long red hair, and the door that Sean kicked in has a huge gap in it as a tribute to his efforts. We hear the sounds of music and revelry outside and, as Mary Kate looks out the window, she sees a party of people approaching the cottage. Still brushing her hair, she opens the half-door to get a better look and the sound of music and laughter grows louder.

1:17:30

Sean is seen sitting upright in his sleeping bag by the wicker basket smoking his first cigarette of the morning. As he throws away his match he is amused to see Mary Kate's agitation as she hurriedly prepares for the unexpected visitors, tidying up furiously and casting him appealing glances. She picks up all the debris she can gather and then comes over and kneels by his side.

"Sean," she appeals to him with just one word – his name.

1:18:00

"How did you sleep?" he asks her with surprisingly good humour – he does not bear any grudges and she knows it.

"Don't be shaming me, in front of your friends," she stutters, and he suddenly realises how the scene would appear to visitors and how the news would spread like wildfire through Inisfree.

"What? Oh, OK," he reacts and quickly packs his sleeping bag into the basket before retiring into the bedroom to pretend he has been sleeping there all through the night.

Now the remnants of the wedding party arrive on the scene, and clearly the drinking has gone on all night. Assistant director Andrew V. McLaglen relates that on the set he suddenly realised that although none of the revellers had been to bed, some of them were dressed in different clothes from those they had been wearing at the reception. When he pointed this out to Ford, the director, annoyed by such petty details, pretended he had written a note about this point and placed it in his shirt pocket. However, when McLaglen later glanced at the piece of paper, he saw it was completely blank! Such were the ways of the great man who felt that if moviegoers were looking for such details they were not worth bothering about. How he would have felt about this current chapter does not bear thinking about.

The party passes by the camera, in front of what is very clearly a painted backdrop of the barn beside the cottage. The motley crew is led by a dishevelled Owen Glynn, bottle and glass still in hand, and just behind him is Hugh Forbes, also the worse for wear with a champagne glass in his hand. Next comes the uncomfortably besuited Feeney leading a pair of horses who in turn are pulling a cart laden with Mary Kate's furniture. On the front of the cart is Dermot Fahy complete with bubaleen cap and of course he is lustily playing the accordion. However, the eagle-eyed will notice that the actor involved is not Ken Curtis, who perhaps was not available for this scene. The double involved keeps his back and the back of his head to the camera throughout, except for a few frames at the beginning of the scene, which gives the game away. Beside him still in formal dress is publican Pat Cohan, ornately framed, glass in hand, to resemble an oil painting. Bringing up the rear and facing backwards is Michaeleen Oge Flynn, complete with cigar and bowler hat. In fact, this is just the sort of jolly party of visitors that any newly married couple would be delighted to see arriving at their house on the first morning of their honeymoon. In actual fact, the party are travelling along a path that did not exist in front of the original Irish cottage.

1:18:30

Throughout this scene the party are singing to musical accompaniment a rollicking old Irish comic ballad called *Mush Mush* in praise of the traditional Irish love of fighting at the slightest provocation. For the record, the words go something like this:

It was there that I learned all me courtin'
Many lessons I took in the art

'Til Cupid the blackguard while sportin'
An arrow drove straight through me
Mush mush mush tooraliaddy
Me mush mush mush tooraliay,
So I lathered him with me shillelagh
For he trod on the tail of me
Mush mush mush tooraliaddy
And just like the Dingle puck goat
I lathered him with me shillelagh
For he trod on the tail of me coat.

The composer of this masterpiece is unknown or in hiding.

The party arrive in the yard in front of the cottage using an entrance that is not in the yard of the original cottage. We notice too that the thatch in the studio replica is much longer in proportion to the height of the cottage than in the real White O'Morning. As Feeney clambers up onto the cart, Forbes and Glynn, suddenly sober, place a chair on the ground and give Michaeleen a lift onto it to prevent his imminent collapse. Forbes turns to the door and shouts loudly, "Hello the house, anyone up?" using an Irish idiom that existed in Frank Nugent's imagination only. Actually, his words are a bit unnecessary after all the music, singing and general racket the party have made.

1:19

Inside, Mary Kate is busying herself lighting the fire and stands up in mock surprise as Forbes and Glynn enter. She curtsies as they both say "Good morning" in turn, just in time for Sean to emerge from the bedroom, acting out his part of the dutiful husband.

"I suppose it is a bit early to be calling," explains Forbes apologetically, with a suggestion of wink, wink, nudge, nudge.

1:19

"Well," says Glynn, pouring himself a drink from his mobile bar, "after you left last night, Mary Kate, a couple of us persuaded Danaher to change his mind."

"It's what you might call a sort of belated wedding present," adds Forbes helpfully.

It is obvious that many of Glynn's lines have been added in the studio or taken directly from what Forbes was meant to say. Forbes and

Glynn almost always appear together in *The Quiet Man* and, although Charles Fitzsimons was on location in the West of Ireland, most of his scenes were shot in the studio with Sean McClory.

"My things, my furniture," gasps the stunned Mary Kate excitedly before rushing out the cottage door like a little girl to watch the unloading. The men smile and Glynn explains, "We'd have brought them over last night, Sean, but due to the circumstances we thought you'd be needing your sleep."

"Thanks, thanks," drawls Sean sarcastically as he peers out the door at the action in the yard. Glynn is quick to notice that Sean is not as happy as he expected him to be.

0:00

Glynn rushes to the right as Mary Kate reverses into the cottage directing the furniture removal. "Oh easy, easy now," she says as Feeney and Pat Cohan enter carrying the spinet as if it were a coffin with two candlesticks perched on top.

"God bless all here," says Feeney in an undertaker's tone, invoking the traditional Irish greeting on entering a house, and echoing Michaeleen's entry into the Danaher house earlier.

"That's right – oh be careful," bosses Mary Kate. "Over there by the wall," she adds as she shepherds them along, echoing her driving of the sheep earlier on. There is no doubt that she is revelling in her position as the central figure in the drama as woman of the house. Sean looks on with a sort of bemused amusement.

"No, no, now turn it around so that the light shines on the music," she continues, making a totally unnecessary rotatory movement with her arms, and Feeney and Pat Cohan duly oblige. Finally, Mary Kate smiles and says, "That's grand, that's grand," just as Michaeleen enters carrying a traditional Irish wooden rocking cradle which he places on the floor with the words, "Where, where do you want this?"

As the cradle rocks to and fro the four men turn smirkingly towards Mary Kate with a touch of Twenties' stag-night Irish-style tone. Mary Kate is suddenly stopped in her tracks,

and as Sean casts an eye over the cradle he puts his hands on his hips and looks at her with a semi-serious look of accusation, as if to remind her that they have not taken any of even the preliminary action necessary for filling the cradle. "Mighty handy," he says to her.

"It was my mother's and my mother's mother's before," says Mary Kate by way of diversion before leaping over the cradle and running out the door, slamming it behind her. This is an echo of their original meeting in the cottage, but this time Sean does not pull her back – now there is a full door of a barrier between them.

1:20:30

"Where will I put it?" asks Michaeleen practically and Sean answers, "Where do you suppose?" stepping over the cradle, opening the door and walking out. Michaeleen repeats the answer, "Where do you suppose?" in that infuriating way of his, mimicking the other person.

Outside, the mood is still jovial. The minstrel Dermot Fahy is definitely not a removal man and is now playing *The Wild Colonial Boy* on the melodion as Mary Kate climbs up on the cart in her excitement. Sean and the twins follow and Glynn explains, "We're sorry about the dowry, Mary Kate."

"We couldn't make him change his mind about it," adds Forbes. "Not even Father Lonergan could do it."

Mary Kate and Sean seem to be the only ones working now as she hands him a chair which he places on the ground.

"Well, let him keep it," says Sean rashly – he still hasn't learned to keep his mouth shut when he should.

"Keep my fortune?" exclaims Mary Kate from her position of high dudgeon on the cart.

"Sure, you got your tables and chairs about you – what do we care about his money?" says Sean with perfect masculine logic.

1:21:00

"My money," says Mary Kate with emphasis. "Well, let him have it if it means that much to him," snaps Sean before shouting, "Gangway" to the others as he carries a trunk into the cottage.

Mary Kate sits on the cart in mock despair and says to Forbes, "What manner of man is it that I have married?"

"A better one, I think," answers Forbes, "than you know, Mary Kate," as he and Glynn unceremoniously dump her from the cart. Behind them Feeney and Pat Cohan are struggling with Mary Kate's big circular table.

Meanwhile, Michaeleen has arrived in the bedroom with the cradle and, as he places it gently on the floor, he is astonished to see the bed broken and clothes strewn all over the place. Assuming that the cause is a wedding night of continuous passion, he gives the bed a look that only Barry Fitzgerald can manage, before taking a puff on his cigar and uttering the immortal line: "Impetuous, Homeric." As a spoiled priest or failed cleric, Michaeleen would have studied Ancient Greek and have been familiar with the works of Homer. However, as a celibate, Michaeleen is a bit shocked at the consequences of the match he has helped to engineer. Moviegoers love this scene, because, for a change, they know the facts of the matter better than Michaeleen. Rather surprisingly, this innocent little scene fell foul of the censor and was cut when *The Quiet Man* was shown in the state of Ohio. Equally surprising perhaps is the fact that it was not in the original screenplay, but a little reflection will reveal that it bears all the hallmarks of a brilliant studio insertion, very probably suggested and written by Ford himself.

1:21:30

The scene now switches to the living room of the cottage a couple of hours after the visitors have departed. Mary Kate has been hard at work and her precious furniture is all in place. On the polished table there sits a fine bunch of roses. Having finished her housework, she is taking some time out to play her favourite music on the spinet.

The air of course is the by now very familiar *Isle of Innisfree* and, although Richard Farrelly's original words fitted perfectly both the mood and the plot of *The Quiet Man*, Ford, Maureen O'Hara and possibly Frank Nugent got together to write their own lyrics for this short extract. Why, it is hard to say, but it would have

been nice to hear even a snatch of Farrelly's poetic words. The song of course was sung here by Maureen O'Hara herself who had a fine singing voice. For the record, these are the words that she actually sang to the *Innisfree* air:

1:22

Oh Innisfree, my island, I'm returning
From wasted years across the wintry sea
And when I come back to my own dear island
I'll rest a while beside you, grá mo chroí.

"Grá mo chroí" in Irish means "the love of my heart", a term of endearment used by lovers for each other but more particularly by a mother for her child. Amusingly, the Spanish version of the movie, *El Hombre Tranquilo*, does not dub the words of the song here but gives subtitles instead. Not realising that the final words are in the Irish language, the translator renders the last line as: "Decanso un rato junto a ti, Cromer Creek." Cromer Creek is thus a *Quiet Man* location existing in the Spanish version only, but rather a clever phonetic guess nevertheless. Incidentally, the eagle-eyed may here wish to observe the inauthentic American spelling on Mary Kate's music sheet.

As she sings the last line of the song and in particular the words "grá mo chroí", a look of intense sadness yet prospective happiness comes over Mary Kate's lovely face. Suddenly she feels sorry for Sean and for the hard time she and her brother have given him. Then she smiles as if suddenly realising she is deeply in love with the man she has married. She jumps up excitedly and readjusts the candlestick on the spinet and, like a little girl playing house, dusts the table with her apron. She looks around proudly at her possessions adorning the fine dwelling that her husband has provided her with, before rushing out of the studio cottage into the garden of the cottage in the Irish countryside. It comes as a shock to learn that very nearly twenty minutes of screen time have passed without Ireland being seen, because all of the action since the couple walked hand in hand through the fields has taken place in the studios.

1:2.

The rose garden

Sean is digging in the little square rose garden about fifty yards south-east of White O'Morn (**Location 4H**). With the usual cigarette in his mouth and wearing his traditional Irish-American farming outfit, he is finding the going tough. As Mary Kate runs gaily towards him, he digs up a large rock and throws it away left-handed, remarking in truth, "Now I know why you have so many rock walls in this country." To his left is a traditional Irish basket he is probably using to keep his rose cuttings in.

As he turns to face her, the two of them are shown together in glorious, glorious colour – a scene with superb composition. Now, however, a close-up of a rose-bush is seen – in the background *Innisfree* is being played lushly and, almost imperceptibly, a church bell is pealing.

The ever-practical Mary Kate Thornton begins to chide him with her hands on her hips.

"Roses," she asks him, "are you planting roses?"

"Yeah," he replies casually – doesn't Mary Kate know that one of the main reasons he has come back to Ireland is to plant roses and relive his mother's dreams? There are at least two echoes here – the first of his mother's voiceover when he first saw the cottage, and the second of the way he stormed out of the Danaher house throwing aside his bunch of roses when his overtures were rejected. Ah, those Danahers are a hard-hearted, rose-hating people!

"Fine farmer you are," she continues to scold him. "Not a turnip or a cabbage or a potato round the place." This was changed from the original line, but if a local script consultant had been employed – and throughout *The Quiet Man* could have done with one – he would probably have had Mary Kate say, "Not a turnip, or a head of cabbage or a spud."

"Or children," adds Sean very nastily – this is below the belt and he knows it. Anyway, what does he expect? The couple have been married only a couple of days – maybe Sean feels that children should appear on an American-style production line.

At this, the cock crows, quite a deliberate symbol of betrayal on the director's part, and Mary Kate, hurt to the quick, sits down on the bank. This cruel line too was an afterthought added at the time of shooting.

"Sorry," drawls Sean lamely as Mary Kate looks in despair at the ground.

The church bell has now stopped ringing – it has rung eighteen times in the pattern 3–3–3–9, the traditional peal of the Angelus calling the faithful to prayer twice a day, usually at noon and at six in the evening. This is quite a deliberate insertion by Ford who was very fond of religious symbolism – he probably thought it would never be noticed, but now it has. From the bright sunlight and the angle of the shadows it appears that it is the Angelus at noon that is ringing.

But Mary Kate is not going to let Sean's tactless remark ruin her happy mood. She forgives him on the spot, perhaps conscious of how hurt he is at their current impasse.

"Well, I suppose they will make a very fine display around the cottage," she concedes in a gentle voice. "It is a pretty cottage isn't it?" she adds, repeating a line she had used earlier, as if to reassure herself – but of course that was in reference to the studio cottage and maybe it had to be said again in case the Little People who lived around the Irish cottage got to hear about it and in their jealousy wrecked the place!

"I think so," Sean agrees as he picks a little daisy and gently hands it to her in a touching act of floration. She presses this little fertility symbol to her breast and looks uncomfortably first towards him and then away from him. The green, white and gold daisy may also be a symbol of the Irish Tricolour.

With their relationship cemented just a little, Mary Kate swings her red petticoat over the bank at the edge of the rose garden and announces her plans to turn Sean into a proper farmer.

Unfortunately, as Maureen swings her legs over the edge of the rose garden the heel of her shoe accidentally catches Duke's right hand on the very sensitive area between the nail and the knuckle. He winces and flexes his fingers, but like a true professional he carries on with the scene as if nothing has happened. Some viewers claim they can see blood on Duke's fingers when he later raises his hand to the handle of the spade. Naturally, both Maureen and Duke expected a retake from Ford when the details were explained, but none was forthcoming from the hard-as-nails taskmaster!

"Well, let's see now," she says smiling enthusiastically. "We'll need a plough and a cultivator and seed for planting and about that horse for the ploughing, we could sell that black hunter of yours."

"I'll buy another horse for the ploughing," says Sean generously, but then another thought strikes him – "Or why not a tractor?" he suggests to her. But Mary Kate will have none of it.

"Oh, a tractor," she says contemptuously. "Nasty smelly things, and besides they're an awful price. With a horse you get other advantages."

"Yeah, for the roses," smiles Sean, pointing in the direction of the flowers, and echoing the earlier line of Missus Playfair.

"Roses again," she scolds him playfully as they come closer together in feeling.

Then Mary Kate has a suggestion. "You…" she begins and then pauses to choose her words more carefully. "We could do our shopping in Castletown," she suggests, "and if we put a good foot under us, we could be there and back by suppertime."

"Five miles?" he scoffs, but when she replies, "Well, that's just a good…" he finishes "…stretch of the legs." Clearly this is a standing joke between them and bodes well for the future but it does point out a fundamental

difference between the foot-based Irish society of the 1920s and an American culture already firmly wedded to the automobile.

Actually, this reference to five miles being just a good stretch of the legs is meant to be an echo of a deleted line spoken by Malouney in the opening scene at Castletown Station: "Inisfree? Oh that'd be five miles and a half over … a good stretch of the legs."

For a few moments there is silence between them during which the background music changes from the sombre *Innisfree* to the more playful *Kerry Dances*, indicating a change of mood.

"All right," he tells her, "get on your walking shoes," and she turns to him agreeably and says, "I'll be a minute." As she heads for the cottage, Sean gives her a playful but full-blooded slap on the rump cowboy-style and we can see why Ford referred to *The Quiet Man* as "A Western shot in Ireland". Mary Kate gives a shriek and then a throaty laugh as her bright-red petticoat flashes across the screen. Then she runs towards the cottage, this time by the direct route, glancing back to check that her husband is real.

Inside the studio cottage Mary Kate changes into her best going-to-town clothes and puts on her traditional Aran cap before the mirror, but as she is putting on her jacket she suddenly hears a loud honking sound. Puzzled, she ignores it and continues dressing but then she hears it again. The sound is such that Harpo Marx could easily have arrived in Inisfree, and Mary Kate rushes out the cottage door to see where all the commotion is coming from. She sees Sean sitting proudly holding the reins of a glistening trap to which his horse has been hitched.

"So you're not a woman to be honked at, hah?" he mocks her, echoing her remarks during the courting scene.

"Why, it's beautiful," she responds, visibly impressed. "Did you ever see such a…why, it looks like it could fly!"

"It's only one horsepower," says Sean with a sweeping gesture of his hand, "but it's all yours."

"Mine?" asks Mary Kate in amazement, putting her hand on her breast in characteristic pose, as if there were dozens of people Sean might have bestowed this gift upon.

"Sure," says Sean. "Think you can drive it?"

"Hold onto your hat," says Mary Kate laughingly as she jumps into the trap and takes the reins.

This supposedly outdoor scene was shot in the studio and one wonders why. The horse and the trap were available at the real White O'Morn, but Ford resorted to a backdrop of the scene rather than show the scene itself. Perhaps the reason was that he needed the illusion of Mary Kate emerging from the cottage where the inside was clearly visible, because we never see any of the inside of the Irish cottage. Incidentally, Mary Kate steps into the trap and leaves her front door wide open while they speed off to town – it was traditional in rural Ireland to leave doors open because the crime rate was so low, but that applied only when people were in the house and certainly not when the entire family was away on a shopping trip!

A few awkward questions could very well be asked here. How did Sean manage to dress in his going-to-town outfit so quickly? Where did he dress and where did he keep his clothes? Where had he concealed the trap and why hadn't the alert Mary Kate noticed anything? But never mind – *The Quiet Man* is a romantic fairytale and not a detective story.

With skilful editing, the trap moves from the yard of the studio cottage to the laneway leading down from the Irish cottage and crosses the little river beside the stepping stones. As they set out for their shopping trip in Castletown, Mary Kate gives a few honks on the horn, maybe to let the neighbours know that the Thorntons have acquired a posh new mode of transport. In the background is the towering corrie of Knockagussy, and as the trap goes out of shot we get a glimpse of the lovely old Teernakill bridge on the main road.

Next there is a short studio shot with a backdrop of the Irish countryside while the couple look at each other and smile and Sean gives a few more honks on the horn. Maureen O'Hara and the Duke seem to be enjoying themselves enormously in this scene, carried along by *The Kerry Dances*. As usual, Ford uses the opportunity to show off some spectacular Irish scenery. Indeed, Nugent notes:

"I think this could be a helluva gay little chunk of picture if you have time for it and prolong this one little stretch of honeymoon mood."

There were of course proposals for some slapstick scenes here, such as knocking Sergeant Hanan off his bicycle, but these were not included in the final cut.

The first place we see is the road separating the two halves of Pollacappul Lough on the way from Leenane to Clifden in County Galway **(Location 15B)**. To the left of this narrow neck of land, but out of shot, is one of the most sublime views in the world – that of Kylemore Abbey, set like a gem against the 1600-foot-high Doughruagh mountain, but again perhaps Ford felt this beautiful building, now one of Ireland's premier tourist attractions, smacked too much of grandeur (it was built by an Englishman for his wife!) and the world of aristocracy. Instead, all we get is a splendid view of Pollacappul Lough as the trap is driven across the little metal bridge, now vanished and replaced by a stone one. This location is about a mile away from the place where Sean and Mary Kate rode their tandem downhill through the trees.

Doubles Mary Maguire and Bill Maguire

5:00

Approach to Clifden

This scene was shot by the second unit and Wayne and O'Hara were not present. Their places were taken by doubles Bill Maguire and Etta Vaughan but the camera never gets close enough to give the game away. Indeed, Bill Maguire's sister Mary Maguire was all set to play this scene when Etta Vaughan showed up. The camera was placed on a little hillock overlooking the bridge and the scene is a very joyous one as the couple trot along to the music of *The Kerry Dances*. The background hills behind the lakes are the Twelve Pins of Connemara from yet another angle.

Next, the couple, with Etta Vaughan and Bill Maguire still doubling, are seen coming along the Ballyconnelly road at Clifden **(Location 5B)** past the picturesque Owenglin River, no relation to Owen Glynn. The camera was placed on the bridge and this is a beautifully composed scene of the type not available in Cong, so the second unit, driven by Jack Murphy, now owner of Cohan's pub, made its way in the station wagon to Clifden masquerading as Castletown. As the church bell rings out, the trap is driven around the corner through a little group of people and past a man leading a little black donkey – shades of Padraig O'Conaire.

1:26:30

Now the couple have arrived in Castletown proper. The northern end of the village of Cong **(Location 7)** serves as Castletown, presumably the bigger village, if only because of its railway station, while the southern end of Cong, where Cohan's is situated, serves as Inisfree. It is "fair day" or market day in

Castletown where cattle and sheep are bought and sold by local farmers on the street. This rather messy practice no longer prevails and such sales now take place in a purpose-built mart.

This was the last scene of *The Quiet Man* to be filmed in Ireland. During the fine weather of the summer of 1951 in the West of Ireland, Ford waited several days for rain to come but, as the sunshine continued, he finally decided to hose down the streets and drive in the cattle. In the little square of Cong we see the cattle milling about being controlled by men with sticks. In the background is O'Connor's grocery store with its advertisement for Lyons Tea prominent in the window. The proprietor painted the name of his mother, Emily O'Connor, on the shopfront specially for the occasion. As Sean and Mary Kate come to a halt in the middle of the action, several extras are prominent – among them Robert Foy who drove the cart containing Sean's bed across the river, and the man with the hat and glasses is John Gibbons who made the windows of the cottage. And in front of Curran's pub **(Location 7C)**, now occupied by Ryan's excellent hotel, stands Red Will Danaher surrounded by other cattle jobbers with whom he is doing business.

1:2

Ford in the Director's chair outside Curran's

"You take care of that, Feeney," says Red Will, smiling for a change as he puts a big wad of notes into his wallet and hands it over to his second in command. Red Will then spits on his hand, echoing his sister's action when sealing the bargain with Michaeleen. Then he allows the buyer, played by extra Pat Conroy, to slap his hand before shaking hands with him and doing the same with his assistant.

We recall that in one of Ford's early films *The Shamrock Handicap* (1926) he felt obliged to include a subtitle to explain away the disgusting custom of spitting – in Ireland, spitting on the palm and shaking hands binds a sale.

"Now then," says Red Will affably, "let's have another pint, and I'm buying this one."

"High time," mumbles Feeney, half under his breath. Feeney is the only one of the company without a drink and it does not seem to have occurred to Red Will that he might like a drink or even deserve one.

"What's that?" asks Red Will, hardly able to believe his ears.

"I said that's fine, Squire, fine, fine," replies Feeney, who as usual is as slippery as a bucket of eels, managing to pull back from the brink of one of his few moments of open defiance in the movie.

Red Will has his doubts, expressed in the grunts "Ooh, oh," but he has other more important things on his mind, so he lets it pass for the moment. Holding his pint glass in a most peculiar manner, certainly not customary in Ireland, he proposes a toast to the buyers. "Good health to you all," he says as he takes a long draught of the black stuff. Poor Feeney still remains drinkless.

Meanwhile, Mary Kate, at **Location 7H**, which in reality is facing in the opposite direction away from where Red Will is, has observed the scene.

"Look," she says excitedly to her husband, "he's sold the cross-breds."

"The what?" asks Sean, to whom farming is still something of a mystery. (A cross-bred is an animal not of pure pedigree – a mixture of two breeds, a bit like Sean himself!)

"The sheep he's been planning on," explains Mary Kate.

In fact, no sheep have been seen yet at the fair, but that situation will be remedied in a moment. Sean smiles at his wife's observation, little knowing what is to come and says merely, "Oh."

"Hurry," says Mary Kate, "now is a good time to ask him. Well, go on, go on," she urges him, pushing him in the chest.

"Ask him what?" says Sean, still a bit mystified.

"About my money," explains Mary Kate, just a little bit annoyed at his density. "He can't say he hasn't got it with him now," she adds with irrefutable logic.

"Can't you get it through your head," says Sean still patient, "that I didn't marry you for your fortune? I don't give a hang about the money."

"But he does," says Mary Kate sharply, "and that's the whole point of it. Now will you go and ask him?"

Here Mary Kate shows that she doesn't give a hang about the money either and is more interested in putting her brother in his place and having her husband prove his virility in public, before they settle down to a happily married life.

"No," Sean tells her, "why shame ourselves?" as he gets out and goes to the other side of the ponytrap. But Mary Kate's temper is rising – that red head of hers is no lie.

"Shame?" she says bitterly. "The shame's on you, not on me – oh, on me too if I've married a coward."

Now we see the sheep at last, but maybe chickens would have been more appropriate, although Sean's temper is rising too.

"Is that what you think of me?" he asks her. At this stage perhaps it is appropriate to ask why Sean had not told Mary Kate all about his boxing career and its tragic end before they were married – surely a case of deception that could lead only to trouble.

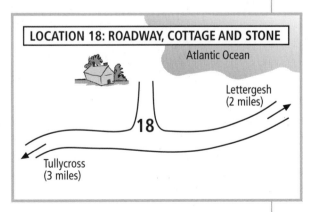

LOCATION 18: ROADWAY, COTTAGE AND STONE

Atlantic Ocean

Lettergesh (2 miles)

18

Tullycross (3 miles)

"What else if you let him rob me out of my money," she continues, with the temperature rising all the time.

The word "money" to Sean is like a red rag to a bull. In the ring he killed a man for money; money was at the centre of his land dispute with Red Will Danaher; and now money is coming between himself and Mary Kate.

"Money," he says angrily, "I'm sick of the talk of it. Is that all you Danahers ever think about, money?"

1:28:00

Mary Kate's escape route from Clifden

With fire in her eyes, Mary Kate gives him no answer but takes the buggy whip in her hand as if to strike him. However, she brings the whip down with great force on the horse's back and he takes off like a shot, leaving Sean standing in the centre of Castletown, a forlorn figure publicly humiliated by his wife. It is interesting to note that he still refers to Mary Kate as one of "you Danahers", indicating that he does not regard himself and his wife as a properly married couple. Not for the first time, Sean feels alienated – an innocent American who has blundered into a complex society whose ways he just does not understand.

He stands looking ruefully after the departing Mary Kate and proceeds to walk slowly in the direction she has gone.

In the original script he is meant to run after her calling, "Mary Kate, come back here," while Danaher, Feeney and several others laugh and jeer at him. But this scene was not shown because maybe Ford realised that certain scenes and emotions are sometimes better imagined than seen.

Next we see Mary Kate driving the trap home at a furious rate, but here Etta Vaughan is again doubling for Maureen O'Hara. This scene was shot in Clifden (**Location 5C**) with the camera placed on the bridge in precisely the same position as that for **Location 5B**, but turned in the opposite direction so as to seem like a completely new scene – an old trick of Ford's. The trap rushes past the lovely Ivy Lodge, on a road heading off in a completely different direction from the one by which they entered the town. As Mary Kate trots off into the distance, we realise that the happy *Kerry Dances* background music has been replaced by the more ominous *Rakes of Mallow*, the tune played when Sean's train entered the station. This echo reminds us that Mary Kate too has entered a new world – a world of open conflict with her husband.

1:2

Sean now has to walk all the way home – quite a good stretch of the legs. First we see him venting his spleen on the stones of a little laneway about a mile south of Lettergesh beach where the horse race took place (**Location 18**). We note the Duke's fine follow-through on the stone kick, reminding us that he did once star as a college footballer. When he reaches the top of the lane, he looks both left and right as if he literally does not know which way to turn in this strange country. Cinematically, he makes the right decision – he turns north up the hill by the turf-stack, towards Killary Harbour and the towering Mweelrea mountain. The laneway and the cottage near the sea look exactly the same today as they did fifty years ago, right down to the high hedges on either side.

Next we see Sean at Carrowgarriff (**Location 10H**) crossing over the wall into a field. Ironically this is the very field where he and Mary Kate romped together during their courtship, but you would never know unless you had been told. Just a few yards to the left, but of course out of shot, is the gap in the wall where Mary Kate sat so enticingly – in fact, this

Which way to turn?

field is shot from four different angles with four different backgrounds and made to appear like four different places!

White O'Morn lies at the base of the hills seen in the background, so technically Sean is at the moment walking away from home! He crosses the wall into the field, picks up a stick and breaks it in anger over his knee before throwing half away. Sticks play an important role in *The Quiet Man* from now on – mostly as a symbol to express the domination of husband over wife. In fact, none of this walk home of Sean's was in the original script and Ford used it as just another opportunity to show off some Irish scenery.

0:00

In the meantime, Mary Kate is repentant but decides to express her sorrow for her behaviour to Father Lonergan in the confessional rather than make up with Sean – a common enough reaction. The original script envisaged an indoor confessional scene in St Anselm's Chapel at twilight, but as usual, any outdoor scene filmed in Cong beats any Hollywood studio scene all ends up.

The location chosen for this outdoor confessional scene was the Cong river **(Location 1H)** not far from where Sean and Mary Kate walked along the bank during the courtship scene. As Mary Kate arrives at the riverbank in her ponytrap, Father Lonergan is busy at his favourite recreation – fishing. Ward Bond was a keen angler and did indeed land several fish in Cong during the shooting of *The Quiet Man*. Indeed, in 1994, at that very spot,

the author witnessed a fine salmon being landed, so not everything in the movie is fiction!

Mary Kate realises she must tread warily because the ultimate sin would be to come between Father Lonergan and his fishing. She sees him walking calmly along the bank, casting his line upon the waters, a man perfectly at peace with himself. In the background is the bridge from County Mayo to Ashford Castle **(Location 1C)**, but as usual the actual castle itself is not seen on the screen.

Wiping the tears of remorse from her eyes, Mary Kate decides to risk disturbing the priest's tranquillity, so putting her rug aside she jumps down from the trap and creeps slowly to the tree on the bank of the river. So intense is the priest's concentration that he does not notice her at all, but she looks back towards her trap to make sure they are alone before running up to his side to attract his attention.

"Father, could I see you about…" she starts, but he has only one thing on his mind.

"Quiet," he says to her rudely. "See that, see milter behind that rock, ah, he's the king of all salmon, he's winking at me. I've been trying to get this one for ten years. There he is, there he is."

1:29:30

There is a strong suggestion here of the Irish legend of the Salmon of Knowledge. The old sage and teacher Finegas the Bard lived on the banks of the river Boyne a little north of where Dublin is now. In the river lived the Salmon of Knowledge whose flesh would confer on the first person who tasted it universal knowledge. For many years Finegas had tried in vain to catch the fish, but finally it was caught in the company of his pupil Fionn MacCumhaill. His master ordered him to cook the salmon on a spit but under no circumstances to eat any of it. The obedient pupil did as he was told, but as he was turning the salmon on its spit he touched it with his thumb to see if it was cooked. The contact burned his thumb, so he instinctively put it in his mouth to ease the pain, thereby inadvertently tasting the flesh of the fish. Thus it was Fionn, and not his master, who acquired universal knowledge, and in later years, when he became leader of the Fenians, if asked any question, all he had to do to obtain an answer was to put his thumb in his mouth.

Given that universal knowledge may be at stake, Mary Kate is fighting a losing battle to gain Father Lonergan's attention, but she persists nevertheless.

"Father, it's very important," she tells him. "I've got to talk to you, Father. It's…but Father, I've got to talk to you, Father, it's important, it's about…it's about my husband and myself."

Now we see them from the reverse angle and there is growing frustration on the priest's face as he turns his attention away from the fish, if only partially, and listens to her with half an ear. With a deep sigh he begins to hear her confession but without any eye contact with her whatsoever, because his gaze is still on his line in the water.

"Father, I…I…" begins Mary Kate, but she is too shy to say the words she wants to say, so, overcome with emotion, she puts her scarf to her mouth, unable to continue for weeping.

"You see…" she begins again, but breaks down once more.

1:30:00

"Father, could I…could I tell you in the Irish?" she asks him.

There is a touch of stage-Irishry here – it would have been more natural to say, "Could I tell you in Irish?"

"Ah, sea, sea, sea, sea," says the priest, meaning "Yes, yes, yes, yes" – possibly the only word of Irish that Ward Bond of Red Indian descent knew.

This introduction of Irish or Gaelic was a very clever device on Ford's part, though it was not intended in the original script. Not alone does it introduce an element of mystery into the proceedings but it also gets around any censorship difficulties that might have arisen because of the delicacy of the subject matter. Ford spoke just a little Irish, but liked to give the impression that he was fluent in the language. There is one delicious story that when he received the Medal of Freedom from Richard Nixon he impressed everyone at the dinner by making his acceptance speech in

Irish. However, the words he actually spoke were just those of the Lord's Prayer in Irish! But he was quite safe – those who didn't know were impressed and those who did wouldn't give him away!

Mary Kate continues: "Níor lig mé m'fear chéile isteach i mo leaba liom aréir. Chuir me faoi ndeara dhó codladh i…i…i mála codlata, mála codlata!"

"Mála codlata," echoes Father Lonergan. "Céard é sin bag?"

(Roughly translated, this means: "I didn't allow my husband into my bed last night. I forced him to sleep in… in… in a sleeping bag, a sleeping bag!" "A codlata bag," says the priest. "What kind of bag is that?")

"A sleeping bag, Father," she tells him coyly in English. "With buttons," she adds as she suggestively fingers the buttons of her blouse, before lapsing into sobs again and covering her mouth while waiting for the priest's reaction.

1:3◦

"Mo spré," she continues, "níor throid sé ar a shon – an peaca é?" ("My fortune, he didn't fight for it – is it a sin?")

Presumably Mary Kate is asking him if her behaviour over her husband's marital rights is to be considered sinful and not his disinclination to fight for her dowry. The mention of the fighting and the dowry are by way of explanation and justification for her actions.

Father Lonergan is furious, mostly because his fishing has been interrupted over what he considers is a trivial incident and he lets Mary Kate know his feelings in no uncertain terms.

"Woman," he tells her angrily, "Ireland may be a poor country, God help us, but here a married man sleeps in a bed and not in a bag, and for your own good I'll tell you a thing…"

And now the real action begins – Father Lonergan has a bite! The confession is forgotten by both parties as the priest shouts, "Halt, halt, there he is," as he lets out his line. Mary Kate too puts first things first and rushes about shouting incoherent encouragement which is drowned by the priest's raucous cries. In reality of course there was no bite – just local man Jim Morrin, the extra already seen thatching the roof of White O'Morn, pulling tightly on the line, out of shot.

"Hold it," continues the priest excitedly, "this is the one I've been waiting for, for ten long years," as Mary Kate runs about shouting helpfully, "Keep his head up, keep his head up."

"There's that cutie," says Father Lonergan now in a frenzy of excitement. "That's the man, that's the man."

"Keep his head up, Father," she encourages him. "Get a tight line."

"Tight line," he echoes, now almost totally out of control both physically and verbally as he moves deeper and deeper into the water.

"I've got you, I've got you," he roars, holding on to his hat, now knee deep in the river. "I've got him, a tight line it is, I've got him."

"Keep his head up, keep his head up," shouts Mary Kate from the bank rather repetitively.

"Humph, his head is up," he roars back. "Will you get the gaff?"

The gaff is a barbed fishing spear – a stick with an iron hook for landing large fish, so Father Lonergan must feel the fish is tired of fighting and is ready to give up. This of course is most unlikely after such a short struggle.

As Mary Kate runs for the gaff, an unauthorised dog, one of the many in *The Quiet Man*, appears on the bank of the river, barking furiously in the general confusion. The dog actually belonged to Jim Morrin, the man holding the line in the middle of the river, and perhaps he had come just to admire his master's off-camera action. Ford good-humouredly left the dog in and even added a little barking as a sound effect.

"For ten years I've...ten years I've...I said get the gaff, woman, get the gaff," shouts the manic priest, totally out of control.

Maybe Mary Kate is confused, but instead of the gaff she brings just a net designed for a much later stage in the proceedings. She too feels that the fish has given up the struggle because she shouts, "Oh, you've got him, you've got him, Father," but forgetting herself, she adds, "Well, keep his head up, you fool." Then realising that she has spoken irreverently to a clerical gentleman, she quickly covers up her mouth, almost too quickly.

This incident in *The Quiet Man* was perhaps inspired by the story of the Indian rajah fishing in the West of Ireland with his gillie. When the rajah hooked a fish, the gillie exhorted him as follows:

"Play him, your Worship, give him more line, your Highness, reel him in, your Holiness, he's nearly there, your Eminence; ah, you've lost him, you dark foreign bastard."

The moral seems to be that when the chance of landing a fish is missed, respect for authority is the first casualty.

The priest is now in very deep water shouting like a lunatic, "Get the gaff, get the gaff, woman," when suddenly the line snaps and the fish gets away. As he stands in the river staring up at his broken line, all he can say is, "Aah, God help us."

It is of course possible to read too much into a director's intentions, but one wonders if the continued use of the phrase "God help us" is in any way connected with the sarcastic motto of County Mayo, in whose river border the priest is standing – "Mayo, God help us". The water in the Cong River is, by the way, very cold, emerging from underground caverns.

Mary Kate has the good sense to realise that from time immemorial women invariably become the scapegoats for men's misfortunes, whether it is expulsion from Eden or an escaped salmon. With a knowing "Ooh" she drops the net and rushes away from the scene as fast as she can. Meanwhile, Father Lonergan throws his rod into the river with great force to vent his anger, saying as he does, "Sleeping bag, is it?" But he retrieves his rod before he leaves realising as a true fisherman that he will fight that fish another day – not for nothing is he called Peter after the apostle fisherman. It is ironic that modern research strongly suggests that the presence of human female sex hormones definitely seems to attract fish, so maybe Mary Kate was the reason why the salmon took the bait in the first place.

Incidentally, Maureen O'Hara relates, in connection with the previous scene, that Ford asked her what she thought of shooting the confession scene by the river. "Let me write it down," she said. So she wrote it down in longhand and gave it to him to read. He looked at it, tore it up into little bits and threw it in the wastepaper basket. That's the scene they shot in *The Quiet Man* – it was acceptable as long as Ford felt that the original idea had come from him.

Meanwhile, Sean is still walking home, without the benefit of transport. With the northern shore of Lough Corrib in the background, he approaches a hillside wall **(Location 10I)** which is, surprise, surprise, the very wall that Mary Kate sat on earlier in the movie, and just a few yards away from Location 10D where he stepped over the roadside wall.

In the background in the lake inlet we can see the little island fortress of Caislean Na Circe (Hen's Castle), anglicised as Castle Kirke. Like many ruins in the West of Ireland, it has an interesting legend connected with it. It was built one night by a local witch who gave to a chieftain called O'Flaherty a magic hen and told him to guard it well, for as long as the hen lived, he would never want for food even in the longest siege. Stranded on the island with the hen, he lived happily for a time eating just eggs, but one day he fancied some meat, so he killed and ate the hen. The very next day two men arrived on the island, killed O'Flaherty and left the castle in the rather flattened condition seen in *The Quiet Man*. Maybe John Ford planned to film that story some time too.

Sean first takes a stone from the ground and hurls it at the wall to let off steam, echoing his hurling a stone through the window in the cottage. Then he sits on the very gap where Mary Kate sat so alluringly, but unless one visits the location it is virtually impossible to tell that it is the same spot. With a sombre and bass *Rakes of Mallow* playing in the background, he sits down, one suspects to give us an even better view of Castle Kirke. In close-up, he strikes a

Time out at Ashford

Ashford Castle

match on a rock and lights a cigarette from which he takes just one pull before throwing it away with some force. He walks out of shot leaving the stones on the wall exactly as they are today. To the left, we see the steep hill which necessitated all the camera trickery during the courting scene because it was too steep for the couple to run down.

We next see him walking in the Ashford Deerpark **(Location 6E)** with the castle towers plainly visible through the trees. This is a very beautiful scene visually, and legend has it that Ford and his party were passing by the field

1:3

when the director saw the flock of birds on the grass and realised the cinematic possibilities at once. Duke Wayne was told to go into the field and walk across it until the birds took flight in a piece of visual poetry. Fact or fiction? It's hard to tell, but it has become yet another part of *Quiet Man* lore.

It is now later in the evening. In a studio scene all the usual suspects are gathered in Cohan's pub – Glynn, Michaeleen Oge Flynn, Pat Cohan himself and Hugh Forbes are standing by the counter drinking pints of black stuff. A sing-song is in progress, during which Michaeleen attempts to light a cigar on the bar candle and nearly burns his face off in the process. The song being sung is *Galway Bay* and, consistent with the theme of the movie, it concerns the dreams of an emigrant who wants to return to his native place. In many ways it represents Ford's own dreams and ambitions. The sentimental words and beautiful melody are both by Dr Arthur Colahan. Here they are in full, though they are not enhanced by Pat Cohan's excruciating falsetto.

If you ever go across the sea to Ireland
Then maybe at the closing of your day,
You will sit and watch the moon rise over Claddagh
And watch the barefoot garsuns as they play.

Just to hear again the ripple of a trout stream
The women in the meadows making hay
And to sit beside a turf fire in the cabin
And see the sun go down on Galway Bay.

For the breezes blowing o'er the seas from Ireland
Are perfumed by the heather as they blow
And the women in the uplands digging praties
Speak a language that the stranger does not know.

For the strangers came and tried to teach us their way
They scorned us just for being what we are

But they might as well go chasing after moonbeams
Or light a penny candle from a star.

And if there's going to be a life hereafter
And somehow I am sure there's going to be
I will ask my God to let me make my heaven
In that dear land across the Irish Sea.

The melody is both beautiful and distinctive – and being recorded by Bing Crosby (who also recorded *The Isle of Innisfree*) helped its international popularity too. Incidentally, it is only in the words of this song that the name of Ford's beloved county "Galway" is mentioned in *The Quiet Man*.

Red Will Danaher and Feeney are drinking at the bar too, though not taking part in the singing of course. Feeney has a beautifully balanced cigarette butt stuck in the corner of his mouth, and Pat Cohan contributes to the sentimental atmosphere by putting his bowler hat over his heart at the mention of the sacred name of "Galway". All in all, it is a cosy and relaxed scene, but the music abruptly stops as Sean suddenly enters, slamming the bar door behind him. There is a tense silence as the drinkers turn in his direction and now we can see Dermot Fahy on the left of the screen.

"Ah, you're just in time to stand me a drink," says Michaeleen facetiously.

"Join us, Sean," says Forbes invitingly, and "You will have a drink," pleads Owen Glynn.

But Sean has other things on his mind. "No thanks," he says gruffly, walking past his friends and over to where Red Will and Feeney are standing – there is no evidence that Feeney's lord and master has bought a drink for him.

"I want to talk to you in private," Sean says to Danaher, but the big fellow continues drinking before he answers.

"If there's anything you've got to say to me," he retorts at last putting down his glass, "say it here."

"I'd rather talk to you in private," repeats Sean quietly, his temper still under control.

"Well, what's the matter, you're among friends," Danaher taunts him. "They fought for you once didn't they? Maybe they'll fight for you again!"

Behind Danaher's head is a picture of a boxer in classic pose as if to emphasise his superior position.

"I'm not asking anybody to do my fighting for me," says Sean humbly.

"Oh, ha, ha, ha," laughs Red Will, "so you're willing to do your own, are ye?"

"You know what I came for," says Sean.

"I do," says Red Will with a scowl, "but I just want to hear you ask for it. Just ask for it, Yank, and you'll be chewing your teeth for a week."

The use of the word "Yank" here is contemptuous. Danaher believes that Irish-Americans are sissies, descendants of people who got out of Ireland when the going was tough, and that he represents the true tough Irishmen who stood their ground. This theme was taken up many years later in Jim Sheridan's movie *The Field* (1990), which in many ways is a darker and gloomier version of *The Quiet Man*.

"You've got twenty pounds on him, Danaher," interjects Forbes.

"And so I have," agrees Red Will. With that he picks up poor Feeney by the scruff of the neck and hurls him against the wall, where he stands almost lifeless, like the puppet that he is. This is a marvellously comic moment, skilfully inserted by Ford in a tense scene, perhaps to show that he, like Sean O'Casey, could blend drama and comedy in a uniquely Irish way.

"How would it be if I put one of me fists in me pocket?" asks Red Will sarcastically, raising his fists and lowering them again.

Then he says to Sean, raising his fists for a second time, "Go on, right or left, now you choose, now go on; go on, that's fair enough isn't it?"

(The identity of the plump man in the black hat framed between the protagonists in this shot remains a mystery.)

In utter frustration, the seething Sean merely slaps his opponent on the fists, turns his head

and walks out of the bar. His friends are astonished and can interpret his actions only as those of a coward.

"Ha ha ha ha ha," roars Red Will, "the fighting Thorntons," and slaps the bar counter in delight, continuing with guffaws audible to the departing Sean.

In the bar, Michaeleen walks slowly and sadly over to the doorstep, sits down and puts his head in his hands. He is full of despair and all of his schemes have come unstuck. This is the low point of the movie, but one from which the climax will build.

But why did Sean come to Cohan's in the first place at this time? Surely it would have been more logical for him to go home directly after his long stretch of the legs and perhaps make up with Mary Kate. The truth is that a scene was cut here which throws quite a bit of light on the situation. Before he went to Cohan's, Sean was meant to return to the cottage where we, but not Sean, see Mary Kate sitting on the edge of the bed, knees close together, and a frightened expression on her face. However, there is food on the table with a candle burning before it, so maybe things are looking up; but as he turns the knob on the bedroom door and calls her name, she still doesn't speak to him and we are left in doubt as to whether she is hoping the door will open or if she is dreading it. Sean looks from the door towards the fireplace and his scowl returns with full intensity, because he sees the damned sleeping bag stretched out on the floor for him in front of the fire. He glares at the bag, the closed bedroom door and the plate of food, then turns on his heel and slams the door as he leaves the cottage. As Nugent remarks, the gauge is rising but had not yet reached explosion point. Sean then proceeds to the pub to confront Danaher.

This would have constituted a very powerful scene and one wonders why it was not included in the movie. Perhaps it was just too powerful, too suggestive and spelled out the marital difficulties between Mary Kate and Sean too explicitly, and Ford felt that the more left to the imagination the better. In addition, he was

1:34:00

working within fairly stringent censorship laws in the United States and may just have been playing it safe.

However, the cut scene is in very sharp contrast with the next scene which is among the longest and most tedious in the entire movie. In this scene, set in the Playfairs' house, there seem to be two conflicting objectives. The first, and possibly the more serious of the two, is a plea for understanding the Anglo-Irish Protestant community whose numbers were seriously declining since Irish independence – in this context the phrase "We are Irish too" is very significant. The second objective is a quite blatant send-up of that very same Anglo-Irish Protestant community. It is almost as if *The Quiet Man* is parading its own ambivalence towards the subject in the most public way possible. Incredibly, the scene lasts almost five minutes of screen time and, while it does help to fill in some details about Sean's past and Mister Playfair's present situation, it could have benefited from a good deal of editing.

We see the Reverend Mister Playfair at night in his study, described as "half study for a theologian, half den for a sporting man". Books line the walls but there are sculling oars, cricket bats, sporting trophies and other memorabilia of his youth too. Prominently seen too is a tall pulpit-like reading-stand on which rests a large leather volume, which could be a theological work, but which in reality is Playfair's sports scrapbook.

As the scene opens, the reverend gentleman is seated, just like his real-life brother Barry Fitzgerald whom we have left seated in the previous scene. But unlike Michaeleen, Mister Playfair hasn't got a care in the world and is concentrating with all his might on a game of tiddlywinks – just about the most ludicrous game imaginable under the circumstances. While the Catholic priest is lustily fighting with a huge fish on the river, his Church of Ireland counterpart is busily engaged in propelling little counters into a cup. Tiddling like an expert, he smilingly sinks his last wink into the cup –

clearly, he has been playing the game with his wife, and the implication is that they have long abandoned what Sean has on his mind. Missus Playfair has answered the door and shown in their visitor Sean Thornton, now cooled off a little from his heady encounter with Danaher in Cohan's.

1:34:30

"It was Mister Thornton, Cyril," she tells him, "so I brought him in," the implication being that not everybody is fortunate enough to be invited into the Playfair inner sanctum.

"Bless my soul," says Playfair, getting to his feet, "come in, sit down." With this mild expression of surprise, he welcomes Sean by shaking his hand vigorously.

"Have you tiddled your last wink, Cyril?" she asks him with no hint of embarrassment as Sean stands between them sheepishly.

"I have," answers Cyril.

"No cheating?" she asks him cheekily.

"I have not," he answers indignantly (what a question to ask a Playfair!) and in this childlike exchange there is surely a strong element of satire, especially in the benign smile his wife flashes at his indignation. Actually, the portrayal here of the class to which the Playfairs belong is quite subtle as well as cruelly hitting the mark.

Sean is clearly uncomfortable, but the Playfairs make no concessions to intruders into their cosy world. Things are made only worse when Playfair puts the ultimate question to an ex-boxer, "Do you play tiddlywinks?"

"No, I ah…" mumbles Sean in reply, feeling that he has landed on yet another alien planet and continues, "maybe I shouldn't have butted in like this," awkwardly fingering his cap.

"Nonsense," says the tactless Missus Playfair, and compounds the situation by asking Sean: "How is your lovely bride?"

"Fine," answers Sean very hesitantly and at long last the penny drops with Playfair – Sean has come for a man-to-man talk and it is time for the lady to depart.

"Elizabeth," he orders her, "say goodnight to Mister Thornton."

1:35:00

"But he's only just come," she protests, still not comprehending the situation, but suddenly she too twigs. "Oh, oh, very well, good night, Mister Thornton," she says, shaking hands with him.

"Good night," says the relieved Sean smiling gratefully.

"Good night, Cyril," she says then and, as he responds with "Good night, Elizabeth," she kisses him chastely on the forehead and he adds, "Pleasant dreams."

Sean looks at the little loving drama being enacted in front of him perhaps contrasting it in his mind with his own situation.

In *The Rising of the Moon* made by Ford in Ireland in 1957, Eileen Crowe plays the part of the wife of a policeman who has let a reward of £500 slip through his hands by inadvertently letting a condemned prisoner escape. As she kisses her husband good night on the dockside she adds, "I'll have the bed warm for you," definitely not what Missus Playfair would have said!

Frank Nugent's screenplay instructions for this scene are quite explicit:

> She approaches her husband for the
> ceremony of their goodnight kiss and the
> poor man is the picture of embarrassment at
> this public display of their love life. But like
> a well-trained child he lowers his head; she
> places a hand on each temple (this became
> shoulder) and kisses him primly right in the
> centre of the forehead. She waits for
> the rest of the ritual until he says, "Pleasant
> dreams." Completely satisfied now, she
> smiles brightly at Sean and goes out the
> door.

Naturally, being female, she is intensely curious about why Sean is consulting her husband. It is of course ironic that while Mary Kate is consulting Father Lonergan, Sean, supposedly a Catholic, is consulting the Protestant clergyman. The movie's wry comment is that while the priest is interested only in fishing, the rector is interested only in sports and boxing.

Missus Playfair makes one last desperate attempt to remain in the action and perhaps overhear something. Just before she goes out the door she turns and says, "Are you sure there's nothing…?"

"Good night, Elizabeth," says Playfair very firmly and she smiles meekly as she closes the door.

"You're the only one I can level with," says Sean urgently, "and I gotta talk to someone or I'm gonna blow my top."

In the originally intended screenplay, Playfair here cautions Sean silently with an upraised finger and then quickly reopens the door, catching his wife with her ears open.

"No, we will not want any tea," he anticipates her, and when she says, "In that case…" he thunders: "GO TO BED, WOMAN." This time she scuttles off and he locks the door. This scene would have been totally out of character and was wisely not included.

"Danaher, of course," says Playfair to Sean, perhaps relieved that it is not the problems with Mary Kate that he has to deal with.

"Yeah," says Sean and continues, "since you know who I am, or was, you know why I don't want to fight him."

1:35

"Yes," says Playfair, "I was reading about it again this evening," moving over to the big lectern and opening his sports scrapbook.

"Some men collect butterflies," he says as he turns the page, "some stamps; my hobby has always been sports, sporting events."

The classification of all men into those who collect butterflies and stamps on the one hand and those who collect sporting clippings on the other hand is of course yet another dig at the genteel pleasures of a country clergyman, but admittedly even Playfair seems a little embarrassed.

The first page we see briefly has five pictures of boxers and whether they are well-known or obscure is hard to tell. The next page features a boxer in training, but some of the routines are unorthodox to say the least – what looks like rock climbing for example. The next page seems to show preparation for the lighting or filming of a fight – perhaps studio stills were conveniently to hand. Recent information indicates that the scrapbook belonged to former Irish heavyweight boxing champion Martin Thornton, who once fought the British boxer Bruce Woodcock. The photographs were those of his own training sessions and were borrowed by The Quiet Man production team and used in the studio scenes.

Then we come to what Playfair is looking for, so that the audience will more fully understand the dilemma that Sean now finds himself in. For the benefit of the illiterate, Playfair reads out the headline:

TROOPER THORN QUITS RING
Heavyweight challenger hangs up gloves after fatal knockout, vows he will never fight again.

The words "Heavyweight challenger" and "fatal knockout" have been heavily underlined for emphasis. However, what is perhaps more interesting is the text which appears underneath the headlines. It is flashed across the screen for less than ten seconds and of course it was not intended to be read, but with the magic of modern technology it has been possible to decipher it, although only with great difficulty. This is what it says:

Trooper Thorn declares he has quit the ring for good and has hung up his gloves for the last time. Thorn's last fight was a knockout over Tony Gardello and so decisive was Thorn's victory that it will be some time before Tony can resume the fight game. Thorn has come up in the fight game the hard way, and it [will come as a disappointment?] to his many fans that he is retiring from the ring.

Is this a little joke that Ford is playing on the audience, little realising that video technology would some day catch up with him? Tony Gardello is dead, so it certainly will be a long time before he resumes the fight game!

"It's a very understandable reaction," Playfair says as he attempts to console Sean and continues, "Still, the papers all say it was an accident, just one of those things."

"You mean it's just one of those things in the scrapbook," replies Sean. "But not when you carry it around in here," touching his chest and toying nervously with his cap as he turns away. "Tony Gardello was a good egg," he continues. "Nice little wife and home, couple of kids, clean fighter, but I didn't go in there to out-box him, I went in there to beat his brains out, to drive him into the canvas, to murder him, and that's what I did, for what? A purse, a piece of the gate, lousy money."

All the time, Playfair looks on and listens sympathetically. "And now money is behind your troubles with Danaher," he adds.

"They think I'm afraid to fight him," says Sean sadly, "all the friends I've made here, even my wife."

"Well, aren't you in a way?" says Playfair slyly, suggesting that Sean's fear is more psychological than real.

"Did you ever kill a man?" Sean asks him bluntly and getting no answer, continues, "Well, I have, and all this talk about her big fortune, it's not that important."

The question "Did you ever kill a man?" that Sean asks Playfair is yet another in-joke that Ford is playing on his audience. In *Drums Along Mohawk* (1939), Arthur Shields plays the part of the preacher and fighter Father Rosenkranz, in John Ford's first feature film in colour. When the Indians capture Joe Boleo (played by Francis Ford) and are about to burn him to death in a cart of straw outside the fort, Rosenkranz decides that he will shoot Boleo to save him from a slow and painful death. Later, however, he suffers from extreme remorse and sits staring into space repeating endlessly "I killed a man".

At this stage one might again wonder why Sean never told his prospective wife either about his boxing career or the man he killed in the ring. Since it was clearly an accident, she would not have held it against him and would understand why he didn't want to fight her brother, but then we would have had no plot to sustain the movie!

Playfair now skilfully tries to reconcile the Irish custom of the bride's fortune with Sean's obvious dislike of money being part of the marriage process.

"Perhaps it is to her," he tells Sean, leafing through his sports scrapbook again. "It must be strange to you," he continues, "from America, but it's an old, old custom, and believe me it's a good custom. The fortune means more to her than just the money."

"Not to me it isn't," says Sean sadly. "It's not worth fighting for."

"Is your wife's love worth fighting for?" Playfair asks in a most unclergymanlike manner.

It is impossible for us not to entertain a suspicion that Playfair, sportsman that he is, wants the big fight to take place no matter what the cost, but maybe deep down he feels that the catharsis of a fight is the only mechanism to resolve the situation.

"I don't know," says Sean. "All I know is I can't fight or won't fight unless I'm mad enough to kill, and if that means losing her, I don't know, maybe she doesn't love me enough."

As they sit down together by the fire, Playfair remarks, "It's a difficult situation, but I think you'll find the right answer in God's good time; and when that time comes, I hope I'll still be here."

"You're not figuring on leaving, are you?" Sean asks him, genuinely concerned.

"It's a possibility," replies Playfair philosophically. "You see, my bishop is coming here tomorrow on his annual visit and I've got such a small congregation, just two or three people at the service. He may transfer me."

"The place wouldn't be the same without you, padre," smiles Sean, his other troubles forgotten for the moment.

"Elizabeth and I just love this place," Playfair muses, leaning towards nostalgia. "We were born here too, you know."

Here Ford is acknowledging that the Anglo-Irish Protestant community is as much part of the rural Irish scene as is the Catholic community, albeit a diminishing one.

"Ah well," continues Playfair, "the Bishop's a good egg, maybe it will be all right." (This is the second good egg in as many minutes in the movie.)

But back to more pressing matters – Playfair changes his tune completely.

"Oh, by the way," he tells Sean, "don't underestimate Danaher. He may be clumsy, but he's got a tremendous right and a jaw of granite."

The die has been cast – although nothing has been mentioned explicitly, both men now realise that Sean has to go through with the fight, come what may.

"I did a little bit of boxing in my time," smiles Playfair by way of explanation.

"Oho," grins Sean, now feeling happier because a resolution to the conflict is in sight, as the reverend gentleman goes to fetch an ancient photograph of himself from a drawer.

As Sean stands up to inspect the many sporting trophies on the mantelpiece, Playfair produces the picture saying self-consciously, "You won't be laughing now, will you? It was at Trinity," he explains, mentioning his Alma Mater, Trinity College, Dublin University, in those days a stronghold of Protestant education.

The photograph, which may very well be authentic, shows a young Arthur Shields, dressed in a striped T-shirt and long black shorts assuming a classic boxing pose.

"Lightweight champion," reads Sean, "nineteen hundred…"

"Oh, the year doesn't matter," interrupts Playfair, "it was long, long ago," wisely not fixing *The Quiet Man* in any particular time frame.

However, the movie is supposedly set in the 1920s, and the date of Playfair's boxing win is still prefixed by "nineteen" so it couldn't have been "long, long ago". Shields was fifty-six at the time of the filming and looks even older, so he would have been out of Trinity for at least thirty years and this would have put *The Quiet Man* well into the 1930s. It's a small point but shows how careful one

200   The Complete Guide to The Quiet Man

has to be with every line of dialogue in a script.

Sean hands him back the photograph and says, "All right," imitating Playfair's old-fashioned stance and the two men laugh together comparing their boxing backgrounds.

9:00

"By the way," says Playfair, "would you like to join me in a glass of…" But before he says the word "port", he suddenly remembers – "But no, no, you'll be in training now of course."

The smile vanishes from Sean's face and he lowers his eyes sadly as the sudden realisation dawns on him that he must, for his wife's honour, break his vow never to fight again.

The scene dissolves skilfully and rather beautifully and we are back again in the interior of the studio White O'Morn. Mary Kate is standing by the fireside staring dreamily into the flames as Sean enters. She is dressed in the same lovely outfit as the day he first saw her and this scene echoes their stormy first meeting in the cottage when she first came to clean it up for him. In the background tender violin music is playing as Sean comes in and puts his jacket to one side. He stands by the fireside and faces her, person to person, as she looks up sadly at him. Then she slowly and deliberately hands him a stick to beat her with, perhaps Ford's idea of the traditional method of punishment of an errant Irish wife, but he throws it into the fire before sitting down without a word. This is of course just a gesture on Mary Kate's part, because she knows very well that he is not the sort of man to beat his wife with a stick.

9:30

As the soft violin music continues, Sean sits on a fireside chair and takes out the cinema's favourite prop – a cigarette. Mary Kate rushes to light a twig in the fire to meet his needs and, as the twig slowly lights, it seems to rekindle the flames of the passion between them. She lights his cigarette, blows out the taper and they stare into the fire together.

0:00

"Did you have any supper?" she asks him, ever the practical woman.

"Nope," he replies tersely, "I'm not hungry."

"The drink sometimes does that to a man," she comments, probably from experience with her big brother.

"I haven't had anything to drink," he adds. "If you want to know, I was talking to the vicar, Mister Playfair."

1:40:30

Now we see the pair of them from the reverse angle – a more mature couple now, being much more understanding towards each other and starting to come to grips with the situation in which they find themselves.

"That's strange," says Mary Kate, "I had a long talk with Father Lonergan." Not quite true, Mary Kate – it was quite a short session and it would be exaggerating to describe it as a talk.

Very tentatively she sits on the arm of his chair and the music suddenly changes to the romantically suggestive *Innisfree*. As they come closer together, we sense that something important is about to happen between them and we are not wrong. Sean looks up hopefully and puts his arm around her shoulders sensing her newly found tenderness towards him.

1:41:00

Here we must comment that the camera angle, the make-up and the lighting do absolutely nothing for Maureen O'Hara and John Wayne in this scene – she a lady of thirty-one and he a man of forty-four, instead of the more youthful characters they are meant to portray. But then *The Quiet Man* was a long time in the making.

Sean takes a last drag on his cigarette and throws it in the fire. As they stare into the flames together, Mary Kate closes her eyes momentarily and he takes her hand into his. He then takes her right arm, puts it around his shoulder and the pair entwine their necks like swans.

1:41:30

Nugent's screenplay instructions are quite explicit at this point:

> Sean suddenly realises there is no sleeping bag on the hearth between them. He looks up and in that moment her eyes meet his and without a word the two slowly move towards each other.

Ford is very strongly suggesting that intimacy

takes place between Mary Kate and Sean and that their marriage is consummated, but the details are left to the powerful imagination of the viewers. Ford did not approve of screen nudity or explicit sex scenes and yet his audiences always got the message, often in a vastly more erotic way than a present-day director would in attempting to achieve the same effect. Another famous director of Irish ancestry, Alfred Hitchcock, also understood very well the power of imagination – he carried this principle to its ultimate limit by ensuring that the character Rebecca in his *Rebecca* (1940) never actually appeared in the movie, but the millions who have seen it all have their own idea of what she looked like and how she behaved.

We come now to the finale of *The Quiet Man*, a slow crescendo to one of the most lengthy and explosive fights in movie history. Sean's conflict with Danaher has been like a festering sore – now it is coming to the surface and the boil is about to burst. Sean has made the decision to fight but he doesn't know when or where. Fate, a conspiracy, or perhaps his wife's impulsive behaviour, is about to give him the spur he needs.

The climax of *The Quiet Man* is controversial and deserves careful analysis – it has at least four different interpretations each possessing some validity and we will look briefly at each in turn.

Interpretation One is the standard interpretation and the one definitely intended by Frank Nugent in his screenplay. After a night of happy intimacy, Mary Kate rises very early in the morning and bolts for the Dublin train, driven by Michaeleen, who is then despatched to inform Sean of the situation. This is intended to give him the excuse he needs to confront and fight Danaher, and the implication is that she will not return to White O'Morn until the affair is settled. Sean's anger and his dragging of his wife across the countryside were meant to be real, as was Mary Kate's feeling of shame that her husband would not fight for her fortune.

There has already been a major conspiracy in *The Quiet Man* so it is no surprise that Interpretation Two involves another conspiracy – this time between Mary Kate and Sean to force Danaher's hand and shame him into paying the dowry. This seems to be the way Ford directed it and Maureen O'Hara, who should know, told me in a personal interview that this is the way that she and the Duke were told to play it as the movie was being shot.

If this is the case, then it changes everything – *The Quiet Man* is not anti-woman, the drag across the field is all a sham, a comic caper, and Mary Kate, far from being abused, is merely going along with the act towards her eventual triumph. This is all very much in keeping with Ford's assertion that *The Quiet Man* was "A Western set in Ireland", a love story, a comedy, a romance and not a serious movie. It is also consistent with the comic nature of the big fight in which clearly nobody is really hurt.

Interpretation Three is a long shot, but it cannot be ruled out. Perhaps there was a conspiracy between Mary Kate and the wily Michaeleen Oge Flynn to force Sean into action. Any conspiracy without Michaeleen would be unthinkable and before we can dismiss this, there are several questions to be answered. Why was Michaeleen sitting outside the cottage as soon as Sean got up out of bed? Why was he chosen to convey Mary Kate's message of love to her husband? Why does he give one of his exquisite eye glances when telling Sean that Mary Kate would be in time for the Dublin train, all the time closely monitoring Sean's reactions? Why does he refuse to saddle Sean's horse (in Nugent's script Michaeleen tells Sean he had already saddled the horse ten minutes ago) and why is he so elated at the prospect of Sean angrily following his wife to the station?

There is, however, Interpretation Four, unveiled here for the first time, and the author believes that it offers a comprehensive explanation of the climax to *The Quiet Man*. As Sean and Mary Kate lay together in their marriage bed, it is very possible that they hatched a plot along the following lines. Early in the morning, Mary Kate would knock on Michaeleen's door and ask him to take her to the Dublin train. Sean would then follow and pull her from the train just in time, before frogmarching her to Danaher where he would either get her dowry or throw her back to her brother. However, there was a great danger that the sharp villagers, especially Michaeleen, would see through this plot, so Mary Kate hatched a second little conspiracy with Michaeleen. After leaving her at the station, she told him to return to White O'Morn, inform Sean what was happening and goad him in every possible way into following her, letting subsequent events appear to be the natural consequences of Sean's anger. The beauty of this explanation is that neither Sean nor Michaeleen knew that the other was involved in a deception instigated by Mary Kate and it is perhaps fitting that a mess created by two men should be cleared up by the wiles and cunning of a woman. Admittedly, all of this would require a great deal of acting by the principals but that is exactly what they appear to be doing!

So, dear reader, pick whichever interpretation you like, but remember that John Ford was one of the most devious and enigmatic movie directors who has ever lived and was capable of every trick in the book as far as leading his audience up the garden path was concerned.

Meanwhile, back at the action, it is early morning in the cottage and Sean with his usual cigarette in his mouth, emerges from the bedroom in a happy mood. He is wearing a dressing gown that looks suspiciously like his Trooper Thorn outfit with the lettering removed, because there is still a little cross on his back. Taking his cigarette in his hand, he bends down to smell the roses on the table before shouting good-humouredly, "Woman of the house, where's me tay?", a line perhaps inspired by the dialogue in *Mungo's Mansion* (1946) by the fine Galway playwright Walter Macken.

"Woman of the house" is a direct translation of the Irish-language description of not just a housewife but the mistress and queen of all domestic affairs, "bean a tí". Sean also pronounces "tea" as "tay", a pronunciation still found in some parts of rural Ireland and a relic of Elizabethan English. Witness Alexander Pope's rhyming couplet:

> Here thou, great Anna! Whom three realms obey
> Did sometimes counsel take, and sometimes tea.

Which of the four interpretations is Sean's behaviour here consistent with? On the surface it appears to be Interpretation One, but was Sean perhaps aware that Michaeleen was on the premises and putting on an act for his benefit? Had Mary Kate perhaps jumped the gun and put the whole scheme into operation a lot sooner than Sean expected? Nugent has Sean waking up and stretching his arm to embrace his wife who has already fled the nest.

1:42:00

Not seeing Mary Kate in the cottage, Sean opens the half-door and smiles out at the world.

"Mary Kate," he shouts, still grinning, but all he can see, sitting on a rock by the side of the door is the little leprechaun himself, Michaeleen Oge Flynn.

"Save your breath, boy, save your breath," says Michaeleen sadly but philosophically. "She's gone from ya, and small wonder."

"What are you talking about," asks Sean in (mock?) surprise, opening the bottom half of the door. "Where is she?"

The pragmatic Michaeleen continues his story. "She came tapping at my door and the sun not up," he tells Sean. "'Will you drive me to the train?' says she."

"Why?" asks Sean.

"Me very question. 'Why?' says I," replies Michaeleen. "'Because I love him,' says she, 'I love him too much to go on living with a man I'm ashamed of.'"

There is a little silence and all we can hear is the chirping of a few recorded birds round the studio White O'Morn.

"What time was this?" Sean asks him.

"Oh, in time for the Dublin train," replies the oracle, giving one of his famous glances designed to see if his verbal ploys are having the right effect. Yes, without a doubt there's a plot afoot in Michaeleen's mind all right – maybe he's doing the whole thing off his own bat, but we must not get carried away with conspiracy theories.

Sean stands still taking a last few deep pulls from his cigarette. Acting or not, his anger and passion are steadily rising and when he finally throws his cigarette on the ground, he has come to a decision – the time has come for action and fighting if necessary. Michaeleen is now looking at him gleefully – after all he is the local bookmaker and the prospect of a fight between Sean and Red Will Danaher could herald the biggest money-spinner of all time in Inisfree.

1:42:30

Sean turns on his heel back into the cottage, presumably to dress for the fray, and says to Michaeleen, "Saddle up my horse will you please?"

"Saddle his horse?" says Michaeleen to nobody in particular as he prepares to light his pipe. Then he shouts tauntingly to Sean, "I'll have no part in helping you to put more shame on her," before again saying to himself, "Hmph, saddle his horse," as if it were the most unnatural thing in the world to be asked. Then puffing on his pipe he smiles contentedly to himself and begins to lilt one of the movie's themes – *The Rakes of Mallow*.

1:43:00

In Nugent's original screenplay there is a great deal of additional dialogue here with much toing and froing of boxing mitts and threats against Danaher. Outside, Hugh Forbes and Owen Glynn sit on their own horses, holding Sean's saddled black jumper between them. Sean thanks them and gallops off furiously towards Castletown Station. None of this dialogue or action appears in the final cut.

The scene now moves to Castletown Railway Station **(Location 2)** with Michaeleen's lilt of *The Rakes of Mallow* merging skilfully into Vic Young's orchestral version. This is of course the tune to which Sean's train came into the station

at the beginning of the movie. Naturally, all of the scenes at Ballyglunin were shot at the same time although they were shown at the beginning and end of the movie.

At the station, shot from the opposite end of the platform than that appearing previously, we see Mary Kate very apprehensively and almost sulkily walking alongside the "Dublin" train **(Location 2E)** unable to make up her mind what carriage to enter. (In reality this is the Sligo–Limerick train via Tuam.) She looks around her to make sure she is being observed, then turns and enters a third-class carriage, putting her little bag on the floor and slamming the door behind her. This is an echo of another door she has slammed so many times in Sean's face – the bedroom door – and represents yet another barrier between them.

If Mary Kate is really serious about leaving her husband then the way she goes about doing it constitutes a serious weakness in the plot. She has no money and a minimum of luggage; there is no evidence that she has any close relatives in Dublin – certainly no brothers or sisters or nieces or nephews. Where is she going to stay, who is she going to stay with and how is she going to support herself? No, it is more likely that Mary Kate had no intention whatsoever of going to Dublin or anywhere else for that matter. She has boarded the train in a most public and ostentatious manner so that as many people as possible would see her do so and she is just waiting for the moment when her husband will snatch her back either in anger or as the result of a pre-arranged plan.

Here a scene was cut that would have been nice to see – the arrival at Castletown Station of the Bishop, welcomed by Mister Playfair, on the very train Mary Kate is catching. The Bishop, played by English actor Philip Stainton, later to star in Ford's *Mogambo* (1953), is described as a portly, gaitered clerical-looking gent; he is an agreeable fellow, obviously fond of his port and his roasts. He turns as a porter comes along with his bag and he beckons the man to follow. As the two men move towards the entrance, the train starts with a small jerk and then stops again. Mary Kate is in turn terrified that the train will pull out of the station and then that it won't. Then she turns in the other direction and stares out the window, hardly believing the sight that meets her eyes – Sean charging down the line on his horse.

Instead, here Ford inserts a scene that was not in the original script. It is clearly intended as comic relief, and is a rather funny sequence based on the many differences of opinion between the train crew and the station staff at Castletown. This is a dispute as old as that of Cain and Abel, the farmer and the cowman, the city slicker and the rural redneck. Ford liked this scenario so much that he repeated it and indeed extended it in *The Rising of the Moon* (1957).

Since this scene was not in the original screenplay, it was obviously written on the spot and it is thick with local colour and references. We see the engine driver Costello (Eric Gorman) climbing onto the train with his fireman (Kevin Lawless).

"Well, we're off," says Costello, wiping from his lips the froth of what has obviously been a welcome pint of porter.

3:30

However, the stationmaster, Hugh Bailey (Webb Overlander), uses the opportunity to reprimand his long-standing enemy.

"And might I suggest, Mister Costello," he upbraids him, "the train already being four and a half hours late, it's high time that..." but despite wiggling a gold pocket watch in the driver's direction, he never gets to finish the sentence.

Lateness of trains is a perennial Irish comic theme – for example, it was said of the legendary West Clare Railway that the only function of the timetable was to show how late the train was and that a calendar would have done equally well!

There is a little problem here, however, that nobody seems to have noticed – if the train is four and a half hours late, has Mary Kate been hanging around the train station all that time? Or is the train so perpetually late that the actual time of arrival each morning has now become the official time? The length of the shadows at the station would seem to indicate that the morning is well advanced and just how long would it take Sean to ride the five miles from Inisfree to Castletown Station?

Back at the action, Costello does not take his reprimand for punctuality lying down and like most Irishmen, he has a plausible excuse at the ready. From the safety of his engine he retorts:

"Now is it my fault, Mister Bailey," he argues, "that there's a hurling match at Ballygar" (of earlier fishing fame) "and that the champions of all Ireland are playing..."

He is interrupted, albeit on his side of the argument, by the guard of the train, Mister Malouney (Joseph O'Dea). By now the porter Paddy O'Donnell and the fishwoman May Craig have joined the platform party, just as they did in the opening scenes.

"If you knew your country's history," says Malouney to Bailey, tapping him provocatively on the shoulder with his flag, "as well as you claim to know it, Mister Bailey, you'd know that the Mayo hurlers haven't been beaten west of the Shannon for the last twenty-two years."

For those who follow hurling in Ireland, and there are many, this is a huge joke. At the time of filming, Mayo did not even have a senior hurling team and fielded at best indifferent junior and minor hurling teams (the author should know – he played for them!). They scarcely ever won a hurling match, let alone remaining unbeaten west of the Shannon for twenty-two years. Mayo hurling has often been described as "compulsory tillage" and elevating such a topic to the status of the country's history is a further joke.

But perhaps there is here a veiled reference to a famous legend or maybe a famous historic event. North-east of the village of Cong lie the Plains of Moytura (incidentally the summer home of Sir William Wilde and his son Oscar Wilde). Here legend has it that a great battle was fought between the two ancient Irish tribes – the Firbolg, dark wiry men from the Mediterranean, and the Tuatha de Danaan. It is said that the Tuatha de Danaan, supposedly with the help of magic, won the day and so acquired supremacy over Ireland. The weapons used were hurls, sticks made of ash wood used in playing the game of hurling. The battlefield is still known as the "field of the hurlers" and it may have been the venue of the first hurling match played in Ireland. Cong itself has always been a stronghold of Mayo hurling but naturally many of the associated legends have been hotly disputed by some historians.

But the real reason for this reference to Mayo sport is probably more subtle. The really popular game in Mayo is Gaelic football, the sister game of hurling. Mayo first won the All-Ireland Senior football title in 1936 and, despite being a county where the football support reaches an almost religious level of fanaticism, they had to wait until 1950 before winning their next title. In 1951, the year *The Quiet Man* was filmed, Mayo were embarking on the defence of their title. They had already qualified for the All-Ireland semi-final and actually went on to retain their title against Meath in September 1951. During the filming, Cong and all of County Mayo were agog with football talk. No doubt the reference was Ford's acknowledgement of the importance of sport in the location area. In the previous year, 1950, Mayo had won the All-Ireland Junior Football championship, and the captain of that team was Stan Mellotte, brother of Joe Mellotte, who was stand-in for John Wayne in *The Quiet Man*.

Sadly, Mayo's football fortunes have not flourished since then. They were beaten by Cork in the final in 1989, by Meath in the final in 1996 after a replay, by Kerry in the final in 1997 and again by Cork in 1999. A current joke claims that the Mayo football team have hired a new Chinese coach appropriately named Win Wan Soon! Incidentally, when Ford repeated his hurling reference in *The Rising of the Moon* (1957), he ran into a storm of controversy with hurling's ruling body, the

Gaelic Athletic Association (GAA), because a player in the victory celebration was carried around by four others on a stretcher!

Meanwhile, back at the action of the movie, May Craig clearly agrees with the assertion about the Mayo hurlers.

"True for ye, Mister Malouney," she shouts encouragingly. But the stationmaster, Hugh Bailey, is not convinced and clearly there is a matter of honour at stake.

"It's a lie," he shouts to Malouney and then turning to the engine driver continues, "It's a lie, Costello," pointing an accusing finger at him while May Craig screeches her disagreement in the background.

It is clear that only a bare-knuckle fist fight can settle the truth of this vital matter, so the combatants prepare. Costello takes off his cap and spits on his hands; Malouney leaves down his flag and removes his cap and glasses, and even Bailey takes off his cap and unbuttons the jacket of his uniform. The proposed curtain-raiser fight, however, is of the "Hold me back and let me at him" variety, and the combatants will quite willingly abandon their struggle when Sean Thornton rides down between the railway tracks and into Castletown Station **(Location 2F)**.

As Duke and Blackjack gallop through the steam from engine No. 59, the cowboy saddle flown in specially from the United States just for his use is clearly visible. As he dismounts we see the metal railway footbridge in the background. As Sean marches up onto the platform, his horse obediently follows but then turns out the gate **(Location 2G)**, attracted no doubt by John Daly who was waiting for him. Sean quickly passes the would-be combatants, still rolling up their sleeves preparing to fight. They turn and gaze after him in amazement as they suddenly realise what is happening.

1:44

Sean now begins to search the train carriage-by-carriage for his beloved wife. Standing on the platform beautifully positioned between the lamp and the pillar is John Horan, a young Galway solicitor and member of the Taibhdhearc Players, who was responsible for recruiting many of the theatrical extras for *The*

Quiet Man. With his suitcase by his side, he is smoking a cigarette and is the archetypal man in an Irish railway station, probably trying to decide if it is worth his while emigrating or not. John Horan is a most delightful fellow and in a lengthy interview he told the author that this scene was shot three times, during which he smoked three different brands of cigarette – a Camel, a Lucky Strike and a Woodbine, before quipping to Ford, "Which cigarette company is sponsoring this scene anyway?" He manages to look suitably surprised as Sean thunders by him down the platform.

This is one of the best scenes in *The Quiet Man*. The music is punctuated with the slamming of each carriage door as Sean seeks out his errant wife, quickly glancing into each compartment in turn. Looking out of her window, echoing the last time she looked at him through the window as he departed from the Danaher house, she sees him coming, so she retreats from her carriage window as quickly as she can and attempts to hide in the corner. This of course is another powerful echo of the time she attempted to hide in the cottage bedroom, but again she has no chance of escape.

From the reverse angle we see the scene from the point of view of the onlookers, a man with a cap and braces and two men with bicycles. In the background John Horan stands, rigid as a statue, engulfed in steam. As the tension mounts, Sean is getting nearer and nearer, slamming doors as he goes, until finally he reaches Mary Kate's compartment where she is cowering in the corner. In his previous attempts to get through to her, Sean first slammed shut a door in the cottage and then broke down a door; now without ceremony he pulls open the door and literally yanks her out of the carriage. Mary Kate's case is catapulted in front of her and left on the platform – perhaps it was empty anyway!

Again there is a strong echo of an earlier scene – in the cottage Mary Kate attempted to escape from Sean and he pulled her back in to kiss her; now she is attempting to escape from him on

the train and he pulls her back out again onto the platform. They become entwined around one of the pillars – for a split second they pause eyeball to eyeball but this time there is no kiss. But just as Sean left the train at Castletown to begin a new life, Mary Kate is leaving the train also to begin what turns out to be a new life for her also.

According to Maureen O'Hara, it was at this moment, when Mary Kate and Sean looked each other in the eye, that Ford directed them to play it as a deception for the benefit of the community and to triumph over Red Will. It has to be a very serious and elaborate deception, because Red Will is no fool, at least when it comes to money matters, but so well did the couple play their parts that they fooled several generations of moviegoers into the bargain.

Michael Donohue of Ballyglunin relates that he and a friend, Mattie Hynes, cycled to the railway station during the filming to get a closer view of the action. They parked their bicycles on the grass (near where Michaeleen's sidecar was parked). Suddenly an American appeared and asked the boys if they would like to rent out their bicycles as movie props and they delightedly agreed. Michael Donohue's Sunbeam bicycle was ridden into movie history behind Duke Wayne as he dragged Maureen O'Hara up the platform, and when the scene was all over, Ford dipped into his pocket and took out a handful of silver. "Is this enough boys?" he asked, handing them about sixteen shillings, which they regarded as a fortune.

The background *Rakes of Mallow* warns us to expect action and we get plenty as Sean pulls Mary Kate along the platform by the cuffs of her jacket. One of the men with a bicycle mounts his vehicle in anticipation as Sean drags Mary Kate in a straight line regardless of suitcases or luggage. As she athletically jumps over a trunk, Mary Kate shows her underwear in just two frames, thus providing what is possibly the only rude split second in the movie – this is not visible at normal speed. John

4:30

Ballyglunin tracks from the reverse angle

Horan jumps back in alarm as she hurdles his suitcase but recovers quickly to pick it up and follow the throng which is increasing by the minute.

Meanwhile, back at the fight between the train crew and the station staff, the combatants are only too glad to abandon their little difference of opinion in deference to the main bout.

"If this means what I hope it means…" says Malouney, undoing all his preparations for battle, but Costello finishes the sentence for him.

"Danaher vice versus the Yank," he says with a delicious malapropism in a tribute to the land of its birth.

"Ah, there'll be wigs on the green this time," continues Costello, referring to the custom of aristocratic duellists placing their hairpieces on the village green so as not to damage them while fighting.

Back on go the jackets of the crew as they abandon their train, as do the station staff their station. There will be no complaints from the passengers, however, for they too have put all thoughts of Dublin aside as they abandon their seats and head for the big fight. This is an episode straight out of the life of Maurice Walsh.

Again, sadly, a scene was dropped here that would have added to the comedy. By now the Bishop and Playfair are about to depart from the station when the Bishop demands an explanation for all the commotion. At first he suspects it is a rail strike but Playfair, who knows very well what is happening and is only itching to see the fight himself, puts him at his ease. But then the Bishop overhears a man saying that he does not wish to be late for the hostilities, so the Bishop says to Playfair in horror, "Did he say hostilities? Merciful heavens, Snuffy, you people are not at war with us again, are you?"

Now Sean pulls Mary Kate out of the little gate of Castletown Station where she vaults another huge obstacle giving a delicious little squeal as

she does so. They are followed at close quarters by Bailey, Costello, Malouney, the fishwoman, the porter, the fireman and assorted passengers on bicycle and on foot.

At last we see the Bishop and Mister Playfair for the first time together. The car used was a period piece – an old 1920s' Morris Cowley. It belonged to Thomas O'Sullivan of Cornamona, a cousin of Bernard O'Sullivan who was later to marry Etta Vaughan, stand-in and double for Maureen O'Hara. The car had registration

The drag begins

number IM 2234 and had been discovered by Ace Holmes who was the prop man for the production.

Gate at Ballyglunin station

Although the car did travel to Ballyglunin, this scene involves yet another piece of cinematic deception. The car containing the Bishop and Playfair is seen, not outside Castletown Station, but near one of the many exits from Ashford Castle back in Cong **(Location 1I)**. This location was extremely difficult to find, now being blocked off and built over.

The Bishop and Mister Playfair sit in the car, turning around in open-mouthed amazement as Sean pulls Mary Kate along, Sean touching his cap in deference to their reverences with a terse "Morning". Mary Kate has other things on her mind and anyway to salute the clerics would give the game away. Playfair's eyes light

up in anticipation at the sight of Sean's actions, knowing that the climactic fight cannot now be far away. The Bishop pokes him quizzically with his umbrella demanding some sort of explanation but all he gets is a smile – there is no mention of rebellions or anything else that might be controversial.

The rest of the field then pass through the Ashford tunnel **(Location 1J)**, and through the gates we can see the Bishop peering backwards from the car in continuing amazement. In a frame-by-frame analysis of this scene something else emerges – opposite the car is a jaunting car on which a man is sitting. The author speculates that this man is John Ford, making a Hitchcock-like appearance in his favourite movie. The evidence is scanty, just the shape of the man's black hat, the scarf, the colour of his jacket and a strong hunch that on this occasion at least, Ford could not resist the temptation of leaving his personal mark on his masterpiece. This is all of course mere speculation, but it would be nice if it were true.

The Bishop is now so flabbergasted he is sitting up in the back of the car like a goose with his mouth open. In the front, Playfair is smiling inanely and clearly enjoying the situation. As the railway employees pass by the car in a hurry, they all show respect for the cloth by doffing their caps and mumbling a hurried "Good morning". May Craig, the fishwoman, has not forgotten her basket and finds time to stop, curtsy, and say, "Good day to you sirs," before hurrying on.

The bishop arrives

The bishop and Reverend Playfair wait

Ashford tunnel (Tower gate)

The action now switches back to Castletown Station to a picturesque spot **(Location 2H)** situated about two hundred yards south-west of Ballyglunin Station. This is Pallas Bridge and Sean approaches it, pulling Mary Kate behind him and followed by a motley crew of railwaymen, passengers, members of the general public and just about anybody who wants to join in the fun. If weddings and funerals are public events, why shouldn't marital and family disputes be for public consumption also? In the United States, people had to pay to see Sean fight; in Ireland, people prepared to travel can watch for free, with Mary Kate as an added sideshow. This scene is a very beautiful one showing a lovely old limestone bridge from a masterly angle. Sadly, nowadays the bridge and this view are almost totally obscured by trees and foliage.

Throughout these scenes, *The Rakes of Mallow* is played at an increasingly frenetic pace and provides an ideal musical backdrop for the hotting-up action.

The action now switches to the interior of Cohan's pub, a studio scene. Hugh Forbes is on that new-fangled instrument, the electric telephone, that the ever-progressive Pat Cohan has installed. Forbes is deep in conversation with an unknown informant who is keeping him and the viewers up to date with the action. It was originally intended to show a man at the other end of the line furiously cranking the handle of the phone and shouting, "Yes, fifteen minutes ago – save a place for me!"

Riding whip in one hand and telephone receiver in the other, Forbes repeats to the assembled gathering of American extras the news he is hearing on the phone.

"Five minutes did you say? Right," he announces before hanging up.

"He's walking her back," he shouts happily. "The whole long way," with a peculiar emphasis on the word "long".

At this stage we may ask what is happening to Sean's horse now that he is walking his wife back? Is the unfortunate animal condemned to wander forever around Castletown, because he is not seen again in the movie?

The assembly now knows that the confrontation with Danaher and the fight are only a matter of minutes away and the smiles broaden.

"It's Homeric, that's what it is, Homeric," says Michaeleen Oge Flynn, echoing his earlier use of this classical word when he sees the collapsed bed the morning after the wedding night.

"Post a lookout at Maam Cross," says Forbes to Michaeleen. "They may go home first."

This mention of Maam Cross, a road crossing just a few miles south of where White O'Morn was located, was in keeping with Ford's policy of mentioning as many Irish place names as possible in the movie, although Maam Bridge might have been a more appropriate place to mention. Incidentally, Maam Cross has for many years housed a tourist-attracting replica of

Pallas Bridge

The Quiet Man cottage; this of course has recently been superseded by Collins' White O'Morn replica in Cong.

Now for the first time we notice the taciturn General (played by "Major" Sam Harris who was a judge in the race scenes) calmly reading his magazine and sipping his whiskey and soda, totally unmoved by the important events that are unfolding about him. In this scene he is a late addition to the script, presumably portraying Ford's idea of the impassive and unflappable character of the Anglo-Irish ruling classes, in contrast with the emotional and excited behaviour of the Celtic-Irish.

"Pat, where's your parabellum?" asks Michaeleen of Cohan as he volunteers to be the lookout.

1:46:00

"In the same place," answers Pat, pointing to a box in the corner between the General and the wall.

"Excuse me, General," says Michaeleen as he grabs the firearm and, freely adapting the words of Paul Revere, shouts, "One if by land, two if by sea and if it's Danaher's, I'll fire the lot – horse, foot and artillery." Whereupon he rushes out the door in a state of great excitement.
The phrase "Horse, foot and artillery" comes from Sean O'Casey's play The Plough and the Stars. In Ford's production of The Plough and the Stars (1936), Fluther Good speaks these words and the part of Fluther Good was played by – Barry Fitzgerald.

Here even Pat Cohan, a man not noted for his emotion and enthusiasm, is moved to make the ultimate gesture.

"Ah, what a day for Inisfree," he shouts (not "What a day for industry" as several commentators have claimed). "On a day like this, I can say only one thing – gentlemen, the drinks are on the house."

There is a stunned silence and Owen Glynn splutters into his drink. Clearly this outburst of generosity is totally unprecedented on Pat Cohan's part and, as the customers stare at the proprietor in silent amazement, he is forced to

repeat his offer by saying, "Well, they are!" There is perhaps an implied joke here relating to Cohan's surname.

Meanwhile, Sean is pulling Mary Kate across the countryside. We now see them on the road leading to Ashford Farm (Location 9J). They are in tandem now but a different sort of tandem to the one they rode down this very road during the courting scene – the ironic echo is obvious. For the geographically minded, their present location is only a few yards away from their final destination, but the director makes them cover many miles of countryside before they get there. The stirring Rakes of Mallow and the excited behaviour of the swelling crowd, many of them on bicycles, are all part of the crescendo that will explode in the fight.

1:4(

Next we see the happy couple on the Ashford Deerpark (Location 6F) as Sean drags his bride under a tree. Then, still holding her by the cuffs, he pulls her across open ground (Location 6G) looking resolutely in front of him and scarcely acknowledging her presence. The followers now emerge from under the tree as Mary Kate, almost inevitably, loses a shoe and hobbles along on one foot. She points back to tell him of her loss, but Sean marches ahead with just one thing on his mind – to have it out with Danaher once and for all. Mary Kate is now feeling the pain of her bare foot on the twigs and the rough grass but Sean never deviates from his path.

The crowd following are quick to spot the lost shoe, and the guard, Mr Malouney, who is leading the pack, picks it up and, taking off his cap because he is about to address a lady, waves the shoe in the air to attract Mary Kate's attention. However, it is May Craig who gets to speak the line, "Here, ma'am darling, here's your shoe," which in all probability is a Ford ad lib.

Sean still pulls Mary Kate along, oblivious to her cries and the shouts of the crowd. As they go down a little incline (Location 6H) the inevitable happens – she falls to the ground with a scream, but he continues to drag her along. She begins the scripted line, "You... [big

1:4

Francis Ford, May Craig and Barry Fitzgerald

bully]" but he cuts her short by dragging her painfully down the incline. Sean helps her up by the scruff of the neck as she splutters incoherently and he pushes her along his chosen path saying sarcastically, "It's just a good stretch of the legs!" If the Thorntons are acting, they are certainly putting on a good show for the local inhabitants. The waiting crowd have politely hung back, but now they rush forward en masse, some of them riding bicycles over the fields.

As they proceed under another tree on the Deerpark **(Location 6I)**, Malouney finally catches up with the pair, brandishing the lost shoe in his hand.

"Mrs Thornton ma'am, you've lost your shoe," he says to her – this is the one and only time in the movie that Mary Kate is referred to as "Mrs Thornton".

"Thank you very kindly, sir," she replies with extraordinarily good manners under the circumstances, but this would be consistent with the interpretation that her perceived anger towards Sean is just an act. Mary Kate attempts to put her shoe on standing up, but fails, and finally sits down on the grass, where she manages to get the shoe on as Sean continues to drag her along.

She rises and Sean spins her around so that she is now free of him for a moment as she gasps several "oohs" and "ahs". Now she throws a full-blooded left-handed punch at him,

echoing the punch she threw in the cottage, but again the ex-boxer sees it coming a mile away and ducks. Mary Kate swings full circle and while she is turned away from him he gives her a little kick in the behind, echoing the playful slap on the rump he gave her in the rose garden. Then, deaf to her shrieks and protests, he continues to pull her along. The crowd of followers, polite as ever, stand off until the couple are on the move again, whereupon they charge forward with great excitement. May Craig is seen to pick up a stick from the ground.

1:47:30

The lovers pass under another tree onto the little road through the Deerpark **(Location 6B)** with the rabble close behind. Mary Kate twists and protests to no avail but she is bearing up remarkably well under the circumstances.

And now we come to what is perhaps the most famous and best line in *The Quiet Man*, spoken by May Craig, just as a mother-in-law would chastise her errant daughter-in-law. As she hands Sean the two-pronged stick she has picked up she shouts, "Mister, Mister, oh, sir, sir, here's a good stick to beat the lovely lady." Mary Kate gasps at this, but the way Sean says "Thanks" as he takes the stick is meant to convey to the onlookers that this time he might very well use it. The shape of the stick is another story – a deep Fordean joke.

Drag scene site

It comes as something of a shock to realise that this extended drag scene was not in Nugent's original script but seems to have been inserted by Ford himself for complex reasons. All Nugent suggested was a short scene described as follows:

> Sean and Mary Kate come to a brook – this is the same brook we have seen before, the one she waded through on the day of their courting. They come to it and she hesitates – thinking to take off her shoes, but without a pause Sean wades in and drags her in after him. And up they go to the other side, she with her bedraggled skirts and he with his set face.

That is all Nugent suggested and expected but Ford let his imagination run riot and gave us a never-to-be forgotten scene, which is of course the most controversial in *The Quiet Man*. Was Ford's motivation sadistic? Did he take a perverse delight in seeing Maureen O'Hara dragged across the countryside like this, even if he directed the players to play the scenes as an act of deception? Local people, the Irish in general and Irish–Americans took the treatment of Mary Kate at face value and interpreted it in terms of brutality, wife-beating and the social humiliation of a woman. Many people in Galway and Mayo felt it brought the West of Ireland into disrepute, and even today many people worldwide find it totally unacceptable.

Of course such physical treatment of women never took place in the West of Ireland, at least not since caveman times and maybe not even then.

And yet the dragging of Mary Kate Danaher across the countryside is, interpreted even in its very worst light, no more than a symbolic ritual, even a comic act. At no stage does she appear to be physically hurt; indeed she appears to be remarkably well groomed throughout, with little mud or dirt on her face or clothes, even at the end of the drag. Is this not *The Taming of the Shrew* all over again, and the handing over of the stick seems to suggest that, in this society at least, the onlookers approve of what is going on and feel that Mary Kate deserves all the punishment she is receiving? After all, nobody is suggesting that Sean really wants to do what he is doing – he is doing it solely for his wife's idea of what her honour is. As Duke Wayne himself was wont to say, "A man's gotta do what a man's gotta do."

Nevertheless, the drag scenes are controversial and one wonders if they were strictly necessary. Sean could just as easily have snatched his wife from the train, seated her on his horse and after riding madly across the countryside with her behind him and hanging on for dear life, flung her at her brother's feet. This would have been just as effective but it would not have made for such spectacular cinema! From Sean's point of view, perhaps the raw physical contact with Mary Kate is merely a substitute for the tender loving contact he has been denied. But whatever the interpretation of these scenes, they are central to *The Quiet Man* and give it, for better or worse, a unique place in the history of cinema.

Incidentally, Maureen O'Hara shared with the author many insights into the amazingly complex character of John Ford or Pappy as she always referred to him. Though lovable and deeply loved, he could be incredibly perverse. For example, he insisted that the drag scene not be rehearsed. O'Hara and Wayne as experienced professional actors, knowing full well that they had to rehearse it, did so in secret at odd moments snatched from film-making. When the scene turned out to be such a success, Ford said triumphantly, "There, what did I tell you – it was better to do it spontaneously." The irony is that he probably knew very well they were rehearsing together but they couldn't tell if he knew or not. What a man!

As we have said, Nugent's conception of this section of *The Quiet Man* was radically different from Ford's and yet several vestiges of Nugent's ideas survive. He had written an elaborate sequence involving Michaeleen standing lookout on a hill and seeing Sean and Mary Kate reaching a fork in the road, one branch leading to White O'Morn and the other to Danaher's. When they take the road to Danaher's, Mary Kate was meant to ask, "But… but aren't you taking me home?" and when it becomes obvious where they are going, Mary Kate's manner changes. She smiles to herself and steps along with a right good will. When Michaeleen sees that they are heading for Danaher's, he fires the gun in the air three times as pre-arranged, and it is only then that the huge crowd of followers begins to materialise.

Meanwhile, back in Cohan's bar, the patrons, having wasted no drinking time by following the feuding couple, are eagerly awaiting news of the venue for the impending fight. When Michaeleen "fires the lot", they know that Danaher's is the venue. Downing their drinks, Forbes and Glynn lead the charge from the pub, but the mock exterior scene here is of course a studio set and not the original in Cong. The giveaway clues are the presence of Sean McClory and the shadows cast by the studio lights on the bicycle leaning against the wall.

The American extras now emerge from the door of the pub, some still carrying their drinks – first things first. Among them is Dermot Fahy, the melodeon player who stands to the left of the doorway playing *The Rakes of Mallow* with all his might. Back inside, even Pat Cohan is shutting up shop in honour of the impending fight, but the unmoved General still sits impassively sipping his whiskey and soda and reading his magazine (probably *Tatler* or *Field and Stream*) as chaos reigns all around him. Even the sound of Pat Cohan's slamming down the heavy counter-top twice does not disturb his tranquillity as he reaches once again for his glass. Like the captain of a sinking ship, Cohan himself is the last to leave, and as he does so he hurriedly fastens a sign to the door. As Dermot Fahy quickly follows him, we see that the sign reads:

1:48:00

GONE TO TEA

– a pretty feeble joke in the circumstances. The General by the way is in the happy position of being locked alone in the pub, but such is his strength of Anglo-Saxon character that he can be trusted not to exceed his whiskey-and-soda quota.

The scene now switches back to the Ashford Deerpark (**Location 6B**) where the fight followers from Castletown Station meet up with the fight followers from Cohan's pub near the spot where Sean first met Father Lonergan. As the two groups meet up and coalesce to become a frenzied mob, Sean and Mary Kate become the meat in the sandwich as it were. Amid shouts and roars of approval, the crowd, intent on seeing a free fight, parts to make way for the couple. Sean is still striding forward confidently, but the strain is beginning to tell on Mary Kate as she sways from side to side. The crowd follows, some still on bicycles, and the pace of the background music quickens as the climax nears. The railway staff, showing remarkable stamina for men of their age, run in formation within the crowd, smiling and grinning all the time.

Now there is another poignant echo of happier times as Sean pulls Mary Kate through the magnificently tall beech trees (**Location 6D**) where he was standing when he first saw her. Then no word was spoken between them; now no word is being spoken either but the circumstances are utterly different. The magic spell of their first encounter has been broken and now the couple are living in the real world.

Nearing the end of the drag

Danaher awaits his in-laws

In the earlier scene Mary Kate was a vision of loveliness; now she is a sight to behold. The crowd follows through the stately trees with May Craig leading the ladies' race by a short head.

Now the end is in sight because we suddenly see Danaher, Feeney and the farmhands in a medium-long shot **(Location 9K)**. The observant will notice that the farmhands are a completely different group from those sitting round the Danaher table earlier, but that scene was a studio shot while the present one is outdoors in Ireland. It's a bit like American football where different squads come on for defensive and offensive situations. Local man and handball champion Paddy Clarke is seen prominently on the left in close shot, holding a long-handled hay fork in his hands.

But the centrepiece of this lovely scene is the magnificent turf-powered traction engine with its tall smoking chimney stack and glowing firebox. Nugent's screenplay instructions had given a choice between a sheep-shearing scene or a harvest scene depending on the physical circumstances and the weather. The hay harvest with its splendid and docile white-footed horses and its eye-catching engine was by far the better choice. One shudders at the loss of dignity this scene would have suffered with bleating sheep all over the place.

Actually, there is something of a visual contradiction in this scene. The crop being harvested is clearly hay and not a grain crop such as wheat, oats or barley. Only a grain crop would need a firebox to drive a threshing machine, so in reality there was no need for a firebox at all! But without it we would not have the red hot climax to *The Quiet Man*.

The traction engine had been hired from Mayo County Council in Ballinrobe about ten miles to the north of Cong. It stood on the roadside near the top of the hayfield **(Location 9K)** where legend has it that it had been towed the previous night by Charles Fitzsimons. Nugent had asked merely for "a machine or gadget with a firebox in it; a harvester or blacksmith's forge." What he got was a magnificent period piece – a star of the scene in its own right.

Red Will Danaher seems to be the only person in Inisfree who doesn't know what it going on, and he certainly has no idea of what is about to hit him. He stands truculently, fists on hips, a giant guarding his domain. Feeney has his inevitable little book and pencil in his hands with which to record the details of the crop and it is he who first notices the approaching storm. With an impish grin he casually remarks to his lord and master, "I think your in-laws are coming to visit you, Squire darlin'," – one of the great lines of *The Quiet Man*. The slow-witted Danaher looks in the direction of the approaching crowd in a manner more puzzled than alarmed.

Now we see the huge wave that is about to break on Danaher's shore – upward of a hundred people, probably the entire able-bodied population of Cong and the surrounding area, are following at a discreet distance behind Sean who is sometimes dragging, sometimes pushing, Mary Kate. As they make their way through the haystacks **(Location 9L)**, the men loading hay onto a horse and cart look on in polite amazement. Quizzically Danaher comes forward for a better view and as usual he is slow to react, but at least this gives us a chance to see the engine in all its glory, before his huge frame obscures it. Feeney stands in front of the machine smirking, and as Danaher comes forward to the camera his lips tighten and his facial muscles tense as he plants his hay fork in the ground. At last it slowly dawns on him that something very significant is happening.

The camera turns once again towards the advancing crowd. Sean is dragging Mary Kate more roughly now, all the more to impress or fool Danaher. Mary Kate falls to the ground for a third time and we are immediately put in mind of the way of the cross, with perhaps Sean being the cross she has to carry. *The Quiet Man* could have of course been interpreted in messianic terms but perhaps we have speculated more than enough already.

Now even Danaher's farmhands join the throng out of curiosity, while one of the railwaymen signals the crowd to keep their distance, but they advance immediately as Sean roughly pulls Mary Kate to her feet by the scruff of the neck and then drags her forward, Aran cap in her hand. For effect, he pushes her so that she falls again on the side of the little hill on which stands the towering figure of Red Will. Mary Kate gets up and makes one feeble "Oh no" groan of protest, but to no avail. As we have remarked previously, for a woman who has been dragged five miles across the countryside, she looks in pretty good shape.

Holding Mary Kate by the hand, Sean squares up to Red Will and shoots from the

Heavy Meitheal

hip, in Duke Wayne-style.

"Danaher," he says bluntly, "you owe me three hundred fifty pounds. Let's have it."

Red Will appears confused and looks around for support but finds none. For the first time, he is isolated and, instead of support, he finds his flanks covered by Hugh Forbes and Michaeleen who have appeared out of nowhere. Owen Glynn is conspicuous by his absence – he seems to have emigrated to America.

"So the IRA is in this too, ah?" says Red Will looking for some sort or any sort of scapegoat.

(This is the one surviving and probably token mention of the Irish Republican Army that remains in *The Quiet Man*, a far cry from its central role in the stories of Maurice Walsh.)

"If it were, Red Will Danaher," smirks Forbes, with an insidious leer, "not a scorched stone of your fine house would be standing," and he points in the direction of the Danaher farmhouse with his riding whip.

"A beautiful sentiment," echoes Michaeleen and these lines at least are authentic, because the IRA had a habit of burning down the houses of unpopular landlords and gentry.

Red Will, gambler that he is, tries one last throw of the dice. Defiantly he turns to Sean, looks the couple up and down and says contemptuously with an evil grin, "I'll pay ye – NEVER!" There's no answer to that he probably thinks to himself, but Sean does have an answer.

"That breaks all bargains," he says, and hurling his gasping wife at her brother's feet in an almost choreographed action he adds, "You can take your sister back. It's your custom, not mine; no fortune, no marriage, we call it quits."

Mary Kate rises hesitantly from the ground and gives her husband a shocked look – whether this is real or just for Danaher's benefit, it's pretty convincing.

"You'd do this to me, your own wife, after, after what happened…" We are in no doubt that she is referring to the intimacy of the previous night, but she cannot bring herself to say this. Anyway, Sean cuts her short with a curt "It's done" – a messianic *consummatum est*!

Red Will Danaher is perplexed, outmanoeuvred, in checkmate and he knows it.

The railway porter nudges the stationmaster who winks at him in return, and Red Will is literally the laughing stock of the whole village and further afield as guffaws ripple through the gathering. Incidentally, Mr Bailey has a pint of porter in his hand – where he got if from is a mystery because he came from the station and not the pub, and how he managed not to spill it during the cross-country run is an even deeper mystery which defies the laws of physics.

Finally, faced with the inevitable, Danaher gives in, as ungraciously as possible of course. He cannot possibly take Mary Kate back, because she would give him hell in his own house and besides that would rule out any faint hope he has of winning the widow's hand. Mary Kate puts her hands to her face, scarcely believing what she is seeing, as her brother extracts the money in banknotes from his wallet and throws it at Sean's feet, snarling as he does so, "There's yer dirty money, take it; count it, ya spawn! And look," he continues, "if I ever see that face of yours again, I'll push that through it."

In the original screenplay Red Will is given his purse by Feeney (maybe he is in the filmed version too because we do not see where the wallet comes from). What Feeney is doing with £350 (maybe $20,000 in today's money) on his person in a hayfield is not to be explained – Feeney doesn't look the type to be trusted with a cent!

Sean is neither impressed nor intimidated by Danaher's tough words. He picks up the money from the ground and brushes past Danaher's threatening fist. He and Mary Kate look each other in the face and without any word being spoken sense what has to be done – or maybe all part of the pre-arranged plan, depending on whatever interpretation one puts on their actions. Sean heads for the firebox of the engine and Mary Kate backs towards it eyeball to eyeball with her husband all the time. With her cap conveniently in her hand to absorb the heat, she opens the door of the firebox. Inside we see the fierce orange flames furiously licking the inner surface of the engine. For about three seconds Mary Kate and Sean stare at each other

The red-hot firebox

iron in furnaces so hot a man loses his fear of hell. And when he's tough enough and hard enough, other things, other things. Well, now Sean has been through his personal hell and his affairs have come full circle to be sorted out in another red-hot furnace. But still there are other things – one big other thing in particular – he has to fight Danaher.

Paradoxically, John Ford claimed that the climax to this powerful scene was the one thing about *The Quiet Man* that he regretted. Afterwards he felt that the money should not have been burned – it should have been given to the poor, or even to Father Lonergan, who probably didn't need it. For a change, Ford was completely wrong and this scene is one of the most dramatic and forceful episodes in the entire movie. Mary Kate is vindicated and publicly regains her honour, her pride, and her standing in the community.

For the utterly cynical and the conspiracy theorists, yet another twist of interpretation is possible. Since the money destroyed in the fire is paper and not gold, the banks can compensate the owners by issuing new banknotes, so Mary Kate and Sean need not have suffered financially – doubtless Danaher kept the serial numbers of all the banknotes he ever owned and in his later good mood would have shared them with the happy couple.

Danaher is clearly appalled by the destruction of his money. In the original script he was meant to roar, "My money! My good money," but in the filmed version he merely stands there brooding and biding his time. Sean gently takes his wife by the shoulder and they walk arm in arm away from the engine in a straight line past Danaher. Mary Kate holds her head high and looks from side to side as she swaggers along beside her husband. However, as everybody knows, there is unfinished business, and Red Will must express his anger by means of a fist fight before the entire affair can be settled.

Danaher is clearly a sneaky street fighter with little respect for the rules of boxing (in reality, as

for dramatic effect and then, without averting his gaze, Sean plunges the paper money into the flames where it is at once consumed.

Then Mary Kate violently slams the door shut on all their troubles, still staring at her husband and no other. Here we have a superb echo of an earlier scene in the movie. On that occasion Mary Kate slammed and bolted the bedroom door to exclude her husband and they were on opposite sides of the door; now she slams and bolts the door to include him completely in her life and they are on the same side of the door. Moreover, just like the firebox, she is red, aflame with passion, red-hot and belongs to him only. Sean can spend his money in her firebox any time he wants! (Your author has now taken a cold shower and is back to normal.) As Michaeleen would say, it's Homeric.

Several other echoes spring to mind too of the couple separated by half-doors and the door of a railway carriage, but there is an echo from a completely different angle. Sean started his career in Pittsburgh working with steel and pig we have already mentioned, Victor McLaglen was an accomplished boxer of world heavyweight class). As Sean passes by, Danaher suddenly throws an unexpected punch. However, he telegraphs it and misses by a mile, as Sean ducks and retaliates with a crippling punch to Danaher's solar plexus. He scarcely needs Forbes' hurried warning cry of what sounds like "Shornton".

As Danaher lies on the ground writhing in pain attended by the faithful Feeney, Mary Kate speaks her lines to Sean but in reality they are for all the world to hear.

"I'll be going on home now," she tells him. "I'll have the supper ready for you." The implication is that she will also have the bed warm for him as Eileen Crowe promised Denis O'Dea in *The Rising of the Moon* (1957).

Mary Kate is announcing to the world at large that she is now a properly-married woman because her fortune has been paid and her husband is not afraid to throw a punch on her behalf. However, it is still early in the day, so her mention of supper shows that she realises that Sean has a hard day's fighting in front of him and would be lucky to be finished by nightfall. Probably from past experience, she knows that her brother is no pushover in a fight.

Mary Kate's sudden change of demeanour would seem to indicate that she and Sean were involved in a conspiracy to fool Danaher and that the drag was just an elaborate charade. If it was otherwise, surely she would not have forgiven him so quickly when she could still feel every bruise and bump on her body? On the other hand, Sean's behaviour suggests that he is flabbergasted at Mary Kate's sudden change of attitude, considering all that has happened. He seems totally confused, with the look of a man who will never understand either the Irish, the mind of a woman and in particular the mind of one Irishwoman, his ever-loving wife. Nevertheless, Sean does manage a broad Wayne-like grin – for the moment all of his problems seem to have been solved so he can afford to relax and feel happy. Did they or didn't they conspire? Perhaps the ambiguity is

deliberate on Ford's part, just to keep us guessing.

Mary Kate continues her triumphant walk through the men in the crowd who politely part to allow her through. She swaggers down the field towards the women of Inisfree who, as befits their sensitive and gentle natures, stand in a huddle in the background, dressed in their coloured shawls. With her public self-respect won back, Mary Kate is as happy as a lark as she strolls home.

But like the monster in a horror movie who refuses to stay dead, Red Will Danaher is not yet done. There now follows one of the longest, most hilarious and geographically widespread fights in movie history – with a few judiciously placed breaks, it lasts nearly eight and a half minutes of screen time. Of course it is not a real fight and nobody on screen pretends it is; it is more of a lusty brawl and, as in Tom and Jerry cartoons, it is obvious that nobody really gets hurt. The fight is the sort of comic climax that Ford sometimes gave his Westerns and why should *The Quiet Man* be an exception?

What many moviewatchers do not realise, however, is that there are two quite separate fights, one in Ireland and one in Hollywood, and these have been seamlessly edited together to give the appearance of one continuous piece of action. The clues to watch for are the presence of Sean McClory in Hollywood scenes only; the studio set of Cohan's pub; changes in lighting, shadows and costume colour; and most of all, a complete change of the cast of minor brawlers as we cross back and over the Atlantic. We shall refer to the Irish fight as Fight A and the fight scenes in Hollywood as Fight B.

The jaunty rendition of *The Rakes of Mallow* accompanying Mary Kate's triumphant walk gives way to more sombre music as the onlookers close ranks to form a makeshift and highly mobile ring within which the fight will take place.

Danaher spits on his hands, echoing his several earlier spitting exploits and, egged on by a smiling Feeney, catches Sean unawares with a foul blow and knocks him to the ground. As Sean rolls over, he is assisted by Hugh Forbes who comments, "That was a dirty blow, Sean," but this scene contains what can be described only as a major cinematic catastrophe. In the rolling motion, Sean loses his cap only to reveal that Duke Wayne is not wearing his hairpiece, his toupee, his rug, call it what you will! The crowd has now gathered round the fighters with shouts of encouragement such as "Will ye let him up", "Get back there", "Go on, get back" and "Come on, Sean, give it to him" amid the general mayhem.

1:30

Sean is not angry, but as he replaces his cap to cover up his nakedness, he has decided that the time has come to take the fight more seriously. He spits on his hands, assumes a fighting stance and says sarcastically, "Come on, Danaher, you asked for it," before advancing towards his opponent. Danaher swings a lusty blow at him, but Sean ducks and hits him a sickening blow in the jaw, knocking him to the ground.

Now we see the fight from behind the crowd, a long shot, to enable McLaglen's double to slip into the action. Wayne, it seems, played himself in most of the fight scenes, but McLaglen's double was Martin Thornton from Spiddal, a professional boxer himself and allegedly a cousin of Ford's. He was a "character" and a hard drinker who was involved in some outlandish drinking sessions with Wayne and other members of the *Quiet Man* cast. Many stories are told about his own boxing career including one incident in which, having secured his purse, he sat down in the middle of the ring and refused to fight. Thornton, on whose family name Sean's was probably based, appears prominently as an extra in the later fight scenes.

Red Will gets up and, as he rises, connects with Sean on the jaw knocking him down again, as the crowd mills around excitedly shouting and cheering, but giving the fighters very little space. Danaher now seems to be getting the worse of it, falling to the ground from two successive punches as the fight moves down the hill. Feeney is in his element, jumping around like a cat on a hot tin roof, delighted no doubt to see his boss getting a taste of his own medicine and the hammering he so richly deserves.

Local legend has it that on the morning of the big fight in Ireland, Ford addressed all of the assembled extras and told them to "go into the threshing field and raise hell". Doctors and nurses stood by in case of injury and there was mention of an ambulance concealed in the bushes in case of emergency. Some of the local fighters took Ford literally and a few genuine injuries were sustained; Jack MacGowran in particular got caught up in some real action and had to receive medical treatment.

Michaeleen too is in his element – it's the biggest informal sporting event that Inisfree has ever seen and he has sole rights on the bookmaking franchise. With his riding whip under his arm he shouts, "Three to one I'm giving on Danaher, three to one on Danaher," with his hand raised in the air. This is an echo of the generous odds he offered on Danaher in the Inisfree Cup. In fact, the odds on Danaher the local champion with a long-standing reputation are surprisingly generous. Does Michaeleen know that Sean was a world-class contender? Very probably, but he has kept quiet about it because there is money at stake.

Echoes abound here of previous events and situations in the movie. Michaeleen is clutching his little book and pencil, echoes of Feeney's writing kit, but now Michaeleen is putting Danaher's name in his book.

The first man to place a bet is Hugh Forbes. "I'll take some of that," he declares loudly. "Ten pounds on Thornton." (Paradoxically this is now the name of both fighters.) Clearly Forbes' IRA unit has been gathering intelligence and knows Sean's real identity or maybe Maureen O'Hara has tipped off her brother as to the probable outcome of the fight to keep some money in the family.

"Done," says Michaeleen. "Anyone else

1:52:00

favour my friend the Yank?" he asks of nobody in particular because he suddenly realises that the fight has moved to another part of the field down the hill. Even Michaeleen it seems is being left behind by the pace of the action. The crowd is now almost too closely surrounding the fighters as Sean hits Danaher another haymaker of a punch, landing him in the hay where double recognition is difficult. As Forbes and others struggle to hold back the ever-pressing crowd, Sean jumps on top of his opponent in the swirling hay and drags him roughly to his feet before something rather extraordinary happens even by Ford's standards of cinematic deception. Admittedly this is visible only in a frame-by-frame analysis, but what happens is that as Sean picks up McLaglen's double, Martin Thornton, whom he has just punched into the hay, it is almost as if he realises he is not the real thing and drops him again. McLaglen appears out of nowhere stage right and Sean then punches him!

Instantly we jump into Fight B in Hollywood. One wonders why Ford went to the trouble of having two totally separate fights. Perhaps when he arrived in Hollywood for the studio scenes he realised that he didn't have enough fight footage or that what he had filmed was in some way unsatisfactory. Alternatively, maybe he wanted to give some action to extras and actors on the other side, in particular Sean McClory. However, the most likely explanation is based on the following observation: it will be noticed that in Fight A the Irish extras did not join in the fighting action, whereas in Fight B the American extras did so with some enthusiasm. Ford wanted to create a Donnybrook, a Maurice Walsh-style faction fight in which the main bout between Red Will and Sean served merely as an excuse for everybody to join in and settle old scores. He could not achieve this with untrained and uninsured Irish extras in Cong, but it was possible in Hollywood.

However, to the close observer, the transition to Fight B is very obvious – we go in one frame from bright sunlight to studio lights with heavy shadows coming from several directions at once; the hay is more straw-coloured and in fact

may even be straw; the colours of the clothes, especially Danaher's shirt, are different and the faces of the extras are definitely American rather than Irish. Sean's punch has propelled Danaher six thousand miles into a stack of straw.

Actually, the man we see spinning across the screen in the opening frames of Fight B is not McLaglen but an American double, possibly Steve Donoghue. Cut, and the real Danaher emerges from the straw with a surprised look on his face. He is met by a deluge of water from the water carriers, a rather heavy-handed joke prominent in Nugent's script but so overused that it soon loses its comic impact. There are meant to be four water carriers, one of whom is Feeney, operating two large tubs, and their function is to refresh the fighters with a generous torrent of water each time one is knocked down. The thin joke is that they come closer to drowning the fighters than helping them. They stumble along after the fighters with a great air of importance and complete seriousness at all times – neither fighter is knocked down or even pauses without being liberally splashed. In fact, it is fair to say that the water carriers are more of a hazard to Red Will and Sean than they are to each other.

In the background to the right we see the thatched White O'Morn studio set in an early stage of construction, indicating that this fight scene was filmed early in the schedule.

Now all hell breaks loose as Sean, in speeded-up action, rushes at Danaher and punches him back into the stack of straw from which he has just emerged. A free-for-all now develops as just about anybody who wants to joins in throwing punches in all directions regardless of where they land. This is a fight for men who enjoy fighting and not fighting anybody in particular. One enterprising fellow seizes the nearest bare leg to him in the straw and sinks his teeth into it as a startled roar of pain is heard. Now virtually all of the bystanders are involved in the general mayhem and the fight is totally out of control.

1:52

As more and more people join in the fun, that great believer in law and order, the proprieties at all times and structured behaviour on all occasions, Michaeleen Oge Flynn, steps in to quell the chaos. With a whip in his left hand and Pat Cohan's revolver in his right, he steps up on the cart and fires two shots towards the cottage to attract the fighters' attention. For an ex-IRA man he appears to be rather squeamish about gunfire because he uses his hat to muffle the sound of the second shot. Alarmed by the gunfire, the combatants all stop fighting immediately. Danaher emerges wet and spluttering from one part of the straw while Sean, tweed cap miraculously intact, emerges from another. Sean suddenly realises that he is not sitting comfortably in the straw, and reaches in to draw a sharp four-pronged fork from underneath him. Unsurprised, he throws it to one side and looks up at Michaeleen.

"Gentlemen," announces Michaeleen from his platform high up on the cart, "this is a private fight." In the circumstances the word "Gentlemen" is used loosely and the distinction between a private fight and a public free-for-all is somewhat academic. "The Marquis of Queensberry Rules," continues Michaeleen, "will be observed on all occasions."

3:00

"Now the Marquis of Queensberry Rules, mind you now, Squire," says Feeney to Danaher, who is still sitting like a turkey in the straw. We know and Feeney knows that there is not the remotest possibility of Danaher's complying with these or any rules − in fact there is more than a hint of sarcasm that a lusty Irish fight should be governed by the rules of an English Marquis. Granite-faced, Danaher rises to continue the fight while Sean good-humouredly goes along with the suggestion saying, "OK with me, Michaeleen." He is halted in his tracks by another drenching contribution from the water carriers. Wiping the water from his eyes he says, "Thanks" sarcastically.

"Non-belligerents will kindly remain neutral," intones Michaeleen. "Now shake hands and come out fighting, I thank you," waving his hat to restart the fight. Again one wonders if Michaeleen's motivation is not personal and financial − if the fight is not seen as fair and above board, maybe the losing punters will demand their money back.

"Do you hear that, everybody?" shouts Danaher standing shoulder to shoulder with Sean and raising both of his hands in the air in acclamation of Michaeleen's suggestion. "The Marquis of Queensberry Rules." Feeney points an accusing finger at some of the onlookers and repeats, "Now, now, the Marquis of Queensberry Rules." Even Sean relaxes for a fatal few moments repeating the mantra, "The Marquis of Queensberry Rules," before the rascally Danaher gives him a full-blooded kick under the chin, probably not one of Queensberry's better-known rules.

As Sean falls back he is cushioned by the straw and two strategically placed extras. Now he is fighting mad, so he gets up quickly and hits Danaher a haymaker of a punch, knocking him down. Not content with this, he picks him up before sending him to the ground again with a left hook, commenting sarcastically, "Come on, get up, Marquis of Queensberry."

1:53:30

The foregoing section of Fight B is not contained in the original script and it is likely that it was added at the last minute as Ford decided to play the fight scene just for laughs. It replaces a long and tedious scene involving the Widow Tillane and Missus Playfair of which we see just a small fraction of the intended original. Missus Playfair was meant to stand at the french windows of her living room observing the fight through a pair of opera glasses. She is madly excited and gives a running commentary to Sarah Tillane who is sitting down pretending to read a book (which turns out to be upside down) and feigning total indifference to the outcome of the fight. Missus Playfair hopes that the Bishop will not see what is going on while Mrs Tillane begs her to come away from the window; eventually, however, she drops her pretence and the two women view the fight from the window together.

In the short scene that survives, Mrs Tillane is observing the fight very keenly through her opera glasses.

"I hope Thornton beats him senseless," she says excitedly to Missus Playfair.

Filming on the river

"Mister Thornton is a married man, Sarah," replies the shocked Missus Playfair.

"Who cares about him?" replies the widow. "It's that big bellowing bully concerns me." She mimics him, "'I'm the best man in Inisfree,' as though I didn't know that."

Although they do not appear in the final cut the remaining few lines of this scene are worth recording because they throw light on her remarks which are otherwise difficult to interpret. Mrs Tillane continues, "But he'll be a better man when he stops thinking he's the best one! I hope Thornton beats him to his knees." Missus Playfair stares, then smiles a little, relieved that she was right after all in her conspiracy.

So, the widow did fancy the macho Danaher after all! If Red Will had played it just a little bit cooler, stopped boasting, bought her the odd bunch of flowers and above all, kept his big mouth shut about her in public, he would have had no difficulty winning her hand years ago.

We are now back in Fight A in the grounds of Cong Abbey **(Location 8G)**. Cong Abbey is one of Ireland's most famous and most beautiful monastic sites – it was founded for the Augustinian Canons Regular in about 1120 by Turlough O'Connor, High King of Ireland, on the site of a sixth-century church associated with Saint Feichin. It is a gem of Romanesque architecture and although many of the surviving buildings date from the thirteenth century, it was partially restored in the nineteenth century. In its heyday as a centre of learning it attracted more than three thousand scholars and students. The priceless Cross of Cong from the monastery now resides in the National Museum in Dublin.

The river seen in the foreground is described in the script as a "brook" – in reality it is a very pretty tributary to the Cong river. The crowd mills along the river bank as Sean and Red Will are supposedly slugging it out in the middle, but it is just a long shot we see from the bridge, so it is hard to tell if Wayne and McLaglen are in there or not – probably not. However, the civil authorities at long last have become aware that there is at very least a disturbance of the peace and they spring into action. We suddenly find ourselves in the little Inisfree police station or Garda Barracks as it would have been known locally – an Irish policeman is known as a "Garda Siochana" which means "Guardian of the Peace"!

In this studio scene the policeman Sergeant Hanan, played by Ford veteran Harry Tenbrook, and his constable, played by David H. Hughes, are looking out the door and the window respectively at the fight and feeling that perhaps they should do something about it. Suddenly

Sergeant Hanan springs into action. "Call up Ballinrobe," he says to the constable. "Tell them to send the inspector down here; send reinforcements immediately, there's a riot here."

The constable cranks the telephone, picks up the receiver and shouts, "Ballinrobe, Ballinrobe," into it, as if half expecting to be heard there without an operator intervening.

4:00

Meanwhile, Mister Playfair and the Bishop have stopped pretending to each other that they are not interested in the fight and leap from the car to get a closer view of the action. The car is parked on the bridge over the Cong River connecting Ashford Castle with Ashford Deerpark (**Location 1C**). In fact, geographically, the car has moved only a few yards from where it was when the fight started. Playfair and the Bishop take up position on the bridge looking down the river towards Lough Corrib. Interestingly, they are looking directly away from the fight which is taking place right behind their backs in Cong Abbey.

The Bishop, who really looks the part with his hat, gaiters and umbrella, is so excited that he impatiently beckons Playfair forward and grabs his binoculars, all the better to see the fight with. The fight has in fact progressed just a little to the clearing along the river bank – the scene was shot from a large platform erected over the river off the bridge opposite Playfair's house. We see Sean being catapulted from the crowd by a huge punch thrown by Danaher, as a result of which he lies flat on the river bank. With his back to the camera, he picks himself up again and takes his stance.

The unlucky Bishop is clearly impressed by this example of Danaher's prowess and since he has the binoculars, he knows that Playfair cannot see what is going on at the moment. The Bishop decides that he will make a little money – little does he know what the wily Playfair knows.

"Five to one on the big chap, Snuffy," he says to Cyril, calling him by what was presumably his public-school nickname.

"Giving or taking," asks the cautious Playfair, checking if it is odds or odds on the Bishop has in mind.

"Giving," says the Bishop.

"Taken," smiles Playfair, as they shake hands on the bet.

The morality of all this is very questionable on Playfair's part. Nowadays it is known as "insider dealing" and the perpetrator if found out can receive a lengthy jail sentence. On the other hand, Playfair could claim that the bad egg Bishop was trying to put one over on him and deserved all he got, but surely Playfair should have taken into account the effect that losing the bet would have had on the Bishop's plans to transfer him or not.

Meanwhile, back at Fight A, Sean has suddenly gained the advantage, probably to the Bishop's dismay. Going for the kill, figuratively if not literally, he hits Danaher a mighty blow which lands him in the water. In this spectacular shot, Danaher's double is Pat Ford, the director's son, whom we have already seen in the line-up for the horse-race.

The fall into the river is a superb stunt which happens so quickly that one does not notice the differences in hair colour, height and bulk between Pat Ford and McLaglen. It is possible that there was some material covering the river bed onto which Pat Ford had to fall – the stony bed of that particular river would have made this a very dangerous stunt indeed. In fairness to Pat Ford the stuntman, the slow-motion running of his fall rivals that of an Olympic diver, and it is one of the highlights of *The Quiet Man*.

Pat Ford splashes about in the water for a few moments and, with very skilful editing, a very wet McLaglen rises from the murky water doing a passable impression of the Lough Ness Monster. Despite being dripping wet and spouting water, he instinctively puts his fists up in a fighting stance. On the river bank, Sean and Michaeleen and the rest of the crowd are smiling almost pityingly and Danaher is at a disadvantage both in terms of his physical position and his points-ranking in the fight. Prominently seen on the bank between Sean and Michaeleen is Martin Thornton who doubled for McLaglen earlier in the fight; he is still dressed in his blue shirt. We notice too that Sean, sans cap, seems to have sorted out his hairpiece problem mentioned earlier.

1:54:30

Typically Danaher goes on the attack but he is fooling nobody.

"You've had enough?" he asks Sean in the hope of securing an honourable draw, but Sean answers loudly, "No" to dash his hopes.

Totally stymied, Danaher rubs his hand over his face and contemplates his immediate future. He holds his right hand out to Sean, not in friendship but seeking help in getting out of the river, with the memorable words, "Well, give a man a hand then," as he moves towards the bank knee-deep in the water. This is an echo of Father Lonergan in the water asking for Mary Kate's help.

The trusting Sean, innocent American that he is, reaches out and pulls him onto dry land as the bystanders crane their necks to miss nothing of the action. Some of the extras are dressed in their Sunday-best double-breasted suits – hardly the best attire in which to follow a cross-country fight. As Sean pulls Danaher out, several people are brought to the front of the crowd – Martin Thornton, Bill Maguire,

Wayne's double, and Joe Mellotte, Wayne's stand-in.

Once Danaher is safe on dry land, his true, unsporting, but very comic nature re-emerges. While holding Sean's right hand and thereby rendering it harmless, he hits him on the jaw with a well-aimed left hook which sends him reeling, almost knocking down several of the railway employees. In fact, throughout the fight Danaher has thrown hardly a single fair punch, but his foul and unfair tactics are just what his supporters have come to see, though they would probably never admit it. While they all dislike Danaher, he is still the local boy against the stranger, and even if he is destined to lose the fight, they all want him to put up a good show for the honour of Inisfree and the glory of Ireland. And of course the longer the fight goes on, the more free entertainment they will enjoy.

A feature of *The Quiet Man*, often unnoticed because of its very nature, is the surreptitious way in which Ford introduces places of interest as background to the action. Indeed, a reviewing of the entire movie looking just at the background scenes is a rewarding experience. Here as background to the fight scene we see the ruins of Cong Abbey, and at times one feels that Ford wanted to make sure that such scenes were included as an integral

At the fight – Martin Thornton, Maura Coyne and Jack MacGowran

part of the action, maybe even to preserve them for posterity.

Meanwhile, back at the police station, word has arrived from the inspector's headquarters in Ballinrobe on how to handle the current public disorder. Sergeant Hanan is on the phone listening intently to his superior officer and saying, "Yes Inspector, thank you sir." When he hangs up the phone, the constable, like the viewers, full of curiosity as to what the official reaction is, asks, "What did he say?"

The response is pure stage-Irish – "He said to put five pounds on Danaher's nose."

Both men rush off to carry out their orders.

Thus, as in the life of Maurice Walsh, even the official authorities feel that the fight must be allowed to continue and that the rule of law must be temporarily suspended. In fact, the fight draws the whole population of Inisfree together as a communal activity and it is interesting to list the characters who have an interest in the outcome. For Sean it is a chance to deserve his wife's love; for Mary Kate her public honour and womanly pride are at stake; for Red Will it is a chance to whip the upstart Yank and revenge himself on the conspiracy; for the Widow Tillane it is an opportunity to have Danaher put in his place before she seriously considers a romance with him; for Mister Playfair and the Bishop it is a chance to enjoy a wager and see a good scrap; for Missus Playfair it is a chance to have a little flutter and see her plot vindicated; for Father Lonergan it is a chance to release some of his repressions by imagining himself as the hero of the hour; for Dan Tobin it is a rejuvenating experience, literally; for Feeney it is a chance to see someone else do to the squire what he would probably like to do himself; for the railwaymen it is a break from the intolerable boredom of their job; for Michaeleen it is perhaps the biggest bookmaking money-spinner of his career; and for Pat Cohan it means a lot of extra drinking and celebrating no matter what the outcome – the fight has something for everyone in the cast!

Meanwhile, back at the action of Fight A at the corner where Collins' replica of White O'Morn now stands **(Location 7D)**, bookmaker Michaeleen is doing a brisk trade.

"Another ten on Thornton," says Hugh Forbes, and Michaeleen mumbling "Another ten on Thornton," puts the name of one Sean Thornton in his book, but there is no striking out his name this time because the advantage is to Sean.

Between Hugh Forbes and Michaeleen in this scene we see clearly the towering figure of Joe Mellotte, stand-in for Duke Wayne for the movie. Joe was also one of the many local extras in the fight scenes. In his later years he became something of a celebrity in the Cong–Neale area because of his connection with the movie. His restaurant and tavern became a mecca for tour buses whose occupants stopped to shake the hand and even demand the autograph of the man who stood in for the Duke. Success never went to Joe's head, however. Even while handing out postcards of himself side by side with Wayne, signing autographs for *Quiet Man* fans from all over the world, he retained his innate modesty, courtesy and gentlemanly behaviour towards all. Sadly, Joe passed away late in 1997, one of the last of the quiet men.

Back at the action, Mr Malouney, the guard of the train, places his bet – "A pound on Danaher," he tells Michaeleen as befits a railwayman of modest income.

"A pound on Danaher," mumbles Michaeleen to himself in a daze as he puts the note in his pocket, only to be pulled roughly from the other side by Costello the train driver, placing his bet.

"Two pounds on Mister Danaher, Mister Flynn please," says Costello, most respectfully.

"Two pounds on Mister Danaher," repeats Michaeleen and Costello says, "Yes" as he scuttles away.

The local support for Danaher is mystifying considering the hammering he is taking in the fight and both railwaymen who have just bet were on the bank when he was punched into

1:55:00

Stand-in and double, Joe Mellotte and Martin Thornton

opening his eyes, nods several times in agreement. With remarkable presence of mind for a dying man, he places a thermometer in his mouth to take his temperature.

Suddenly we hear noise and commotion from the outside world. Somehow the old man senses that "the fight" is on, the moment he has been waiting for to see the big bully Danaher put in his place at last. As Father Paul looks out of the window to see what all the excitement is about, Dan Tobin suddenly perks up, takes the thermometer from his mouth, and decides that he will not die just for the moment. He smiles like a happy baby and jumps out of bed, ready to take his place as an important spectator at the fight.

This scene could almost have been lifted from the works of the Irish playwright Boucicault or the biblical story of Lazarus. There were several changes from the originally intended script. Dan Tobin was meant to stick his head out the window to hear "a stripling" announce, "Will Danaher is fighting the Yank from America," and the old man is carried to the fight on a bed by a quartet of volunteers.

1:55

the river. Perhaps it is the generous odds of three-to-one that Michaeleen is offering (Sean's odds have not been announced but we know from a later line that they are even money). However, it is likely that many of the punters are letting their hearts rule their heads by backing the local man against the Yank.

We now switch to the interior of Dan Tobin's cottage which is a studio scene. The gaffer himself is meant to be on his deathbed, slowly expiring, though from the frontal camera angle he looks pretty healthy. By his bedside Father Paul is reading, not from the prayers for the dying as was originally intended but from a bloodthirsty Celtic saga. In the little bedroom are several shawled women crying quietly and in particular there is Dan Tobin's daughter played by Mimi Doyle. She is sobbing into the apron covering her face for a very good reason – the more she covers her face, the less we will realise that, when she steps outside the door of the cottage in the Irish scene, the part is being played by another actress!

Dan Tobin lies on his bed, eyes closed, with a rosary in his hand, while Father Paul reads:

"Con of a hundred battles, aye and a thousand besides, stood alone on the victorious field, his mighty buckler bent, his broken sword clutched in his mighty hand, the blood of a thousand wounds oozing from his open veins, dripped on the bodies of the slain…"

Dan Tobin clearly approves of this story and,

Outside, back in Ireland, several latecomers to the fight are arriving by bicycle at the bottom of Cong's quaintly named Blazes Lane as Father Paul in his cassock emerges from the cottage **(Location 7E)**. Sizing up the situation immediately, he takes a couple of steps forward, then turns and runs up the laneway as fast as he can, lifting up his cassock as he goes. Clearly he is on his way to inform his superior Father Lonergan of what is happening. At the top of the laneway we see Curran's pub outside which Red Will sealed the bargain after selling the cross-breds **(Location 7C)**.

As Father Paul emerges from the doorway there is yet another "oops" moment in *The Quiet Man*. Opposite him, with its shadow clearly across the lane, is one of the new-fangled electricity poles specially erected to bring current to Cong for the movie. Worse still, as Father Paul sprints up the laneway, two other poles are clearly visible, totally out of keeping

Dan Tobin's house

with the supposed 1920s setting of the movie. Earlier in the action the keen-eyed may be able to find further electricity poles and even wiring on the front of Cohan's pub.

Back at the cottage, Dan Tobin is emerging from the doorway pulling his trousers on over his nightdress and carrying a big stick in his hand. His daughter, now played by Galway actress Maureen Coyne, a member of the Taibhdhearc Players, is simultaneously attempting to help him dress and to restrain him from doing further injury to himself. However, for a dying man, he is showing remarkable enthusiasm. As he flails down the lane we notice that by some sort of miracle he seems to have acquired a pair of shoes in the short time since he has arisen from his deathbed. At the fight itself, the token woman in the crowd, May

Craig, is seen urging the fighters on.

Meanwhile, geographically less than a mile away from the fight **(Location 1H)**, Father Lonergan is still patiently angling for the "king of all salmon" when Father Paul suddenly appears shouting, "Father, Father Lonergan."

"Ssh, ssh, ssh, ssh, ssh," says the parish priest, but the curate will not be silenced.

"It's a big fight in the town," he insists, pointing incidentally in the direction away from the town.

"Listen," says Father Lonergan, never taking his eyes off the line, "there's a big fight in this fish right here too."

"I'd have put a stop to it," gasps Father Paul, still holding his prayer book, "but seeing it's…"

Father Paul is having little success in distracting his superior from fishing, an echo perhaps of the lack of success of his real-life sister Mary Kate on the very same spot.

"You do that, lad," replies Father Lonergan. "It's your duty."

(There is a bit of a clanger here – Ward Bond gives us a very American pronunciation of "dooty" rather than the Irish "juty".)

"But seeing it was Danaher and Sean Thornton," says Father Paul desperately.

"Who?" asks Father Lonergan in amazement.

"Danaher and Sean Thornton," replies Father Paul as the parish priest repeats the

1:56:00

Maura Coyne with cast members

second name in unison with him.

"Well, why the devil didn't you tell me, oh you young...?" roars Lonergan and, throwing down his fishing rod, starts to run as quickly as he can. The two priests sprint along the river bank towards the fight (well, away from it actually!). Some things, some once-in-a-lifetime events it seems are even more important than fishing and this is one of them. In front of Cohan's pub around the Market Cross of Cong, Fight A is still raging **(Location 7A)**. Indeed, so dense is the crowd that it is almost impossible to see the fighters. Moviewise, they could very well be absent from the fight, and maybe they are, but who cares. This violent scene is a harsh echo of Sean's placid arrival in Inisfree at this very spot – little did he think that in such a short time he would be involved in a community brawl.

The vaulted gate

However, help is on the way. Father Lonergan, now miles away on the Ashford Farm **(Location 9M),** vaults a five-bar gate with surprising athleticism for a man of his age and heads towards the fight. Father Paul, more politely, opens the gate and walks through, but, naughty man, he does not close it behind him according to the country code or even the Marquis of Queensberry rules either.

Father Paul rushes along the gable end of the barn **(Location 9N)** to join his parish priest who is pretending to watch the fight around the corner, though in reality it is quite a distance away. The sound effects of punches landing and the exciting music do a good job in convincing us that the two priests are actually watching the

Where the priests watched the fight

fight as the senior cleric holds his curate back from the vision of the crowd.

Ward Bond deserves at least an Oscar nomination for overacting in this scene as he follows every punch and connection with gestures and gasps of his own, based on the tired old cliché that the repressed priest likes to release his inhibitions through physical violence or watching others fight.

"Father, shouldn't we put a stop to it now?" asks the anxious Father Paul, as Father Lonergan bobs and weaves in time with the fight.

"Ah, we should, lad, yes we should, it's our duty!" replies Father Lonergan. (The "juty" is more Irish-sounding now.)

Finally he gives a groan of "enk" as he fields an imaginary punch and sports a most inane smile upon his face.

Back outside Cohan's the mayhem continues at Fight A. The crowd of supporters has grown if anything and is milling around the fighters. The pub sign reading:

THE SARSFIELD ARMS
P. COHAN PROP.

is visible to the sharp-eyed. Legend has it that it was sold to an American collector for £25 – if he is reading this please make contact! The Irish water carriers are in evidence, but unlike their American counterparts they seem unable

1:56

to penetrate the crowd. Again one wonders if the fighters are actually in there at all in the medium-long shot. In close-up Wayne is there all right, but it is definitely Martin Thornton instead of McLaglen – in fact there is no evidence that McLaglen took part in Fight A outside Cohan's at all.

Now we get a splendid close-up of Michaeleen's white-faced horse, parked in front of Cohan's for no other reason than to disguise the fact that McLaglen is not present in person. Sean Thornton punches Martin Thornton under the horse in Fight A and he magically becomes McLaglen as Danaher in Fight B. Feeney provides the continuity as he stoops over his fallen master, and the two people to Feeney's right, underneath the horse, are Patrick and Michael Wayne.

In Fight B now, Danaher is getting up as Feeney encourages him with a number of incoherent exhortations which sound like "Boy, get up like a man, come on, come on, come on," and other inspiring phrases. The water carriers arrive and give Danaher a liberal dousing but by now this joke has worn very thin – there were of course meant to be two sets of water carriers to cover the fact that the Irish and American pairs look so different. The Irish wear caps and jackets, while the American aquarians wear tam-o'-shanters and are in their shirt sleeves. Differences in colour and lighting are also quite obvious here.

As Danaher recovers from his first drenching and begins to sit up he gets a second splash which more than takes his breath away. As he is dragged to his feet by two helpful bystanders, we note the presence of Pat Ford without his glasses as an extra with a cap to McLaglen's right. Suddenly we switch back to Fight A where May Craig is visible as a valuable marker just behind the horse – she did not travel to Hollywood for the studio scenes. Patrick Wayne gets his head in front of the camera again also.

In Fight A now, Sean Thornton, for some reason best known to himself, mounts the horse and sits there safely until Danaher gets his second wind and the crowd gives them a little

more room to manoeuvre. Now Michaeleen gets up on the back of the sidecar and throws Sean his cap, maybe just in case he has another accident with his rug in the fight.

"How's the betting going?" Sean asks Michaeleen, who replies, "Even money, Sean, even money, but don't ruin me." This is the first time we learn Sean's odds but, although most of the local money has been on Danaher, a few big bets like those of Forbes on Thornton could bankrupt Michaeleen. As Michaeleen takes off his hat and characteristically scratches his head, the smiling May Craig, who seems to be everywhere at once, joins the two men on their elevated platform. Is this Sean's mother come to protect him during the fight?

Sean uses his elevated position to jump once again from Fight A into Fight B to the alarm of May Craig and the ever-present railwaymen. He lands beside Danaher outside the studio Cohan's; although very wet, Danaher stands in typical fighting pose. In the background we notice Owen Glynn swept along by the crowd in the company of Hugh Forbes, and Pat Ford is never far from the action in the background beside Dermot Fahy. Now Glynn and Forbes have decided that it is time for a drinks break or maybe even time for the fight to come to an end, so they stand between the two combatants.

"Well, Danaher," says Sean, "you're a good fighting man, I'll say that for you."

"Well, if it comes to that," smiles Red Will, "it's been a pleasure beating ye." He turns round to shake hands with one of his supporters but then he turns back suddenly to hit Sean a foul blow in the stomach, one of his favourite tactics. Indeed, it would be difficult to find a single fair or legal punch that Danaher threw in the fight and no doubt he is proud of the fact. For once, Sean, smiling to the crowd, is caught unawares and takes the full force of the blow, falling to the ground as Owen Glynn tries to restrain Danaher. Sean, surprisingly, lands in Fight B where the punch was thrown, and the dreaded water carriers arrive again, emptying the full contents of their tub on Sean and the extras who cushioned his fall. At this stage Sean fears the water carriers a lot more than he fears Danaher and shaking his hands dry he gives

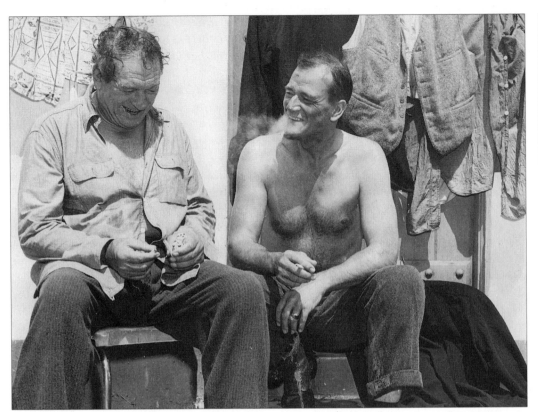

McLaglen and Wayne relax between takes

them a scathing look before rising to his feet again with a highly sarcastic "Thanks".

Still in Fight B (and the movie does not return to Fight A again) Michaeleen the bookmaker is still being offered business. Forbes cheekily comes and asks him, "Will you take another twenty on Thornton?" but Michaeleen replies, "No, no, the book is closed, the book is closed," because that bet would certainly bankrupt him. He puts his hand first to his head and then to his mouth as he tries to calculate his overall winnings or losses in his little book.

But there is one other would-be punter who wants a piece of the action when he is pretty sure of the outcome. In his second big moment of defiance in *The Quiet Man*, Feeney climbs up beside Michaeleen and, having looked carefully around to check that he is not being observed, says slyly into his ear, "A pound on Thornton against the Squire!" Feeney is serious because he has a pound note in his hand, wherever he got it. Maybe it's Danaher's money he is holding, which would be a neat trick to play on

his boss, winning some money by betting the Squire's money against the Squire!

However, Michaeleen will have none of it, and his response is immediate and very significant in the light of Irish history – "Go away, ya traitor ya."

Traitors and informers were universally despised in the Ireland of the time and still are in many parts of the country. Even if Michaeleen knew he would gain financially from Feeney's bet he would have no hand or part in this transaction. Furthermore, it is ironic that the man betrayed, McLaglen, was himself the informer in Ford's Oscar-winning movie of the same title. Finally, in just one frame of this sequence, on the "t" of "traitor", Michaeleen actually spits on the despised Feeney, whether deliberately or not we cannot tell. The spit, which is not clearly visible at normal speed, was first pointed out to the author by Gerry Collins. It is a compulsory exercise for every *Quiet Man* fan who has access to a video playback machine to locate the relevant frame, so get cracking right now!

Forbes and Glynn again separate the combatants as the fight grinds to a halt.

"How about a drink before you kill yourselves?" suggests Forbes.

"The drink will be on the house," adds Pat Cohan helpfully, with another generous rush of blood to the head.

"Ah, it's a good idea, Sean," interjects Owen Glynn. "The people from Ballyglunin are coming over by bus – thousands of them."

Ford liked to have mentioned by name places which had made a big contribution to *The Quiet Man*, if only to please the local people. Ballyglunin was of course the railway station used in two major sections of the movie. However, the "thousands" travelling from Ballyglunin by bus are doomed to be disappointed as the fight will have finished before they arrive.

7:30

Maybe Red Will Danaher is feeling the pace because he surprisingly agrees with the suggestion saying, "Ay, that's a good idea." But he adds in a fighting pose, "Not that I'm tired, mind you, I'm as fresh as a daisy."

"You look more like a black-eyed Susan to me," retorts Sean, and adds "Let's go," as they turn to enter the pub. A black-eyed Susan is a flower very different from a daisy and a much better description of Danaher's current appearance.

We notice that the only railway official prominent in both Fight A and Fight B crowds is Webb Overlander, stationmaster and Duke Wayne's make-up man. None of the other actors who played railwaymen travelled to Hollywood for the studio scenes.

As the crowd makes its way to the pub door the wily Pat Cohan shouts, "Principals only," with a view to keeping expenses down since he has announced that the drinks are on the house.

The scene now switches to Mister Playfair and the Bishop who are standing behind the wall of the potato garden in front of Danaher's house **(Location 9G)**. All they can see from here is

an empty house, but what matter, it's a nice shot.

The puzzled Bishop, binoculars in hand, remarks to his immediate inferior, "Is that a public house?"

"Yes, your lordship," answers Playfair.

"Are they going in?" persists the Bishop, who does not seem very quick on the uptake.

"Yes, your lordship," the patient Playfair answers.

"Does that mean the fight's over?" asks the Bishop in a disappointed tone of voice.

"No, no," smiles Mister Playfair, "that's just the end of round one."

"Oh," says the Bishop philosophically as Playfair looks through the binoculars.

Meanwhile, outside the studio Cohan's, the crowd is pressing around the entrance, but only Sean and Danaher are allowed in.

"All right now, stand back, stand back, let them have their drink in peace," Owen Glynn marshalls the crowd, while Hugh Forbes adds, "Keep away, now keep away."

Inside, Pat Cohan makes elaborate preparations for the fighters' drinks break, doffing his hat and bowing in an exaggeratedly theatrical manner. The General, wise man, is still sitting in the bar where we left him before the fight, unmoved and still reading his pictorial magazine. Naturally he pays no attention whatsoever as Pat Cohan, Sean and Red Will enter the bar. He vibrates not even an inch as Pat Cohan noisily slams the bar-top entrance just behind his back. Clearly, the General is a true member of the gentry who prides himself on paying no attention to disputes among the peasantry.

Pat Cohan realises that he is treading on eggshells and that he must chose his words carefully and diplomatically if he is to prolong the uneasy truce between the two fighters.

"Ah now let me see," he says, "whiskey? Naw, that would be too warm, it would get your blood up. Porter's the very thing," (cheaper too!) and he proceeds to draw two pints of porter.

"Ah," says Danaher to Sean, "it's peaceful and

1:58:00

quiet in here, isn't it?" Ironically these are the first civil words he has addressed to Sean in the course of the entire movie.

"Yeah," says Sean laconically as he takes a sip of his porter.

"You know…" says Danaher, and then stops suddenly as he realises there is something in his mouth. It is a tooth, loosened by the punches he has taken, but he casually spits it out and continues as if nothing has happened. This has all the hallmarks of an on-the-spot humorous addition to the script by Ford.

"You know," continues Danaher with a superb Irish bull, "this has been a fight I'd come a long way to see," as he picks up his drink and takes a long draught.

"I hope you can stick around for the finish," says Sean with an American bull in the spirit of the conversation. Danaher does a double take, first laughing, but then, as he slowly understands the implications of what Sean has said, he reverts to his sullen ways.

"Don't worry about that," he snaps as he takes another big mouthful of his drink. But Danaher is definitely mellowing, impressed by the only thing that he can be impressed by – Sean's fighting ability. He turns to Sean smilingly and says, "You know, Yank, I've taken quite a likings to yez."

"I'm getting real fond of you too," replies Sean, but the sarcasm is lost on the big hulk as Pat Cohan beams benignly on the pair of them.

Now Danaher turns to the barman with a wink and decides to take a rise out of Sean with his heavy-handed wit.

"Your widow, me sister," he says to Sean, "she could have done a lot worse."

This is a standard Irish bull because you cannot have a widow until after you are dead, but Danaher is suggesting that Sean will not survive the remainder of the fight, so Mary Kate is virtually a widow already.

"True, true," agrees Cohan, going along with the gag.

"Poor woman," says Danaher in mock sympathy.

"Thanks," says Sean in his usual sarcastic tone, and then adds to Cohan, "Fill them up again."

"Ah, you'll buy me no drinks," says Danaher unaccountably, as Sean takes some money from his pocket.

"The… the drinks are on the house of Cohan, sir," says Pat the peacemaker nervously to Danaher.

In fact, the glasses are still half full, so why all the fuss?

"And I'm takin' no drinks from you, you little squint," says Danaher ungraciously to his host, despite the fact that he has just taken one. The description of Pat Cohan as a little squint echoes Mary Kate's description of Feeney earlier on in the movie.

"I'm buyin' the drinks," insists Sean stubbornly putting his money on the counter.

Danaher rudely knocks Sean's money to the floor with a fine reverse sweep of his hand. This is a very deliberate and ironic echo of the incident at the wedding reception where Red Will scattered Mary Kate's dowry of gold pieces on the floor. In a curious twist of circumstances, both men are now very anxious to press money on each other. The moral of the story seems to be that it is not the money that counts, but the principle of the thing.

"You can buy me a drink at your wake, ha, ha," laughs Red Will, "and not before," – another original Irish bull from the pen of Frank Nugent.

Danaher smiles at Pat Cohan, full of admiration for his own wit, as he throws his money on the counter. Now it is Sean's turn to assert himself – maybe he feels he has stood for too much nonsense already. He scatters Danaher's money on the floor and says crossly, "I'm buyin'," and taking some more money from the reserve fund in his trouser pocket, slams it on the counter with some force. One wonders how the fight took place at all with all the copper and silver the men were carrying on their persons. Remarkably too in the cool climate of Ireland, the men's clothes seem to have dried out rather quickly, seeing that Danaher spent a lot of time in the river and remembering the enthusiastic activities of the water carriers.

Danaher has had enough of these verbal skirmishes and has decided that the time has

1:58:30

1:59

234   The Complete Guide to The Quiet Man

come for fighting action again. Crudely, he throws the remains of his pint of porter full into Sean's face. Sean splutters and calls, "Bar towel," whereupon Pat Cohan hands him the smallest and most miserable towel in the entire world. As he dries his eyes, Sean comes to a decision – things have gone far enough, and the fight ends here and now. Learning from Danaher's unfair tactics of distraction followed by a surprise attack, he asks Cohan, "What time is it?" as Danaher, off-guard, peers with interest.

"Half past five, sir," answers Cohan in his best brogue, but the correct answer is "Time to finish the fight," because it's been a long day since Michaeleen drove Mary Kate to the station that morning. To make things worse, Sean has had no breakfast and doesn't seem to have taken any break for food during the drag or the fight, so he is now drinking on an empty stomach.

Having distracted Danaher, Sean summons up all his energy and all his experience and hits him the mother of all punches, sending him crashing through the obviously fake studio door, shattering it to pieces. As the punch lands and Danaher flies through the air, the bell rings for the end of the fight and presumably Sean is the winner by a knockout. This is a benign echo of his knocking out Tony Gardello in that fatal fight, for although Danaher is knocked out, he is not dead, and Sean will not have to quit his ring of friends in Inisfree. McLaglen's double (again probably Steve Donoghue) lands with such force outside the pub that he knocks over several of the crowd who of course cushion his fall. The double wisely keeps his face covered as much as he can and rolls out of shot.

High up on his perch on the sidecar, Michaeleen is completing his calculations on how his credits and losses stand after the day's betting. As Danaher emerges head first through the door, Michaeleen exclaims, "Glory be to God," closing his eyes and putting his hand to his head. He has very mixed feelings about the outcome of the fight – he is glad that Sean won, but because of his victory he faces financial ruin from which it will take him a long time to recover. One mystery remains – what is Michaeleen doing outside when there is free drink in Cohan's?

In the originally intended script, the fight does not end here – indeed punching Danaher through the door was merely the beginning of round two, as Mister Playfair's earlier remark to the Bishop indicates. Michaeleen, cheering Sean, suddenly says to himself, "What am I saying? He's ruining me!" Father Lonergan pays more lip-service to stopping the fight but does nothing; finally, after Sean has downed Danaher with four consecutive punches, he fails to rise again, despite Michaeleen's impassioned plea of "Get up, Danaher, I'm a ruined man."

Now the authorities and the forces of law and order were meant to spring into action. Sergeant Hanan and his constable arrive to move along the crowd and prevent a disturbance of the peace. Father Lonergan bawls at a bunch of unfortunate shawled women for having the audacity to watch the fight. He confronts Sean and Red Will, asks them if they have been fighting and describes their behaviour as disgraceful. He forces the two men to shake hands, which would have been an echo of their earlier unfriendly and painful handshake. At this stage Danaher was meant to remark affably, "Well, it's all in the family anyway!"

Some of these scenes had great comic potential and would have been nice to see, but it appears that they fell victim to Herb Yates' draconian time constraints. The great fight scene in particular thus ends in a very unsatisfactory manner with too much left to the imagination. On the other hand, maybe some would argue that the fight had already gone on long enough and had become a bit boring. One would be loath to give advice to John Ford, living or dead, but a more satisfactory decision might have been to cut more of Fight B and give a little more of the comic aftermath of Fight A.

As it was, Ford chose to turn his attention to the clerical gentry, the Playfairs and the Bishop. We see Missus Playfair stealing back sheepishly to her house from the Widow Tillane's while outside her husband is tinkering with his car (**Location 8F**). As he looks up she says, "I hope you won't be vexed with me, Cyril, but I've lost three pounds to Mrs Tillane. I know I shouldn't have bet but…"

It is clear that Mrs Tillane has bet on Thornton, while Missus Playfair has backed the local man Danaher.

1:59:30

Playfair stares at his wife quizzically as if betting and winning were the most natural things in the world, but their conversation is interrupted by the arrival in their doorway of the Bishop, blowing on a cheque freshly written, no doubt with a Parker fountain pen.

"There you are, Snuffy," says the Bishop, "fifteen pounds," and Cyril Playfair smiles happily to himself as he folds the cheque and pockets it.

At last the Bishop notices Missus Playfair and shakes hands with her enthusiastically saying, "Hello there, Elizabeth." She curtsies and replies, "Your Lordship."

"And what have you been doing all day?" he asks her, as her husband smiles fondly at the two of them.

She does not reply, but a good line was cut from the script here – Playfair with a twinkle was meant to reply on her behalf "Charity calls," later amended to "Parochial visits." Ford, it seems, did not risk using this witty line because it involved Playfair's deceiving his bishop, albeit Irish-style on screen. Interestingly enough, while all the many references to the Catholic parish priest's betting (and there were quite a few) were removed, all of those relating to the betting of the Protestant clergy remained – a curious sense of values.

Now Elizabeth Playfair realises she has nothing to be ashamed of except losing and that in fact she has ample reason to be quite annoyed at her husband's extravagant gambling activities.

"If you'll excuse me," she says to the two men, "I'll get your tea, Snuffy." Clearly, this public-school nickname has been concealed from his wife up to this, but now the secret is out, and the name will be used to great effect in future tricky situations. The Bishop, innocent of the whole situation and complex rural plots and customs, smiles sweetly after her.

The movie is now virtually over but there are still a few questions to be answered and several loose ends to be tied up. How real is the bonding between Sean and his brother-in-law Red Will? Will Sean and Mary Kate live happily ever after? Will the Playfairs remain in Inisfree or be transferred to another parish? Will Father Lonergan catch his big fish and will Michaeleen recover financially? Will the train ever leave the station on time? And will Red Will Danaher find romance, happiness and a much bigger farm and income with the Widow Tillane? Some, but not all, of these questions are answered in a superb final four minutes or so, allowing us the luxury of a happy ending for all the characters as befits a great comic masterpiece.

Firstly, we are left in no doubt that Sean and Red Will have become lifelong friends and in fact Danaher is quite proud of having a brother-in-law who is such a good fighter. Drinking ability is another trait that Danaher respects and from the next scene it looks as if Sean has passed this particular examination with flying colours. We see both men, with arms around each other's shoulders, crossing the stream in front of White O'Morn in its Irish location. The pair of them are "well-oiled", as the local phrase has it, and are staggering through the water together singing *The Wild Colonial Boy*. This echoes the singing of the same song at a time earlier in the movie when they were completely at loggerheads. They sing:

2:00

There was a wild colonial boy
Jack Duggan was his name
He was born and bred in Ireland
In a place called Castlemaine
He was his father's only son
His mother's pride and joy
And dearly did his parents love
This wild colonial boy.

"Aieee," they finish on a raucous shout of laughter.

As the two men manage with difficulty to cross the little river towards White O'Morn, we see the faint figure of Mary Kate silhouetted in the doorway. Next we see a close-up of her standing outside of the studio cottage staring in amazement at the sight of her husband and her brother staggering home together arm in arm; she can scarcely believe her eyes. At first, standing hands on hips, she is quite indignant, but then her face breaks into a broad smile as she realises that all is well and that the two most important people in the world to her have become friends. Suddenly, however, a look of terror crosses her face – will her housekeeping, her cooking and everything else meet with the approval of the two men? In a state of mild panic she reverses into her cottage.

Inside, the studio cottage is as pretty as a picture. There is a colourful tablecloth on the table which is laid for two, and two candles shine brightly in the centre. Mary Kate looks around to see what needs to be done – whether the table is meant for Sean and herself or Sean and her brother, we cannot tell. She rushes over and brings the bread and butter to the table and stands to attention by the doorway. Then she notices that a chair may be out of place so she brings it nearer to the table and stands stiffly again; but in moving the chair closer to the table she has dislodged the tablecloth, so that must be fixed up too. However, she is in position, standing to attention when the two men arrive at the door.

0:30

As the two brothers-in-law appear in the doorway, arm in arm, they present a pathetic sight. They are still battered, bloodied, torn and dirty from the fight and they have drunk so much that it is a miracle they have made it home at all.

"Woman of the house," says Sean, "I've brought the brother home to supper."

Mary Kate is now truly *bean a tí* or woman of the house and the reference is no longer sarcastic. It is a recognition that she is now officially wife and housewife, mistress of all she surveys, a fact accepted by herself, Sean, society in general, including her brother Red Will.

Danaher is now "the brother" and not just Mary Kate's brother – he is family.

"He is kindly welcome," replies Mary Kate, smiling and curtsying at the same time.

This scene is chock-a-block with echoes from earlier scenes in the movie, maybe to remind us of all the trouble and strife that has preceeded it. In particular, we now have a mirror image of the scene where Sean and Michaeleen call to the Danaher house to pay court to Mary Kate. Then Sean was too late for supper, now Red Will is in good time for supper. There is lots of "something wet" in the cottage, and Red Will, now sure of his welcome, says, "God bless all in this house," echoing Michaeleen's earlier "God save all in this house" and Feeney's "God bless all here". Finally, Red Will is told by Mary Kate "Wipe your feet," just as he was ordered by the Widow Tillane's little maid Nell when White O'Morn was being sold. Then he resented the order, but now he replies, "Thank you, ma'am." Meanwhile, Sean is indulging in a few significant echoes of his own. He takes off his cap and hurls it into the bedroom with great force. Wasn't it in this very cottage that Sean hurled a rock through the window to start Mary Kate from the bedroom like a frightened rabbit from the undergrowth? Didn't he throw his hat over a Connemara wall to signify his liberation from the courtship rituals of rural Irish society? Now he is throwing his cap through the very door he had to break down on his wedding night. However, now at last Sean is sure that he has broken down all barriers between himself and Mary Kate.

As he pulls out his chair, Sean says to Red Will, "Sit down, sit down, that's what chairs are for," the exact words sarcastically spoken to him when he was totally dependent on Red Will's whim in seeking Mary Kate's hand. As the two men sit at the table, Mary Kate brings a big jug of porter and Sean first attempts to pour himself a glass, but then remembers his good manners and pours his guest's drink first, rather messily spilling a good deal of it.

"Hurry it up," says Sean to Mary Kate with

2:01:00

typical American impatience as the ceremonial candles flicker on the table, but for once Mary Kate does not mind being honked at by the man in her life as she brings the joint to the table and dishes out the meat. Sean clinks glasses with Red Will and takes a long draught of his porter, surely the most satisfying drink he has ever partaken of in Ireland. Red Will too celebrates by downing his pint, but Mary Kate finishes as she began – serving meals to her menfolk.

The Quiet Man could very easily have ended here but Ford has still a few loose ends to tie up and indeed a few tricks up his sleeve.

In a rather beautiful shot we see a close-up of the Market Cross of Cong **(Location 7A)** beside which is standing a comely Irish maiden draped in her Galway shawl. The inscription on the cross in ancient Irish lettering reads in translation:

A PRAYER FOR NICOL AND GILBERT O'DUFFY

These were Abbots of Cong Abbey about the fourteenth century, but according to local tradition the stone cross also marks the spot where an unpopular judge was murdered. It is said that he had just sentenced to death a man he had found guilty of murder when he himself was slain by the brother of the accused at the very spot where the cross was afterwards erected. It's just another of those charming legends for which Ireland is justly famous.

The narrator, Father Lonergan, seems to be winding up the movie just as he began it on a fine soft day in the spring – it is now a sunny day in late summer.

"Well then," he begins, "so peace and quiet came once again to Inisfree, and we were up…" as the church bell rings and a dog lazily crosses the road. He is about to continue in the same placid tones when he is rudely interrupted.

"Good heavens, what's that woman up to now?" he shouts as Missus Playfair zooms around the corner at full speed on her tandem,

just in front of where the White O'Morn replica cottage is now situated **(Location 7F)**. This is an echo of the breathtaking ride of Sean and Mary Kate round the adjacent corner on the same tandem.

"Make way, make way," shouts Father Lonergan in another burst of overacting and overbrogueing, "she'll be running you down with that juggernaut."

A juggernaut for the uninitiated is an idol of Krishna at Puri, Orissa, annually dragged in procession in an enormous car under whose wheels, it is said, devotees used to throw themselves. It is hence figuratively used to describe any institution or notion to which persons blindly sacrifice themselves or others. One can see immediately, therefore, the aptness of Father Lonergan's unscripted metaphor.

Missus Playfair flashes past the segregated crowd of shawled women and rides on at full speed towards the crowd of men which parts to admit her as she dismounts from the tandem **(Location 7G)**. Eager hands grab the tandem as Missus Playfair makes her way through the crowd to reach Father Lonergan and Father Paul who are standing by the wall in front of the tree-lined stream. The youths in the left of this frame are Michael and Patrick Wayne, again masquerading as local inhabitants.

Site of farewell scene

Echoing the previous conspiracy to bring about the marriage of Sean and Mary Kate, Missus Playfair and Father Lonergan are hatching another plot. Previously it was Danaher that had to be fooled, this time it is the Bishop, because now, most untypically, they are hatching a little ecumenical plot to keep the Playfairs in Inisfree, by making the gullible episcopal gentleman believe that there is an unprecedented increase in the Protestant population. Such outbursts of Protestant–Catholic co-operation were not common in the Ireland of the period and indeed there is a long-standing and rather cruel joke that the only time that Irish Protestants and Catholics ever truly got together was to get rid of ecumenism!

Missus Playfair whispers something in Father Lonergan's ear, supposedly in Irish, a most unlikely ability for a clergyman's wife, echoing the confessional scene with Mary Kate. Father Lonergan replies with the only two words of Irish he seems to know, "Sea, sea," ("Yes, yes,") as Missus Playfair points to the direction in which the car bearing the Bishop will arrive as Playfair drives him to the station presumably.

Father Lonergan now elevates himself above the crowd **(Location 7G)** and makes his announcement.

"Now when the Reverend Mister Playfair, good man that he is, comes down," he says, "I want yez all to cheer like Protestants. Now spread out, spread out."

How one cheers like a Protestant as distinct from cheering like a Catholic, an agnostic or an atheist, the parish priest does not specify. The original script alternatives were clearer – they were "Now remember! I want you all to cheer him as if you were Protestants" and "Now remember! I want you to cheer him as though you meant it."

So saying, Father Lonergan takes a handkerchief from his pocket and ties it into a little scarf with which to disguise the clerical collar around his neck. The crowd of men rushes forward towards the huddle of shawled women as the camera cuts back again to show Father Paul lowering his hat and covering his collar as Father Lonergan does likewise. Between them, Missus Playfair, the one genuine Protestant in the crowd, is smiling happily but trying to keep out of the Bishop's sight. The boy to the left is Patrick Wayne. Finally, the priests take off their hats and Father Paul sports a blackthorn stick for added effect.

Then, right on cue, the car, with horn blaring, comes around the corner driven by the unsuspecting Cyril Playfair with the Bishop sitting regally in the back seat, a most impressive figure. If they are driving to return to the train, naturally they are heading in the wrong direction geographically, but we have grown used to this by now. Father Paul, Missus Playfair and Father Lonergan are shown leading the cheering and the crowd shout, "Hip hip hurrah," not just once but four times and raise their hats in the air.

The Bishop beams and nods benignly to the crowd. Mister Playfair smiles in delight and amazement at the splendid gesture of his Catholic neighbours – the poor man is close to tears with happiness. However, we must remark that if the Bishop is this easily fooled about the size of the local congregation, one wonders how he ever made it into the hierarchy, but maybe that was a lean year for bishops.

As the Morris Cowley crawls through the crowd in a cloud of pollution we see its registration number, IM 2234, quite clearly – IM was the Galway registration code of the period. Recently, the Playfair car has been located in perfect working order, but for legal reasons its owner and whereabouts cannot be revealed. But it will not be long before it is driven in style through the Emerald Isle once again!

The Bishop gets a couple more "Hip, hip, hurrahs," and one of the last of the crowd to cheer him before he departs is Joe Mellotte, Wayne's famous stand-in, seen in a full frontal shot – a little tribute from Ford to acknowledge his unique contribution to *The Quiet Man*.

1:30

2:02:00

Now the white face of the horse Napoleon comes into view **(Location 7F)** pulling the sidecar driven by Michaeleen Oge Flynn who seems to have missed out on the little ecumenical conspiracy. But who are the courting couple he is conveying? None other than the Widow Tillane and her macho beau, Red Will Danaher! And why, we may well ask, are they allowed to sit on the same side of the vehicle when Sean and Mary Kate were not? An outbreak of patty fingers in this situation would be almost impossible to control, but the real reason for the novel configuration is more mundane. It has nothing to do with their age, maturity or status in the community or even with local customs and clerical sanctions. It is simply a matter of having the couple face the camera at the same time.

As Michaeleen brings the sidecar to a halt with a shout of "Whoa" to give us a better view of the couple, we see that Red Will is dressed in his Sunday best, complete with trilby hat, buttonhole, walking stick and even a bunch of flowers in his hand. However, he is still somewhat the worse for wear following the fight and his face bears several patchwork plasters. He looks most self-conscious and uncomfortable as if to say, "The things I have to do for a few extra acres of land," but the scene is a masterpiece of comic underplay by the then sixty-five-year-old Victor McLaglen.

Beside him, the Widow Tillane looks equally uncomfortable but probably for different reasons. Mildred Natwick was not normally a comic actress and does not seem to have entered into the spirit of this scene. On the other hand, maybe the noble and aristocratic nature of the character she is portraying means that she must hold herself aloof from this vulgarly public courting ritual. Nevertheless, she is splendidly turned out in a fetching frock and a magnificent flower-covered bonnet on her head. In her hand she carries a discreet umbrella so that there is no danger of Red Will's taking advantage of her in a sudden thunderstorm.

Michaeleen inspects the couple with a view to spotting improprieties and seeing nothing amiss, just issues his usual warning, "No patty fingers if you please," echoing his admonition to Sean and Mary Kate, "the proprieties at all times". Mrs Tillane raises her eyebrows in surprise at being lectured thus, but Danaher nods in agreement – maybe he doesn't want any patty fingers. However, whether by accident or design, Michaeleen shows a complete disregard for his female passenger by ludicrously nudging her bonnet over her eyes with his shoulder as he prepares for the take-off with a cry of, "Hold on to your hats. Come up." These are the last words heard in *The Quiet Man*.

The couple set off on their courtship journey to the same music as Sean and Mary Kate did – *The Kerry Dances*. This time there is genuine enthusiasm and feeling from the crowd of bystanders as they throw their hats and caps in the air and cheer loudly. After all, there is to be a big society wedding in Inisfree with in all probability a big wedding feast with free food and free drink all round, and who knows what other prosperity the amalgamation of two large estates may bring?

Now Red Will and the Widow Tillane are off in earnest as the grinning Michaeleen accelerates the sidecar. Even Mildred Natwick manages a smile but Red Will remains impassive and granite-faced as they pass by the camera. Maybe his facial muscles for smiling have been damaged in the fight and he still hurts too much to do to anything but just sit there, but let us not forget that he was fighting for the widow's hand and respect in the fight too. If he hadn't taken up the challenge, he might have had Mary Kate back again and no chance of wedded bliss with his darling Sarah. Paradoxically, and little does Red Will know this, if he had won the fight and not been humiliated, he wouldn't have won her either. However, all's well that ends well and we are to assume that Mr and Mrs Danaher lived happily ever after, though whether Red Will gave Sarah any kith or kin is hard to say.

Now it is really time for the cast of *The Quiet Man* to say goodbye and take their leave of us, and Ford and Nugent decide to do it in true theatrical style by having many of the main characters take a bow as if they were on stage.

2:02

Farewells

Duke waits

This seems quite an appropriate way to end a comedy but it is not always suitable for a tragedy – the sight of people who died during the action suddenly coming alive again and taking a bow can be a bit disconcerting. The happy ending is emphasised by the fact that we hear for the first time in the movie as background music one of the most stirring and joyful of all Irish tunes – *Saint Patrick's Day*. This is the recessional hymn of *The Quiet Man*, and was also featured in Ford's *She Wore a Yellow Ribbon* (1949).

The first members of the cast to say goodbye are Father Paul and Father Lonergan, smiling with regret at having to leave us. Father Lonergan has uncovered his collar and is back to normal clerical dress. Next we see a beaming Elizabeth Playfair – all of her plots and schemes have come to a successful conclusion and for her it is certainly a happy ending with the prospect of living with her husband in Inisfree indefinitely. Next to her is Hugh Forbes – the script naturally called for Forbes and Glynn to say goodbye together but of course Glynn was not available in Ireland. Forbes waves us goodbye with his cap.

Next, May Craig the fishwoman and Sean's mother-figure gives us one of her loveliest smiles and a gracious curtsy. She is symmetrically surrounded by the railwaymen Mr Costello to her right and Mr Malouney to her left. The faces of these three cast members are bathed in gentleness and any harsh comments in the movie are soon forgotten.

Now, we have a mystery – who is the splendidly dressed gentleman with the pipe pretending to be Guppy? In 1996 the author had the man's picture printed in the movie section of the RTÉ Guide, Ireland's national radio and television guide, in the hope that some reader would recognise him, but nobody did. However, Martin Summerville, whom I met while hawking the photograph around the Cong area, was of the opinion that the man's surname was Barton and that he came from Dublin. If this is the case, he could very well have been an angler staying at Ashford Castle whom Ford plucked out of obscurity for a moment of immortality to impersonate Guppy. Feeney, one of the most underrated members of the cast, is by the mock Guppy's side and indeed casts him a sideways glance just to let us know that the two of them do not come from the same planet.

Then we have three more railwaymen – none of them in fact a professional actor. Paddy O'Donnell the porter and Kevin Lawless the fireman were both car-drivers, and Webb Overlander the stationmaster was Wayne's make-up man. Conscious as ever of the punctuality of the train, Mr Bailey is looking at his pocket watch. Maybe this was Ford's way of saying that all members of the cast, from big stars and professionals down to bit players and amateurs, were important and made their particular contribution to *The Quiet Man*.

Dan Tobin, played by John Ford's brother Frank, is given a nostalgic final few moments alone before the camera. Rejuvenated by the fight, an echo of his earlier threat against Danaher with his stick ("If I had the floor") he has made a full recovery from his final illness. Dressed in his traditional Aran costume, he raises his blackthorn stick in defiance and if we could hear him speaking he would be saying, "Up the rebels."

Frank Ford featured in one of the first incidents recorded on the Irish shooting which demonstrates just how contrary his brother Jack could be. He told assistant director, Andrew

McLaglen, to have the whole cast on hand in costume and make-up for the morning of the first day's filming. McLaglen felt that this did not include Frank, whose scenes were later in the movie and who needed at least an hour to have his elaborate beard fitted. When Pappy arrived on the set, he looked around and seeing everybody except Frank said, "OK, we'll have Frank." There was a mad rush to find Frank and fix up his beard and make-up and wardrobe which delayed proceedings for nearly an hour. When he was ready, Ford looked at his brother a few times through his viewfinder and then proceeded to film other scenes that did not include Frank. He just had to show people who was the boss.

Frank Ford was given very many scenes in *The Quiet Man*, far more than the importance of the character he portrayed merited. Garry Wills in his book on the Duke, *John Wayne – The Politics of Celebrity* (1997), suggests that this prominence was an attempt on his brother's part of making up for the many years of inglorious bit parts and cameos he had played in Ford movies, but it could just as well have been in recognition of all Frank had taught Jack about the movie business. As it was, Frank is the only *Quiet Man* character to give a solo bow in the farewell scene and it would be nice if this had been his final appearance on screen. However, he was to appear in just two more movies – Ford's *The Sun Shines Bright* where he played the part of Brother Finney, and *The Marshall's Daughter* where he played Gramps. Both of these movies were released in 1953, the year he died.

But, quite appropriately, the final scenes of *The Quiet Man* belong to Sean and Mary Kate as they take their leave of us in front of White O'Morn. They stand smiling side by side, equals now, on a grassy knoll by the stepping stones over the stream **(Location 4I)**. First they wave furiously to the camera, which is us, as if to thank us theatrically for our interest in their problems and for watching the movie. In his hand Sean is holding a stout stick, the phallic symbol of brutal control and forced dominance throughout the ages. This is an echo of the many sticks seen throughout the movie – Danaher's, Dan Tobin's, the one Sean broke over his knee, the one Mary Kate handed to him and the one May Craig handed to him. Then Mary Kate, serious for a moment, stops smiling and makes that famous whisper in her husband's ear. What does she say? Maureen O'Hara, in an interview, put it to me as follows:

2:03:00

> Only three people know what I whispered in Duke Wayne's ear. The first was Pappy and he's dead. The second was Duke and he's dead too. The third was myself and I ain't telling.

Despite earnest pleas and all sorts of inducements she says she has not and will not divulge it to anyone and will carry it to the grave with her. Nor would she leave it to the author in her will in a sealed envelope if I outlive her! I have enlisted the services of at least two expert lip-readers but, because the whisper was filmed sideways and not full frontally, they were unable to decipher the words used. Nevertheless, there are a few clues we can latch onto, a few straws in the wind.

According to Maureen O'Hara, Mary Kate does actually say something into Sean's ear and does not merely mumble. Secondly, the line was an unscripted suggestion of Ford's and when he first directed her to say it she replied, "I couldn't say something like that to Duke." Next, she confirms that the line was "pretty rude" and could not have been spoken aloud without getting into trouble with the censor. Finally, and perhaps most surprisingly, she told me that Duke did not know what was coming and that one of Ford's reasons for the whisper was to shock Wayne and see his reaction. Certainly, he does seem to do an unintended double take and stares at her untypically for a few seconds as if he cannot believe his ears.

Of course there has been no shortage of suggestions, printable and unprintable, as to what Mary Kate whispered in Sean's ear. One of my favourites is an old Irish romantic suggestion that could very well have been used

– "How would you like to go halves on a baby with me?" But whatever was said, it remains and probably will remain one of the most enduring mysteries of the movie. So great is the mystique of this scene that it was used over forty years later as a television advertisement in the United States for a perfume called "Whisper".

John Ford always maintained that to be suggestive or erotic, a movie should leave as much as possible to the powerful imagination of the viewer, and that tactic certainly seems to have succeeded in this instance. Nothing Mary Kate actually whispered could be half as suggestive as what people imagine she has whispered. Perhaps it is just as well that we don't know the content of the whisper – maybe some mysteries are better not solved and the continuing speculation can only increase the popularity of *The Quiet Man*. Trust Ford to give us a happy ending but to leave us with a mystery to keep him on our minds.

Anyway, whatever the content of Mary Kate's whisper was, it has the desired effect on Sean. He gives her a startled look. As he looks at her, she smiles, reaches down and takes the stick from his hands and throws it away with great force. There is no need for force or a stick now – she is his and his alone without compulsion. Then believing that it is nice to be chaste but even nicer to be caught, Mary Kate turns away from Sean and runs towards the stepping stones. Halfway across, she turns towards him invitingly but he is already following her. Leaping across the remaining stepping stones, Mary Kate turns again just to check that Sean is still coming, knowing full well that he is. As she leaps over the last gap athletically, she stays out of his range but close enough to tantalise him. As he leaps the final gap, she waits for him and they walk arm in arm up the little lane. Finally, just to show him she is not yet fully tamed and so that Sean will not take her for granted, she attempts to break away again and run to the cottage door. Sean, however, is having none of it and playfully restrains her by the arm as they enter the cottage door together. We have no doubt they lived happily ever after, and so perfect is the ending that there is no need for a sequel.

It is fitting that the musical background to the final scene is *Saint Patrick's Day* because *The Quiet Man* is shown most on television worldwide when the Irish celebrate the feast day of their national saint. Ford has given *The Quiet Man* a tremendous ending – powerful, happy, yet deeply erotic, just the sort of feelings which millions of moviegoers have left the cinema with after watching it for over fifty years. More significantly, the ending gives us potent echoes of two of the most important earlier scenes in the movie.

In the courting scene Sean and Mary Kate crossed the stream one after the other – both get their feet wet and when they arrived on the bank they weren't sure where they were going. Now, in contrast, they cross the water on well-placed stepping stones and keep their feet dry. Now their goal is clearly in sight – the cottage which is to be their home where they will spend their life together and one hopes they will have a family of tough young boys and beautiful red-haired young girls.

In the final chase up the laneway to White O'Morn there is a strong echo of the scene in which Mary Kate is dragged across the country-side. Then, whether in collusion with Sean or not, she was dragged, broke away from him and threw a punch at him. Now he chases her gently, she stops and waits for him and then runs ahead teasingly, and the atmosphere is totally affectionate, the very antithesis of the earlier scene.

In John Ford's movies there is frequently a strong sense of family – we have only to cite *The Grapes of Wrath* (1940), *How Green Was My Valley* (1941) and *The Searchers* (1956), but none more so than *The Quiet Man*. As the words THE END and the eagle logo signifying A REPUBLIC PRODUCTION flash on the screen, we are left with great hope for the future and an optimism about the ability of human beings to cope with conflict and sort out their problems using intellect and action. Above all, we are left with an overwhelming belief that love conquers all.

The whisper

Maureen and Duke wait

Chapter Six

Influences

No work of art exists in isolation and the movie *The Quiet Man* is no exception. We have already traced the development of the screenplay from the original story by Maurice Walsh, through the amended version in *Green Rushes* and the too-political novella by Richard Llewellyn, to the proposed version by Frank Nugent. However, as we have pointed out on numerous occasions, the final print included many changes and on-the-spot improvisations, mostly due to Ford's ingenuity and wicked sense of humour.

When Nugent was commissioned to write the final version of the screenplay, it is very likely that he looked carefully at as many movies made in Ireland or movies with an Irish theme as he had access to, probably following Ford's advice. Both Frank Ford and John Ford had previously taken part in and directed several movies with Irish themes that are nowadays accessible only as archive material. Among these are *The Shamrock Handicap* (1926), which may have inspired *The Quiet Man* horse-racing sequence; *Mother Machree* (1928), in which Victor McLaglen appeared; and *Hangman's House* (1928), based on the Donn Byrne novel in which an exile returns to Ireland to get rid of a scoundrel, starring both Wayne and McLaglen. Ford's production of the Sean O'Casey play *The Plough and the Stars* (1936), starring Barry Fitzgerald, Eileen Crowe and Arthur Shields, also seems to have had some minor influences on *The Quiet Man*.

Of more immediate interest, however, are five movies made in the thirties and forties which we believe very strongly influenced Nugent's screenplay and inspired many of the sequences and lines of dialogue in *The Quiet Man*. Indeed at times it appears that Nugent and Ford "borrowed" rather freely from these earlier productions, and true *Quiet Man* fans might be advised not to watch these movies if they wish to preserve the illusion of originality

of their favourite movie. With regard to certain themes, lines of dialogue, treatments and musical backgrounds, it might be too extreme to suggest that they were "lifted" from these earlier productions, but there seems little doubt that *The Quiet Man* was very strongly influenced by the following earlier movies - *The Informer* (1935), *How Green Was My Valley* (1941), *The Foxes of Harrow* (1947), *Captain Boycott* (1947) and *Saints and Sinners* (1949). This list is of course not exhaustive and there may be others, but we believe these are the main ones. We now give a short account, in chronological order, of these influences and points of similarity.

1. THE INFORMER (1935): John Ford was not the first person to film Liam O'Flaherty's novel *The Informer*, set during the Irish struggle for freedom. There had been a British-made film of this powerful story directed by Arthur Robinson in 1929 which was made and recorded in London. This version, which incidentally was banned in Ireland, was quite a competent production but suffered from its total neglect of Irish accents and customs. All of the actors and actresses spoke with middle-class or upper-class English accents which at times turned the proceedings to farce.

Ford's version of *The Informer* is set in 1920 shortly before *The Quiet Man* is set and has a strong IRA theme. Gypo Nolan, played by Victor McLaglen, is a heavy insensitive fighter, of limited intelligence and with a short temper, yet underneath he is not really malicious, more of an immature child than an adult rascal. Red Will Danaher could possibly be described as the Gypo character with a sense of humour added, albeit a primitive sense of humour. Gypo betrays his fellow rebel Frankie McPhillip to the authorities to obtain the twenty pounds needed to take himself and his girlfriend to America, whereas Sean Thornton uses the blood money he earned in the ring to come to Ireland to acquire a girlfriend.

As the British officer (played by Frank Baker – a man in the bar in *The Quiet Man*) hands over the twenty pounds he says, "You'd better count it," and Forbes' line, "You have twenty pounds on him, Danaher," could be a reference to this also. When Gypo changes the notes to coins, the thirty pieces of silver, the coins are thrown first on a table and afterwards at the wake onto the bare floorboards, exactly as in *The Quiet Man*. As he squanders his money on drink and fish and chips for the hangers-on around the streets of Dublin, Gypo is accompanied by Terry, played by J.M. Kerrigan, on whom both Michaeleen and Feeney could have been based. Terry insults the proprietress of the shebeen by calling her an "ould squint", and his catch phrase is "up the rebels", a phrase with which Nugent littered the *Quiet Man* script but which did not make it to the final print.

Many lines and incidents in *The Informer* resurface in *The Quiet Man*. Gypo "has the floor" and "has an announcement to make". He says "And another thing" and "Get out, get out", and throws a stone through the window of the fish-and-chip shop. The "vice versa" joke is aired for the first time and so is Francis Ford's outrageous beard – he appears in *The Informer* as Judge Flynn in the IRA court scene, but never opens his mouth because of accent problems. Towards the end of *The Informer* there are two scenes which very closely resemble scenes in *The Quiet Man*. Dan Gallagher (Preston Foster) asks his girlfriend, Mary McPhillip (Heather Angel), "What time is it?" and she replies, "Half past five," and when Gypo Nolan enters the church just before he dies, we see the altar from the back of the church with the altar boy quenching the candles on the left-hand side.

The Informer leans heavily on Irish music as a background to many of the scenes, but because of the seriousness of the theme we get little light-hearted stuff. However, Moore's melodies are extensively used, and at least two of the songs used in *The Informer* are repeated in *The Quiet Man* – *The Wearing of the Green* and *Believe Me If All Those Endearing Young Charms*.

At times one feels that Ford and Nugent in *The Quiet Man* are mocking *The Informer* and engaging in self-parody, but there is also the possibility that because *The Informer* was a double-Oscar winner for McLaglen as best actor and Ford as best director, maybe they felt that some more of the same formula might achieve the same result.

2. HOW GREEN WAS MY VALLEY (1941): This was another Oscar winner for Ford, so again maybe he felt that he should retain as much of a winning formula as he could. His first choice for the screenplay of *The Quiet Man* was Richard Llewellyn, but as we now know the result was too political, so he turned to Frank Nugent instead. *How Green Was My Valley* is quintessentially Welsh, but strangely enough it is often grouped with Ford's "Oirish" movies and quite a few of the actors and actresses were Irish, largely from Dublin's Abbey Theatre. It was Maureen O'Hara's first movie for Ford and her performance was outstanding in the part of Angharad Morgan. She later called her only daughter Bronwyn in honour of another character in the movie. Several other *Quiet Man* cast members appear too – Arthur Shields as the fire-and-brimstone Mr Parry, a Christian as unlike Cyril Playfair as could possibly be imagined; Barry Fitzgerald as the feckless and hard-drinking Cyfartha, not a million miles removed from the Michaeleen character; and Mae Marsh and Frank Baker in very minor roles.

Themes, incidents and lines of dialogue which reappear in *The Quiet Man* include the following: the new preacher, Mr Gruffydd (Walter Pidgeon), drinks with his parishioners and joins in the celebratory singing to everyone's surprise just as Father Lonergan did; one of the Morgan's sons was called Will, perhaps the inspiration for Danaher's name; the dinner scene involving Danaher's workmen is reminiscent of the family dinner in the Morgan house; the doctor arrives in a pony and trap and Angharad looks at the departing Mr Gruffydd through the window pane; Angharad and Gruffydd stand by the open fireside as Mary Kate and Sean did later and he says to her, "I have no right"; the mine-owner Mr Evans arrives at the front door with his obnoxious son to ask for permission to court Angharad, who is at once told to leave the room; Angharad then once again looks through the closed upstairs window at the object of her desires; she goes to his cottage at night and sits there in the dark until Mr Gruffydd finds her and, as she goes to the door to leave, she kisses him in a gentle prelude to the more powerful *Quiet Man* scene.

The Irish actress Sara Allgood (Mrs Morgan) treats us to an Irish bull – "Another beating like that and he will walk home dead," and Barry Fitzgerald delivers the line, "It is, it is," exactly as he was later to deliver, "I do, I do," before the courtship scene; there is no tea for the boxer in training but a glass of beer if you please, and when the teacher is being beaten up, Cyfartha invokes the Marquis of Queensberry and his rules; Mr Gwilyn Morgan (Donald Crisp) advises that two women should not try to co-exist in the same house, and the growing Huw Morgan (Roddy McDowall) breaks into falsetto as Michaeleen and Mary Kate were to do in The Quiet Man. Finally, Ford chose to have a narrator for *How Green Was My Valley* just as he later chose one for *The Quiet Man*. All mere coincidence and just circumstantial evidence? Perhaps, but a prima-facie case at least has been established.

For *How Green Was My Valley* Ford chose the very best Welsh songs and melodies so, of course, there was no Irish music involved. But the movie won a great number of Oscars, outgunning even the much-vaunted *Citizen Kane* (1941). However, it is fair to claim that the acting awards at least went to the wrong people. Donald Crisp took best supporting actor for a very ordinary performance as Mr Morgan, and Sara Allgood, making no attempt at all to cover up her broad Dublin accent and sound like a Welshwoman, scarcely deserved her nomination.

The performance of child actor Roddy McDowall as Huw on the other hand was quite superb, and Maureen O'Hara has never looked more beautiful or acted so well – it is to those two that the nominations should have gone.

3. THE FOXES OF HARROW (1947):

This movie, itself a *Gone With the Wind* (1939) clone, starred Maureen O'Hara, Victor McLaglen and Rex Harrison as a very unlikely Irishman, Stephen Fox, who leaves Ireland as a young man to seek his fortune as a gambler in the United States. Except for one very important scene, the influence of *The Foxes of Harrow* on *The Quiet Man* is not as great as the other movies we are considering. There were of course a number of superficial resemblances, which could be mere coincidences that some would say could have occurred in a dozen other movies, but we list these just for the record: Rex Harrison takes his stocking off on a sandbar and kisses Maureen O'Hara against her will – then he fixes up Harrow to attract her and, when she comes to the house, she sits at the piano and sings; Victor McLaglen gives Rex Harrison a hand out of the river and the line, "How's your blushing bride?" is used.

However, one major scene in *The Foxes of Harrow* has a very clear analogue in *The Quiet Man*. On their wedding night, Odalie (Maureen O'Hara) locks Stephen (Rex Harrison) out of their bedroom because he has chosen to spend time drinking with Mike Farrell (Victor McLaglen) and his cronies. The bolt on the door is very similar, and when Stephen, even though he hardly looks up to the task, kicks down the bedroom door, we feel as if we could be watching Sean Thornton in action. The dialogue that ensues is pure *Quiet Man* too. Odalie says, "I'll wear your jewels, Stephen, I'll preside at your table. Will there be anything else?" Stephen replies, "Nothing else. The door will be repaired, the only bolt on your side."

Later in *The Foxes of Harrow* the bolting of the door or otherwise becomes a major issue as it was intended to be in *The Quiet Man*, and there seems little doubt that one of the most powerful scenes in *The Quiet Man* had its origins in an easily forgotten earlier movie.

4. CAPTAIN BOYCOTT (1947): This

movie, based on the novel *Captain Boycott* by Philip Rooney, and starring Stewart Granger, Alastair Sim, Cecil Parker and Noel Purcell, had a huge influence on *The Quiet Man*. For a start it was shot in the Cong–Maam area and Cong, Ballinrobe, Mayo and other *Quiet Man* place names are mentioned frequently throughout. The Land League activist Hugh Davin rides his horse across the Connemara landscape jumping walls – in a couple of cases the very walls which Sean's double jumped! The very field in which Mary Kate sat on the gap in the wall and Sean broke the stick in anger over his knee is shown, as is the old mine in the background. Hugh Davin's costume looks exactly like Sean's outfit when he paints the cottage and both the interior and exterior cottage designs look for all the world like those of White O'Morn.

Alastair Sim as the parish priest is an obnoxious inspiration for Father Lonergan, and the plot crucially depends on the outcome of the Currane races where one spectator remarks, "Boycott is holding back" and another wonders aloud if, like Feeney, he should traitorously back Boycott to win the race. The rebellious peasants meet for military drilling in an old abbey and, as the soldiers come to help the beleaguered Boycott, the tune they march to is *The Rakes of Mallow*. To cap it all, as Hugh Davin runs towards the final fight, he vaults a gate!

The dialogue too has several lines later heard in *The Quiet Man*. Among these are, "Come fill up the glasses", "I want to offer a toast", "You're just in time" and "The drinks are on the house".

Captain Boycott was a mediocre movie, not least because of Stewart Granger's excruciating Irish accent, but it seems undeniable that Ford and Nugent lapped up many of its features for use in *The Quiet Man*.

5. SAINTS AND SINNERS (1949):

This is a rather dreadful British-made movie set in Ireland with a lot of cringe-making performances from the principals offset by solid performances from the usual Irish bunch of supporting actors and actresses. Produced and directed by Leslie Arliss, with script by Paul Vincent Carroll, *Saints and Sinners* has a trite storyline – Michael Kissane (Kieron Moore, with another excruciatingly contrived Irish accent) returns to the village of Kilwirra after

having been wrongly imprisoned for stealing the funds meant to buy the new church bell. In the space of a mere eighty-five minutes, he establishes his innocence, unmasks the true villain (Eddie Byrne) and wins back his girl (Sheila Flaherty) from him. There are two sub-plots – the return of the rich American O'Brien (Tom Dillon) and his supposed wife Blanche (Christine Norden) to find O'Brien's mother's grave and make amends for the way he treated her; the other sub-plot concerns the local "witch", Ma Murnaghan (Marie O'Neill), whose horse-racing tips prove to be correct but whose prediction for the end of the world, unsurprisingly, fails to materialise. Only one *Quiet Man* cast member is involved, Eric Gorman (Costello, the train driver) who plays here the part of Madigan the shopkeeper, but the many borrowings by Nugent from *Saints and Sinners* for *The Quiet Man* appear undeniable.

Saints and Sinners opens with a train pulling its way across the Irish countryside as *The Quiet Man* was meant to and as a segment of *The Rising of the Moon* (1957) later did. As the train pulls into the little station of Kilwirra (translated: Cill Mhuire/Mary's Church), we see the porter walking along the platform as Michael Kissane emerges from his carriage carrying a holdall. The close-up of his opening the carriage door is almost precisely the same as that of Sean Thornton performing the same action. Michael Kissane, like Sean, is trying to escape from his past and unhappy dealings with money. The locals ostracise him but he is welcomed by the parish priest, Canon Kinsella (M.J. Dolan) just as Sean was welcomed by Father Lonergan. There is a great deal of talk about horse-races and betting, but the Canon seems to be the only person in Kilwirra who does not spend all his spare time thinking about horses. The bell calls the locals to prayer as it called Sean to Mass.

The Kilwirra village pub is suspiciously like Cohan's both internally and externally and of course there is a Celtic cross in the middle of the street. When Michael takes Sheila to witness a village eviction, they ride in a sidecar with back projection of the countryside and he lifts her down from her seat by the waist. There is a ruined church on a little island that looks exactly like Castlekirk and in fact may even be Castlekirk; there are cottage half-doors – and a salmon is caught; the phrases "That's darn nice of you", "Name the happy day", "The drinks are on the house" and "It's a great day for Flaherty" are heard at various points in *Saints and Sinners*.

When Michael and Blanche go off together there is a sudden storm and they take shelter in the old abbey where Blanche raises her skirt and shows Michael her legs. There is a fight in the pub which unfortunately never gets off the ground. In Kilwirra Church the organ is playing gently after Mass, and when Michael takes Ma Murnaghan back to her very White O'Morn cottage, *I'll Take You Home Again, Kathleen* is played as she warns him not to put water in her whiskey. O'Brien buys a stained-glass window for the church and the prophesy of the end of the world is conveyed through a close-up of a newspaper clipping. Finally, Ma Murnaghan is suddenly revived from her fatal illness by the noise of the crowd and Michaeleen's exclamation of "Glory be to God" is heard. To cap it all, in the final scene O'Brien and Blanche plan to marry as Red Will and Mrs Tillane do.

The number of points of coincidence in detail between *Saints and Sinners* and *The Quiet Man* is quite astonishing and thus it appears that an Oscar-winning movie took much of its inspiration from a very ordinary British movie which is now virtually forgotten.

We could go on – for example, in *Rio Grande* (1950), the first movie in which Maureen O'Hara and John Wayne appear together, the Marquis of Queensberry rules are invoked and the dreaded water carriers make their appearance, and the more one investigates such coincidences, borrowings and liftings, the more one feels that nothing in movies is original. Given that the evidence of *The Quiet Man*'s lack of originality is overwhelming, if circumstantial, are *Quiet* maniacs to think any less of their favourite movie? Certainly not! Ford and Nugent may have used similar locations, scenarios, lines and characters as previous

productions, but it's almost like criticising an author who uses the same letters and words as previous authors. The skill lies in how the components are treated, how the ingredients are put together and above all in the camera angles and colour photography. Almost no director other than Ford could have turned such mundane bits and pieces into a masterpiece.

If *The Quiet Man* was inspired by earlier productions, then it in turn inspired a whole string of clones and imitators. In fact, it is fair to claim that every movie either with an Irish theme or made in Ireland since 1952 owes something to *The Quiet Man*. We will examine just a few of the most obvious of these and mercifully we will be as brief as possible.

1. The first of these was *Happy Ever After* (1954), known in the United States as *Tonight's the Night*. This was directed by the Zampi brothers, Mario and Giulio, and given the success of *The Quiet Man* one can imagine them saying, "Hey, there's money in these Irish movies; let's make a Paddy film." The script was by Jack Davies and Michael Pertwee, with additional dialogue by Irish writer L.A.G. Strong for added authenticity. Barry Fitzgerald is the only *Quiet Man* star involved and his part as Thady O'Haggerty is very similar to his role as Michaeleen Oge Flynn.

The very slim plot concerns the death of the eighty-four-year-old General O'Leary (A.E. Matthews) while foxhunting, and the arrival in Rathbarney of his caddish heir, Jasper O'Leary (David Niven) from England. Jasper reverses and overturns all the popular policies and customs of his uncle, so much so that the General's tenants spend the movie trying to murder him, but naturally all ends happily and Jasper departs penniless accompanied by femme fatale Serena McGlusky (Yvonne De Carlo).

The locations were all in the English countryside masquerading as Ireland and much of the action centres on the local pub, The O'Leary Arms. At times we feel we are watching a watered-down version of *The Quiet Man*, albeit in glorious technicolour. Barry Fitzgerald is seen betting and driving the old car. The horse is Cleopatra rather than Napoleon and the odds are three to one the General doesn't jump the wall. There is a train pulling into the station and the passenger is driven away on a sidecar. There is a sub-plot involving a widow trying to win the doctor away from his true love and Jasper O'Leary is referred to throughout as "the squire". Regan the bookie has a shifty assistant with a pencil and little book who behaves very like Feeney. The design of The O'Leary Arms bar is very similar to Cohan's and for the hunt, the drinks are on the house. The part of the policeman Milligan is played by Bryan O'Higgins, who may have been intended for the policeman in *The Quiet Man*. The script is littered with Irish bulls such as "You'll be shot dead and sent to prison afterwards."

Happy Ever After was a shameless attempt to cash in on the success of *The Quiet Man*, although viewed in isolation it is a pleasant and harmless enough production. However, Irish newspaper critics immediately saw through it. *The Irish Press* said:

> Mario Zampi just wades into the thing and doesn't give one begorrah about any form of reality. He manages to make *The Quiet Man* look as exact and realistic as a statistical survey.

The *Sunday Independent* was even more perceptive. It said:

> It is a feeble imitation of *The Quiet Man*. John Ford's masterpiece satirised the real Ireland. There was substance and subtlety in his script… Beneath the exaggeration was a basic reality and one could in every instance visualise a prototype in real life. His village was an Irish village. His pub was an Irish pub. Beneath its disguise, the village in *Happy Ever After* is essentially an English village. The tidy pub is an English pub.

On the positive side, the theme song *My Heart is Irish* written specially for *Happy Ever After* is a pleasant enough song, and the many Irish players seem to have enjoyed their parts enormously. Many of them were probably kicking themselves that they hadn't been involved in *The Quiet Man*.

2. Ford's next Irish movie was *The Rising of the Moon* (1957), known in the United States as *Three Leaves of a Shamrock*. The fourth proposed leaf of the shamrock was James Joyce's short story *The Dead* which Ford did not film. However, it was given the full cinematic treatment by John Huston in 1987, starring Sean McClory with Donal Donnelly in the part of the dishevelled Irishman which could have been written for Jack MacGowran, had he not died in 1973.

To say that *The Rising of the Moon* took much of its inspiration from *The Quiet Man* would be putting the case mildly. Ford developed and repeated many of his successful earlier ploys and indeed completed a lot of unfinished business left over from *The Quiet Man*. Over a dozen of the same Irish players reappeared in *The Rising of the Moon* and this time there were no foreign box-office principals, which probably accounted for its lack of financial success. The producer was Michael Lord Killanin and the Four Provinces production was meant to be a flagship of the home-grown Irish film industry but, alas, this did not happen.

The Rising of the Moon consisted of three segments introduced by Tyrone Power standing in a Dublin Georgian doorway. Power, who died shortly afterwards in 1958, came from a long line of Irish-American actors and played his Irish ancestry for all it was worth – even his introduction echoes *The Quiet Man* when he describes the Irish as "a quiet and peace-loving people".

The screenplays of all three segments are by Frank Nugent and the background to the credits includes the Cliffs of Moher, filmed for but not shown in *The Quiet Man*, and Ross Errily Abbey from a different angle. Leaf one of the shamrock is based on the Frank O'Connor story *The Majesty of the Law* in which the principled old Dan O'Flaherty (Noel Purcell) chooses to go to jail rather than pay a fine for assaulting his insulting neighbour. Police inspector Michael Dillon (Cyril Cusack) talks about "walking the whole long way" and as he nears the cottage he is observed by neighbours Eric Gorman (Costello in *The Quiet Man*) and Micky J. the poteen maker (Jack MacGowran with his rightful Mac instead of Mc). Making moonshine in a national monument is indicative of having "no sense of the proprieties" and the cottage is a White O'Morn clone inside and outside. The china is willow pattern and the unneeded cork of the whiskey bottle is thrown into the fire. Eric Gorman prays "God bless all in this house" as he enters the cottage, and Irish bulls come thick and fast, for example, "the falling population is due to the fact that this year people are dying who never died before". Does all this sound familiar? If it does, there is more to come.

In the second leaf of the shamrock, Nugent and Ford develop the theme of the chaotic Irish railway system in a hilarious sequence based on Martin J. McHugh's short play *A Minute's Wait* about a train that never seems to depart from a nightmare station. The opening shows the arrival of the Ballyscran and Dunfail Railway into a Castletown clone railway station. A sidecar waits at one gate of the level crossing, opened because the staff are "half-expecting a train". May Craig, again the woman at the station, makes a match for her niece as a dowry of £300 changes hands – her niece Mary Ann kisses her lover Christy and then slaps his face. The train driver (Paul Farrell) shouts, "We're off" after indulging in a superb malapropism – "I'll return sometime when the company is more congenital!" *Quiet Man* porter Paddy O'Donnell appears pushing a wheelbarrow full of lobsters for the Bishop's jubilee and there is good-natured Protestant-Catholic banter. There is a threatened fight between the train and station staffs, and the train is delayed yet again to transport the victorious hurling team. The bewildered English couple left behind in the station deliver the Bishop's line deleted from *The Quiet Man*: "Is this another of their rebellions?" as the train steams out of the station to the air of *The Rakes of Mallow*.

The final leaf of the shamrock was meant to be deadly serious – 1921, based on Lady Gregory's play *The Rising of the Moon*, about the springing from jail of an IRA prisoner Sean Curran (Donal Donnelly) just before he is due to be executed. Martin Thornton, Victor McLaglen's double in *The Quiet Man*, is prominent as a Black and Tan soldier, as is Joseph O'Dea as a prison guard. Eileen Crowe is splendid as the strong-willed wife of police sergeant Denis O'Dea (the original choice as Michaeleen), and John Horan, the man at the station in *The Quiet Man*, is the bill-poster at the Spanish Arch in the Galway docks. Micheal Ó Brían fusses about the escaping prisoner and there is talk of treason. Finally *The Peeler and the Goat* gets another outing as everybody retires to Martin Thornton's for a pint.

The Rising of the Moon is an underestimated and a very entertaining movie which never claims to have the depth or vast complexity of its earlier ancestor. All of the local cast give splendid performances and it manages to avoid being stage-Irish throughout. It should be made compulsory viewing for all *Quiet Man* fans who will have a lot of fun spotting the resemblances.

3. Not all *Quiet Man* clones were rip-offs and *Love With A Perfect Stranger* (1986) seems to be more of a gentle tribute than anything else. It is a Harlequin Romance movie, made for television with screenplay by Terence Brady and Charlotte Bingham, based on the novel by Pamela Wallace. Although gushingly sentimental, it is not without charm, with fine performances from the leading players. The plot concerns the romance of a successful American business woman, Victoria Ducane (Marilu Henner), and an eccentric Irish aristocrat, Hugo De Lacey (Daniel Massey), who meet on a train in Italy on their way to Florence. At one stage the dialogue runs as follows:

"It's almost dawn."

"You've never seen an Irish dawn."

"I've seen *The Quiet Man* three times."

"So you don't reckon that you could live in a whitewashed cottage with roses around the door?"

"Not unless it had a telex."

Throughout, the opening few notes of *The*

Isle of Innisfree are played without ever breaking into the melody proper, but the ending is a very obvious and deliberate tribute to *The Quiet Man*. When Victoria Ducane returns to the United States, she wanders around in a stupor unable to decide between her true love in Ireland and her career but realises she cannot have them both. An attractive offer to buy out her company comes from a company called *Qutamine Holdings* and, against her directors' advice, she sells and takes the flight to Ireland. At Shannon Airport she is met by a little man called Mike (John Delaney) in a bowler hat who utters such gems as "Would you be the American lady?"

Victoria is ferried away from Shannon in a horse-drawn sidecar over a bridge through the grounds of an Ashford-type estate, as Mike delivers several Barry Fitzgerald-type lines. When they arrive at Hugo De Lacey's luxurious country house he helps her down from the sidecar by the waist and it emerges that his house was not stolen from his family by the Druids but that Hugo is the Third Earl of Dromore. He then explains to his wife-to-be that QUTAMINE is an anagram of QUIET MAN and that it was he who bought her company. Romantically he offers it back to her as a wedding present and the movie ends in a blissfully happy manner as the couple discover their shared love of racehorses and their breeding.

Love With a Perfect Stranger puts no great strain on the intellect, but it is quite entertaining, and its tribute to *The Quiet Man* gives it a charm missing from many similar romantic productions of its kind.

4. The Field (1990) is a powerful and high-quality movie for which Richard Harris won a deserved Oscar nomination and might have won the award were it not that his co-star Brenda Fricker and Daniel Day-Lewis had won the awards in another Irish movie *My Left Foot* (1983), which also won the Oscar for best film. *The Field* has been described as a dark and sombre *Quiet Man*, but it would be more accurate to describe it as a *Quiet Man* with the humour removed. There appears to be an enormous number of points of resemblance between the two movies which deserve close examination.

To begin with, *The Field* was based on an original story by a writer from the North Kerry literary triangle, John B. Keane, born and bred near where Maurice Walsh lived. Secondly, although the action was set in North Kerry, when it came to be filmed, the location chosen was Mayo and West Galway, just as it was for *The Quiet Man*. In the opening scene we see "The Bull" McCabe (Richard Harris) and his son Tadgh (Sean Bean) drawing seaweed from the beach – the very beach at Lettergesh where the *Quiet Man* race scene was shot. The seaweed (bullock manure in the original) is for use in the field that the McCabes have rented from the widow (Frances Tomelty) who has neither kith nor kin, poor soul. "The Bird" O'Donnell (John Hurt) is a sort of idiot Feeney who aids and abets Tadgh to torment the widow by smoking her out of her half-door cottage – we see a close-up of the smoking chimney as in *The Quiet Man*. The widow refuses to sell the field to the Bull despite his many offers but decides to put it up for auction instead. The Bull sports a distinctly Dan Tobin-type beard and we see him at dinner with his wife Maggie (Brenda Fricker) despite the fact that they have not spoken to each other for eighteen years.

Much of the action was filmed in the lovely village of Leenane (not unlike Cong) called Carrigthomond rather than Inisfree, and the pub is Flanagan's rather than Cohan's. The publican Flanagan (John Cowley) is also the auctioneer, and the widow takes exception to having her affairs discussed by the local men in his pub. Tadgh McCabe is attracted to a lovely red-haired tinker girl named Kate with whom he tries to run away at the end of the action.

The Bull McCabe knows that none of the locals will bid against him for the field that several generations of his family have rented and nurtured, but the apple cart is upset by the arrival of an unnamed American (Tom Berenger) with money to burn. In the original play, the stranger was an Englishman with a name – William Dee. The American has great difficulty being accepted by the locals and tries to win their approval by buying drinks for everyone in Flanagan's as he smokes several cigarettes á la Duke Wayne. "What right has he to land he has never worked?" the locals ask – it's really McCabe land.

When the inevitable and savage fight between the American and the McCabes takes place, by the river naturally, the American by his stance and tactics clearly shows that he is a trained boxer, but the McCabes carefully avoid the Marquis of Queensberry rules and Tadgh gives his opponent a boot in the groin while the Bull fells him with a blow of his Danaher-like stick, after asking the Yank if he's had enough. This time it is the American who is killed more or less accidentally and there is a Playfair-type plot to conceal the identity of the killer.

There are many other points of similarity – graveyards with Celtic crosses; the Yank returning to Ireland because his father had died; Tadgh running across the stream in the storm; the widow's declaration that she feels alien in Carrigthomond; a chase across the countryside with a herd of cattle; an end view of the church at Mass time; and above all the use of the superb scenery of the West of Ireland to enhance the movie visually.

The Field started life as a very successful stage production but almost all of the additional plot needed for the movie version appears to have been lifted from *The Quiet Man*. The result is powerful but humourless, but then *The Field* was intended to be a very serious movie based on one of the most fundamental of all human problems – the right to ownership of property and whether that right belongs to those who work the land or the owners who take the wealth produced for them. In Russia and Palestine, *The Field* has been interpreted as part of the class struggle between labour and capital and between colonist and tenant. Jim Sheridan's direction of *The Field* was a major achievement but the movie is unlikely to attract the cult following that *The Quiet Man* has.

Two other Irish movies, *Ryan's Daughter* (1970) and *Far and Away* (1992) also exhibit *Quiet Man*-like features but we will be merciful and leave the analysis, as the schoolbooks often say, as an exercise for the reader.

Chapter Seven

In Conclusion

As the shooting of the Irish location scenes for *The Quiet Man* was completed, even before the Hollywood interior scenes were shot, everyone involved began to realise that they had a hit, even a masterpiece, on their hands. Even the normally indifferent Ford was enthusiastic and believed that he had achieved all he had set out to accomplish. A perusal of the papers of Lord Killanin donated to the Irish Film Institute in Dublin reveals something of Ford's feelings at this time – some would say that what follows is pure theatre – Ford at his ambiguous Irish-American best, but surely some of his emotional reaction is genuine, even if it is awkwardly expressed. Several points emerge from the Killanin papers that are worth recording.

Meta Sterne

First of all one senses the importance in Ford's life of a lady rarely mentioned – Meta Sterne. For many years she was Ford's script girl, but also his girl-Friday, his right-hand woman and in effect his secretary. She accompanied him to Cong for *The Quiet Man* but kept very much out of the limelight – her name appears nowhere in the screened or unscreened credits, and she is to be found only in a single still photograph during the shooting. By all accounts she was a formidable lady who did not suffer fools gladly, but perhaps Ford liked her

style as a reflection of his own gruff approach to life. Most of the letters, extracts of which follow, were dictated to and typed by Meta Sterne.

On 2 October 1951, Ford wrote to Killanin:

> I apologise for any abrupt leave-taking at Shannon. I remember Michael going to the plane with me, but I was all choked up at leaving our beloved Ireland. I was afraid I would burst into tears – which I did upon reaching my berth and thereupon fell fast asleep and awoke in New York. I don't recollect anything at all hardly – it seemed like the finish of an epoch in my somewhat troubled life; maybe it was the beginning of jespere? Galway is in my blood and the only place I have found peace.
>
> Hey, *The Quiet Man* looks pretty good. Everybody here is enthused and I even like it myself. It has a strange humorous quality and the mature romance comes off well. I am now in the throes of cutting, dubbing music – that indeed is the tough part, requiring meticulous attention to detail. I think the Irish might even like it...
> ...Well the quiet men and women all send love and regards – they still have that faraway look in the eyes mirrored in green hills and brooks. The Duke is sitting opposite and says, "Can I come back too?" I corrected him, "May I come back too?"
> Love and affection to all.

On 25 October, Ford writes:

> *The Quiet Man* looks better every day. If you are still talking to Huggard [Manager of Ashford] which I am not, you might tell him and the Tourist Board that they may expect an influx of American film companies in the next eighteen months.

Other interesting snippets emerge from later correspondence. Ford asks if it would be possible to locate the Mayo parish of Dunfeeney from which his ancestors were allegedly driven (by the Druids?). In fact, it lies right next to the famous Céide Fields, now one of the West of Ireland's premier tourist attractions centred around what is probably the oldest farming settlement in the country, and over four thousand years old. Ford would have been really pleased about that.

On 30 July 1953, Ford asks Killanin to request that Nora Connelly or Martin O'Feeney would remember his brother Frank Ford in the rosary. During Frank's final illness Pappy visited him in the hospital every day, putting a lie to the stories that the two men were not on speaking terms.

After the release of *The Quiet Man* in 1952, the rest of the world began to sit up and take notice also. Ford was chosen by the Directors' Guild of America for their top award for 1952 for his work on *The Quiet Man*. This award traditionally pointed towards the choice for the Academy Award for best director and when the Academy Award nominations were announced *The Quiet Man* received seven nominations in a very tough year. These nominations were:

1. Best Picture: *The Quiet Man*

2. Best Supporting Actor: Victor McLaglen

3. Best Director: John Ford

4. Best Writing, Screenplay:
   Frank S. Nugent

5. Best Colour Cinematography:
   Winton C. Hoch and Archie Stout

6. Best Art-Direction, Set Decoration, Colour: Frank Hotaling, John McCarthy Jr, Charles S. Thompson

7. Best Sound Recording: Republic Sound Department – Daniel J. Bloomberg

Sadly, out of seven nominations received, there were only two Oscars for *The Quiet Man*, but then the competition was intense. Best Picture went to De Mille's *The Greatest Show On Earth*, which also edged out Kramer's *High Noon*. Subsequent history indicates, that in the mind of the public at least, the award for best picture should have gone to *The Quiet Man*.

McLaglen was edged out by an actor of Irish ancestry, Anthony Quinn, for his part in *Viva Zapata!*, but if McLaglen had not already received an Oscar for *The Informer* (1935) it might have been a different story.

Ford received an unprecedented fourth Oscar as best director and he had two others for shorts. The names of the people he defeated in 1952 speak for themselves – De Mille, Huston, Mankiewicz and Zinneman, some of the greatest names in movie direction. Because of illness, Ford could not attend the presentation ceremony and Duke Wayne accepted the statuette on his behalf.

The other Oscar went, quite deservedly, to Hoch and Stout for their superb colour cinematography which would possibly have won an Academy Award in any year. Frank Nugent must have been disappointed, because his screenplay was outstanding, but the award went to Charles Schnee for *The Bad and the Beautiful*.

Perhaps as a consolation prize there was a special Oscar for Merian C. Cooper, for his many innovations and contributions to the art of motion pictures. Nowadays he is remembered mostly for *King Kong* (1933) and *The Quiet Man*.

More surprising perhaps than the small number of Oscars was the omission of *The Quiet Man* from the nominations in some other categories. Wayne and O'Hara deserved at least a nomination as Best Actor and Actress and the editing of *The Quiet Man* merited at very least a nomination. But most surprising of all was the ignoring of Vic Young's music in the category of Scoring of a Dramatic or Comedy Picture and *The Isle of Innisfree* as Best Song. *High Noon* and its song *Do Not Forsake Me, Oh My Darlin'* of course took these Oscars, but the merits of *The Quiet Man*'s music seem to have been lost on the members of the Academy.

There were many other awards too. *The Quiet Man* scooped three awards at the Venice Film Festival, including the coveted Silver Lion. It was voted Best American Picture of 1952 at the National Board of Review Awards and it was one of the Japanese Kinema Jumpo Best Ten Films for 1953. In France, *L'Homme Tranquille* was voted Best Catholic film of the year. As recently as 1996, the readers of *The Irish Times* newspaper overwhelmingly voted *The Quiet Man* the greatest Irish movie of all time. In 1999, *The Quiet Man* appeared as No. 66 in the top movies of the millennium in an Internet survey.

The Quiet Man is a comedy, a Western, a serious movie, but above all it is a love story. Why have millions of *Quiet Man* fans worldwide for fifty years regarded it as the greatest movie ever made? Why has it achieved cult status to the extent that every summer the West of Ireland is crawling with fans from the United States, Italy, Japan, the United Kingdom, and Ireland itself, both North and South, following the trail of Sean and Mary Kate, Michaeleen and Red Will, the Widow Tillane and the Playfairs? Well, think of baking a Christmas cake. Take the finest ingredients, gleaming utensils, a warm oven, a skilled cook – and not just a skilled cook but one who loves the task and puts heart and soul into the job – and pretty soon you are looking at a culinary masterpiece.

John Ford was one of the cinema's greatest directors, if not the greatest. The electric chemistry between Wayne and O'Hara is one of Hollywood's greatest platonic love stories, and Ford's stock company lent every ounce of support and experience that was necessary; Barry Fitzgerald stole the show and McLaglen was superb; Nugent's screenplay based on Maurice Walsh's original story was masterly, and Hoch and Stout's cinematography quite magnificent. Throw in the Irish Players, the incomparable scenery of the West of Ireland and the wholehearted enthusiasm and cooperation of the people of Cong, Cross, the Neale and Clifden, and the ingredients are complete. Finally, the whole package was conceived and delivered with loving care, affection and Irish-American sentiment by Pappy Ford, using a highly skilled technical crew, as part of a burning and lifelong ambition to pay tribute to his Irish ancestry. These are some of the reasons why *The Quiet Man* is regarded as a masterpiece by so many people and why it will remain popular worldwide for a long time to come. And to those who claim that the place portrayed in *The Quiet Man* never existed, we can do no better than to adapt the famous line from Ford's *The Man Who Shot Liberty Valance* (1962): "This is the West of Ireland, sir. When the legend becomes fact, print the legend."

Ford the Director in Cong

INDEX Page numbers in italics refer to illustrations

Index compiled by Yann Kelly, Cover to Cover

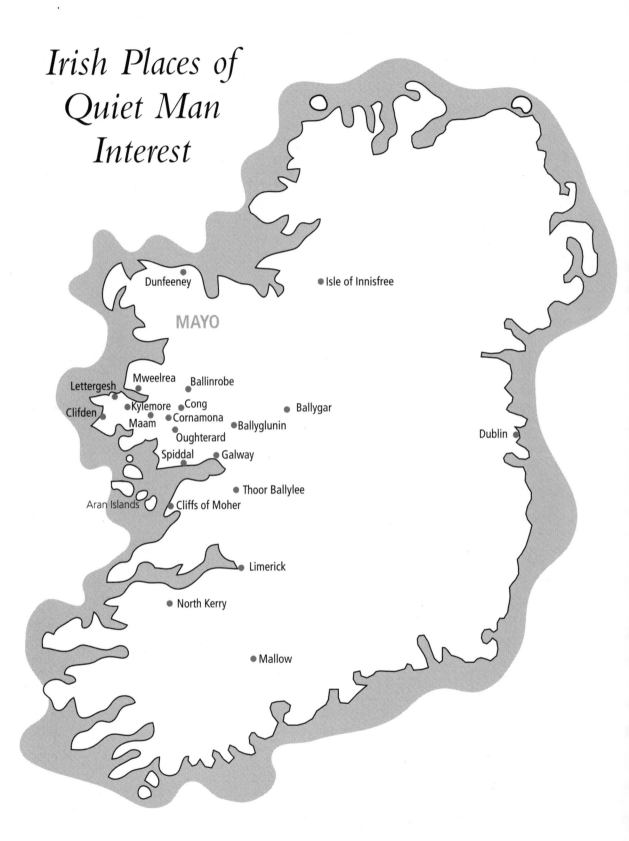

Irish Places of Quiet Man Interest

MAYO

Dunfeeney

Isle of Innisfree

Mweelrea   Ballinrobe

Lettergesh

Kylemore   Cong   Ballygar

Clifden

Maam   Cornamona   Ballyglunin

Oughterard

Spiddal   Galway

Thoor Ballylee

Aran Islands   Cliffs of Moher

Dublin

Limerick

North Kerry

Mallow

The Complete Guide To

The Quiet Man

The Quiet Man

The Complete Guide To
The Quiet Man

The Complete Guide To
The Quiet Man

The Complete Guide To
The Quiet Man

The Quiet Man

The Complete Guide To The Quiet Man

The Complete Guide To The Quiet Man

The Complete Guide To The Quiet Man